1979

709.95
Wigoder, G
Jewish art a

W9-BQJ-843

3 0301 00082282 1

Jewish Art and Civilization

Jewish Art and Civilization

Volume II

Editor-in-Chief:

GEOFFREY WIGODER, D. Phil.

Head, Oral History Division,
Institute of Contemporary Jewry,
Hebrew University, Jerusalem;
Editor-in-Chief of the
Encyclopaedia Judaica

LIBRARY
College of St. Francis
JOLIET, ILL.

 WALKER & CO. NEW YORK

© 1972 by Office du Livre, Fribourg (Switzerland)

All rights reserved.
No part of this book may be reproduced or transmitted in any form or by any means, electronic or mechanical, including photocopying, recording, or by any information storage and retrieval system, without permission in writing from the Publisher.

First published in the United States of America in 1972 by the Walker Publishing Company, Inc.

ISBN: 0-8027-0394-1

Library of Congress Catalog Card Number: 72-80540

Printed and bound in Switzerland

Contents

709.95694
W663

8-14-79   Graber Art Books $31.64

8 6 7 15

Contributors to this volume

CHAPTER VIII   ENGLAND
Dr. Vivian D. Lipman
Former President of the Jewish Historical Society of England;
Lecturer on Anglo-Jewish History at London University

CHAPTER IX   NETHERLANDS
Dr. Jozeph Michman-Melkman
Cultural Director, Ministry of Education and Culture, Jerusalem

CHAPTER X   POLAND AND RUSSIA
Dr. Yehuda Slutsky
Lecturer at Tel-Aviv University

CHAPTER XI   UNITED STATES OF AMERICA
Rabbi Abraham J. Karp
Professor of History and Religious Studies University of Rochester;
President, American Jewish Historical Society

CHAPTER XII   SOUTH AND CENTRAL AMERICA
Dr. Haïm Avni
Lecturer at the Institute of Contemporary Jewry, Hebrew University, Jerusalem

CHAPTER XIII ISRAEL TODAY
Yaakov Tsur
Formerly Israel Ambassador to Argentina and France; Head of the Jewish National Fund,
and former Chairman of the Zionist General Council

CHAPTER VIII

England

by Dr. Vivian D. Lipman

The Character of England

In England, various factors hastened the change from medieval Western society based on feudalism and the Church to the modern concept of a national state with a centralized government: its geographical situation as an island; the loss of most of its Continental possessions at a relatively early date; the Black Death, after which a new and free form of agricultural society gradually replaced the feudal system. Because England had a head start on her Continental neighbors, she experienced her anti-monarchical revolution a century and a half earlier than France and almost three centuries before Russia. And though after a brief interlude the monarchy was restored, never again was the power of the Crown able to stifle freedom of thought or conscience.

Faces of medieval English Jews, thirteenth century. These six faces come from caricatures drawn on thirteenth-century English official documents and show individuals as they appeared to their contemporaries. Reading downward these are: a) the great financier Jurnet, son of Isaac, of Norwich, shown crowned, with three faces; b) Mosse (Moses) Mokke, son of Abraham, also of Norwich, wearing the Jewish spiked hat (?); c) Mosse's wife, Avegaye (Abigail); d) Aaron, 'son of the devil', of Colchester, wearing a cowl and with the Jewish badge in its English form of the two tables of the law; e) an unnamed English Jew of 1234, with a pair of scales; f) Hake (Isaac), another Norwich Jew, of 1289. Jewish Historical Society of England.

As a result, England subsequently enjoyed practically three hundred years of growth, during which she was for a period indisputably the richest and most powerful nation in the world. Even the struggle for political emancipation of the mass of the population was conducted within constitutional limits despite the fact that at times the atmosphere was dangerous. By the end of the 19th century, therefore, England was the envy of the less privileged nations of the world.

The image which has impressed itself on outsiders—and one that persisted until the mid-20th century, when it has been replaced by that of a permissive society—was a land where it was 'always afternoon', where the country house weekend was the epitome of pleasant and gracious living; where freedom of the individual and the press were supreme; where no secret police knocked on the door at night.

England in modern times has on the whole adhered to this image in respect of the Jews. When the *Jewish Chronicle* wrote on the outbreak of the 1914 war, 'England has been all to the Jews, the Jews will be all they can to England', it was expressing the sentiments of an Anglo-Jewry composed mainly of immigrants and the sons of immigrants, which had been absorbed into the established community and many of whom had no other aim than to live as 'Englishmen of the Jewish persuasion'. Even in the half century which has followed, loyalty to Britain has not, on the whole, conflicted, except perhaps temporarily, with Zionism and pride and affection for the State of Israel. For the appeal of life in England since the Resettlement has been the tolerance and freedom which has facilitated the absorption of people from different backgrounds and with different ideals and has molded them into a national entity while allowing them to preserve their separateness in matters of religion in its widest sense.

It was not, however, always so. Anglo-Jewish history falls into three clearly defined periods: the Middle Ages when Jews were a restricted, more or less tolerated, minority until they were expelled in 1290; from then until 1656 when Jews were not supposed to be in the country openly at all; and from 1656—the Resettlement—since when they have enjoyed virtually complete social and, from 1858, political equality.

The Medieval Period

Jewish society is, to some extent, a reflection of its environment, and thus in the Middle Ages the Jews in all countries were particularly conditioned by the surrounding society, a state of affairs that applied to medieval England as well as to Continental communities. Since the Anglo-Jewish community was an extension of northern French and Rhineland Jewry, the same conditions could, to a large extent be found. The Jews were the king's chattels, driven to moneylending because all other means of livelihood were denied them. (In England, they could not hold rural land in a feudal society, and were debarred therefore from agriculture. Even in the towns they could not practice a craft because they were denied membership of the craft guilds which operated on a religious basis.) While they were useful in providing money they were generally protected; but exploitation eventually reduced their profitability both as moneylenders and as royal 'milch cows' to be taxed on every conceivable pretext and sometimes none at all. This was the pattern of the Anglo-Jewish medieval settlement, which began under the Norman kings and was summarily ended by Edward I in 1290 when he realized, after a trial run in Gascony, that the impoverished community brought him in less than he could obtain by confiscation of their effects on expulsion. His action, the first general expulsion of Jews—as distinct from local expulsions—set a precedent which was followed by Philip the Fair of France, who banished the French Jews in 1306, and by Ferdinand and Isabella of Spain in 1492.

Yet during the two centuries of Jewish settlement in England there had been periods of reasonable security. The Jews had first come to England either in the reign of William the Conqueror or in that of his successor William Rufus, who hardly rates as an orthodox Christian and who is reported to have offered to turn Jew if the Jews could defeat the bishops in theological disputation. Some crossed the Channel after disturbances in Rouen at the time of the preaching of the First Crusade (1096). Certainly in times of strong government in the 12th century the Jews were favored by the Crown. The Charter granted them under John in 1201 confirmed the privileges they had enjoyed under Henry I and these were substantial. They were free to travel, a right to which medieval rabbis attached great importance as indicating a free status; they enjoyed a large measure of communal autonomy; they were exempt from the courts of the local lords and of the Church and subject only to royal justice. In twelfth-century England they were thus a favored class, but their position was eroded as the 13th century advanced and the power of the Church with its growing intolerance and anti-Semitic legislation permeated all sectors of English life.

Earlier the Church as a whole, as distinct from particular dioceses, had been prepared to tolerate the Jews. They were the descendants of biblical characters with whom the populace, through the stories told them by their priests, were familiar. True, they were infidels but they were regarded as witnesses to the origins of Christianity and it was hoped that they would eventually accept conversion. Bernard of Clairvaux, for example, had condemned attacks on Jewish communities by Crusaders and the papacy never at this time supported accusations of ritual murder and indeed often tried to combat them. But with the Third Lateran Council in 1179 the attitude changed. Social intercourse between Jews and Christians was discouraged; Jews were even forbidden to employ Christian servants. The measures were largely ineffective in England at that time though no doubt they contributed to the anti-Jewish feeling which found expression in the attacks on Jews in 1189-90. The 1179 decrees, however, were only a prelude to the harsh impositions of the Fourth Lateran Council in 1215, which not only repeated earlier decrees but also insisted that Jews should wear distinctive dress. In England, this was generally avoidable on payment until in 1253 the wearing of a badge was made compulsory, as were restrictions on building new synagogues, employing Christian servants and settling outside established communities, for which a licence was hence-

forth required. And under Edward I the screw was turned still tighter with the expulsion of Jews from certain towns which were the dower of the queen mother, who was fanatically anti-Jewish.

The influence of medieval Anglo-Jewry on its environment was small. The social and neighborly intercourse which evidently existed in the earlier period when Jews and Christians often rode together on journeys or visited one another's homes and drank together, was later forbidden by both the Church and secular authorities, though this did not prevent a number of Christian guests attending, despite ecclesiastical warnings against doing so, a particularly lavish Jewish wedding held in Hereford in 1286, for which they were placed under the ban of the Church.

It is of interest, however, that the Jews of medieval England did not live in ghettos. True they congregated in certain streets—one of which was generally called 'the Jewry'—close to a place of royal protection, to the market, and to their synagogue, but their houses were not separated by any physical barrier from those of their Christian neighbors.

Nor were all urban houses which have survived inhabited by Jews. Often a house has been wrongly attributed to Jewish ownership because it was thought that only a Jew could afford such dwellings. In fact, most Jews could not afford them either and it is only a minority, such as the so-called Music House of the Jurnet family in Norwich and the Jew's House at Lincoln identified with Belaset, which can definitely be stated to have been built and lived in by Jews.

It is thus obvious that it would be a mistake to assume that all Jews were rich magnates. The Anglo-Jewish medieval community, consisting at its peak of between four and five thousand souls, produced a number of rich financiers during the two hundred years of its existence. But there was a much larger number of individuals who existed by negotiating small loans among villagers or petty burghers, probably by a bit of pawn-broking or by working for richer coreligionists either directly, or by producing the consumer goods they needed. There also seems to have been a criminal element among the Jews and there are records of crimes of violence as well as offenses against the Forest Laws.

MEDIEVAL PREJUDICES

England has the doubtful distinction of being the first European country in which was heard the accusation of ritual murder in the Middle Ages. The story of the murder of William of Norwich in 1144 is an unpleasant example of the use made by calculating interests of an incident which, in fact, probably need never have been connected with Jews at all. But once the suspicion had been aroused that the boy found buried in a wood outside Norwich at Easter had been the victim of Jews celebrating the festival of Passover, there were unscrupulous persons prepared to make a martyr of the boy for the material benefits accruing to the Church from pilgrims who would come in the hope of miraculous cures or to do penance for their sins. However, it is only fair to record that the accusations were not accepted unanimously and that there were local churchmen who opposed the assertion that William was a martyr murdered by the Jews. Since the 19th century attempts have been made to discover from the evidence the true cause of William's death. The present author, having regard to the state of undress of the corpse, the ill-treatment of the body and the fact that he was gagged, has come to the conclusion that the boy was the victim of a sexual crime.

The surprising part of the matter would seem to be the small amount of anti-Jewish feeling aroused. The sheriff as the king's representative extended protection to the Jews of Norwich and accompanied them to the ecclesiastical court to which they were summoned, reminding the clerics there assembled that the Jews were accountable only to the king. The matter soon died down and the subsequent murder of a leading local Jew was not really due to it.

How different, though, the hostility aroused and the massacres perpetrated when the preaching of the Third Crusade—the first to make any impact on England—inflamed Christians against the 'infidels' in their midst. Debtors seized the occasion of the current anti-Jewish feeling to cause riots and to burn the records of transactions in which they were involved. The massacre of the York community in 1190—during the festival of Passover—has taken its place in medieval martyrology with the destruction of the Rhineland communities at the end of the 11th century. The situation in Norwich in 1144 must be compared, too, with the story of St. Hugh of Lincoln, another tale of a boy martyr but one which occurred in 1255 when the climate of opinion had hardened against the Jews. Though the boy, it is now accepted, probably died accidentally while playing, a forced confession was extracted from the Jew living nearest to the spot where he was found and a large number of Jews was arrested, many of whom perished.

Deteriorating relations between Jew and non-Jew were aggravated in the long reign of the weak, pious and anti-Semitic Henry III (1215-72), who was ably abetted by his violently anti-Jewish wife. The Jews suffered from the increasing exactions of the Crown, from the worsening climate of opinion and from the disorders following the baronial rebellion against the king.

LEARNING AND POETRY

Within their own community, however, Anglo-Jews often led a rich intellectual life. In an age when only a small percentage of the population could read and write, the Jews were generally literate in Hebrew and often in Latin and Norman-French as well. Indeed many business documents which have survived were obviously written by the signatories themselves. Anglo-Jewry kept in close touch with the communities of Northern France, particularly before 1204 when Normandy was lost to the English king. They received eminent scholars from abroad. Abraham Ibn Ezra is reputed to have visited England in 1158, and it was while Yomtov of Joigny was living in York in 1190 that he was among the Jews who committed suicide in Clifford's Tower.

The community also produced scholars of its own. Probably the greatest Jew in England in the Middle Ages was Elijah Menahem of London who was scholar, financier and physician and who lived from about 1220 to 1284. Various commentaries, including one on the Passover *Haggadah,* survive as well as a series of halakhic decisions. The *Etz Hayyim* of Jacob ben Judah Hazan of London was written as late as 1287, only three years before the expulsion. A code of law with liturgy and poems, the codification takes the same general form as other contemporary works of a similar type, such as the *Mishneh Torah* of Maimonides. It is in two parts, sixty chapters in the *Sepher ha-Torah* which is largely concerned with liturgical, ritual and matrimonial law, and forty-nine chapters in *Sepher ha-Mishpat,* mainly on civil law. It also contains the complete prayer-book of medieval Anglo-Jewry and their Passover *Haggadah.* Incidentally, the text of the medieval Grace after Meals would seem to confirm that scholars enjoyed high status, for unlike the modern version, there is a prayer for their increase.

It might appear that medieval Jewish scholarship was unequal, concentrating on Talmud, responsa, and grammar, the last particularly favored not only in Jewish learned circles but among the Christians. In actual fact, a famous medieval Hebrew poet, Meir of Norwich, who survived the expulsion and whose works were preserved for centuries in the Vatican Library, provides evidence that the standard of Anglo-Jewish literature was in no way inferior to that of Continental Jewry. The story of the discovery of his existence is a remarkable one. He might have remained completely unknown but for the fact that a fourteenth- or fifteenth-century scholar, probably German, copied out the poems and that they reached the Vatican. Still the poet's name might not have been known but for the fact that his signature is there in acrostic form—'Meir' in some of the short poems; 'Meir son of Elijah the *Hozeh* (seer)' on another occasion; and in a long poem on the Exodus, 'I am Meir, son of Rabbi Elijah from the city of Norwich which is in the land of the Isle called Angleterre...' If his work survived so fortuitously, is it not likely that there were other authors of caliber whose works have disappeared?

There were, too, patrons of scholarship and scholars among the medieval magnates of Anglo-Jewry. For until modern times scholarship was not generally a separate occupation. To devote time to study and to esteem scholars was the pride and pleasure of many businessmen (aided, no doubt, in the Middle Ages by the fact that moneylending left time for other pursuits). Many had libraries or at least collections of books, and in a number of cases the rich financier was also steeped in religious learning and capable of sitting on a *Bet Din* (rabbinical law-court). Some, like Elijah Menahem of London, were physicians. And, in a period when herbs were important in the treatment of illness, it was a Jewish doctor in Norwich who owned the first private herbarium in England.

The 'Synagogue' statue outside Rochester Cathedral, mid-thirteenth-century. Mid-thirteenth-century figure, one of a pair of the conventional Church and Synagogue contrasted figures, with a broken banner and tablets of the law reversed. Dean and Chapter of Rochester Cathedral. Photo R.H. Langden.

Menasseh Ben Israel, 1636. Menasseh Ben Israel (1604-57), rabbi, author, and printer, of Marrano origin, came to London to appeal to Cromwell to allow the Jews to resettle in England. Although his name is indissolubly associated with the Resettlement, he probably died a disappointed man, believing his mission to have been unsuccessful. He was drawn by Rembrandt in the Jewish quarter of Amsterdam, where he spent most of his life. Amsterdam, Rijksmuseum.

CHRISTIAN HEBRAISTS

Jewish doctors certainly treated well-to-do Christians and there were other social relationships between Jews and Christians. But at a time when there was quite an important school of Christian Hebraists in England, it would be interesting to know where these obtained their knowledge of Hebrew. Not necessarily, the evidence would seem to show, from Anglo-Jews. Just as the Jews of England and Northern France were closely linked, so too were English Christian scholars with their colleagues in Paris, and in Paris there was a lively school of Hebrew studies. There, Jewish commentaries, particularly Rashi, were extremely popular among Christian students of the Hebrew Bible. But in view of the fact that the aim of Christian Hebraists—such as the thirteenth-century Dominicans and Franciscans who studied the Old Testament to draw its heirs closer to Christianity—were not always the pursuit of learning alone, Jewish scholars would have been chary of

teaching them and thus putting a weapon into their hands voluntarily. On the other hand, converts would have had no such scruples. Nevertheless, there is some reason to believe that Roger Bacon, the Franciscan friar and philosopher, Herbert of Bosham, and Maurice, Prior of the Augustinians at Kirkham, may have studied with Jewish teachers. Maurice mentions that in his youth he spent three years learning Hebrew and transcribed forty Hebrew Psalms, the Jews themselves admiring his calligraphy. Roger Bacon, a friend and admirer of the famous thirteenth-century Bishop of Lincoln, Robert Grosseteste, who sponsored a literal version of the Psalms, wrote that there was no difficulty in finding Hebrew teachers for 'there are Jews to be found everywhere'.

Two cases are known in Anglo-Jewish medieval history of Christians whose study of the Hebrew language had unexpected results in an age which took its religion seriously. The Dominican friar Robert of Reading became a proselyte and died as a martyr in 1275 under the Hebrew name Haggai. A more romantic story is that of the unnamed deacon who came from Coventry to Oxford University and whose study of Hebrew and of the charms of a local Jewess with whom he fell in love led to his conversion and marriage. Charged with desecration of the host, he was found guilty and burned alive, though his wife seems to have escaped punishment.

We cannot attribute to Anglo-Jewry any *Haggadot* or other manuscripts of artistic workmanship, like those of Continental Jewries, although it is conceivable that English examples of this type of work may have been produced but may not have survived. On the other hand, there remain in England stained glass windows and medieval statuary and it is tempting to speculate on how far the Christian artists used models from the Jewry for their Old Testament characters. Was Terah, for example, still looking out from the window of Canterbury Cathedral, drawn from life? Was he based on a Jew seen by the artist walking in the street, even down to the detail of his medieval Jewish spiked hat? Indeed were characters in morality plays later in the Middle Ages based—apart from biblical stories in the Vulgate—on earlier representations when the Jews were there to be observed or on some folk memory handed down from generation to generation?

For after the Expulsion what remained was a memory—a few streets bearing ever afterward the name 'The Jewry' or 'Old Jewry', a few stone houses, a few converts to Christianity in the Domus Conversorum, a few visitors, Jewish physicians, for example, called in by monarchs and important personages and allowed to practice their religion during their stay. In Norwich, the tradition of Abraham's Hall (the property of Abraham, son of Deulecresse, a wealthy Jew, burnt on what was probably a trumped-up charge of blasphemy in 1279) survived until the 18th century, for an inn on the site had as its sign Abraham offering Isaac for a sacrifice. The cult of boy-martyrs persisted

Portrait of a medieval Jew, Canterbury, c. 1178. Stained glass window of c. 1178 in Canterbury Cathedral, showing Terah, father of Abraham, wearing the characteristic medieval Jewish red pointed hat and the long robe. Dean and Chapter of Canterbury Cathedral.

until the Reformation particularly in literature. A century after the Expulsion, for instance, the Prioress's Tale in Chaucer's *Canterbury Tales* describes such a killing. It purports to take place in a town in Asia, where:

> '...all these Jews conspired
> To chase this innocent child from earth's face
> Down a dark alley-way they found and hired
> A murderer who owned that secret place;
> And as the boy passed at his happy pace
> This cursed Jew grabbed him and held him, slit
> His little throat and cast him in a pit.'

But as the last verse showed, the inspiration was:

> 'O Hugh of Lincoln, likewise murdered so
> By cursed Jews, as is notorious...'
> (transl. Nevill Coghill)

Finally, there remained in some English cathedrals a symbolic reminder in the form of two statues contrasting the Church Triumphant and the Synagogue Dejected, a motif found elsewhere on the Continent, notably at Strasbourg Cathedral.

THE SECRET SETTLERS

The Expulsion of the Jews from Spain in 1492 and their forcible conversion in Portugal in 1497 added a new element, which heralded the eventual Resettlement. It also coincided with one of the turning points of world history, the discovery of the New World, and the subsequent movement of trade and civilization from their Mediterranean past to the Atlantic. Antwerp and later Amsterdam and London superseded Venice and Genoa as the richest entrepots; they became key centers in Jewish life, and in the return of the Jews to England.

The Marranos, the new Christians from Portugal, played an important role in this process. Jews at heart, they masqueraded as loyal Catholics and attended Church services but found also the opportunity to attend secret Jewish services among themselves. The courage of these people; the risks they ran day after day, year after year; the fear of exposure—with its awful consequences—which they faced as they went about their everyday pursuits; the natural decline in their religious knowledge generation by generation through lack of Jewish education and practice until all that remained were vague memories of an ancestral cult—all these factors might have influenced a less determined race to forget the past and accept the advantages that conformity offered. Yet such was not to be. Obviously many were lost to Judaism but there remained a vital element to play a significant part in Jewish history and to convert the term of contempt 'Marrano' (meaning 'pig') into an honored name in the course of the centuries to come.

One portent for later times was that the Marranos' safety depended on their being indistinguishable in dress and behavior from their neighbors. This normally meant living as Catholics, and after the Reformation in England (although some in the Low Countries and England eventually did live as Protestants), as Catholic foreigners. Since in England they were obviously 'Portuguese', it would be expected that they should be Catholics. Dissimulation was essential for survival. The Inquisition kept close watch on all suspected of Judaizing—indeed our knowledge of the Marranos in England is basically derived from denunciations and spies' reports in the Inquisitorial archives. Discovery, once a Marrano fell into the Inquisition's hands, meant prison, with examination under torture; if he refused to recant, the stake.

Marranos were in England from the end of the 15th century, but while there were probably individuals present throughout the 16th and early 17th centuries, life in organized communities was not continuous. Established groups there were secretly holding religious services and following Jewish practices, both in London and, for one period at least, in Bristol. A woman such as Beatrice Fernandez of Bristol was able to observe the dietary laws even when traveling and staying at inns on the journey. And the great house of Mendes of Antwerp employed a Marrano agent who boarded ships at Southampton to tell Portuguese travelers whether it was safe for them to continue their journey to Antwerp in search of greater religious freedom or whether it would be wiser, if at the time the Inquisition was particularly active in the Low Countries, to disembark in England and wait awhile. Probably by the end of Elizabeth's reign the Marranos were often known to be Jews and 'Portuguese merchant' was synonymous with Marrano. But their usefulness as doctors or providers of intelligence to the ministers of the Crown made it expedient not to seem to notice their real character.

Jews did arouse, however, hostility among the foremost writers of the age, especially in the period when Rodrigo Lopes, Queen Elizabeth's Marrano physician, who dabbled in Portuguese politics, was executed in 1594 for allegedly plotting to poison the sovereign. It is now generally accepted that, while he may have been involved in some intrigue, he was not engaged in treason against his royal patient. Christopher Marlowe's *Jew of Malta,* first performed in 1592, is supposed to have been based partly on the career of Joseph Nasi, who became the sultan's minister and duke of Naxos; reports about him, combining truth with lurid imagination, had long been circulating in England. Shakespeare's Shylock was surely an amalgam of all the anti-Semitic accounts that he had ever heard in a country where no professing Jews were to be found and where Lopes, though a foreigner, would not have had outward characteristics which in other circumstances would have been regarded as Jewish. Yet Shakespeare was too great a playwright to make Shylock unmitigatedly villainous. There is a pathos, which though it may have owed nothing to any insight into Jewish teaching or suffering, does, nevertheless, bear witness to the playwright's comprehension of a fellow human being's capacity for feeling, even though he was a despised Jew. It also shows that Shakespeare had no illusions that Christianity automatically engendered goodness:

'Hath not a Jew eyes? hath not a Jew hands, organs, dimensions, senses, affections, passions? fed with the same food, hurt with the same weapons, subject to the same diseases, healed by the same means, warmed and cooled by the same winter and summer, as a Christian is? If you prick us, do we not bleed? If you tickle us, do we not laugh? If you poison us, do we not die? and if you wrong us, shall we not revenge? If we are like you in the rest, we will resemble you in that. If a Jew wrong a Christian, what is his humility? Revenge. If a Christian wrong a Jew, what should his sufferance be by Christian example? Why, revenge. The villainy you teach me, I will execute, and it shall go hard but I will better the instruction.'

By the mid-17th century the climate had changed again. When the Resettlement of the Jews in England was achieved in 1656, it was due to a combination of factors in the English environment—political, religious, economic, and social.

Politically, the Civil War and the republican government which followed occupied a period of less than twenty years, but their effects for English history were lasting. Gone for ever was absolute monarchy as conceived by the early Stuarts. Gone was the power of the Church of England to impose conformity, as was found when attempts were made after the Restoration. Even though those outside the established Church did not obtain full political rights until the 19th century, they were not, except for brief periods, such as the time of the so-called 'Popish plot', in any physical danger. And the fear that a Catholic monarch with Catholic descendants might endanger the *status quo* (religiously and politically) which had been built up, led to the Revolution of 1688 and the replacement of James II by William of Orange.

THE INFLUENCE OF THE OLD TESTAMENT

The religious factors were perhaps even more important. The Puritans, divided into sects though they were, read and loved the Bible, and particularly the Old Testament, for its own sake and not merely as a prelude to Christianity. Their interest had been aided by the availability of printed books in the century since the discovery of the printing process. In 1611, the publication of the Authorized Version gave Englishmen the opportunity to read the Bible in magnificent and poetic English, translated from the original Hebrew and not from garbled versions of other translations. And until the 20th century, when the Bible is no longer required reading, generations of Englishmen responded to its inspiration. Both as creative writers or as regular readers they knew and were influenced by its contents and noble style. Even now, often without realizing it, English people (and perhaps Scots and Welsh even more) use biblical expressions or phrases as part of everyday speech: for example, 'there is nothing new under the sun', 'nation shall speak peace unto nation', 'how are the mighty fallen', 'the voice of the turtle', 'the little foxes', (the last two were titles of plays also). Shakespeare was reared on an earlier translation of the Bible and was familiar with its contents, as were his audiences. It was said of Milton that he thought in Hebrew though he wrote in English. Everywhere in the early part of the 17th century—and indeed in the non-conformist religious revivals at the end of the 18th century and in the 19th century—preachers, outside the court circles, modeled

their discourses on the language of the Bible, and used long quotations from its pages. They and the reading of the Bible itself helped to form not only the moral outlook but also the literary style of future generations. The imagery and the Bible-based simplicity of Bunyan's prose, for instance, had a distinct effect on eighteenth-century prose writers.

The Hebrew Bible's influence on the English-speaking world was not limited to speech or sermon. Biblical ideas on individual liberty as analyzed by seventeenth-century Puritans influenced the framing of the Bill of Rights in 1689 (which in turn was the basis for the American Constitution). In this connection, it is interesting to consider how the pride of place given to various books of the Bible has changed with the centuries. Thus the subjects which had influenced earlier generations, such as those concerned with Law, history and political theory, were superseded in the 19th century by the Prophets. Their ideas on social justice accorded well with the growing social conscience of the economic and social reformers who were campaigning for legislation to prevent the exploitation of the poor.

Of course, until the religious indifference of the 20th century, the Jews themselves, despite a minority of defectors, had been conditioned by their biblical heritage, reading it both in the original Hebrew and in the vernacular; taking pride in its records as their own history; studying its laws and relating its contents to contemporary conditions. They gloried in being the People of the Book, irrespective of their own religious Orthodoxy—a state of affairs which exists in modern Israel where Bible study and Bible reading are not exclusively the preserve of the religiously observant as it is, to some extent, in modern Britain.

It is not surprising, then, that in the Bible-conscious society of seventeenth-century England, many of the Puritans should have felt a sympathy for the descendants of the biblical characters they revered, and should have been prepared to have them living openly in England. Some advocates of readmission had, of course, an ulterior motive, hoping that freedom and toleration would lead to eventual conversion of the Jews; others believed that a great ill had been done to the Jews by England in the Middle Ages and that the time had come for redress; while still others thought that they were really members of the Ten Lost Tribes of Israel and should honor their brethren. Puritan terminology often spoke in Hebraic terms, even referring to their enemies as the 'uncircumcised'.

THE RESETTLEMENT

Crucial, of course, for the Resettlement was the personality of the absolute ruler, Oliver Cromwell. Tolerant in religion, prepared to let those of other faiths live freely so long as the security of the state was not endangered, he saw the economic advantages which could accrue to England from the readmission of the Jews, who, he hoped, would enrich London at the expense of Amsterdam.

This economic factor was brought to the fore by the small group of Marranos who settled in England from the 1630s. Led by Antonio Fernandez Carvajal, a wealthy merchant and shipowner who had lived in the Canary Islands, several of them had connections with the Islands and their trade. Others came from Brazil (where Marranos had flourished in a brief period of Dutch rule) and from the Marrano settlements in Amsterdam and Hamburg. In addition to their economic importance as importers of bullion, precious stones, dyestuffs and sugar, some at least acted, like their Elizabethan predecessors, as suppliers to the Government of military intelligence, which their overseas commercial relations made it easy for them to collect. Although living outwardly as Catholics, they met privately for Jewish worship in Carvajal's London house. An incident in 1656, however, induced them to declare themselves openly as Jews.

England was at war with Spain and the ships and cargoes of Spanish nationals were therefore liable to seizure. Information was laid against one of the Marrano merchants, Antonio Rodrigues Robles, and the seizure of his goods followed as 'enemy property'. Robles appealed to the Lord Protector for restitution, claiming that he was not an enemy alien but a Jew. He was supported by the evidence of a number of his fellow Marranos, who likewise declared their real identity.

Menasseh Ben Israel

This incident occurred during the one-man campaign for open Resettlement of the Jews in England conducted by Menasseh Ben

The Bodleian bowl, c. 1280(?). Bronze bowl with Hebrew inscription, found in Norfolk about 1696. Apparently 13th century and possibly originating in the medieval Jewish community of Norwich in Norfolk. Oxford, Ashmolean Museum.

Israel, Amsterdam rabbi, scholar, and publicist, himself of Marrano origin. Menasseh Ben Israel's own life bears out the contention that in certain parts of the world, at least, the lot of the Jew was easing. He had lived most of his life in Amsterdam, where the worst he had to fear was periodic bitter quarrels with his own congregants and with his professional colleagues. By the outside world he was regarded as an authority on Jewish affairs, the representative Jew of his era. Diplomats sought him out, savants consulted him. Theologian, writer, acquaintance of Rembrandt, who has immortalized his features, he was a celebrated and respected figure in the non-Jewish world, a noted preacher whose large audiences included many Gentiles as well as Jews. His advocacy of Jewish Resettlement in England, because the exclusion of the Jews from that one country prevented the messianic redemption, set the seal of respectability on the movement. His book, the *Hope of Israel,* published in 1650 in Latin, was soon translated into English and was a 'runaway best seller'. When, therefore, he added the weight of his prestige to the pleas for readmission already made, the strength of the case both on practical economic grounds and on the grounds of religion was well-nigh unassailable.

Menasseh Ben Israel had arrived in London in September 1655 and in October waited on the Council of State, presenting to Oliver Cromwell his *Humble Address to the Lord Protector* and a petition for the repeal of laws against the Jews and for their readmission on specified, and somewhat restrictive, terms. This petition was eventually referred on December 4 1655 to a distinguished assembly of lawyers, politicians and merchants. Almost at once the two senior judges answered that there was no legal bar to the readmission of the Jews but the four succeeding sessions produced opposition on points ranging from theological prejudice to mercantile jealousy; and even those who favored official readmission would have imposed severe social, as well as political, disabilities on the Jews. At the end of the fifth session on December 18 1655, Cromwell dissolved the Conference. The Robles incident, already described, followed in March 1656 and on March 24 another petition was presented to Cromwell. This was signed not only by Menasseh but by the leading Marrano residents, who had admitted their true faith in the Robles case. This petition had no political implications, no messianic overtones. It asked simply for tolerance for the right to meet privately for prayer and to bury the dead according to Jewish rites.

Until recently it was thought that this petition was never answered and that, since Robles' property was ordered to be restored on May 16 1656 by the Council of State, this was as far as the Council went; that because there was no record of a specific permit to resettle, none was given, and that Cromwell, unable to extract a positive decision, merely connived at the Resettlement of the Jews. That theory has been called into question by Cecil Roth who discovered that in the minute book recording the proceedings of the Council on precisely the day (June 25 1656) it was due to discuss the matter, the relevant pages had been torn out deliberately. The discussion therefore is likely to have taken place and the conclusion to have been favorable, a result which was conveyed to the waiting Jews, including Menasseh Ben

Israel, either by word of mouth or by a written communication (perhaps both) which has since been lost. Who suppressed the pages of the minute book is unknown but it is likely that the responsibility lies with one of the opponents of Jewish resettlement, wanting the next government to regard the return of the Jews as a personal whim of Cromwell's which did not have to be honored by his successors.

Menasseh Ben Israel, however, was disappointed that the terms on which he desired a settlement to be based—including communal autonomy, control over immigration and a special oath of allegiance—were not conceded. In fact, his ideas belonged to the past, to a different age and one to which Anglo-Jewry to its advantage never had to subscribe. Even though there were some attempts in the next half century to make terms and conditions, neither Charles II nor his successors would agree and Anglo-Jewry developed, as have all the best British institutions, without any written constitution at all. It was this quiet, unobtrusive beginning of the modern community which has molded it and influenced its history ever since.

It must be admitted, however, that England from the Resettlement until modern times has always been a backwater so far as Jewish intellectual life is concerned. It has had neither the numbers nor the Jewish learning of Continental communities; neither the traditional scholarship of Eastern Europe nor, when it came, the scientific and philosophical approach of the German *Wissenschaft*. Even when the reservoir of scholarship moved from its traditional environments, the new centers were the United States and later Israel, and Great Britain was bypassed. Anglo-Jewry has, nevertheless, played an important part in modern Jewish history though this has often been conditioned by the attitudes of the host society and, in some cases, by accident rather than by conscious design. The leading role of Britain in world affairs in the 19th century gave British Jews an opportunity to seek to intervene to improve the conditions of Jews in other lands; and the relationship of Britain to Palestine and the Jewish national home in the 20th century also meant that British Jews had a special position in world Jewry. But the prominence of Anglo-Jewry after 1945 was due largely to the fact that, after the European Holocaust, it was the largest Jewish community in Europe, apart from that in Russia which was sealed off from the mainstream of Jewish life for half a century. Numerically it has been overtaken in the 1960s by France which has received a large influx from North Africa. Anglo-Jewry's importance has thus been, in its different ways, out of all proportion to its size or capacities.

The Early Sephardim

The Jews from the Resettlement enjoyed a social equality with all other dissenting groups in England. There were one or two attempts to levy special taxes on them, but these did not persist; and while they suffered from certain political disabilities, these were shared until the 19th century by others who were Christian Englishmen, not members of the Established Church. Perhaps the most important special disability, since so many of the Jews were

Jacob Sasportas (1610-98). Sasportas was *Haham* of the Spanish and Portuguese Congregation in London from 1664 to 1666, when he left for Amsterdam on account of the great plague. Engraving by P. van Gunst. London, Spanish and Portuguese Jews' Congregation. Photo Freeman, London.

immigrants, was their inability to be naturalized, even by private Act of Parliament, because of the need for a Christological oath. But endenization was a workable substitute; and the Jews of England had less of a special status than any other Jews in Europe until the end of the 18th century (probably even less than the favored Jews of Holland).

It was, of course, easy for the Sephardim to pass unremarked among the general populace. After all, they were Westerners. And though they were after 1656 free to meet for prayer in their synagogue, outside they demonstrated no special mannerisms which marked them off as Jews, though they were obviously recognized as a distinct group by Addison, writing in the first issue of *The Spectator* in 1711: 'I have been taken for a Merchant upon the *Exchange* for above these ten years, and sometimes pass for a *Jew* in the Assembly of Stock-Jobbers at Jonathan's.' They quietly went ahead in the years that followed the Resettlement, consolidating their position, welcoming other Sephardi merchants into their ranks, and, in the reign of William III, having their numbers reinforced by the wealthy Amsterdam Jews whom the

Haham David Nieto, 1654-1728. The most scholarly and versatile of Anglo-Jewish rabbis, writing in Italian, Spanish and Hebrew on many subjects. Painting by David Estevens, engraving by J. McArdell. London, Spanish and Portuguese Jews' Congregation. Photo Freeman.

tions); and Princess Anne (the future queen) who was reported to have visited the synagogue in 1681, later, according to tradition, presented a piece of timber from a man-of-war to serve as one of the beams in the roof of the Bevis Marks building (since her husband, Prince George of Denmark, was Lord High Admiral, there is some plausibility in this story).

The Sephardi community continued to grow. A recrudescence of the Inquisition between 1720 and 1735 caused perhaps 1,500 refugees, whose families had remained secretly loyal to Judaism for over two and a quarter centuries, to emigrate to England. Increasing numbers arrived from Italy, especially from Venice and Leghorn—families like the D'Israelis and the Montefiores; others came from Morocco and Gibraltar (especially in 1781 when the civilian population was evacuated at the beginning of the siege).

In the early years of the Resettlement, the Sephardim had been the sole, and later the dominant, Anglo-Jewish religious group. But soon their numerical predominance was challenged (although their social and financial leadership remained throughout the 18th century).

THE COMING OF THE ASHKENAZIM

When the medieval communities of France and Germany had been faced with expulsion in the 14th and 15th centuries, the trend had been to move east, particularly to Poland, which, under enlightened rulers, had welcomed a Jewish middle class and the economic benefits they had brought. By the middle of the 17th century, however, the era of tolerance was over and the ruling class was intent on persecuting the Jews and restricting their activities. In 1648, the Chmielnicki massacres unleashed migration westward, a movement which continued for the next three centuries (see chapter on Russia and Poland). Though the first Ashkenazi immigrants in England worshiped in the London Sephardi synagogue, the only one in existence, they were soon sufficiently numerous to organize their own synagogue about 1690 and buy their own burial ground, and they had sufficiently wealthy members to facilitate their endeavors. The Great Synagogue was opened in 1726 (it was to be tragically destroyed by enemy action in 1940). Unlike the situation of the Sephardim, Ashkenazi sources of recruitment never dried up and by the end of the 18th century they had become numerically the stronger element in Anglo-Jewry, though the prestige of the Sephardim, with a community of only about 2,000, still remained paramount.

The first Ashkenazi immigrants—and the wealthiest—came from Hamburg. This is true of both Benjamin Levy and Moses Hart as well as Hart's rival Mordecai Hamburger (the son-in-law of the woman diarist Glückel of Hameln), the founder of the Hambro synagogue—which, in fact, may owe its name as much to its patronage by immigrants from Hamburg as to its connection with Hamburger. Of the leading characters of Anglo-Jewry in the earlier part of the 18th century, both lay and religious, many others also had some connection with Hamburg or with its sister community Altona. But by the end of the century the notable

monarch encouraged to settle in England. Their synagogue flourished, and they were fortunate to appoint as a *Haham* (chief rabbi) David Nieto, a man of outstanding scholarship and personality who guided their affairs from 1701 to 1728, and who headed a modest flowering of literary activity in his own congregation.

By the end of the century the first synagogue was too small and was replaced by the magnificent Bevis Marks synagogue, which was opened in 1701.

The impression made on non-Jewish visitors to Sephardi services varied with the occasion. Pepys, attending on *Simhat Torah,* found the synagogue 'a bear garden'; John Greenhalgh, another observer, being present on a Saturday, was impressed (as much by the wealth of the community as by its religious devo-

Bevis Marks synagogue, London, 1701. The oldest surviving synagogue in Britain was opened in 1701 in Bevis Marks in the City of London, for the Spanish and Portuguese Jewish community. It is similar to, but smaller than, the Spanish and Portuguese Synagogue of 1675 in Amsterdam. The scene, a color engraving from a watercolor, was painted in 1817 by a member of the community, Isaac Mendes Belisario, an artist who exhibited at the Royal Academy. London, Collection of Spanish and Portuguese Jews' Congregation. Photo Freeman, London.

19

personalities, such as Levi Barent Cohen, Aron Goldsmid and Eliezer Isaac Keyser had come from Holland, or from some other great city such as Vienna (as Baron Lyon de Symons) or Frankfurt-am-Main, the home of the Rothschilds. By this time, some of the scholars and religious functionaries were being drawn from the great reservoirs of learning in Poland.

Among the poorer immigrants, there was a different trend, and one which has not yet been fully investigated. It would seem that many of them came from small German communities, particularly from towns in the south of that country. The pressure to move, until 1768 at least, was not caused so much by active persecution as by economic needs. Rules in the German states about the activities of Jews were often stringent. Prussia under Frederick the Great, while almost encouraging rich Jews, would hardly tolerate poor ones. In many cases, while a man was permitted to earn a living sufficient to bring up a family, this right would not be extended to his sons, who, when they were ready to found families in their turn, would have to move on. England, in which they were free to operate, proved attractive, and in the earlier part of the century, the agents on the Royal Mail packet boats would grant free passes to the poor and passage across the English Channel for a nominal sum. Alternatively, the gradual immigration of this type of Jew may well have been accelerated by the *Haidamak* disturbances, which reached their climax in 1768, causing refugees from Poland to crowd into Germany and to displace German Jews who then moved west. This influx of Polish Jews into small towns with limited economic opportunities may have caused some of the more enterprising among the native population to seek a livelihood elsewhere. Such a situation was seen in England in the 1840s when the poor Irish immigrants drove the Jews out of much of the market trade.

In any case, the 18th century saw additions to the Jewish population in England, causing its increase from about 1,000 in 1700, to 6,000 by 1740, 8,000 by 1750 and 20,000 by 1800. Since the Napoleonic Wars caused a considerable decline, though not a complete halt, to further arrivals, it may be assumed that this figure remained substantially the same in 1815, though natural increase has to be taken into account in a period when the general population was rising too and when some estimates put the Jewish population in 1815 at between 25,000 and 27,000.

The Enlightenment

In the 18th century, both Sephardim and Ashkenazim were conscious of the importance of education, though in the early part of the century the Sephardi schools were superior in the teaching they provided. There, boys were taught Hebrew, English and Spanish or Portuguese (the conservative Sephardi community,

while using English freely in their everyday lives did not see fit to replace Portuguese by English in synagogal minutes until as late as 1819).

The onset of the eighteenth-century Enlightenment had its effects even among the English Jews. There were some early attempts at freethinking. For example, the German-born physician, Meir Loew Schomberg, who built up a large fashionable practice but quarreled with both his Jewish coreligionists and the Royal College of Physicians, wrote a Hebrew treatise in which he not only worked off a good deal of personal spite but also suggested that one could be a good Jew by belief in God without observance of the practical and ritual commandments (it is perhaps significant that five of his six sons became Christians).

Another eighteenth-century Jewish preoccupation with intellectual problems is that of an anonymous writer who dealt with the problem of Jewish education in an open society and the purpose to which it should be devoted in a work written in Judeo-German: *Sepher Giddul Bannim* (The Education of Children), published in London in 1771. The anonymous author may have been the physician George or Gompertz Levison (a pupil of the pioneer of surgery, John Hunter). His book advised on methods of teaching Judaism to children from their earliest years so that they might learn to love and appreciate their heritage, but its author accepted the view that religion existed in a secular context.

Eventually, the modernizing trends which on the Continent produced the Enlightenment, were not without their more modest parallels in the Anglo-Jewish establishment. About 1770, there began, after a period of intellectual stagnation, a revival of Hebrew printing in London and the production of prayer-books and Bibles with English translation—notably by David Levi, the humble but indefatigable scholar who, while eking out a living as a tradesman, was a one-man Jewish publication society.

A revolution in the wider field of education was brought about by Hyman Hurwitz and Joshua van Oven. Hurwitz, an immigrant from western Poland, an area within reach of the influence of the Mendelssohnian Enlightenment, opened a private school in Highgate, where he became a friend of Coleridge. In his school he introduced modern methods of tuition, hitherto unknown in the *heders* of Anglo-Jewry and brought a scientific attitude to the mapping out of a program of Jewish education. This school, subsequently transferred to Kew, became under Hurwitz's successor, Neumegen, the school to which most of the leading families of the communal Establishment sent their sons in the second and third quarters of the 19th century. Hurwitz subsequently became the first Anglo-Jewish professor as Professor of Hebrew at the newly founded University College, London.

Perhaps even more widespread was the influence of Joshua van Oven. The physician of the Great Synagogue and an amateur Hebraist of note, he was a pioneer of communal reorganization. Van Oven made a lasting contribution by converting in 1817 the small charity school of the Great Synagogue (which dated from 1732) into a voluntary school on the lines of those being founded by the National and British Societies for the Church of England and Nonconformists. It was this school which, as the Jew's Free School, became the largest primary school and gave

◀ *Portrait of Dr. Fernando Mendes,* by Catherine da Costa, 1722. Dr. Mendes, a Marrano court physician (d. 1724), who accompanied Catherine of Braganza when she went to England to marry Charles II, was painted by his daughter, the first Anglo-Jewish woman artist. London, Jewish Museum.

Sir Moses Montefiore, 1840. Painting by Solomon Hart, R.A., 1840. Sir Moses Montefiore (1784-1885), the famous philanthropist, is shown in Lieutenancy uniform and holding the Ottoman sultan's *firman* condemning the Damascus ritual murder libel. He was the first English Jew in modern times to be knighted. London, Spanish and Portuguese Jews' Congregation.

Rabbi Solomon Hirschell (1762-1842). Painting by F. B. Barlin. Born in London where his father was rabbi, he was brought up in Germany. He embodied the forces of tradition and was also the first rabbi of the Great Synagogue to act as chief rabbi for the Ashkenazim of Britain and the British colonies. London, National Portrait Gallery.

successive generations of the Jewish proletariat a grounding in secular education, an indoctrination in English standards and an injuction to fidelity to Jewish religious tradition.

Even the traditional chief rabbi, Solomon Hirschell, who at the end of his life resisted the coming of religious reform, showed some adjustment to modern ideas—he was, after all, brought up in Berlin, where his father, Hart Lyon (former rabbi of London) was rabbi and acquainted with the circle of Moses Mendelssohn. Hirschell, incidentally, was the first prominent English rabbi to be of English birth (although of European upbringing); and he was the first who could be called a chief rabbi, whose authority was generally recognized by Ashkenazi congregations beyond London and indeed in the British colonies overseas.

SOCIAL LIFE IN THE 18TH CENTURY

As the 18th century advanced, some Jews began to fulfill the hopes that had been entertained by those English Christians who had considered that in the congenial atmosphere of England they would convert. Some of the proudest Sephardi families who had retained their loyalty to Judaism during two centuries of threatened persecution were assimilated and married into the English upper class. Moses Mendes, a minor poet, was baptized, and others, even if they did not convert themselves, encouraged their children to enter the English aristocracy. Samson Gideon, the great financier of the mid-19th century, secretly retained membership of the Sephardi community, but he married a Christian and had his children baptized. He did this to support his unsuccessful claim to a baronetcy or peerage; and it is clear from a letter to his son, when the latter was created a baronet while still a schoolboy at Eton, that Samson Gideon's overriding ambition was to found an English landed family.

Many among those Jews who remained within the fold were accused of worldliness, of ostentation in dress and behavior, of levity. Rabbi Hirsch Levin (or Hart Lyon), rabbi of London's Ashkenazi Great Synagogue from 1757-64, castigates his flock for dressing like Gentiles, while their womenfolk in decollete dresses and fashionable wigs endeavor not to appear daughters of Israel. They associate with English people even on Christian feasts when they dress better than on their own. They eat Christmas pudding, visit theaters and operas, coffee houses and gaming houses. And they are lax about Jewish observances.

Yet the interest in theater and opera which he condemned was a manifestation of the interest which Jews had (and have) in music and which made them patrons of the great musical figures of the time, such as the young Mozart when brought to London by his father, and Handel, whose *Judas Maccabeus* they, together with the composer's royal patron, turned from a failure into a success when Handel was boycotted by the English nobility. It was the same spirit of interest in the arts which George Bernard Shaw a century and a half later praised when he commented on the influence on the theater of the absence of rich nonconformist families and the presence of rich Jewish families.

Jews of the upper class certainly mixed socially with non-Jews; they were among the guests of Horace Walpole and, in an age of laxity, when the clergy were often younger sons of the aristocracy or landed gentry, holding livings donated by their

'*Moses and Aaron*', by Aaron de Chavez. This painting, showing Moses and Aaron with the Ten Commandments in Spanish and Hebrew, was over the Ark in the Creechurch Lane Synagogue. The artist, Aaron de Chavez (d. 1705) was the first recorded Jewish painter to work in England. London, Spanish and Portuguese Jews' Congregation. Photo Freeman, London.

families, and not celebrated for their spiritual qualities, Jewish owners of country houses were even to be found playing cards with the local parson.

Members of the community did not fail to do the fashionable thing and have their portraits painted by the famous painters of the period, Reynolds, Gainsborough or Romney. Judging by what remains in England's historic synagogues and in the Jewish Museum, communal dignitaries and rabbis also patronized lesser artists, so that the interest aroused in the modern viewer is rather that of the historian than the art connoisseur.

EARLY ANGLO-JEWISH ARTISTS

The community was also producing artistic talent of its own. Aaron de Chavez painted a famous picture of Moses and Aaron for the first Bevis Marks synagogue in 1674. Martha Isaacs was chosen to paint the portrait of Rabbi David Tevele Schiff in 1765, though her career in England ended soon after, when she left to settle in India. Abraham de Lopes Oliveira was a silversmith whose ritual objects—particularly ornaments for Scrolls of the Law and Sabbath lamps—were of the highest standard, so that the needs of the community, which, in the early days of the Resettlement had either been supplied from Amsterdam or by non-Jewish craftsmen such as John Ruslen, were at a later date catered for by native-born Jewish masters. By the end of the century, Naphtali Hart, a Jewish silversmith, was in partnership with a Scotsman, Duncan Urquhart, and while their firm specialized in the elegant tea services fashionable at the beginning of the 19th century, they also followed a profitable side-line by making *kiddush* cups for ceremonial occasions. However, the plate presented annually to the Lord Mayor of London from the end of the 17th century by the Jewish community as a gesture of their goodwill, though it depicted a theme of Jewish significance, seems to have been executed by non-Jewish craftsmen.

There were also immigrant artists, Solomon Polack from Holland, and Solomon Bennet from Poland, a portrait painter and engraver. The latter's portrait of the chief rabbi, Solomon Hirschell, which appeared in a pamphlet of 1808 by Levi Alexander, entitled *'The Axe to the Root'; or Ignorance and Superstition evident in the Character of the Rev. S. Hirschell,* did not improve the bad relations already existing between the two men. Bennet, in fact, although considered highly as a painter in Germany where he lived for many years, is better known as a controversialist than an artist among Anglo-Jewry.

Sabbath lamp, London, 1734. English eighteenth-century silver lamps for the Sabbath are rare. This one, dated 1734, is by the Anglo-Jewish silversmith, Abraham de Oliveira, who was responsible for many Jewish ritual objects. This lamp is similar to contemporary Dutch models and contains six parts (hook, crown, ball, lamp with seven burners, drip-pan and pendant finial). London, Jewish Museum.

Lord Mayor's plate, London, 1737. Beautiful silver plate with English inscription recording presentation to 'Sir John Barnard, Knight, Lord Mayor of the City of London by the Body of Jews residing in the said city, anno 1737.' In the center of the plate there is an imaginary coat of arms of the Tribe of Judah. Jerusalem, Israel Museum.

FROM PEDDLER TO PUGILIST

In the 18th century, many of the needs of the rural housewife, who visited a market town infrequently and the metropolis perhaps once in a lifetime, if at all, were supplied by various kinds of itinerant salesmen. Among these was the bearded Ashkenazi peddler, generally a recent immigrant, depicted in caricature by Rowlandson and others or in the porcelain statuettes of the period. He made his way with his pack on his back, visiting the remote and outlying countryside districts and providing the inhabitants of isolated areas with the haberdashery and the baubles they would otherwise have had to go and get from afar. Many of these itinerant tradesmen formed the nuclei of provincial communities, for when they saw the opportunity, they would settle down and turn jeweler, silversmith, tradesman, or, in the ports, navy agent.

At the end of the social scale were the old clothes men, eking out a meager living from buying secondhand clothes and selling them to the lower-class Englishmen who, until the mid-19th century, could not afford to buy new clothes and wore the cast-offs of the more affluent. Poverty and unemployment increased among the unskilled Ashkenazi immigrants, many of whom found that the hopes they had had of making a living in England bore no resemblance to reality. Some took to crime and it was after a robbery with violence committed by Jews on the inhabitants of an isolated farm at Chelsea, that the Government imposed its prohibition on the issuing of free passes which had enabled Jews to come to England from the Continent. Another notable crime, though committed in France in 1791,

A Jewish peddler, c. 1760. Derby ware statuette of a Jewish peddler who is wearing an East European fur-edged hat and long coat. National Art Collection Fund, Lady Ludlow Collection.

86715

LIBRARY
College of St. Francis
JOLIET, ILL.

The Jewish boxer Daniel Mendoza (1763-1836). Daniel Mendoza whose skill made him the most famous pugilist of his time is shown in his second and successful fight with the previous champion, Richard Humphreys, on May 6 1789. Engraving by J. Grozer after Thomas Rowlandson. Alfred Rubens Collection.

had repercussions in England, for the Jewish thieves who stole the du Barry diamonds brought them to their criminal contacts in London. However, in this affair, a Jew was also on the side of the angels, for when the jewels were shown to Lyon de Symons, he not only recognized them but was instrumental in apprehending the criminals. It may be that the character of Fagin, familiar to readers of Dickens' *Oliver Twist,* and considered an anti-Semitic portrait, would have found its place in late eighteenth-century London, though it was out of date when the book was written in the 1830s. For by that time Anglo-Jewry was more typically represented by its sober and respectable middle class.

Previously, however, Daniel Mendoza taught the poor self-defense and by his own success as a pugilist won the respect of the general population for his people. The conscience of the established community had been aroused by the plight of the poor in the 1770s and 1780s. Societies were set up to teach the poor trades and crafts, to give them the means of subsistence, and to apprentice youths so that they might earn a living in tailoring or in one of the other occupations then followed by Jews.

In the mid-18th century, an effort was made to facilitate the naturalization of Jews but the storm caused by the 1753 Jew Bill, though a limited measure, led to its almost immediate repeal. Henceforward the Jews passed out of legislative history until the emancipation of the Roman Catholics and Nonconformists in the early 19th century engendered action to obtain equal political rights for the Jewish community, by then almost all native born.

However, another facet of governmental activity in the 18th century was a happier augury for the future. When Empress Maria Theresa expelled the Jews of Prague in 1774, George II and the British Government, with no ulterior motive, made representations to have the decree rescinded, thus providing the first instance of a European government acting in the interests of an alien minority. In the 19th century, such cooperation between the Anglo-Jewish community and the British Government to help persecuted Jewries abroad was to be a feature of foreign policy.

This later cooperation of Jewry and the British Government was aided by what was originally merely a matter of protocol—the protest of the Ashkenazim at their exclusion from the loyal greetings extended by the Sephardim to the new king, George III, on his accession to the throne in 1760. The compromise solution between the two communities, that the Sephardim and Ashkenazim would join together on matters of mutual interest, though at first resulting in intermittent consultations only, was the nucleus of the Board of Deputies, the representative Anglo-Jewish organization of the 19th and 20th centuries. Its activities and recommendations on behalf of Jewish communities both at home and abroad have been listened to by the British Government and its agencies, though its influence has depended on Britain's relationship with the Jews at the time. Thus, in the 19th century, when Britain's policies coincided with Jewish aspirations, the Board was a powerful organization whose specialized knowledge was respected. On the other hand, the exact opposite is true of the 1940s, when the Zionist-orientated Board was in conflict with the Labor Government which was rigid in its opposition not only to a Jewish state but to the admission of all those survivors of the concentration camps who wished to settle in Palestine.

Silver Kiddush cup, London, 1810. Plain goblet with rounded foot. Hebrew inscription recording presentation to the Jewish community in the Kent port of Sheerness by Moses bar Michael in 1811. By the London silversmith Thomas Daniel, 1810. Jewish Historical Society of England, University College, London. – *Silver citron box,* London, 1817. Engraved with Hebrew and English inscription recording presentation by the chief rabbi, Solomon Hirschell, to Aaron Joseph, warden of the Great Synagogue, London, on his marriage, 1817. The box unscrews to hold a citron *(etrog)* used on the Feast of Tabernacles. By the London silversmith Samuel Hennell. London, Jewish Historical Society of England, University College. – *Silver goblet,* 1812. Presented to Dr. Coltman by the Jews of Liverpool for his services to their poor, 1812. By Duncan Urquhart and Naphtali Hart. London, Jewish Historical Society of England.

The Israel-de Symons wedding, 1822. The chief rabbi, Solomon Hirschell, marries under the traditional canopy Samuel Hilbert Israel of Clapham to Fanny, youngest daughter of Baron Lyon de Symons (the couple became the parents of Sir Barrow Helbert Ellis, Indian civil servant). London, Jewish Museum.

NEW ARRIVALS

By the end of the 18th century, therefore, there existed a community of about 20,000, of whom 2,000 were Sephardim and the rest Ashkenazim. While the majority, numbering some 15,000, lived in London, there were provincial communities of varying size in a score of other town-ports like Plymouth and Portsmouth, country towns like Exeter, fashionable resorts like Bath and Brighton, and one or two of the rising manufacturing centers like Manchester.

Not only the numbers but also the composition of the community had undergone changes in the preceding hundred years and it was particularly noticeable among its leadership that very few of the families who had originated among the Marranos remained within the fold. Consequently leadership in the 19th century fell to those families which had arrived from countries such as Italy during the middle of the 18th century. The Mocattas and the Montefiores, fairly modest on their arrival, became the magnates of nineteenth-century Anglo-Jewry.

Among the Ashkenazim, where wealth and social status were not so great, the assimilatory process was slower. Although individual members of famous families and their descendants did convert or marry out of the faith, the likelihood was that the family itself, or at least a branch of it, would remain Jewish so that the name would survive. An example is the Goldsmid family. While Abraham and Benjamin's children were lost to Judaism, Sir Isaac Lyon Goldsmid was a great figure in nineteenth-century Anglo-Jewish history. The Cohen family, founded by Levi Barent Cohen, who came from Amersfoort in Holland in the third quarter of the 18th century, is another instance of a family whose descendants married into every well-known Anglo-Jewish family; while the nineteenth-century Rothschilds made it a definite policy to allow daughters to marry into the general population—where the prize was sufficiently high—but discouraged such practices among the sons, a formula which proved successful until the 20th century.

THE PERIOD OF EMANCIPATION

The 19th century is rich in famous Anglo-Jewish individuals— Moses Montefiore, David Salomons, various Rothschilds, the first Lord Swaythling—men of action and achievement. Anglo-Jewish talent found its outlet in organization, in building up a series of institutions, which, firmly based, have survived continuously for more than a century. The tendency is in keeping with the English environment. The importance of character in Victorian England is stressed over mere book learning; the social legislation of the period bears witness to the growing awareness of the rich and influential that they have a duty toward their social inferiors; the principles of *laissez-faire* are gradually made to retreat before government control; the supremacy of the family and of a puritanical code of morality succeed the permissiveness of the pre-Victorian era.

Nathan Meyer Rothschild and his family, c. 1821. Painting by W.A. Hobday. The founder of the English branch of the Rothschilds (1776-1836) has his fourth son, Mayer Amschel (1818-84) on his knee. His wife holds the youngest child, Louise (1820-94); next are Charlotte (1802-59), Lionel Nathan (1808-79), Anthony (1810-76) and Nathaniel (1812-70). On the floor, Hannah Mayer (1815-64). London, Jewish Museum.

The Jews of England found themselves in sympathy with this code generally. The interaction of Jewish teachings and of Victorian Bible-based morality led to harmony in ideas and practice. The respectable, hardworking Jewish community of the mid-19th century was content to parallel Christian church-going by regular synagogue attendance; to strive for better material conditions for themselves and their families; and to support their communal leaders in the struggle for political equality, which entered its long final phase when the granting of Catholic emancipation in 1829 made it seem unreasonable that only the Jews should be excluded from political power.

It is probably true that, like the suffragettes more than half a century later, the emancipationists were a minority movement, the mass of the Jews being prepared to accept the *status quo*. In the period after the 1832 Reform Bill which gave a limited extension of the franchise, the momentum gradually grew, especially since in local government and in such privileges as the freedom of the City of London—without which retail trade within the City was forbidden—the barriers were falling fast. By 1855 there was a Jewish Lord Mayor of London, Sir David

Baron Lionel Nathan de Rothschild, 1835. Painting by Moritz Daniel Oppenheimer. A protagonist in the struggle for Jewish emancipation and the first Jew to sit as a member of the House of Commons (1858). He financed the purchase of the Suez Canal shares in 1875. London, National Portrait Gallery.

Sir Isaac Lyon Goldsmid's house at 20 Spital Square. The house of a Jewish patrician in East London, before the wealthy merchants and financiers moved their homes westward. Goldsmid (1778-1859), wealthy banker and the first Jewish baronet in England (1841), built himself a villa at Regent's Park in the 1820s. Historical Buildings Section, London County Council.

Salomons, and neither he nor Sir Moses Montefiore, who had been Sheriff of London from 1837 to 1838, had to compromise their Judaism in any way to execute their civic duties. The non-Jewish support was also impressive. Lord Macaulay was a powerful advocate and the approbation of individuals was backed by the voice of the City of London which was prepared, to all intents and purposes, to be disfranchised for eleven years rather than abandon the Member of Parliament it wanted, Baron Lionel Nathan de Rothschild, and elect a more 'acceptable' candidate. The stumbling block through these final years was not the House of Commons but the die-hard members of the House of Lords, many of whom genuinely believed that by admitting Jews to the ranks of politicians, and thereby allowing them to

The first Lord Rothschild taking the oath in the House of Lords, 1885. Painting by B.S. Marks. Nathaniel Mayer, first Lord Rothschild (1840-1915) is shown taking the oath in the Jewish manner, with head covered. Politically a Conservative (unlike his Liberal father), he was the acknowledged lay head of the Anglo-Jewish community. First Jewish peer, he was one of the outstanding Jews of his time. National Portrait Gallery.

become potentially members of the British Government, they would be jeopardizing the survival of Britain as a Christian country. The solution to the problem in 1858 allowed each House to determine the form of oath to be taken by its members—the unacceptable part of the existent oath being the phrase 'on the true faith of a Christian'. By the time Nathaniel Rothschild was raised to the peerage in 1885 such controversies were completely out of date and he was able to take his seat without opposition.

JEWS IN BRITISH POLITICS

But the thirty years' struggle had had the effect of aligning the Jews with the Liberals and Radicals who had supported their claims against Tory extremism, though Conservatives like Disraeli and Bentinck had spoken and voted in favor of Emancipation. By the 1870s, however, Jews were joining the Conservative party and were being elected to Parliament as Conservatives. In 1874, Saul Isaac became the first Jewish Conservative M.P. and he was followed shortly afterward by the more talented Lionel Louis Cohen and Henry de Worms (later Lord Pirbright). Nor did the Rothschilds maintain their former Liberalism. The

second Lord Rothschild was a leading figure on the Conservative benches in the House of Lords in the early 20th century.

The move away from the Liberals in the 1870s was due partly to the growth of anti-Semitism in the Liberal Party due to its opposition to what it considered Disraeli's cynical eastern policies. While the Liberals were hostile to Turkey because of her cruelty to her Christian subjects, Disraeli was prepared to overlook these misdemeanors in the pursuit of his conception of British interests—the protection of the route to India, 'the brightest jewel in the English crown', from Russian infiltration. Nevertheless, the Liberal Party still attracted Jews of the caliber of Sir George Jessel, Solicitor General in 1871, and in the early 20th century, Herbert Samuel (the first Viscount Samuel), the first professing Jew to be a member of a British Cabinet, and Rufus Isaacs (the first Marquess of Reading).

The decline of the Liberal Party in the 1920s and 1930s caused many of its adherents to transfer their allegiance to the growing Labor Party, though numbers of Jews have remained Liberals by conviction. For many years, Jews were out of sympathy with Conservatism, though in local government in the 1960s they featured prominently on Conservative-dominated councils. On the other hand, socialist doctrine proved attractive

The old clothes market in Petticoat Lane, c. 1860. Old clothes dealing was a typical Jewish occupation until the mid-nineteenth century and the old clothes markets were in the heart of London's Jewish quarter. Alfred Rubens Collection.

to Jews, whether the descendants of proletarian Russian immigrants of the 1881-1914 period or intellectuals. Since 1945 their numbers in the House of Commons have been proportionately high, with a considerable number supporting the left wing of the Party. Indeed, until persecution of the Jews as Jews by the Russians, and even as late as the Hungarian rising of 1956, many Jews were members of the Communist Party. For what has happened is that, with the loosening of religious ties, Jews have gone searching after 'other gods' and have sought their redemption in Marxism, socialism or one of the fashionable creeds which have an ephemeral appeal.

THE RUSSO-JEWISH IMMIGRANTS

The most important social change within the life of Anglo-Jewry came with the period of mass immigration from Eastern Europe in the years between 1881 and 1914. Anglo-Jewry increased in these years from 65,000 to 300,000, London Jewry from 46,000 to 180,000. This was only a part of a much wider movement which, as a result of tsarist persecution, brought a million Jews from Eastern Europe to the Western World. There had been a few immigrants, of course, from Eastern Europe into Britain before the 1860s, and a small but steady flow in the later 1860s and 1870s. In 1881, however, the assassination of Alexander II was followed by pogroms spreading a wave of terror through many provinces in south-west Russia. Similar persecutions over the next decades added to the flow of emigrants.

It was not only from the Russian empire that the immigrants came. There was also a steady flow from the Austro-Hungarian territory of Galicia, where the cause was poverty not persecution, and from Rumania, where governmental anti-Semitism became a tradition.

So much alien immigration provoked mounting opposition and a Royal Commission was set up to produce a report in 1903. Although it recommended no general bar against immigration but only attempts to prevent the concentration of immigrants in particular areas, an Aliens Act was passed in 1905 which sought to limit immigration generally. However, in the British tradition, it allowed entry to genuine refugees from religious or racial persecution; and within a few years the number of such refugees obtaining entry to Britain rose again. It was the war of 1914, not the Aliens Act, which really ended the mass migration from Eastern Europe.

The newcomers provided a complete contrast to the assimilated Anglo-Jewish community, in which they were at first not altogether welcome. Their habits and their dress were different, and they knew no English. They were a distinct element overcrowding the East End of London and forming ghettos in the large provincial cities, appearing conspicuous wherever they went. The opposition which alien immigration provoked aroused fears of anti-Semitism; and the Jewish Board of Guardians, feeling that its resources were unequal to coping with the far greater number of applicants for its help, offered them inducements to return to their countries of origin. It was not until

Israel Zangwill (1864-1926). Painting by W.R. Sickert. An author and dramatist of versatile talents, Zangwill will probably be best remembered for his description of life in the London Jewish immigrant quarter, where he was brought up and taught as a young man. Especially popular are *Children of the Ghetto, Ghetto Tragedies* and others in the same vein. London, Jewish Museum.

the Kishinev pogroms that the Anglo-Jewish community accepted the fact that the flow of immigrants would not cease and that the new arrivals had come to stay. Thereafter, a united community fought attempts to restrict immigration. It was largely due to their efforts that the Aliens Act did not, as events proved, turn out to be the complete barrier to immigration which had been feared.

The immigrants formed, in the years before 1914, a world of their own. This world was sympathetically depicted by Israel Zangwill, born in 1864 and himself the son of an immigrant, though like his own 'grandchildren of the ghetto' removed from it by education, by profession, by associates and, in his own case, by out-marriage. He was an early and enthusiastic supporter of Herzl, though he severed his connection with the Zionist movement when the Seventh Congress refused Britain's offer of Uganda as an alternative home for the Jews.

In his famous *Children of the Ghetto,* Zangwill brought to life the East End community, its hopes, its achievements, its poverty, its religion, and its conflict between the Orthodox older generation and the modern younger people. Here is found what no sociological or statistical report could give—an understanding of the effects of their experiences on the people themselves. And because Zangwill was a Jew from the East End, albeit of a generation earlier, before the mass immigrations, the incidents he describes are often based on actual occurrences or on Jewish laws and practices which would be unknown to Gentile writers. Many of the characters in the book are thinly disguised portraits of personalities well known in the East End of London in the last twenty years of the 19th century. The saintly Reb Shmuel, for example, is based on the much loved rabbi Jacob Reinowitz (a *dayyan* or judge of the chief rabbi's court), who combined strict religious practice and great learning with tolerance toward those who brought their problems to him; the ultra-pious mystic N.L.D. Zimmer was the original of Karlkammer in the book; Harry S. Lewis, the editor of the *Jewish Standard* (on which Zangwill worked) was the model for Raphael Leon, who has a leading role in *Grandchildren of the Ghetto;* Melchizedek Pinchas has been identified with Naphtali H. Imber, the composer of *Ha-Tikvah;* and, as the model for Moses Angel, Zangwill used his own father. Like Moses Angel, the elder Zangwill's heart was set on Jerusalem; and, as soon as he could afford it, the son enabled the father to settle there.

Zangwill in his short stories also portrayed Jewish suburbia —Dalston and Highbury—as well as Jewish life in the provinces, in Eastern Europe and in the United States. It is significant that his writings on Jewish themes have proved the most lasting of his many works.

A novel of the Jewish provincial ghetto had to wait a further generation until in 1922 Louis Golding's best-seller *Magnolia Street* did for Manchester what Israel Zangwill had done for London. The book, although popular in its day, does not have the same charm and warmth as Zangwill's work, although it is now of interest as recording a social milieu which has disappeared.

The Elite

Communal authority remained with the Anglo-Jewish elite well into the 20th century. In the Jewish, and indeed the Victorian English spirit, the Establishment was very much a family affair, with the Rothschilds at the top and a group of other closely knit families ruling Anglo-Jewish institutions. These families inter-married with one another; they lived near one another in town; even in the country they clustered their country houses in close proximity, as in the Rothschild territory on the Buckinghamshire-Bedfordshire border, or in Kent.

Some of the magnates derived a special prestige from their association with royalty—particularly 'the Marlborough House set,' the entourage of the Prince of Wales for some thirty years before his accession to the throne as Edward VII in 1901. There had, of course, been contacts between the royal family and Anglo-Jewry before. William IV's brother, the duke of Sussex,

'Brighton Front', 1861. Abraham Solomon (1823-62) depicts Brighton Front in 1861, when it was past its fashionable zenith under the Regency but still a favorite resort for many, not least London's wealthier Jews. Tunbridge Wells Art Gallery.

The North London synagogue, 1868. This synagogue, by the Jewish architect Hyman Henry Collins, was the first public synagogue built in the popular middle-class residential areas of North London of the time (Barnsbury, Canonbury, Highbury, and others). Jewish Historical Society of England.

for instance, was a keen orientalist and a patron of Jewish charities and institutions; but the friendship of the Prince of Wales with members of the Rothschild family was a new departure in that it brought prominent Jews into close regular association with the heir to the throne and thus, *ipso facto,* into the highest rank of English society. The Prince of Wales, excluded by Queen Victoria from any active role in the work of government, took over the leadership of London society which his mother had abandoned in her widowed seclusion. The Marlborough House set, over which the Prince presided, showed by its very position the reaction against the austere thought of Buckingham Palace. Membership of the English landed aristocracy was not a necessary qualification—indeed almost the reverse. Wealth, intellect, charm were the qualifications; above all, the

ability not to be boring. The first Lord Rothschild and his two brothers, the brothers Reuben, Arthur and Albert Sassoon, Sir Ernest Cassel, Baron de Hirsch, Sir Felix Semon, the physician, and Sir George Lewis, the most fashionable solicitor of the day, were all within the circle—although not all were active members of the Jewish community. The prince would stay at the homes of some of his Jewish friends and, where the matter arose, would accommodate himself to their religious duties. The prince's fondness for the company of his Jewish friends and his tastes for Jewish humor naturally aroused considerable comment. It is reasonable to infer that Edward was attracted by the combination of luxury and taste, the sense of something interesting and different, which these Jewish magnates with their Continental or Oriental backgrounds could contribute.

LEADERSHIP AND SOCIAL SERVICE

The Jewish upper class as a whole, however, while less glamorous than the members of the royal entourage, were men with a social conscience. Their prosperity did not make them indifferent to the needs of their poorer coreligionists. They felt it their duty to take communal office, to man the committees of the voluntary organizations, and they spared neither their time nor their energy in the causes they upheld. Not everyone was a Moses Montefiore who retired from business at the age of forty to devote himself to good works. Lionel Louis Cohen, for instance, did his day's work on the Stock Exchange and in Parliament before turning to his Board of Guardians activities.

Much of the work done epitomized the Jewish ideals of charity. It is not enough according to Jewish teaching to make a donation and then to turn one's back; consideration must be given to the use to which the money is put, and to the dignity of the recipient who must not be allowed to feel himself a beggar, of no account to anyone. From this evolved the Board of Guardians' practice, side by side with emergency relief, of helping the poor to help themselves. Loans were granted to start businesses, to tide a man over a period of bad luck, and systematic efforts were made to teach trades. In certain aspects the Board was well ahead of current non-Jewish practice. The employment of a sanitary inspector, although intermittent, was instrumental at least in limiting epidemics in 1855 and 1866; and similar regular work in the housing field in the following decades pioneered environmental health work by voluntary bodies and local authorities.

At the end of the 19th century, the Board of Guardians, though opposed to providing general medical services, was among the first to combat and treat tuberculosis. Moreover, when its methods, advanced in the early days of its existence, fell behind current ideas based on replacing philanthropic action with trained professional staff, the Board was flexible enough to adapt itself to the new techniques. In the mid-20th century, the Board had to fit in to the framework of the Welfare State, dealing increasingly with the needs of old people and of other social groups whose problems do not stem primarily from poverty; and after a century of work as a Board of Guardians of the Jewish poor, it reflected these changes by renaming itself the Jewish Welfare Board.

In education, too, the Jewish community were pioneers. The Jews' Free School has already been mentioned and it was followed by similar schools providing elementary education for large numbers of poor Jewish children in the East End of London. Under the patronage of the Rothschilds and other communal magnates (who patronized their own particular school) these schools flourished. Their standards were high, due to the intelligence and devotion of Jewish schoolteachers and the keenness of the pupils themselves. Many an immigrant child of the 1881-1914 period owed his later success to the anglicization he received in these schools. The Jews' Free School (JFS), for instance, was one of the first to organize vocational training. In the 1930s, when many of its pupils were still living in unsatis-factory conditions, it equipped the senior girls to teach home economics in a Jewish context. It is perhaps significant that, though this East End school was destroyed by enemy action in World War II, its successor, the JFS Comprehensive School is again a leading institution in the field of Jewish and secular education, and one of the more successful examples of the new and not yet fully proven comprehensive education in Britain.

THE RELIGION OF THE VICTORIAN JEW

The location of the postwar JFS outside the former Jewish quarter of East London is only one indication of the movement of the Jewish population away from its traditional home in the East End. In the 1930s, the wealthier children of the immigrants followed the practice of their predecessors and abandoned the East End in search of gardens, bathrooms and the status of suburban living. The attraction of suburbs for Jews had, of course, started in the mid-19th century when there was a similar movement out of the center of London by the growing middle classes. For the Jewish middle class of the 19th century the results of prosperity were new communities followed by new synagogues to serve the growing populations of the West End, North and North-West London. Previous self-imposed limitations on the building of new synagogues had to give way to the realities of a situation in which most synagogue-goers were people still walking to synagogue on Sabbaths and festivals, yet living miles from the synagogues existing at the beginning of the 19th century.

It was as a result of these movements of population and the increase of synagogues in residential areas that in 1870 the London Ashkenazim formed a United Synagogue. Although the United Synagogue was founded and run by laymen as an umbrella organization for the offshoots of the original Great Synagogue, its earlier years were closely associated with the chief rabbinate of the Adlers. Nathan Marcus Adler (1803-90), who succeeded Solomon Hirschell as chief rabbi, had a university doctorate and a German training; he was, while strictly Orthodox, a modern pastor and an organizer. He was succeeded in 1890 by his son, Hermann, who had previously acted as his father's deputy. Hermann Adler, like his father, was a traditionalist, but more willing to consider some innovation. These processes of modernization and adjustment within the Anglo-Jewish religious establishment provide another outstanding example of the Anglo-Jewish genius for organization rather than spirituality. Anglo-Judaism under the Adlers aimed to keep within it the majority of the Anglo-Jewish community, whether doctrinally Orthodox or more permissive in practice. Once again the Anglican compromise set the example for Anglo-Jewish imitation. Perhaps this helps to explain why the Reform Synagogue—whose origins in 1840 had only a limited relation to theological issues and whose early members included individuals like Sir Francis Goldsmid, meticulous in their religious observance—and the later Liberal Jewish movement never attracted a mass membership either in London

Lionel Louis Cohen (1832-82). A *Vanity Fair* cartoon of 1886. As founder of the United Synagogue and the Jewish Board of Guardians, Conservative Member of Parliament and stockbroker, Cohen represented the lay leadership of the Anglo-Jewish religious establishment. (Photo George Miles).

Hyman Hurwitz, 1846. Born in Poland, Hurwitz (1770-1844) became a pioneer of the 'Enlightenment' in England. An educational reformer and founder of a famous school, he was first Professor of Hebrew at University College, London. Litho by J.M. Johnson from a picture by Kirkafer. London, Jewish Historical Society of England.

or in the provinces. At present, the Progressive community numbers 40,000 out of a total Jewish community estimated at some 420,000.

A contributory factor was, perhaps, that the mid-19th century immigrants from Germany who so powerfully developed the Reform Movement in the United States did not make so marked an impression on the Anglo-Jewish community as a whole;

they were probably relatively fewer and many of them, as persons of broad European culture, speedily assimilated into the wider community.

The Russo-Jewish immigrants of the 1881-1914 period, who in other countries created a new and separate community, did not remain long isolated from the previous Anglo-Jewish community; nor did they, on the other hand, completely alter its character and institutions. Instead, they gradually assimilated into the established Anglo-Jewish community while also slowly influencing its ways. The reasons for this phenomenon must be set out in some detail, becuse they provide the key to the understanding not only of the relations between Jews and non-Jews but also of how the Anglo-Jewish community developed as it did in the late 19th and first half of the 20th century.

THE JEWISH ATTITUDE TO ENGLAND

Throughout the 19th century, England had acquired a special reputation in the eyes of Jews the world over. The tolerance of her own attitude toward the Jews compared favorably with the anti-Semitism, overt or implicit, of Continental Europe. In England, Jews could acquire wealth, property, positions of influence, the friendship and sympathy of their Government and also of their fellow citizens. For this was an age when Englishmen could still be aroused to moral indignation by reports of persecutions abroad; and they crowded meetings held, under distinguished auspices, to protest against ill-treatment of Jews in Russia and elsewhere. The completion of Emancipation in 1858 removed any reservations about Jewish political equality. Finally, the unequaled prestige of Britain throughout the world naturally had its effect on the standing of Britain in Jewish eyes.

All these factors come together in the journeys of Sir Moses Montefiore to aid his hapless brethren. He made them with the support of the British Government, traveling at times in a British warship, bearing an English title; he was granted a distinction by the queen to mark his success. His efforts were regarded by some as a demonstration of British influence in the Near East. It was natural therefore that Jews all over the world should see some equation between British and Jewish interests and regard Britain differently from other nations.

The philanthropic and political activities of Montefiore were designed to hasten the day when Jews abroad would obtain similar privileges to those enjoyed by their coreligionists in England. With the belief in the compulsive power of continuous progress current among the Victorians, it was inconceivable that there should ever be retrogression. True, the day of liberation was long in coming but that it would eventually arrive was never doubted. Thus is significant that Montefiore, with all his love for the Holy Land, never advocated mass immigration as a solution to Jewish ills. That was left to a more realistic and cynical age which had learned by bitter experience that general enlightenment was a mirage, though in England there was a group of non-Jewish writers in the mid-19th century who, before the days of political Zionism, advocated a Zionist program.

Novelists, poets, and dramatists in the 18th century had been generally anti-Semitic, or at best neutral, in their treatment of Jewish characters. The 19th century, however, saw a desire among great English writers to do the Jew honor. Trollope, it is true, was anti-Semitic, but Dickens, after Fagin in *Oliver Twist* redressed the balance by creating the too-good-to-be-true Riah in *Our Mutual Friend*. In Scott's romantic medieval novel *Ivanhoe*, Rebecca was noble as well as beautiful and, unlike Shakespeare's Jessica, staunch in her religious loyalty. Disreali made Sidonia a combination of an idealized Rothschild and an equally idealized Disreali, an impossibly heroic and superior figure. Even the

writings of lesser known Jewish authors, such as the poet and novelist Grace Aguilar, helped to give a more sympathetic, and indeed a truer, picture of Jewish life and ideals. As a result the public were given a different picture of the Jew from the old clothes men of caricature or even the characters of missionary novelists who, depicted in the course of exchanging their Jewish darkness for the light of Christianity, were represented with varying degrees of accuracy.

In the later 19th century, however, an unfavorable view of Anglo-Jewry came from certain Jewish writers who castigated the materialism, the ostentation, the lack of religious sincerity of the wealthy middle class whom they classified as card-playing philistines. Two novels particularly set the tone and thereby

The Montefiore family, 1797. Painting by R. Jelgerhuis. Sir Moses' father, Joseph Elias Montefiore (1759-1804), and mother Rachel (1762-1841) with the young Moses, then thirteen, holding a book; his brother Abraham (1788-1824) and two of their sisters. A typical Anglo-Jewish middle-class scene of the period. London, Jewish Museum.

Grace Aguilar

Grace Aguilar (1816-42). A writer of novels on Jewish subjects, Grace Aguilar brought Jewish ideals to the knowledge of the Victorian reading public. Her most popular work, *Vale of Cedars,* describes the trials and tribulations of Spanish Marranos. Alfred Rubens Collection.

give a picture of the social life and attitudes of a section of the population, not necessarily representative of the whole.

In 1888 Amy Levy's *Reuben Sachs* depicted the milieu of Bayswater and Maida Vale, suburbs of fairly recent Jewish settlement: 'Books were a luxury in the Leuniger household. We all have our economies, even the richest of us; and the Leunigers, who begrudged no money for food, clothes or furniture, who went constantly into the stalls of the theater, without considering the expense, regarded every shilling spent on books as pure extravagance.' Another example of her criticism is that: 'Born and bred in the very heart of nineteenth-century London, belonging to an age and a city which has seen the throwing down of so many barriers, the leveling of so many distinctions of class, of caste, of race, of opinion, they had managed to retain the tribal characteristics, to live within the tribal pale to an extent which spoke worlds for the national conservatism.

'They had been educated at Jewish schools, fed on Jewish food, brought up on Jewish traditions and Jewish prejudice.'

But even more contemptuous of Maida Vale society was Frank Danby (alias Julia Frankau, the mother of the novelist Gilbert Frankau) in *Dr Phillips—A Maida Vale Idyll* published in 1887. 'All the burning questions of the hour are to them a dead letter; art, literature, and politics exist not for them. They have but one aim, the acquisition of wealth. Playing cards at each other's houses is their sole experience of the charms of social intercourse; their interests are bounded by their homes and those of their neighboring brethren.'

Yet a little reflection shows how partial were these charges. The cultured cosmopolitan Jew, especially the Central European, was responsible for much patronage of music, the theater, and the arts, not only in London but in provincial cities like Manchester and Bradford.

The great sympathetic Jewish novel of the 19th century was written by a non-Jewish writer. George Eliot's *Daniel Deronda* was published in 1876. It is the story of a young man brought up as a Christian who discovers his origins, reverts to Judaism and, finally, with his Jewish bride, leaves England to settle in Palestine. The inspiration behind the writing of the book is said to have come from Emanuel Deutsch and the character of Daniel was reputedly based on Colonel A.E.W. Goldsmid, himself half-Jewish by birth, but who returned to Judaism and later led the English branch of the early Zionist society *Hovevei Zion* (Lovers of Zion). Through the mouth of one of the characters, Mordechai Cohen, George Eliot voices Jewish aspirations which cannot be faulted in a world where the State of Israel is an accomplished fact but which must have been startling, indeed ludicrous, to many mid-nineteenth-century Jewish men of property: this was made clear by Amy Levy in *Reuben Sachs* where the book is mockingly described by one of the characters as 'George Eliot's elaborate misconception'.

Mordechai's words therefore are more sympathetically received by a later generation than that for which they were written, though there was obviously gratitude for the understanding of Jewish tribulations displayed by a world-famous non-Jewish writer. '...There is a store of wisdom among us to found a new

Professor Samuel Alexander O.M. Bronze sculpture by Sir Jacob Epstein. The Australian-born Jewish philosopher (1859-1938) was awarded the prized distinction of the Order of Merit (in 1930). London, Ben Uri Art Gallery.

Jewish polity, grand, simple, just like the old—a republic where there is equality of protection, an equality which shone like a star on the forehead of our ancient community, and gave it more than the brightness of Western freedom amid the despotisms of the East. Then our race shall have an organic center, a heart and brain to watch and guide and execute; the outraged Jew shall have a deference in the court of nations as the outraged Englishman or American.'

And the last word on the matter came from Daniel himself: 'I am going to the East to become better acquainted with the condition of my race in various countries there... The idea that I am possessed with is that of restoring a political existence to my people, making them a nation again, giving them a national center, such as the English have, though they too are scattered over the face of the globe.'

In an age when Englishmen were traveling to the Middle East, the Jew fulfilled the romantic, exotic role which in the 20th

41

century has passed to the Arab. Lord Shaftesbury, after his period of conversionist activity, was an advocate of Jewish statehood; Laurence Oliphant was another of the pre-Zionists; while Disraeli, though he had been baptized as a boy of thirteen, was profoundly influenced by his Jewish origins, even inventing ancestors from the Spanish Sephardi aristocracy to fulfill his cravings for romance. His visit to Palestine, his Jewish friendships, his novels were the vital background to the Eastern policies he pursued when at last in the 1870s political power was indubitably achieved, even though his pro-Turkish and anti-Russian line did not directly affect Jewish development in Palestine.

However, despite the few who looked to Palestine, the vast majority of Jews in the 1870s were content with their lot in England and, when the immigrants came after 1881, they had no other promised land in mind than England or America, to which some to them were unable to continue their projected journey because of lack of the passage money. Although these Russo-Polish immigrants flocked to Herzl's meetings and thrilled to his words—in contrast to the 'West End' Jews who cold-shouldered him and the chief rabbi, Hermann Adler who called Zionism an 'egregious blunder'—paying their small contributions to Zionist funds, they had no desire themselves to move on again. England, despite the initial hardships they were enduring, offered opportunities to their children and to themselves to better themelves. The scholarship won by the immigrant boy, Selig Brodetsky, to Cambridge University was a cause for pride to the whole East End community and a presage of what might be for their own children in the future.

The Beginnings of Anglo-Jewish Letters

It is a customary generalization on Anglo-Jewish history that periods of religious observance have alternated with laxity and suicidal assimilation. Observance has coincided with immigrations of Orthodox refugees who have either led to their own lives completely separate from the native-born community or have injected their own fervor into it, until such time as they—or their children—have integrated, and the process has has to begin all over again. The Napoleonic Wars, which slowed down—though they did not stop—immigration for a generation, left by 1815 a largely native-born community. It was the educated members of this community which cooperated, under the leadership of Isaac Lyon Goldsmid, in setting up the first secular university in Great Britain, University College, London, at which Jews could take degrees and in which (as already mentioned) for the first time at a British university, a professorship, that of Hebrew was held by a Jew, Hyman Hurwitz. During the next four decades scholars came from abroad either as political refugees or attracted by the greater freedom possible in England: Emmanuel Deutsch, the Silesian-born talmudist who worked at the British Museum; Louis Loewe, who came from Berlin to be oriental secretary to the duke of Sussex, accompanied Sir Moses Montefiore on many of his missions, and was the first principal of the Jews' College and later of the Ramsgate College; Adolph Neubauer of Hungary,

who joined the Bodleian Library in 1868 and was Reader in Rabbinic Hebrew at Oxford from 1884 to 1900 Solomon Schiller-Szinessy, also of Hungary, who fought in the Hungarian rising of 1848, was Minister of the Manchester congregation and subsequently Reader in Rabbinics at Cambridge.

Yet their impact on general Anglo-Jewish life was limited. In spite of the scholars, in spite of men and women who combined Jewish with secular culture, in spite of the various literary societies and the attempts to promote an interest in and knowledge of the Hebrew language and literature, the sole lasting achievement of this period was the foundation of the *Jewish Chronicle,* which outlived all its rivals and remains the only flourishing publication in Anglo-Jewry to this day. It was fortunate in its editors, and particularly in that Abraham Benisch, himself of Bohemian origin, established the paper on a sound commercial basis while not neglecting learned contributions, a reflection of his own scholarly interests. He it was, too, who advocated settlement in Palestine and laid down a practical program for the enterprise; and it is noteworthy that in later years, despite the hostility of the Anglo-Jewish establishment, the Zionist platform always found support from editors of the *Jewish Chronicle.*

While the majority of the Jewish scholars were from abroad, Britain and its colonies were not without native-born Jewish scholars in the 19th century. This was particularly true of the 1880s and 1890s when there was a surge of Jewish literary activity, albeit inspired largely by the Rumanian-born Solomon Schechter. This interest in the Jewish past was symbolized by the great Anglo-Jewish Historical Exhibition at the Albert Hall in 1887, which made a tremendous impact both in the Anglo-Jewish community and outside; it was an achievement, because of its scope and the pioneering work involved, even greater than that of the exhibition held at the Victoria and Albert Museum in 1956 to celebrate the tercentenary of Jewish Resettlement. One by-product of the 1887 exhibition was the foundation in 1893 of the Jewish Historical Society of England, which, because of the European Holocaust, is probably the last surviving Jewish learned body of its age in Europe.

The circle around Schechter included Israel Zangwill; the philosopher and theologian Claude Montefiore; Lucien Wolf, journalist and authority on foreign affairs; Israel Abrahams, later Reader in Rabbinics at Cambridge; and Joseph Jacobs, folklorist and social scientist, who subsequently left for America and was an editor of the *Jewish Encyclopaedia.* It will be noted that, in the slightly amateurish tradition of English scholarship, most of the group of British-born scholars were men with other occupations.

If one seeks to estimate the contribution of nineteenth- and early twentieth-century Anglo-Jewry to English scholarship it must be admitted that they do not play the same role as Jews in Germany, Italy, or France. Even so, there were many brilliant individual contributions: Samuel Alexander (1859-1938), the philosopher, who was born in Australia but educated at Oxford, where in 1882 he became the first professing Jew to be elected to a fellowship, was an outstanding figure by any standards. A systematic philosopher whose *Space, Time and Deity* has been regarded as the most thorough treatise on philosophy to appear in

England since Hobbes, he was not only a metaphysician but a philosopher deeply interested in ethics and esthetics. But, apart from Alexander, one should mention the Shakespearian scholars, Sir Sidney Lee, editor of the *Dictionary of National Biography* and Sir Israel Gollancz, a founder of the British Academy and its first Secretary.

JEWS IN THE ARTS

In art, the scene is varied. The beginnings were conventional enough: Solomon Alexander Hart (1806-81), Royal Academician, Professor of Painting and Librarian of the Royal Academy, painted large historical scenes in the grand manner as well as

Day of Atonement, 1919. This oil painting of 1919 by Jacob Kramer represents the simple, fervent piety of the Jewish immigrants from Eastern Europe. The artist himself was born in the Ukraine in 1892. Leeds, City Art Gallery.

44

pictures on Jewish themes, including some contemporary pieces. Abraham Solomon (1824-62) was a genre painter of scenes of social respectability but executed with careful and effective craftsmanship. Far different was his more gifted younger brother Simeon Solomon (1835-1905). Beginning as a Pre-Raphaelite—Burne-Jones said he was the greatest artist among them—his earlier paintings have, as Swinburne said, a strange beauty in the drawing of the faces. He was, however, an unstable character and succumbed to excesses of sex, drink and drugs. After a spell in prison, he died in an East London workhouse.

Camille Pissarro was in London as a refugee during the Franco-Prussian War and his son, Lucien (1863-1944) married in England, and did most of his work there. His post-Impressionism influenced the work of English painters of his time. Solomon J. Solomon (1860-1921) was a fashionable portrait-painter of Edwardian society and also had important public commissions: he was a committed Jew. In this he differed from Sir William Rothenstein (1872-1945), although the latter, in his early career, painted a number of Jewish scenes in the strictly Orthodox Machzike Hadath synagogue in East London. Rothenstein was, by origin, one of an assimilated German Jewish family of Bradford. But the Russo-Jewish immigration soon produced in England (as in Paris) its own artists. Alfred Wolmark (1876-1961), David Bomberg (1890-1967), Mark Gertler (1892-1939) and Jacob Kramer (1892-1962) were among this group, Bomberg and Gertler being born in England of recent immigrant parents. Wolmark startled Edwardian galleries by his use of color. Bomberg, Gertler and Kramer, however, while seeking for a time to develop in England a Jewish style that would represent the Yiddish culture of their origins, were more restrained, less addicted to fantasy, more sober in their colors than the analogous Russo-Jewish painters elsewhere, such as Chagall—perhaps because of the sobering influence of the English environment. An outstanding sculptor was Sir Jacob Epstein who, coming from New York, settled in London in 1907. His works varied from bronze portrait busts to monumental sculptures (such as the one adorning the rebuilt Coventry Cathedral).

English Jews also played a minor but respected role in other branches of the arts. Thus that most 'typically British' of songs *A Life On The Ocean Waves* was one of eight hundred songs composed by Henry Russell (1813-1900), whose son Sir Landon Ronald (1873-1938) was a noted composer, conductor, and principal of the Guildhall School of Music. But it was essentially as performers that Jewish musicians were best known—among them the pianists Moiseiwitsch, Solomon, and Dame Myra Hess who founded and ran a series of lunchtime concerts at the National Gallery during World War II; the violinists Yehudi Menuhin and Ida Haendel who both made England their home; and Lionel Tertis who was responsible for the renewed recognition of the viola as a solo instrument.

In literature, a number of Jews have made their mark including the poets Siegfried Sassoon, Isaac Rosenberg and Humbert Wolfe who all made their reputation in the World War I period (when Rosenberg was killed), and the historian Philip Guedella. In the 1950s the impressive record of English drama was spearheaded by a number of Jewish dramatists including Harold Pinter, Arnold Wesker and Peter Shaffer with Lionel Barth scoring successes in musical plays. Well-known younger poets included Dannie Abse and Jon Silkin.

THE IMMIGRANTS AND THE ESTABLISHMENT

By the time of the 1881-1914 immigrations, the established community, although generally traditional in religious observance, was culturally assimilated. The immigrants from countries where they had lived self-contained lives were an element distinct from the native-born community. Just as in the cultural field they published Yiddish newspapers, which tried to resist the official community's policy of anglicization, there was some degree of conflict between their religious institutions, grouped around the small *chevrot* or conventicles and the official religious establishment.

Yet this conflict should not be exaggerated. Some groups among the immigrants, regarding the official community as insufficiently Orthodox, maintained their separatism. But the majority realized that they had in common with the United Synagogue establishment the use of the German or Polish ritual of prayer. Thus, although the immigrant may have found services at a United Synagogue somewhat cold and unemotional—and the membership charges prohibitive, at least initially—he would not have been at a loss in following the liturgy nor could he have condemned its Orthodoxy out of hand. This meant that as the immigrants became more anglicized and began to ascend the social scale, they were attracted from their own *chevrot,* which had been formed into the Federation of Synagogues at the instigation of the first Lord Swaythling in 1887, and often joined the United Synagogue, membership of which became a status symbol to them and their children in the same way as membership of a Reform Congregation was a status symbol in the United States. The results can be seen almost a hundred years later. Whereas the United Synagogue, despite much non-adherence, maintains its dominant position in the Anglo-Jewish community, the Federation of Synagogues has lost regular worshipers in its synagogues, many of which, in areas abandoned by Jewish inhabitants, have had to be closed or amalgamated.

ACHIEVEMENT IN INDUSTRY AND COMMERCE

In the economic field, the great increase in the numbers and influence of the British middle class, one of the most significant factors in nineteenth-century English social history, had repercussions on the Jewish community. It created a demand for consumer goods, which the Jews were particularly adept at satisfying,

◄ *Portrait of the artist's mother,* 1911. Born in the Jewish quarter of East London of Polish-Jewish parents, Mark Gertler (1892-1939) depicted the immigrant types of his childhood. London, Tate Gallery.

45

Seder plate, England, 1925. An English modern silver copy of the early 17th century majolica plates used for the ritual constituents of the Passover Eve ceremony and with the headings of the service in the center. Silver versions of the same type are found in Holland in the 18th century and elsewhere. Jerusalem, Israel Museum.

probably the greatest contribution to 20th century merchandising was made through the firm of Marks and Spencer, who, under Simon Marks and Israel Sieff, changed fundamentally the whole pattern of shopping and the attitude toward buying clothes. By dealing direct with the manufacturer and eliminating the middleman, they were able to reduce prices drastically, while, at the same time, because of the size of their orders, being able to insist on a high quality and design.

RELIGION AND EDUCATION

The Jewish immigration of the 1930s from Central Europe, unlike the proletarian influx from Eastern Europe, was a middle class movement, the refugees being wealthy or comparatively wealthy, educated, with technical know-how, and so were able quickly to acquire economic independence. German and other refugee Jewish scholars, scientists, artists and businessmen made a great contribution to Britain in peace and war. Special mention should perhaps be made of the artists, who have influenced their English surroundings in a way even greater than that of their predecessors of previous immigrations. Joseph Herman, born in Warsaw, who came to England in 1940, made his home among the Welsh miners and portrayed their daily life at work; Hans Feibuch, born in Frankfurt-am-Main, became famous as a painter of murals for English churches; Benno Elkan, whose candelabrum is one of the artistic treasures of the Knesset, also executed similar works for England's national shrine, Westminster Abbey.

It is perhaps remarkable that synagogues in Britain have not as a rule commissioned similar works from Jewish artists, or indeed buildings from Jewish architects of the first rank. In the 20th century, particularly since 1945, there have been a large number of Jewish architects but synagogues have generally been designed either by non-Jewish architects or by less prominent Jewish architects, a welcome exception being the small synagogue at Belfast by Eugene Rosenberg. Perhaps this failure to appreciate the contribution that outstanding artists could make to the synagogue is due to the continued 'provincialism' of Anglo-Jewish religious life. Continental Jewry did appreciate this potentiality but the German and other Central European immigrants did not make the overall impact on Anglo-Jewish religious life that might have been expected. If they were Orthodox Jews, they either formed their own communities—where learning was of supreme importance—or joined the United Synagogue. Their influence on that organization was in one sense strong and persistent. Better educated in Judaism than their Anglo-Jewish counterparts, they gave the latter a feeling of inferiority so that the old easy-going

thereby themselves acquiring considerable wealth and moving into the ranks of the middle class. Among them were such men as Marcus Samuel who imported and sold shells from the Far East, later manufacturing the elaborate shell ornaments, without which no Victorian household would have been complete. To this economic enterprise of the father, the world was to owe 'Shell' oil, for when the son (later the first Viscount Bearsted) sought a name for his new oil company, he honored the commodity on which the family's first fortune had been founded.

Primarily, however, Jewish initiative caused innovations in the clothing trade and thereby a social revolution whose magnitude cannot be overestimated. For the first time, a working man in the middle of the 19th century could be as good as his master. He was able to buy new, cheap clothing cut in the same fashion as that worn by the wealthy. It is true that the material was not so fine nor the workmanship of bespoke standard—'one man, one garment' tailoring remained in the 19th century largely the prerogative of the non-Jewish craftsman. But the gap between the classes was narrowed by the fact that all had the opportunity, in the cities at any rate, to wear clothes which superficially looked alike. Tailoring for this new market, itself growing as the prosperity of the country increased, proved a profitable venture.

This contribution of E. Moses and Son (and suchlike firms) in the mid-19th century was taken further by Montague Burton in the early 20th century, with his chain of stores marketing the ready-made clothing manufactured in his modern factory. Yet

The Jewish family, 1913. Russo-Jewish immigrants depicted by Mark Gertler ▶ (1892-1939). The mass immigration of refugees from Russian oppression (1881-1914) produced densely packed ghettos in London and other large cities. The distinctive garb and features of the immigrants attracted the attention of contemporary artists from outside and later from inside the immigrant community. London, Tate Gallery.

tolerance fought a losing battle against the more rigorous logic of the newcomers.

Yet there must be proper appreciation of the reason for the awareness and for the closing of the ranks of the 'faithful'. In the past, when assimilation became strong, there were prospects of new immigrations and new infusions of enthusiasm. Religion was still a force in the land unrivaled by the counter-attractions of materialism. But the position has changed. Those who guard the Jewish heritage in Britain are conscious of the flight away from traditional Judaism, of the indifference to Jewish education and of the growing number of out-marriages. The old aristocratic families have merged or are gradually merging with the surrounding society. And the children and grandchildren of the East European immigrants, often the victims of wartime evacuation and divorce from a Jewish background, have been unable to transmit any Jewish teaching, of which they themselves are often ignorant, to their children. Now the Jewish school—especially the primary school under the auspices of the Zionist Federation, which enjoyed increasing success in the 1960s—stands, in many cases, as the only bulwark against complete assimilation. As in so many aspects of life in the non-Jewish as well as the Jewish world the school has superseded the home, the teacher has succeeded to the rights and duties abdicated by the parents.

In England there is the danger that, for many, the Jewish past will become passé. Already Jewish moral attitudes and behavior, which were cited by non-Jewish observers as being admirable examples for the general community, have been decried and abandoned. While alcoholism and violent crime remain alien to Jews, the strong family life characteristic of Jewish communities is disappearing. The divorce rate matches that of the general community, illegitimate births have risen sharply, and drug-taking is on the increase. The Jewish young, like their non-Jewish counterparts, have succumbed to the persuasive influences of the permissive society.

THE INFLUENCE OF ISRAEL

One hope for Anglo-Jewry lies in its commitment to Israel which has grown with the years and which may be the supreme factor in the retention of Jewish identity. The process has been a slow one and, interestingly, the Zionist connection with England was, in the early days, greater than its ties with Anglo-Jewry. Theodor Herzl, it is true, found support from Israel Zangwill, from Leopold Greenberg, the editor of the *Jewish Chronicle* and from a minority of other English Jews. He was able, by the force of his personality, to win over Lord Rothschild who had previously been hostile. He received the adulation of the poor immigrants in the East End of London. But his great achievement was that, in pursuit of his aim of obtaining legal recognition for his claim to Eretz Israel, he won over such members of the British Government as Joseph Chamberlain, then Colonial Secretary. He was so attracted by the possible English connection that at the Fourth Zionist Congress held in London, he declared: 'England the great, England the free, England with her eyes fixed on the seven

seas will understand us. From this place the Zionist movement will take a higher and higher flight, of this we may be sure.' Although the offer of Uganda by the British Government was rejected by the majority of Zionists whose object was the traditional homeland or nothing, the interest in Jewish nationalism evinced by the British Government at this early date was only the forerunner of things to come.

The fortuitous development, unperceived at the time, was the immigration of Chaim Weizmann, the young Russian scientist who chose to make his home in Manchester instead of in Switzerland or Germany, and thereby changed the course of history. In his spare time, Weizmann indoctrinated a group of young Manchester intellectuals—Harry Sacher, Leon Simon, Simon Marks and Israel and Rebecca Sieff. They became his disciples in Zionism. He won over the influential editor of the *Manchester Guardian,* C.P. Scott, whose newspaper henceforward promoted the Zionist case. Thus when the 1914-18 war prevented communication between Zionist leaders whose national states were not on the same side, the English group, reinforced by Nahum Sokolow, who had been sent by the Zionist Movement to London, was ready to take over the direction of the campaign.

Much has been written in Leonard Stein's definitive book *The Balfour Declaration* about the various motives which led to the granting of the Balfour Declaration by the British Government in 1917. The misconceptions regarding the power of Russian Jews to influence events in Russia in that year of revolution; the effect such a promise would have on American Jewry's attitude to the war; the underestimating of Arab reactions; the benefits which would accrue to Britain strategically from having a Jewish national homeland in Palestine. All these, as well as the desire to do justice to the Jews and the influence of Weizmann and Herbert Samuel— whose importance has been underestimated—affected the issue and made it expedient as well as desirable that some gesture should be made to encourage Jewish aspirations. Lloyd George, Balfour and Sir Mark Sykes were genuinely uplifted by the idea of Jewish independence but even so the original concept of Palestine *as a national home* for the Jews was watered down in the final version of the Balfour Declaration:

'His Majesty's Government view with favor the establishment in Palestine of a National Home for the Jewish people, and will use their endeavors to facilitate the achievement of this object, it being clearly understood that nothing shall be done which may prejudice the civil and religious rights of the existing non-Jewish communities in Palestine or the rights and political status enjoyed by Jews in any other country.'

At the time the difficulties caused by the change of formula and the later interpretations placed on it were not envisaged by anyone. The enthusiasm of the Jews was unrestrained; the fact that the Mandatory Power which was to administer the country would be Britain was felt to ensure a smooth and happy future for those Jews who wished to settle in Palestine. And the first High Commissioner appointed was a Jew, the same Herbert Samuel, whose memorandum to the Prime Minister in 1914 suggesting a national home in Palestine had brought forth the comment from the prosaic Asquith:

'I have just received from Herbert Samuel a memorandum headed "The future of Palestine". He goes on to argue, at considerable length and with some vehemence, in favor of the British annexation of Palestine, a country the size of Wales, much of it barren mountain and part of it waterless. He thinks we might plant in this not very promising territory about three or four million European Jews, and that this would have a good effect upon those who are left behind. It reads almost like a new edition of *Tancred* brought up to date. I confess I am not attracted by this proposed addition to our responsibilities, but it is a curious illustration of Dizzy's favorite maxim that "race is everything" to find this almost lyrical outburst proceeding from the well-ordered and methodical brain of H.S.'

The disillusionment was swift. Difficulties in colonization, Arab riots and a policy of appeasement toward their intransigence, the various Royal Commissions sent out from England to solve the Palestine problem—all led to unsettled conditions and mounting hatred. The German immigration of the 1930s brought a new element into the *Yishuv* (Jewish community) which became a refuge for some of those who could escape from the Nazi terror.

Exterior of Belfast synagogue, Northern Ireland. This is perhaps the only modern communal synagogue in the British Isles by a leading contemporary Jewish architect (Eugene Rosenberg, C.B.E., architect of St Thomas' Hospital, London; of Warwick University and many other university and hospital buildings; and of Gatwick Airport). The main building is circular, with a covered entrance corridor. Yorke, Rosenberg and Mardall.

But the notorious 1939 White Paper, limiting Jewish immigration to a maximum of 75,000, after which the gates would be permanently closed, was followed by World War II, when thousands of Palestinians enlisted in the British forces.

When peace came, the tragic losses to Jewry were fully revealed: 6,000,000 dead. The survivors, broken in mind and body, wanting only to go to Palestine, were obstructed by the restrictive policy administered by the new British Labor Government, which in pique passed the whole problem on to the United Nations. Then followed commissions, a period of suspense and in November 1947, international opinion expressed in the UN General Assembly agreed to the partition of Palestine and the establishment of a Jewish state.

In the twenty years since the birth of the State in 1948, though a massive *aliyah* (immigration) from Britain has not materialized, the moral effects of the existence of the State have been profound, giving Anglo-Jewry a new pride and self-respect. The Jew no longer feels that he should be quiet in the hope of passing unnoticed by his enemies. As the Six-Day War showed, Jewry, whatever views had been held previously and however loose the ties had been, found a unity of purpose in a one-hundred-per-cent commitment to the Israel cause. As a result, there has been an increase in migration to Israel since 1967, particularly of young families from England.

Nor is the interest confined to Jews. Adventurous youth has found in Israel one of the few countries of the world where idealism and endeavor are still considered important. They have spent vacations on *kibbutzim* or following their profession in development areas. When volunteers were required to work on the Masada 'dig' the response from applicants in all walks of life was overwhelming, despite the fact that by joining the enterprise they would be out of pocket.

While there has been no pressure on British Jews to emigrate, there have been those who have responded to the challenge offered by Israel; those who have acted on their belief that only in Israel is it possible for a Jew to live a full and uninhibited Jewish life.

THE FUTURE

Anglo-Jewry's contribution to British life has been undoubted—in commerce, the arts, science, letters, philosophy and in public life generally. To Jewish life, on the other hand, its contribution has been more limited: no giants of piety, no major contributions to scholarship. And yet British standards of conduct, of public life, and even British habits have become readily assimilated by Jews, even immigrants of the first generation, and have thus been passed into the general corpus of Jewish experience.

The future of Anglo-Jewry as a community is at best uncertain. The demographic trends—in so far as they can be discerned—are not favorable: declining rates of births, lower marriage rates within the community than in the general population, and so on. Demographically, the outlook is for a declining community, presumably no longer to be reinforced periodically by transfusions of foreign immigration. The process of assimilation to the general community is what can only be expected in an open society.

The answer to this in Jewish history has been the inner resources of the Jewish community, its spiritual leadership, its tenacity of religious observance, its devotion to its traditional learning. Yet it is precisely these which are lacking in the Anglo-Jewish community today. The struggles of Israel during the last twenty-odd years, culminating in the experience of the Six-Day War in 1967, produced a general feeling of sympathy, of fraternity, of pride. But it is questionable whether sentiment and fund-raising can in themselves ensure the survival of a religious community. Insofar as the feeling of identification is deepened in particular individuals, this logically leads to emigration to Israel and the loss to Anglo-Jewry of some of its younger, more vital elements. If the feeling of identification with Israel led to a widespread study of, and proficiency in, the Hebrew language, things might be different: but of this there is little evidence as yet.

The Anglo-Jewish community has been traditionally based on religious affiliation. Can it remain as an entity in a society in which the cementing force of religion is limited to a minority, however devoted? This is a question which only the future can answer. Yet one thing is clear: the story of Anglo-Jewry is not yet over, nor the unique relationship between Jewish culture and English civilization.

◀ *Interior of Belfast synagogue,* Northern Ireland. The picture shows the eastern side of the synagogue with the Ark in which the Scrolls of the Law are kept, and to the right, a candelabrum used on the festival of *Hanukkah* (dedication). The covering of the Ark and the candelabrum are bronze, the work of Nehemia Azaz, an Israeli sculptor living in England. Yorke, Rosenberg and Mardall.

CHAPTER IX

The Netherlands

by Dr. Jozeph Michman-Melkman

The men we meet at the beginnings of the Jewish community in the Netherlands are remarkable, often impressive, personalities. There had been isolated Jewish families living here and there in the Middle Ages; but there was little to distinguish these Ashkenazi families from their brethren in Germany. They were exposed to persecution from the middle of the 14th century and it is virtually certain that when the republic of the Netherlands began its war of independence against Spain, there were no Ashkenazi Jews in the Seventeen Provinces. Spanish and Portuguese Jews had, on the other hand, already settled in the wealthy southern Netherlands in the 16th century and established their center in Antwerp. But they lived there as crypto-Jews or Marranos, for the Spanish rulers of the country, Charles V and later Philip II, enforced the same anti-Jewish laws as in metropolitan Spain, and enforced them with the same fanaticism. The successful revolt and proclamation of a republic by the seven Northern Provinces offered the persecuted Marranos opportunities of which they began to avail themselves by the end of the 16th and the beginning of the 17th century.

The contrast between the hesitant and slow settlement of Jews elsewhere and their settlement in the Netherlands is striking. Proud of their wealth and lineage, conscious of their economic importance for the young and still insecure commonwealth, they negotiated from a position of equality. Take, for instance, Don Samuel Palache from Fez, who arrived in the Netherlands as ambassador of the king of Morocco (1609), gained the confidence of Stadtholder Prince Maurice, and set out to fight Spain. Tradition has it that his home housed the first *minyan* (group of ten male adult Jews, the minimum required for communal prayer) of the Beth Yaacov community, and when he died in 1616, his funeral cortege included not only Jews, but also representatives of the authorities.

Even before this, Marranos had settled in Amsterdam and elsewhere, though without openly admitting they were Jews. The turning point in the life of the Marrano colony came in 1602. Apparently, they had invited an Ashkenazi rabbi, Uri Halevi or Philips Joosten, as the Netherlands texts call him, to serve as their minister, *shohet* (ritual slaughterer) and *mohel* (circumciser); so much, at least, appears from the minutes of his interrogation when he was arrested in 1603. Of the outcome of this interrogation nothing is known, but it is clear that Uri Halevi and his Sephardi friends now decided to admit their religion openly and establish a community, if not in Amsterdam, then in some other town in the Netherlands. This, at least, appears from a resolution taken by the Aldermen of Alkmaar on May 10 1604: 'At the request of Philips the Jew, in the name of several households of Jews and Jewish associates (i.e. Marranos), of the Portuguese and other nations... it is permitted that they may enter this town and stay and dwell there peacefully and secure even as any other good burghers... and confess their religion.' This was a first victory. It was to be followed soon by another, when the city council of Haarlem, after long negotiations, granted a similar charter to a group of well-to-do mer-

SCEPHER AEMVNOT
five liber
DE CAPITIBVS FIDEI
auctore

Celebri R. SCEHADIAH,
*principe olim Iudæorum
in Perfia.*

Scriptus Arabicé an. 873. Hebraicè an. 1186. tranflatus á
R. Iuda Ben Tibon: Theffalonicæ.
impreffus ante annos 85.
ac nunc recufus.

Amftelodami
Apud Iofephum Ben Ifrael.
An. 1647.

Emunot ve-Deot by Saadyah Gaon, Amsterdam, 1647. Latin title page of Saadyah Gaon's tenth-century philosophical work *Emunot ve-Deot* (Book of Beliefs and Opinions) printed at the press of Menasseh Ben Israel's son Joseph. The printing press set up by Menasseh Ben Israel in 1627 introduced Hebrew printing to Amsterdam, which remained the principal center of Jewish printing for the following century. Amsterdam, Bibl. Rosenthaliana.

chants from Amsterdam who also wanted to bring over their families from Portugal, Turkey, and Italy. The documents show that 'Belchior and Francisco Mendes and Michael Castro, *alias* Abraham and Isaac Franco and Michael Nehemie' were not only rich but also skilled negotiators. One may presume that in their negotiations they always kept an eye on Amsterdam, where the resistance of Church circles to Jewish settlement was much stronger than elsewhere. When finally Rotterdam also decided to invite Portuguese merchants to settle (1610), Amsterdam could not lag behind. Officially, Jews were not yet admitted, but *shehitah* (ritual slaughtering) took place, a prayer-book was published, a plot for a cemetery was bought, and a tender was issued for the building of a synagogue.

It was a strange situation, and even stranger in that not even all Christians enjoyed freedom of religion. In 1618, the Remonstrants (a sect which had seceded from the official Reformed [Calvinist] Church) wrote to Prince Maurice: 'Judge for yourself, high-born Prince, whether it be not a deplorable procedure that the Jews, overt enemies and detractors of our Savior, exercise their religion in the mightiest city of Holland, namely in Amsterdam, while we Christians, yea, even Protestants, are forbidden to do likewise.' It was indeed a problem, which became even more acute when the Jewish religion proved to be attractive to Christians. The rulers of the province Holland decided to solve it once and for all and requested two leading legal authorities, Hugo de Groot (Grotius) and Adriaan Pauw, to draft a Jewish statute. De Groot's report has been preserved; it is by no means as tolerant as one would have expected from so great a lawyer and fighter for intellectual liberty. The States of Holland refused to commit themselves to the detailed regulations which De Groot proposed, possibly as a result of the representations made by the Portuguese merchants in a counter-memorandum. At any rate, it was decided to leave a completely free hand to the different towns.

This amounted to a defeat for the Church circles who wanted to keep the Jews in bounds and found it hard to reconcile themselves to the charters which Rotterdam and Haarlem had granted. In fact, however, the legal situation of the Jews was not to change until the Emancipation. The other provinces followed the lead of Amsterdam, as they usually did, and left the towns to decide matters for themselves. This might well have led to arbitrary decisions; and indeed, there were towns where Jews were forbidden to stay overnight or where settlement was subject to restrictive rules, but they were the exception. In Amsterdam particularly, where, notwithstanding initial opposition, the large majority settled, the authorities took pains to assure that the *status quo* was not violated, and neither the aggressive sermons of the parsons nor the occasional complaints of the artisans had any effect. While the Jews did not become citizens *('poorters')*, they were allowed to exercise any trade that had not been regulated by the guilds.

Emunot ve-Deot by Saadyah Gaon (in Hebrew), Amsterdam, 1647. The title page of *Emunot ve-Deot* by Saadyah Gaon (see previous illustration) in Hebrew. This work is one of the basic pillars of Jewish religious and philosophical thinking. The original Arabic version was translated in Spain by Judah Ibn Tibbon. Amsterdam, Bibl. Rosenthaliana.

COMMERCIAL ACTIVITIES

That was all the Sephardim who settled in Amsterdam wanted; they were not after social or cultural integration in the Netherlands community. Their spiritual home was Spain, with its far higher cultural standards than those of the little republic. There existed a closed community of exiles, a Diaspora of Marranos, who maintained close relations with each other, primarily in the exercise of commerce. For that very reason they were able to make a unique contribution to the economic prosperity of the young republic. They did not—as has occasionally been claimed —lay the foundations for the economic power of the Netherlands empire in the 17th century, for their contribution was at first, certainly until the Twelve Years Armistice (1609-22), far too small for that. But there was a mutual influence: the Sephardi merchants did certainly benefit from the fruits of the enterprise and daring of the Netherlands Golden Age. In turn, thanks to their worldwide connections and the use of their capital, they were able to offer the Netherlands republic opportunities which were readily accepted. Netherlands shippers carried the goods of the 'Portuguese' to all parts of the known world. They sailed for Angola in Africa, for Goa and Cochin in India, for Brazil, the West Indies and North America. Their agents were sent out to North and East Europe: they could be met as far abroad as Danzig, Posen and Zamosc. In those days of inadequate communications it was important that the Amsterdam merchants had relatives dispersed all over the world as a result of the Expulsion from Spain. Particularly close ties with Amsterdam were kept up by Hamburg and Venice, so that the former could become the basis for the Baltic trade and the latter for the Levant trade.

The increase in importance of the Jewish merchants in Amsterdam may be gauged from the growth of their numbers among holders of accounts with the Bank of Exchange. In 1609 only 24 of the 731 accounts were held by Portuguese merchants but by 1620 they numbered 106 out of 1,202. By 1674 there were 265 Jewish account holders out of a total of 2,031, or 13 per cent, while the Jews accounted for no more than 1½ per cent of the population. Though the size of the accounts shows that quite a few Christian merchants were better off than the richest Jews, there were, nevertheless, many small capitalists among the Portuguese Jews and their average wealth was considerably above that of the remainder of the Amsterdam population. The wealth and economic importance of the Portuguese Jews was not a matter of individuals, but of the group and of its contacts with other centers.

There were a few great merchants, like, for instance, Bento Osorio; later, there were Moses Machado, supplier to the Dutch and English armies under William III, and Francisco Lopes Suasso, who was able to lend the same William III two million guilders for his expedition to England. By the end of the 17th century the Portuguese Jews had begun to increase their capital considerably, and their initially minor share in industry grew at the same time. They were in sugar refining and in the tobacco industry—an important field in the beginning of the 18th century —and above all in the diamond industry, which in course of time was to become an almost exclusively Jewish occupation in Amsterdam.

Another trade in which the Jews could engage because it had not been preempted by the guilds was Hebrew book-printing. The first printing press was that of Menasseh Ben Israel (1626), who later was followed by others who achieved a wide reputation. The output of these presses was of such outstanding quality that the Jewish publishing houses of Amsterdam soon outgrew their modest beginnings and exported their books to all parts of the Jewish Diaspora.

Notwithstanding, then, the not inconsiderable restrictions hampering their economic growth, the Jews shared in the general prosperity of the Netherlands republic.

THE GOLDEN AGE OF NETHERLANDS CULTURE

The 17th century was the Golden Age of Netherlands culture, which shone particularly in the field of painting, but flourished in other domains as well, such as literature and science. The mutual influence of Netherlands culture and that of the Sephardi Jews is evident from the many mutual points of contact. One has only to look at Rembrandt's paintings to understand how he was fascinated by the Jewish types of his surroundings; and not by Jewish types alone: Jewish religious conceptions must also have been a source of interest to him, for he made four plates for Menasseh Ben Israel's book *Piedra Gloriosa,* an apocalyptic work interpreting the suffering of the Jews of Poland at that time, as a sign of the coming of the Messiah. There were Christians who converted to Judaism; on the other hand, there were Church authorities who wanted to convert the Jews, scholars who studied the Mishnah and the Talmud, and even a Christian poetess who composed Hebrew poems. But above all, the interest on both sides is evidenced by the disputations which took place in Amsterdam: the first dialogues between Christians and Jews in which the latter could express themselves freely and without having to defer to hostile authorities. The first dispute, as early as 1608, was between the Englishman Hugh Broughton and the physician David Farrar. Menasseh Ben Israel also defended Judaism in his *Vindiciae Judaeorum* and even, though cautiously, attacked Christian tenets in another book, *Conciliador.* So did another, less famous but far more learned author, the Amsterdam rabbi Saul Levi Morteira, whose *Providencia de Dios con Ysrael* specifically attacked the Calvinist doctrine of the official Netherlands Reformed Church; the book has never been printed, presumably because of its aggressive tone. The greatest of the Jewish apologists, though, was Dr. Isaac Orobio de Castro (1620-87), originally professor of medicine in Seville and later physician in Amsterdam, who had a learned disputation with an Amsterdam minister and even dared to publish a book against *La Vana Ydolatria de las Gentes.* So violent were the pronouncements of many of those who had only recently returned to the Jewish fold that the magistrates of Amsterdam finally decided to permit no more disputations between Jews and Christians; they were obviously afraid of a reaction in Church circles.

But it should not be thought that the polemics were directed only against Christians. There were also internal discussions, that were often no less fierce. The first we hear of them is in 1618, when the secular leaders of the Beth Jacob community, led by the physician Abraham Farrar, clashed with R. David Pardo. While Farrar and his adherents were rationalists who took a critical view of the Kabbalah and were even prepared to question rabbinical decisions, R. Pardo regarded this as backsliding into heresy. The conflict became so acute that the rabbi and some of his followers set up a new community: Beth Israel. Soon afterward, the city was to be the scene of an even more tragic dispute. At its center was Uriel da Costa. Uriel, who was born in Oporto in 1585, became treasurer of a church in 1608. He began to observe Marrano customs about 1610 and persuaded many of his relatives to do likewise. He fled to Italy with his mother and three brothers in 1614, and converted to Judaism, assuming the name of Uriel instead of Gabriel. A few years later he had set up in Hamburg; by 1627 he was in Utrecht, then by 1631 in Amsterdam. Riddles surround his life but his ideas, and particularly his argumentation against the immortality of the soul, aroused a wave of indignation in the Marrano Diaspora. Over the next twenty years, Sephardi religious scholars produced a flood of treatises, books, and even poems in defense of the immortality of the soul. Uriel was excommunicated. In 1640 he shot himself, leaving a work, *Exemplar Humanae Vitae,* which has reached us only in a version that has been mutilated by anti-Semitic hands.

Uriel da Costa's principal claim to fame, though, is as the

The Jewish bride. Famous work by Rembrandt. Rembrandt lived in the Jewish quarter of Amsterdam and was attracted by Jewish types whom he depicted in portraits and biblical themes; thirty-seven out of his two hundred male portraits are of Jewish personalities or types. Among his sitters were Dr. Ephraim Bueno and Menasseh Ben Israel. Amsterdam, Rijksmuseum.

Portrait of Benedict Spinoza, c. 1670. Portrait of the famous Dutch philosopher (1632-77) by an anonymous Dutch painter. Though he had received a traditional education and his teachers had included Menasseh Ben Israel, Spinoza's unorthodox religious views led finally to his excommunication from the Sephardi community. The Hague, Gemeentemuseum.

by an 'unbeliever'. The surprising result of his expulsion from the Jewish community was that, notwithstanding the revolutionary nature of his ideas for the period, the authorities gave him less trouble than they did his Christian adherents. His philosophical system may be the most important contribution to Dutch culture any Dutch Jew has ever made, but at the same time it must be said that no Portuguese Jew of his time ever identified himself so closely with the Netherlands commonwealth or kept at such a distance from the Jewish community.

This may well account for why the reaction to his activities was so much less marked than it was in the case of Uriel da Costa. We know of one of his supporters who was also excommunicated: Dr. Juan de Prado, who soon afterward disappeared to Antwerp. He and Spinoza were the targets of an intelligent pamphlet from the fearsome pen of Orobio de Castro. But that is all we known of Spinoza in the Jewish community. This can perhaps be explained in part by the fact that at this time the mystical trend began to predominate in the Portuguese community. The spread of Isaac Luria's kabbalistic ideology in Italy dates from the years 1656-9, and in view of the close relations existing between Amsterdam and Italy, it is hardly surprising that in Amsterdam as well, rationalism had to make way for mysticism. The result was that by 1666, Amsterdam was ripe for the advent of the Messiah Shabbetai Tzevi (see chapter on Muslim Lands). Rabbis and congregants were thoroughly convinced that the Messiah was about to lead them to the Promised Land and refused to listen to the more sober voices of a few skeptics. As the community prepared itself to pay allegiance to the 'King of the Jews', their hopes were crushed by the report of his conversion to Islam. One result of this traumatic disillusionment was that from then on, the Portuguese Jews as a community resigned themselves to awaiting their fate in the Netherlands; returning to Spain was out of the question, and establishing a Jewish commonwealth in Palestine proved impossible. From then on, they regarded themselves as subjects of the Netherlands republic. The most exalted expression of this change of attitude may be found in the splendid synagogue which was built at the instigation of *Hakham* (chief rabbi) Isaac Aboab da Fonseca, a one-time follower of Shabbetai Tzevi. A Christian poet calls it

Chef d'œuvre de tous lieux sacrés,
Du premier temple la mémoire,

and indeed Bouman, its architect, drew his inspiration from the Solomonic Temple—or rather, from its reconstruction by Jacob Judah Leon, who became so famous for the model he had constructed that he was given the nickname Templo. This imposing, fortress-like structure was inaugurated in 1675 in a manner which a contemporary writer regards as fit for 'a festival celebrated in freedom and in the Temple rather than in exile and in a synagogue'.

The synagogue—called 'Esnoga'—was built with a view to the future. The community was flourishing, and its headmen expected membership to grow to larger numbers than was to be the case. The Sephardi immigrants had grown in stature and wealth with the Commonwealth. They were by now playing an important part on the Exchange, the operation of which has

precursor of the best known scion of the Jewish community of Amsterdam: Baruch Spinoza, like him a victim of excommunication. Unlike da Costa, Spinoza had been educated in the Jewish faith; perhaps even more important, he was born in Amsterdam and never left Holland. He refers to Holland as 'mea patria' (my fatherland) and is totally lacking in Jewish national feeling and respect for ancestral tradition. Spinoza was interrogated and excommunicated by the *parnassim* (synagogue wardens) and rabbis before his writings were published. One may assume that his heresies were not the sole reason for the measures taken against him: Spinoza's contacts with the Protestant sect of the Collegiants and with the atheists were regarded as a great danger, not only for the religious views of the Jews themselves but for their place in Dutch society, which might be undermined

Interior of Portuguese synagogue, Amsterdam, 1675. A rare example of a synagogue interior painted by a major artist, Emanuel de Witte, in 1675. The building and interior have remained unchanged until the present day. Jerusalem, Israel Museum.

Festive meal in the Sukkah, Amsterdam, 1722. From an engraving by Bernard Picart, depicting the Festive Meal in the *Sukkah* or the booth for the Festival of Tabernacles, which commemorates the forty-year wandering of the Israelites in the desert. The *Sukkah* seen here is that of a rich family while the one behind is that of a poor family. It has to be a temporary structure through which it is possible to see the stars. Amsterdam, Fodormuseum.

never been better described than by Joseph Penso in *Confusión de Confusiones*. We find many representatives of foreign powers among them, and their relations with the court of Stadtholder William III were close. Wealth also served to stimulate culture. In the stately mansions on the canals of Amsterdam and the luxurious villas on the road to Utrecht beside the river Vecht, the wives and children of the barons engaged in music, dancing, and poetry. The poetry, incidentally, was almost never in Dutch: some poetic societies used the Spanish language, but Hebrew also had its practitioners. Joseph Penso was seventeen when he wrote a Hebrew play, and other poets, like Moses Zacut, Solomon d'Oliveira and—in the 18th century—David Franco Mendes are also known to have produced Hebrew poems at an early age. That they were able to do so was due to the modern educational methods of the famous Talmud Torah school, which

stressed the study of Hebrew grammar and the actual speaking of the language—an approach which was far from general at the time. In their love of music, the citizens of Amsterdam took their cue from Italy. Works were written for religious purposes by such Amsterdam composers as Abraham de Caceres and the non-Jew C.G. Lidarti; from there, it was but a short step to operas and plays. In 1624, a play by Reuel Jessurun (*alias* Paulo de Pina), entitled *Diálogo des Montes* was even performed in the synagogue, but such frivolities were forbidden in 1639.

Not that the rabbis objected to poetry and music. On the contrary: in many of the dozens of pious societies which, in addition to their official activities, also offered an opportunity for the study of rabbinical literature, it was the custom to celebrate the conclusion of a Talmud tractate by the composition and reading of poems and dialogues, and in at least one instance by a play. In 1683, the poet-historian Daniel Levi de Barrios was familiar with at least twenty such societies, and there must have been many other similar associations. Another occasion for musical and theatrical performances was provided by the weddings of the leading families; if the family was particularly wealthy, a poet might be invited specially for the occasion. In this way, two eighteenth-century Hebrew poets have left plays and operas: Moshe Hayyim Luzzatto and David Franco Mendes. We know, however, of no Spanish or Dutch plays—proof that the environment was still felt as too foreign to invite participation in local cultural life. At most, there were rich Portuguese Jews who appeared as patrons of the arts.

THE ASHKENAZI COMMUNITY

The first Ashkenazi Jews must have reached Amsterdam about 1620. They held their first separate synagogue service in 1635, and in 1642 they bought a cemetery which is still in use. From 1648 on, many Jews from Eastern Europe went to the Netherlands. While the number of Sephardim in Amsterdam in 1610 was 400, and in 1674 their total number in the Netherlands—besides Amsterdam, the only place where Portuguese Jews lived was in the Hague—cannot have been much more than 2,500, Ashkenazi Jews in Amsterdam in that year already numbered 5,000. A century later, the Sephardi community had remained

Jewish burial ground, Amsterdam, 1670. Cemetery of the Sephardi community at Ouderkerk, near Amsterdam, from an engraving and etching by Abraham Blooteling, after Jacob Ruisdael. Jerusalem, Israel Museum.

Synagogue. By M. Pool Sculy. No. 1 is the rabbi; no. 2, the Ark coffer; no. 3 the Scrolls; no. 4 the *Hazzan* or cantor. Amsterdam, Rijksmuseum, engravings dept. Inv. no. 16:309.

almost static (3,000), while the number of Ashkenazi Jews in Amsterdam had grown to 19,000, with another 8,000 in the remainder of the country. Nevertheless the cultural impact of the Ashkenazim until the middle of the 18th century was disappointing. Admittedly, the Great Synagogue was inaugurated in 1671 —in other words, even before the Esnoga synagogue—and soon proved too small, so that it was followed by a few large and innumerable smaller ones, which surely indicates that there were at least a few Jews of sufficient wealth. The bulk of the Ashkenazi community, however, consisted of relatively poor Jews. In all

◄ *Ketubbah,* Rotterdam, 1648. Marriage contract on parchment etched by Shalom Italia, 1648. Italia was born in Mantua and settled in Amsterdam. Coming of a family of printers, he made his name as an engraver and miniaturist, doing many copperplate borders for the *Ketubbah* and *Megillah.* Here he depicts wedding scenes from the Bible, those of Eve, Sarah and Rachel on one side, traditional wedding scenes on the other. The name of the groom in this wedding: Isaac Pereira; that of the bride: Rachel, daughter of Abraham da Pinto. Jerusalem, Israel Museum.

those years, the Amsterdam community produced no scholars. It is perfectly understandable that initially its rabbis had to be brought from abroad, but the practice was continued. By 1710, the Amsterdam community was large enough even to be able to invite one of the greatest scholars of the time, Tzevi Ashkenazi, known as *Hakham* Tzevi. It is, however, significant that when a conflict arose between him and the Portuguese chief rabbi, Salomon Ayllon, the aldermen of Amsterdam finally intervened in R. Ayllon's favor and *Hakham* Tzevi was forced to leave the city in 1714. The Ashkenazi community acknowledged its debt to *Hakham* Tzevi to the extent that his descendants held the office of chief rabbi of Amsterdam for more than a century. The family also produced many chief rabbis and rabbis for other places in the Netherlands.

Whether these can be regarded as Dutch rabbis, however, is another question. In the 18th century, at any rate, they cannot, for even Jacob Moses had been educated in Poland and was unfamiliar with the Dutch language and with conditions in Amsterdam. The same goes for his predecessors and for other

Halitzah ceremony, Amsterdam, 1683. This copper etching shows the so-called *Halitzah* ceremony in which the brother of a man who died childless is relieved from his obligation to marry the widow. This ceremony involves the widow removing the brother-in-law's shoe and reciting the biblical formula: 'So shall be done to the man who shall not build his brother's house.' Dutch artist unknown. Jerusalem, Israel Museum, 2725-10-51.

scholars who reached the Netherlands more or less by chance. They often published their works in Amsterdam, because the Amsterdam printers produced good work; but they had acquired their learning elsewhere. Their daily language was Yiddish, and was to remain so until the second half of the 18th century.

The Portuguese Jews also applied themselves by preference to Spanish and Hebrew, but the difference was that they were prosperous and had had a share in the rich Spanish civilization. The bulk of the poor Ashkenazim were unable to reach a cultural level equal to that of the Sephardim. Notwithstanding

וככה תאכלו אתו מתניכם חגרים נעליכם ברגליכם ומקלכם בידכם פסח הוא לה׳

Seder meal on Passover, Amsterdam, 1695. The engravings are by Abraham ben Jacob in imitation of the engravings in Matheus Merian's *Icones Bibliae,* Basle, 1625. The quotation at the bottom is taken from the *Haggadah* service and reads: 'And thus shall you eat it, with your loins girded, your feet shod, and a staff in your hand'. It was a custom among many Jewish communities to enact this scene at the Passover table to recall the Jews in Egypt on the eve of the Exodus. Amsterdam, Bibl. Rosenthaliana.

the steady growth of the Amsterdam community, it continued for years to look up on the one hand to the greater scholarship of the East European centers and on the other to the social position of its Portuguese coreligionists. There were a few rich families who monopolized the office of *parnassim* (synagogue wardens) and who exercised unlimited authority over their communities. Tobias Boas, the Hague banker, was one of the advisers and moneylenders of the stadtholder's court and the government. He even represented the Jewish communities of Amsterdam and Rotterdam in audiences at the court, and presumably had a hand in the *démarche* of the Dutch Ambassador Burmania when he protested to Maria Theresa against the expulsion of the Jews from Bohemia and Moravia. This certainly was the case with another great banker, Benedict Levie Gomperts of Nijmegen, who had followed his family from nearby Cleves in Germany.

Gomperts, member of a widespread family, had interests not only in the Netherlands (particularly in Amsterdam and Amersfoort), but also in Germany and England. The most famous Ashkenazi, though, in the second half of the 18th century, was Benjamin Cohen of Amersfoort, first a tobacco merchant but later also a banker, whose relations with the court were so close that Stadtholder William V and his wife Wilhelmina even stayed at his house.

However, it should not be forgotten that most of the Dutch towns did not admit Jews, or admitted them only subject to restrictions. The great wealth and cultural achievements of a few individuals cannot conceal the fact that few Jews could make more than a bare living. This is particularly the case in Amsterdam, which had a very large Jewish proletariat. As a result, the Ashkenazi Jews found their contacts with their surroundings

65

Circumcision, Amsterdam, 1722. Circumcision as depicted in Picart's *Cérémonies et Coutumes Religieuses,* with, in attendance, the father of the child, the godfather, the *Mohel* (circumciser) and the rabbi. The Chair of Elijah, on which the child is placed before being circumcised, can also be seen. The woman with a cross is a Christian servant. Amsterdam, Fodormuseum, Inv. no. A. 10258.

mainly among the less prosperous classes. If one is to believe stories from the 18th century, there were a fair number of pickpockets and prostitutes among them—hardly surprising in an international port. Significantly, a considerable number of Yiddish words found their way into the slang of the Dutch underworld. On the other hand, Yiddish, which the Jews continued to use until well into the 19th century, soon absorbed Dutch words and expressions.

Relations between the Portuguese and Ashkenazi Jews were to change radically in the second half of the 18th century. By 1762, hints of the incipient changes are to be found in the writings of Isaac de Pinto, a rich and learned Portuguese Jew. As a *parnas* of the Portuguese community, he had to deal with increasing poverty among many of its members, who had lost their money through unlucky speculations and the ill-fortune of the Netherlands republic. Nevertheless, de Pinto felt far superior to his Ashkenazi brethren, as appears clearly in his con-

troversy with Voltaire. But soon afterward, another Portuguese Jew of Amsterdam, Mordechai van Aron de... (the surname is not mentioned) in a Dutch periodical took a very different line: the Portuguese-Jewish nation, he states, has had its summer; the High German Jews (as the Ashkenazim are formally called in Dutch) on the other hand, most of whom arrived destitute, '(are) being regarded by us Portuguese with a good deal of contempt, but (are) in fact more industrious and economical than we are; they have survived their winter and see better times approaching. They are rising, we are sinking.'

EMANCIPATION

But the times that were in store for the Ashkenazim were hardly better ones. The war with England, the subsequent domestic strife, and finally the French conquest in 1795 brought

Preparations for the Passover Festival, Holland, 1725. Etchings from Bernard Picart's *Cérémonies et Coutumes Religieuses* showing the preparations for the Passover Festival a) the search for leavened bread; b) The *Seder* (Passover) meal. The scenes depict a ceremony in a Sephardi community. (a) The night before Passover a search is made for any (leaven) bread inadvertently overlooked which is then burned and a special blessing recited. In fact some leavened bread is deliberately left in a corner so that the ceremony can be carried out. (b) 1) The plate with hard-boiled egg and roast shank-bone of lamb, commemorating the Temple offerings. 2) Plate with bitter herbs which symbolize the bitterness caused by the Egyptians to the Israelites in Egypt. 3) Contains a mixture symbolizing the mortar the Jews were forbidden to have in Egypt. 4) Salt water in which the bitter herbs are dipped. 5) The father is breaking the unleavened bread in his hand. All the Jewish household servants are participating. 6) Serviette under which one piece of unleavened bread is hidden. 7) On the floor the basket where unleavened bread is kept. Amsterdam, Rijksmuseum, engravings dept.

L'EXAMEN du LEVAIN &c.

A. La Maitresse de la maison, qui met du PAIN LEVE en divers endroits, afin que son Mari qui en fait la recherche en trouve.

Dessiné d'après nature et gravé par B. Picart 1725.

1. Le Plat, ou est un Cs. d'Epaule d'Agneau avec un Oeuf dur.
2. Plat ou sont les Herbes Ameres.
3. Plat de Figues, Pommes, Amandes, Canelle &c. hachees et cuites ensemble, representant la matiere dont ils faisoient les Briques en Egypte.
4. Plat avec la Sauce pour tremper les Herbes Ameres.

Le REPAS de PAQUES.
chez les
JUIFS PORTUGAIS.

5. Moitié du Gateau des Levites, dont le Pere de Famille rompt des morceaux, qu'il distribue a tous ceux qui sont a table. &c. tous les Domestiques Juifs sont a la meme Table, avec lui.
6. Serviette, sous laquelle le Gateau a été caché.
7. Panier ou sont les Matzes ou Pain de Paques.

67

hardship to the Dutch, and to the Jews even more. At the same time, almost overnight, an entirely new generation arose that sought to realize the ideals of the French Revolution: liberty, equality, and fraternity. The supporters of the emancipation of the Jews were exclusively members of the upper middle class, and, while their writings and speeches castigated the social evils prevailing in the Jewish communities, for which they held the *parnassim* responsible, it soon became clear that their real aim was civic equality. Strangely enough, they had to fight their battle on two fronts: notwithstanding the victory of the French Revolution and the establishment of the Batavian republic, the revolutionaries in many parts of the country, and notably in Amsterdam, objected vehemently to the admission of the Jews as full-fledged citizens. But the majority of the Jews was equally opposed to change. Both the *parnassim* and the masses remained faithful to the House of Orange and rejected the revolution. Moreover, they feared that equal rights would also mean equal

duties; specifically, they were concerned about compulsory service, abolition of the autonomy of the communities, and the introduction of the Dutch language. Both parties tried to influence the political representatives of the nation. The innovators, such as the lawyer Moses Solomon Asser and his son Carolus, the physician Hartog de H. Lemon or the mathematician Littwak, were closer in their views to the leading figures of the republic. In imitation of the French revolutionaries, they established themselves as a club, Felix Libertate, which engaged in propaganda among the Dutch revolutionaries. On the other hand, the *parnassim* succeeded in gaining understanding for the opposite viewpoint among conservative and religious delegates.

The result was the unique debate which began on August 22 1795, and was wound up on September 2 with the adoption of the Decree on the Civic Emancipation of the Jews. In this debate, two parties confronted each other: those who regarded the Jews as a nation and therefore wanted to deny them citizenship, and

Yom Kippur or Day of Atonement, Holland, 1725. The Day of Atonement as celebrated by the Ashkenazi Jews in Holland. The Day of Atonement is the most solemn day in the Jewish calendar when Jews beg for forgiveness for sins committed. On this day a white garment *(Kittel)* is worn during the service. Amsterdam, Rijksmuseum, engraving dept.

Esther Scroll with case, Holland, mid-eighteenth century. Esther Scroll printed on parchment with copper engravings illustrating scenes from the Bible story printed in Holland in the mid-eighteenth century. The silver case of the same period is from Germany. On the scroll, the beginning of the Esther story is visible, with the blessings (on the right) said before the reading. Tel Aviv, Stieglitz Collection.

those for whom the Jews were individuals. The debate is remarkable for the almost complete absence of any note of anti-Semitism or pseudo-anti-Semitism, and on reading the reports today, one is more than once tempted to side with the opponents, who spoke appreciatively of the Jews' belief in the Messiah who was to lead them back to their ancient homeland. Eventually, the decree was passed by a large majority, presumably due to backstage pressure by the French ambassador. But even though

the decree was adopted at a time when the country was virtually a French province, the Restoration of 1815 brought no attempt to tamper with Jewish Emancipation; and until the rise of National Socialism, no political party ever proposed to deprive the Jews even in part of their civic rights.

In the Jewish community of Amsterdam, the debate was conducted on a less lofty level. While the municipal authorities were on the side of Felix Libertate, the *parnassim* could count on

Rabbi medal, Amsterdam, 1735. Silver medal commemorating the appointment of Rabbi Eleazar ben Samuel from Brody (Galicia) as rabbi of the Ashkenazi community in Amsterdam. This medal caused a great controversy as it portrayed the graven image of the rabbi. Jerusalem, Israel Museum.

Omer calendar, Holland, eighteenth century. The painted wooden *Omer* calendar was used for the counting of the *Omer* — the forty-nine-day period of semi-mourning between Passover and Pentecost. The holes are for a peg which was moved forward from day to day. The Hebrew in the center is the blessing recited before the counting of the *Omer* at the evening service. Jerusalem, Israel Museum.

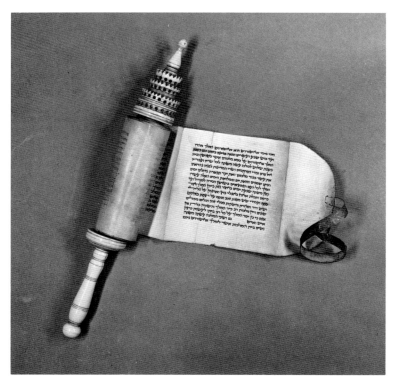

Ivory megillah, Holland, eighteenth century. Handwritten Esther Scroll, rolled on an ivory holder with carved top. Here, the beginning of the book of Esther. Cologne, Stadtmuseum, Inv. No. 1928/418

Etrog box, Holland, mid-eighteenth century. The *etrog* box served to keep the citron fresh during the week-long Festival of Tabernacles. Inscribed below: 'Fruit of Citrus Tree'. Jerusalem, Sir Isaac and Lady Edith Wolfson Museum, Hechal Shlomo, Inv. No. 25/7.

Bookbinding, Holland, 1770. With the inscription *Five Books of the Torah.* Silver, 1770. Tel Aviv, Stieglitz Collection.

the support of the masses, who even threatened the innovators with violence in the synagogue. In 1796, the men of Felix Libertate took an unprecedented step: they left the community and established a new one, Adath Jeshurun, with its own chief rabbi (Rabbi Isaac Ger, son of a Swedish convert to Judaism), its own synagogue and its own cemetery. Adath Jeshurun has sometimes been called the first Reform synagogue; unjustly so, for the changes in the synagogue service were minor and the rabbi was strictly Orthodox. The differences with the old community lay in the field of national and communal politics, though the spokesmen of Adath Jeshurun also used social arguments to incite the masses against the *parnassim.* It is characteristic of the times that the battle was fought mainly with pamphlets written in Yiddish, proof that Dutch had by no means become the daily language among the Jews. At one moment it seemed as if Adath Jeshurun would prevail over the old community. After a coup d'état instating the Jacobin trend in the Batavian republic (January 1798), the new magistrates of Amsterdam deposed the *parnassim* and replaced them by Jews who shared their ideas (*manhigim*). This, however, only increased the unrest, and by June 1798, they had to be replaced by more moderate personalities. The authorities did try to make peace between the quarreling Jews, and in 1802 the government even ordered the two communities to reunite. But in vain: the reunion did not take place until 1808, on the order of Louis Napoleon, Napoleon's brother, who had by then been made king.

To judge by the letter, the reestablishment of unity would seem a victory for the old community, though in actual fact the innovators had won the day. Most characteristic for the

Decanter for Kiddush wine, Holland, nineteenth century. Cut glass decanter for *Kiddush* wine used for the sanctification blessing on Sabbaths and festivals with inscription of the months of the year followed by the names of holidays. Amsterdam, Joods Historisch Museum, Inv. no. 300.

course of development is perhaps the man who became the head of the new organization created by Louis Napoleon: the High Consistory. Its appointed chairman was Jonas Daniel Meyer (1780-1834), a brilliant lawyer who was to play a leading part in Dutch Jewry. As a grandson of Benjamin Cohen, the enormously wealthy banker who had been a *parnas* in Amsterdam, Meyer had connections with the old community. He had a considerable influence on the king, who, unlike his famous brother, wanted sincerely to help the Jews. Meyer had represented the old community at the Assembly of Notables which met in Paris in 1806, but neither the High German nor the Sephardi community sent a delegation to the Paris Sanhedrin, though Adath Jeshurun did. One may assume that Meyer had been able to prevent the king from forcing the old communities to take part in the Sanhedrin.

The 'High Consistory of the High German Communities in the Kingdom of Holland' soon developed activities which were in agreement with the new ideas. External decorum in the synagogue service was encouraged, the use of the Dutch language was promoted by means of a Bible translation, and great efforts were made to reduce the large number of private *minyanim* (Jewries). All these measures had the support of the king, who, on Meyer's advice, sought to remove all obstacles to complete equality for the Jews, such as the refusal of towns to appoint Jews to municipal office. The king even went as far as to decree that wherever the weekly market was held on Saturday, it was to be shifted to another day of the week. Another measure, however, taken by the king at the insistence of his brother, provoked serious resistance: the formation of a special Jewish army corps that was to take part in Napoleon's war against Russia. In spite of the propaganda and pressure of the High Consistory, the volunteers included a number of officers but hardly any other ranks, so that the project had to be dropped.

Our only reason for mentioning this abortive plan is the

Louis Bonaparte's entry into Amsterdam, 1808. The Jewish citizens of Amsterdam, standing on the terraces of their synagogues (Portuguese synagogue, left, and Ashkenazi, right) greet the entrance parade of Louis Bonaparte. An etching by Langendijk. Amsterdam, Rijksmuseum, Rijksprentenkabinett.

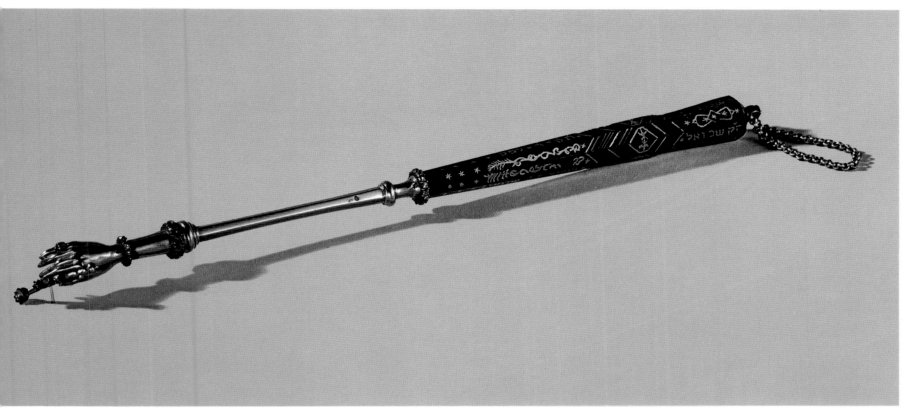

Torah pointer, Amsterdam, 1754. This gold and jasper Torah pointer bears the inscription: 'Samuel Zanwel, son of Simon Polak (or Falk) of blessed memory and his wife Mirele, daughter of Tobias Boaz (famous banker at the Hague) Amsterdam, 514 (=1754)'. Paris, Musée de Cluny, Strauss-Rothschild Collection, 12334.

light it casts on the mentality of the leading figures in the Jewish circle grouped around Jonas Daniel Meyer. They wanted to raise the Jews from their inferior station and bring them up to the level of the best of the other nations. Because of the outcome of their efforts, they are now often judged unfairly and regarded as assimilants who had no higher purpose than to curry favor with non-Jews. This takes no account of the fact that many of the innovators strove for a better future for the Jewish people and were often inspired by Jewish national feelings. Running side by side with the struggle for Emancipation, the second half of the 18th century marked the revival of Hebrew literature among the Ashkenazim, just as it came to its end among the Sephardim. In the Netherlands, it reached its peak in the beginning of the 19th century, when an association of Hebraists, 'To'elet', was founded under the inspiring leadership of Dr. S.I. Mulder. An undoubted influence of Mendelssohn, and perhaps even more of his collaborators Naphtali Herz Weisel (Wessely) and Solomon Dubno, can be felt: the latter two lived in Amsterdam and had great influence on the younger generation. Nevertheless, the Hebrew revival movement shows a specifically Dutch trend, if only in its choice of subjects. Moses Lemans, for instance, an outstanding Hebraist and mathematician, wrote a great epic work on the war between the Netherlands and Belgium, while Gabriel Polak, the most industrious if not the most gifted of the circle, translated many works from Dutch and Latin literature. Even greater is the group's impor-

tance in the field of education. Not only were nearly all of them teachers, but they turned out valuable Hebrew study books and dictionaries, and above all translations of the Bible and liturgical works.

These translations also had an additional function: they helped to make the Jewish masses, who continued to use Yiddish, familiar with the Dutch language. It was one of the means used to turn the Dutch Jews, who in the 18th century had always been referred to as 'the Jewish nation', into a religious community and to organize them into what, following the Christian pattern, called itself a 'Church Association'. In this respect, King William I, crowned in 1815, continued the work of Louis Napoleon. He, too, was strongly influenced by Jonas D. Meyer, whom he appointed as secretary of the National Commission on the New Constitution (1815), where the Jew Meyer had to keep the balance between twelve Protestants and twelve Catholics. The degree of activity which King William I deployed in Jewish affairs is astounding. Even by 1814, he had signed two decrees regulating the structure of the High German Israelite and Portuguese Israelite Church Associations and prescribed where the six chief rabbis were to reside. The celebration of marriages and funerals, the appointment of *parnassim,* budgets—everything was regulated by royal decree. In 1817, a decree was issued on the education of poor Jewish children, and in the same year, provision was made for the examination of teachers and rabbis, teaching by unqualified and foreign personnel was prohibited, and a com-

sions that the Jews felt them as a threat to their life or existence. Admittedly, certain offices, particularly representative ones such as that of mayor, were never open to Jews. On the other hand, there were certain professions in which Jews could easily make a career for themselves from the beginning of the 19th century.

One profession in particular owes its development in the Netherlands to a very large extent to the Jews: the law. We have already mentioned some lawyers, Jonas D. Meyer and the Assers. The latter family produced a host of jurists, the most

Jonas D. Meyer, 1780-1834. Famous jurist, president of the board of Jewish synagogues and secretary of the National Commission on the New Constitution of the Netherlands, shown in a lithograph by J.A. Daiwaille after a painting by Louis Moritz. Amsterdam, Rijksmuseum, Rijksprentenkabinett.

pulsory national syllabus was introduced. In 1818, local authorities were ordered to provide grants for Jewish communities in accordance with their numerical strength. The king also encouraged the building of new synagogues, and in 1827 even awarded a 'medal of honor' for the publication of Jewish educational works. While most of these measures can be attributed to Jewish advisers, it is clear that the king was serious about applying the principles of emancipation: complete equality for the Jews, to be achieved by, among other things, the elimination of all differences between Jews and non-Jews which, in the king's view, were not of a religious nature.

The king's efforts were in the first place successful among the well-to-do Jewish circles. As in Germany, there were those among them who went so far as to abandon Judaism. Conversion never, however, assumed epidemic dimensions in the Netherlands, on the one hand because the Jewish community was a long-standing, closed circle which it was not easy to abandon, and on the other hand because the anti-Jewish feelings rife among a large part of the population never assumed such dimen-

Miniature Sabbath stove, Holland, beginning of nineteenth century. Possibly a model. As the lighting of a fire was forbidden on the Sabbath, these stoves kept the food warm for twenty-four hours. Of brass and iron. Amsterdam, Joods Historisch Museum, Inv. No. 23 b.

famous of whom was the Nobel peace prizewinner, Tobias M.C. Asser. The first Jewish professor of law was J.E. Goudsmit of Leiden, who was to be followed by dozens of others, including E.M. Meyers, whose dismissal from his chair in Leiden by the German occupation authorities in 1940 caused such a degree of unrest that Leiden University had to be closed. The Supreme Council, Holland's highest law court, has probably never been without a Jewish member. As chance would have it, its president at the time of the German occupation was a Jew, L. Visser. On that occasion, Visser proved himself a man of principle and a conscious Jew. Of the five Jews who were Cabinet members during the last century (not a large number as such), four were Minister of Justice.

Another profession in which the Jews had excelled was medicine. Even in the 17th century there were famous Jewish doctors, and in the 18th century, Jews were the first protagonists of vaccination. However, it was only much later that the universities opened their doors to Jewish members of the medical profession.

In considering the part played by the Jews in the life of the Netherlands, we cannot overlook the figure of Samuel Sarphati, a physician whose manifold activities doubtless sprang from a strong social motivation. He founded a company for the manufacture of flour and bread, but when he realized that in doing so he had not succeeded in abolishing poverty, he attempted to provide employment by restoring Amsterdam's position as an international center by such means as the organization of exhibitions. Since there was no suitable space for his purpose, he built an enormous complex to fill this need; and for this building to be put up in suitable surroundings, he exerted pressure on the municipal authorities until they started to follow the example of Paris by establishing new suburbs with wide avenues. This, of course, stimulated the need to provide accommodation for visitors, and it was Sarphati who took the initiative for the construction of the first—and to this day the most representative—modern hotel in Amsterdam.

Sarphati would of course not have succeeded in all this without the help of the bankers. Karl Marx spoke contemptuously of the many Jewish bankers of Amsterdam, though on investigation they are somewhat less ubiquitous than Marx's anti-Semitic cast of mind made them out to be. Most of them, like the Bischoffheims, were branches of foreign enterprises. But there were two financiers who played a highly important role in the Netherlands. The first was Lodewyk Pincoff, whose energy was the driving force behind the development of Rotterdam. The career of Pincoff, who was even elected to the First Chamber (the Netherlands Senate), came to a sad end when the African Trading Company, which he had founded, went bankrupt. He escaped to America and was sentenced *in absentia*. His fall resulted in an anti-Semitic campaign which not only made its mark in the press, but also resulted in a cooler attitude toward the Jews in ruling circles. The man feeling this most immediately was the banker A.C. Wertheim, who in a sense may be regarded as Sarphati's successor. In addition to being a banker, Wertheim was also a Liberal politican, with considerable influence in his

Dr. Samuel Sarphati, (1813-66). The enterprising Dutch physician, whose multiple activities usually had a social motivation behind them, in a lithograph by S. Altmann. Amsterdam, Rijksmuseum, Rijksprentenkabinett.

party. But the most interesting aspect of his personality is his attitude to Judaism. Wertheim was completely detached from Orthodoxy. In Germany he would no doubt have found his place in a Reform synagogue; in the Netherlands, this Jew who desecrated the Sabbath and violated the dietary laws in public was for years president of a 'Church' Association which was committed to a position of rigorous Orthodoxy—a position which Wertheim defended with great spirit. His statement 'Not a stone of the fort' became the slogan of the synagogue, whose Orthodox rabbis and unorthodox lay leaders joined forces to prevent the rise of any Reform movement in the Netherlands, and this attitude prevailed until far into the 20th century.

THE MODERN PERIOD

By the end of the nineteenth century, Dutch Jewry was in the throes of far-reaching economic, sociological, political and cultural changes. In Amsterdam, the Jews had played a major part in the diamond industry ever since the 17th century. When the South African diamond fields were discovered, demand for cut stones rose enormously, causing an unprecedented prosperity in this industry, which attracted more and more Jewish dealers and workers (the 'Cape Period', 1872-6). The boom passed and was

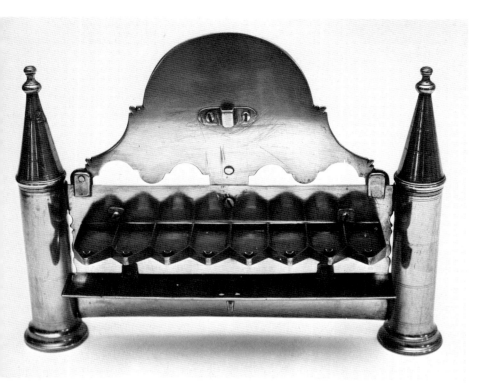

Hannukah lamp, Holland, early nineteenth century. Strasbourg, Musée Alsacien, Société pour l'Histoire des Israélites d'Alsace et de Lorraine.

Brass Hanukkah lamp, Holland, end of nineteenth century. Tree, animal and flower ornamentation, with eight oil lamps. Cologne, Stadtmuseum, Inv. No. 1927/710.

followed by a severe slump. But unlike what had happened in former days, the workers would no longer rest content with the steps their employers proposed to meet the crisis in the old-fashioned manner; Socialism had taken a hold on them, and their demands and arguments in the trade union movement were radical. In these hard times, there developed 'a sharp, almost hostile division between Jews and Christians' among the diamond-cutters. This was brought to an end principally by the great Dutch trade union leader Henri Polak (1860-1943), who founded the General Netherlands Union of Diamond Workers (Algemeene Nederlandsche Diamantbewerkers Bond) in 1894. Owing to Polak's organizational talents, the ANDB was soon to become the strongest trade union in the country and was capable of resisting the anarchistic trends which threatened to overwhelm the Socialist movement. To counter the danger of anarchism, Polak and eleven others founded in 1894 the Social-Democratic Workers Party, in which he played a leading role for many years and which he was to represent in Parliament.

The trade union movement, too, owes much to Henri Polak, who, after a bad disaster for the Netherlands workers, played a major role in establishing the Netherlands Federation of Trade Unions in 1906; in its beginnings, the new Federation was greatly influenced by the ANDB with its excellent organization and ample financial means. The growth of trade unionism and Socialism led at first to serious conflicts within the Jewish community. Henri Polak, of course, played his part in this conflict, though later events were to prove that he held strong Jewish convictions and even supported the rebuilding of the Land of Israel.

In his writings he never denied his Jewish origins and interest. Most of his Jewish fellow-Socialists, however, thought differently. The Jewish proletariat, which turned Socialist in the beginning of the 20th century, regarded the Jewish religion as 'opium' and, unlike the East European Jews, never developed an independent road to Jewish Socialism. Even more hostile was the attitude of the Jewish intellectuals of the Marxist Left, who eventually found themselves in the Communist party and whose leader, David Wynkoop, son of a well-known rabbi and Hebrew grammarian, completely cut his ties with all things Jewish. Still, for all their internationalism and atheism, the Jewish quarters of Amsterdam retained a markedly Jewish feel, reflected in their characteristic dialect and perhaps also in strong intellectual aspirations. Not many years later the sons of diamond-workers, hawkers and small shopkeepers were to be found among the intellectual élite of the Netherlands.

In the hundreds of Jewish communities outside Amsterdam, things were different. Here, there was no coherent Jewish proletariat, and the Jews were strongly aware of being a small minority that was different from the general population. With a few exceptions, they had a hard time making a living. Hawker, market dealer, cattle dealer, butcher—those were their main trades. Here again, things changed at the end of the 19th and the beginning of the 20th century: the hawkers began to benefit from the development of industry, the market dealers from better communications and commercial expansion. Thus they became manufacturers and wholesalers, mainly in the textile trade. In the eastern Netherlands, a number of Jewish families

(Menco, Spanjaard, Hedeman) succeeded in establishing large factories and developed the district of Twente into the center of the Dutch textile industry. Another industry, first established by a Jewish trader in a small village, was the margarine factory of Van den Berg, which was to grow into the worldwide Unilever concern.

This increase in prosperity was paralleled by another development: the Jews began to leave the small villages for the cities. Amsterdam attracted the greatest numbers, but the other cities, Rotterdam, the Hague, Utrecht, and Groningen in the north also saw their Jewish population grow at the expense of the country. Obviously, this process toward urbanization also had the effect of making many Jews, who in their former small communities had kept faith with their religion, lapse into religious indifference or even leave the Jewish community entirely.

The beginning of the 20th century was therefore a time of crisis for the Dutch Jews. Their progress was faster than that of the general population, and at the same time their birthrate, which had been very high, trailed off rapidly. The number of mixed marriages increased; in Amsterdam, even, it was the highest of all the great cities in Europe. The demographic decline was further reinforced by the considerable numbers of those who opted out of the Jewish community on the grounds of atheism.

Not that the role of the Jews diminished. We have already seen how important they were in the Socialist movement: the

Silver circumcision medal, Utrecht, 1845. Circumcision medal given by Judah ben Eliezer, a *Mohel* (circumciser) from Utrecht, to all the children he circumcised. The chair seen here is the Chair of Elijah or circumcision chair; on the other side the name of the child and date of the ceremony were engraved. Jerusalem, Israel Museum.

number of Jewish Labor leaders who were elected to Parliament or municipal office was considerable. The Liberal party, too, had numbered Jews among its leading members ever since Wertheim. No less important was their part in cultural affairs. The first of the Dutch Jewish painters was also the greatest: Jozef Israels (1824-1911). He had not yet detached himself from the Jewish community, and his Jewish identification inspired some of his best works, such as the *Son of the Old People and the Scribe.* His son Isaac Israels, also a talented painter, belonged to a different

period already, in which the rich Jews were embarrassed by their poorer brethren, but still felt most at home in their own circle, the *haute juiverie.* Later painters never came up to the standards of Jozef Israels.

Glass goblet with silver base, Holland, 1860. Glass with Hebrew inscription giving the name of the donor and the person to whom it was destined. Silver base with Dutch silver mark. Hamburg, Museum für Kunst und Gewerbe.

Sculptors were rare among Dutch Jews; one of them, Jozef Mendes da Costa (1863-1939) was not only known for monumental works, but also for figurines and groups in *grès cérame,* which reflect his social consciousness as much as his Jewish ties. He was obviously influenced by the new social movement. The same is true to an even greater extent for the writers, the most famous of whom, Herman Heyermans, was the Netherlands' greatest playwright and whose plays concerned themselves mainly with the sufferings of the working class. When Heyermans wrote about Jews, however, he was usually so critical as to be nearly hostile. In his novel *Diamond Town* and his play *The Ghetto* he depicts figures that are less than sympathetic. To his credit it must be said that he later admitted this bias frankly, at least as far the play is concerned.

The rise of Socialism inspired many other Jewish writers; not a few of them directed their attention to the Amsterdam ghetto or the small Jewish country community, and enjoyed great fame in their time, although they have no message for later generations. An exception must be made in the case of the gifted children of a rural rabbi named De Haan: Jacob Israel and Carry. Jacob Israel, a talented lawyer, regarded himself as a great poet, though in actual fact his gift for prose may have been greater. Swaying from one extreme to the other, he began his career as an atheist-socialist teacher in Haarlem and ended it as a fanatically Orthodox Jew who sought the friendship of Arabs in order to fight Zionism and thus became the victim of the first political murder committed by Jews in the modern Land of Israel. His sister was more consistent in her atheism and her rejection of Judaism, but she never denied her origins, as is shown by her touching description of her youth and her religious experiences in the paternal home.

This love of the Jewish milieu, though often enough combined with a measure of self-hate, is characteristic of the Dutch and particularly the Amsterdam Jews. It is hardly surprising to find it in a city where the Jews had for three centuries accounted for one tenth of the population and thus had created and developed a sphere that was particularly their own. It was a sphere which did not fail to attract non-Jews, many of whom sought to identify themselves with it, a tendency most marked in the world of the theater and cabaret. There have been many great Jewish actors—the greatest of them was Esther de Boer van Ryk, who owes much of her fame to her appearances in Heyermans' plays—while the greatest of Dutch cabaret entertainers, Louis Davids, was also a Jew. In fact eventually even the lines between Jew and non-Jew became completely blurred. Jewish speech and Jewish patterns of living left such clear traces in the world of the arts, that the absence of this milieu was painfully noticeable after World War II.

Zionism

In this prevailing atmosphere, it is scarcely surprising that the Jewish national movement was confronted with specific problems. Most Dutch Jews were so deeply convinced of the effectiveness of the Jewish-Gentile symbiosis in Holland that they could not believe in any danger to the Jews and felt sure that the few existing traces of discrimination would disappear in course of time. Not that Dutch Jewry lacked those who felt strong ties with Jews in other parts. The closeness of the link with the Land of Israel is evident from the establishment of a fund-raising organization for the benefit of the Jews in the Holy Land: Pekidim and Amarcalim of the Holy Land (1810), in Amsterdam. This organization, headed by the bankers Lehren, became a factor of importance in the support of the Jews of Jerusalem and also helped strengthen the Jewish community. The Lehren brothers were pietitst who came into conflict with the prevailing rationalist-assimilationist trend. Their group still had its followers in the 20th century, but its influence was negligible.

Zionism on the other hand, basing itself, as it did, on the principle of emancipation, was able to gather a following from the very beginning. One of the first Zionists was the banker Jacobus H. Kann, who was among Herzl's early collaborators. In the Netherlands, the Zionist movement soon had to fight on two fronts: it was violently opposed by the Orthodoxy and condemned by all the Dutch chief rabbis with the exception of Dr. J.H. Duenner. On the other hand, the Socialist Jews regarded Zionism as a reactionary movement, which was therefore a danger to the worker and must be fought. As a result, there were only two Zionist nuclei until the time of the end of World War I: those Orthodox circles which followed Duenner's lead, and members of the free professions. This situation was changed by that war. Neutral Holland absorbed a number of refugees, particularly from Belgium, and they soon started to deploy an intensive Jewish national activity. Under their influence, the Jewish national movement in the Netherlands began to be more active in propaganda, education, and cultural affairs. Young religious leaders became enthusiastic Zionists and Socialist opposition weakened. A strong Jewish youth movement, which militantly promoted Hebrew and a pioneering movement came into existence. During the 1920s, growth remained comparatively slow, but the great change came with the rise of Hitler in Germany, particularly after 1933. The seven years until the Netherlands themselves were occupied by the Germans were a restless time. The thirty thousand or more German Jews who escaped to Holland brought the Dutch Jews face to face with questions which could not be answered without a complete change of orientation. Who was responsible for their maintenance? Should one insist on keeping the borders open, or would this undermine the position of the Netherlands Jews? Was the stream of refugees a portent of what Holland must expect, or would the country be able to preserve its neutrality again, as it had done in World War I? To look after and help absorb the German Jews, a mighty apparatus was set up under the leadership of the diamond merchant A. Ascher and the historian D. Cohen. This committee to all practical intents took over responsibility from the Government, which was extremely reluctant to admit the refugees. In the discussion over their admission, the vast majority of the Jews spoke in favor of a policy of open borders,

The Jewish Bride by Joseph Israels, 1903. Israels (1824-1911) depicted the general everyday life in Holland as well as specifically Jewish scenes, particularly from 1883 onward. This Dutch-Jewish painter has often been called the most significant figure in Dutch art since the 17th century. Amsterdam, Rijksmuseum.

German round-up of Jews, February 1941. Jews kneeling on the Jonas Daniel Meyerplein after a round-up by the German police during the occupation of the Netherlands. Of the 140,000 Jews in Holland at the outbreak of the war, some 80 per cent perished. There are today 22,000 Jews in the country.

notwithstanding the possible consequences for the Netherlands. Most Dutch Jews, however, fostered illusions as to the inviolability of the country which now appear incomprehensible. Only few had premonitions of the terrible disaster which was to befall Dutch Jewry.

WORLD WAR II

If we are to understand what happened in the Netherlands between the years 1940 and 1945, we must remember that the Netherlands had not known war for more than a hundred years.

Peace and contentment had become national characteristics. The law was obeyed to the letter as were all official orders, for no one considered the possibility that a criminal government might take advantage of this obedience to lead peaceful citizens astray. There was one small group which sided with the Germans, but even one section of the Dutch National-Socialists rejected anti-Semitism. All this, however, did not prevent the Dutch officials from following the German decrees meekly, even if they were contrary to the Netherlands constitution and international law. The eyes of the population were not opened until the Germans began to use brute force and arrested a few hundred Jews in Amsterdam, herded them together and deported them to the concentration camp of Mauthausen. Amsterdam reacted with a total worker's strike (February 1941), which spread to other places in the neighborhood as well. It was a unique and courageous act of solidarity with the Jews; for the Jews, however, the effect of the strike was only moral. The Germans, taught by experience, continued their actions by means of quasi-legal decrees and thus brought the majority of the civil service and the police over to their side. Concentration camps were established;

Interior of Maastricht synagogue, 1839-40. A fine Dutch synagogue interior. The women's gallery can be seen upstairs; the reader's desk is in the center, the Ark at the end, and, above it, the Ten Commandments.

the one in Westerbork served as a transit camp to the death camps of Auschwitz and Sobibor. Of the 140,000 Dutch Jews, more than a 100,000 were deported, and only a few thousand of these returned. Many of the others perished as well. Among the non-Jewish population, a considerable number were prepared to give shelter to the Jews, in spite of the danger to life which it involved. It is assumed that some twenty thousand Jews went underground; about half eventually were found by the Germans.

Even during the war, there had been isolated complaints in the underground press about the failure of the Dutch population to reject German anti-Jewish discrimination unanimously. The complete extent of the disaster, however, did not come out until after the war. The numbers of the victims spoke a language that could not be misunderstood. The terrors of Auschwitz and Sobibor became known. Reports, accounts, diaries appeared, the most famous being that of Anne Frank. The feeling of inadequacy became a trauma of the Dutch people after World War II. Theologians became aware of the relation between Jew and Christian and pleaded for a total revision of the Christian view of Judaism. Artists identified with Jewish suffering and wrote of it, spoke of it, illustrated it. It seemed that the Jews had never occupied the Dutch people's attention so much as when they had become numerically a completely unimportant minority.

And what of the Jews themselves? The shock of the apocalyptic events left unmistakable traces. The Jewish community shook off its self-satisfied attitude and regained an awareness of its links with Jews elsewhere. This appeared first and foremost in the massive emigration to Palestine and later to Israel, which proportionally exceeded that of all other Western countries. Many Dutch Jews, though, also emigrated to other countries, Canada, Australia, and particularly the United States. But there are yet other aspects that reflect the catastrophe. The prose and poetry of the Dutch-Jewish writers is pervaded by the memories of what happened to them or to the Jews in general. More than ever the Jews in the Netherlands are aware of their Jewish identity.

One may ask whether this is not a passing phenomenon. The Catastrophe operated selectively and the intellectual and financial upper strata of the Jewish community were comparatively the least affected. Hence, though only one-sixth of the Jews have survived and remained in the Netherlands, the share of the Jews in Dutch cultural and economic life seems no less than before the war. At an estimate, there are some fifty Jewish professors, and dozens of writers, poets, composers and other artists. Unfortunately, however, this seems to be an Indian summer which presages no new growth. Not only is the community numerically so small that it depends on other countries, mainly on Israel, particularly for its spiritual needs, but the demographic conditions are particularly unpromising. The birth rate is lower than that of the general population. The favorable climate, the absence of discrimination, and the general prosperity encourage further blending with the non-Jewish environment. Jewish consciousness and the sympathy and often admiration for Judaism among the non-Jews are not sufficient to counteract this trend.

The three hundred and fifty years of Jewish existence in the Netherlands thus form a complete self-contained entirety, framed by two great disasters for the Jewish people: the Expulsion from Spain and the Nazi Holocaust. During that period, the Netherlands Jewish achievement, economically and culturally, has been considerable. But while the first part of the period, until the Emancipation, is characterized by a Jewish community which was closed off from its environment and in close contact with Jews elsewhere, the second half presents the opposite picture: separation from the Jewish world and ever greater participation in the Dutch society. The Jewish national revival was on the point of reversing the trend, when the great Holocaust put an end to all thought of independent development, and all that remained was the memory of a great past.

CHAPTER X

Poland and Russia

by Dr. Yehuda Slutsky

The beginning of Jewish settlement in East Europe is connected with the Jewish migration that took place in the Hellenistic period from the Orient and Asia Minor to the shores of the Black and Azov Seas. Traces of early Jewish communities are to be found in the Byzantine settlements of the Crimean peninsula, in the main town of Chersonesus (near Sevastopol), in Theodosia, and on the Bosphorus (now Kerch), as well as along the eastern shore of the Black Sea.

Among the merchants crossing the territories of the Slavs and Khazars from West Europe to the Asian regions, reaching even as far as India and China, the Jews played an important part. In this they were aided by their knowledge of the languages spoken in these countries, including Slavonic, and by their national and religious ties with Jews already settled there. Trade was conducted in spices, cloths, hides, weapons, and slaves. The tenth-century Jewish merchant Ibrahim Ibn Yaakub speaks of Jewish merchants arriving in Prague, one of the entrepots of East European trade, with their wares from Cracow, Rus (Kiev area) and the lands of the Slavs and Turks.

In the middle of the 8th century the chiefs of the Khazar kingdom adopted Judaism. The Khazars, a warrior Turkish tribe, had founded a large kingdom in the region of the north Caucasus and the vast steppelands between the Caspian and Black Seas. The capital of the Khazar monarchs was Ityl (or Atil) near Astrakhan on the river Volga. The Jewish Khazar realm continued in existence for over two centuries, but little about it is known. The Jewish element was apparently constituted from the ruling class—the king, his court, and his military leaders—together with Jews who had migrated from the Islamic or Christian territories that surrounded the Khazar kingdom. The majority of its inhabitants were Muslims, Christians and pagans, who enjoyed religious freedom and civic privileges.

The rumored existence of the Khazar kingdom was a source of encouragement to Jews in other parts of the Diaspora. Hasdai Ibn Shaprut, the counsellor and confidant of the caliph of Cordova (mid-10th century), wrote in his letter to the Khazar king that if it were indeed true 'that there exists a soil and a kingdom where scattered Israel is neither subject nor subordinate to others', he would be willing to renounce his place of honor, to abandon his family, and to journey 'over mountains and hills, over sea and land' to behold the greatness and honor of the Jewish king and the 'tranquillity of the remnant of Israel'.

The Khazar kingdom was involved in constant warfare with its neighbors, in particular with Russian Kiev. The memory of the warriors 'from the Jewish lands' who fought the warriors of the Russians is retained in the early Russian sagas. Svyatoslav, prince of Kiev, destroyed Ityl in 969, and this was followed by the rapid disintegration of the Khazar kingdom, which disappeared from the scene of world history within fifty years.

It is not impossible that the downfall of the Khazar kingdom played some part in the Christianization of the Kiev princes. It certainly strengthened the bonds between Christian Byzantine and pagan Russia. A hint of this is found in the Russian tradition that relates how Vladimir, prince of Kiev, decided to adopt Christianity. 'How is it that you have come here to instruct others,' Vladimir is said to have exclaimed to the Jews who had come to persuade him to adopt Judaism, 'when your God has forsaken you and scattered you among the nations? For, had he loved you, you would not be so dispersed!'

Nevertheless, there were Jews living in the city of Kiev, which became an important commercial center. Early Russian sources speak of the 'Gate of the Jews' in Kiev. The Jews apparently took up residence in the city under the protection of the prince. During the revolt of the townspeople in 1113 the mob attacked not only the castles of the aristocracy, but also the homes of the Jews. There is also mention of religious disputations held between representatives of the Church and the Jews in Kiev. Kiev Jewry maintained contact on matters of Law and religion with the rabbinical scholars of West Europe and the principals of the academies in Babylonia.

After the passing of the Khazar kingdom nothing is known of the fate of its Jewish inhabitants. Many of them must have perished during the Mongol invasions of Europe in the first half of the 13th century. Those who survived probably formed the nucleus of the Jewish settlements in Lithuania and Poland, but they merged with or were assimilated by the large numbers of Jewish migrants now arriving in East Europe from the West. Only a few minute communities have retained their specific language and way of life up to the modern period: the Tatar-speaking Jews of the Crimea, and the small Karaite congregations in Crimea, Galicia, and Lithuania.

This glorious episode of the Jewish kingdom in the Diaspora has been perpetuated in the *Kuzari,* the philosophical opus of the Spanish-Jewish philosopher-poet, Judah Ha-Levi, writing in the 12th century.

In the generations to come, however, East European Jewry was not molded by the Jewish Khazar element, but by the stream of Jewish immigrants from the West.

POLAND—LAND OF REFUGE

While the East Slavic tribes were defeated and enslaved by the Mongols, the great kingdom of Poland-Lithuania began to emerge in the territories inhabited by the West Slav peoples. Over about seven centuries, the fate of the Jews in East Europe was to be linked with the development of this kingdom, and the relationship between the various classes of its inhabitants.

Jewish migration from Central Europe to Poland began at the end of the 11th century, after the destruction wrought on the communities in Germany and Bohemia by the early Crusaders (1096). A contemporary chronicle records that 'many Jews fled, and others secretly transferred their property to Poland.' The new immigrants most probably joined their coreligionists already living in the Polish regions. The rate of immigration increased in proportion to the restrictive legislation, persecutions and expulsions to which the Jews were subjected in West Europe. It was not to cease until the mid-17th century, and reached its height in the mid-16th century. The newcomers brought with them their spoken language, a German dialect with an admixture of Hebrew words and phrases. In Poland this language absorbed numerous Slavic words, and developed as an independent language—Yiddish-Deutsch, or, as abbreviated, Yiddish.

Poland, which began to take shape as a single entity in the 12th and 13th centuries, had need of this immigration for the development of its commerce and industry. Jews are already mentioned in twelfth-century documents as moneylenders to the Crown and nobility, and as farmers of the excise and mint.

The early Polish coins bear Hebrew inscriptions, or inscriptions in Polish in Hebrew lettering, such as the legend '*Mieszko Krol Polski*' (Miesko, king of Poland). Since neither the Polish nobility nor the common people as yet felt the lack of an alphabet, commerce was conducted in Hebrew. This was the language in which the merchants made entries in their ledgers, drew up their obligations, and signed their deeds of credit.

The process of migration and settlement was not accomplished without difficulties. Parallel with the Jewish immigration, there was a considerable German colonization movement of merchants and artisans, who established urban settlements throughout Poland. These immigrants brought with them from Germany the traditional hatred of the Jews, and also viewed them as rivals. The Germans demanded the prohibition of Jewish settlement in the towns, or at least curtailment of their liberties to engage in commerce and crafts. A good many Polish cities obtained the 'privilege' *de non tolerandis Judaeis,* i.e. of excluding the Jews from their boundaries. In other cities Jewish residence was restricted to specific streets or adjacent suburbs. At the end of the 15th century the Jews were expelled from Cracow and Warsaw, the largest cities in Poland.

In their struggle against the Jews, the burghers were aided by the Catholic Church, which constituted an important political and economic factor in the kingdom of Poland. The clergy regarded the prosperity of the Jews as offensive to its status. According to Church doctrine, the Jews were destined to serve as witnesses to the reign of Jesus on earth, and to bear the burden of degradation and scorn, because their ancestors allegedly crucified Jesus. The clergy demanded that Jewish rights be curtailed, that Jews be debarred from holding positions or sources of livelihood liable to give them authority over Christians, that Jewish residence be confined to ghettos, and that they wear a distinguishing sign on their clothing. The Church also accused the Jews of desecrating the host (on the first occasion in Poznan, in 1399), and of ritual murder (first in Cracow in 1406), the priests and monks leading mob attacks on the Jewish population.

The protectors of the Jews were first and foremost the kings of Poland, who regarded them as a useful economic asset and faithful mainstay of the Crown treasury. The Polish monarchs facilitated Jewish immigration into Poland and settlement there, in particular during the 13th and 14th centuries, when the country had to repair the devastations of the Mongol invasions. In 1264 Prince Boleslav of Kalish granted the first charter of privileges to the Jews. The charter, based on similar constitutions granted in Germany, states that the Jews are under the protection of the ruler, and provides that any person causing injury to Jews shall be severely punished. The synagogues and Jewish cemeteries are afforded protection, and the charter guarantees that no charges of ritual murder shall be preferred against them. The Jews are under the direct jurisdiction of the ruler, but litigation among themselves is to be judged 'in their synagogues and according to their laws and usages'. The Jews are permitted to engage in moneylending and trade, and inviolability of Jewish property is guaranteed. This charter became the cornerstone of the general charter of privileges granted to the Jews in 1334 by Casimir the Great. The 1334 charter specifically states that it has been granted to the Jews 'because they are our subjects, and they are required to be prepared with their money to serve us when we are in need of it'. Nearly all the later Polish monarchs ratified this charter. In practice, the extent of its implementation depended on royal requirements and on the amount of pressure brought to bear on the king by the burghers, the clergy and the nobility.

The influence of the nobility—the *Shliakhta*—in the country increased in the course of time until, by the 15th century, Poland had become a 'Republic of the Nobility'. The position of the Jews, therefore, was to no small extent determined by their relationships with this group. These magnates acquired property, reducing the peasants to serfdom, and obtained wide concessions from the government, including the right of propination, i.e. the manufacture and sale of alcoholic liquors, the consumption of which was an inseparable part of life in Poland for persons from every sphere. The magnates also controlled the large tax-farming enterprises, and ousted the Jews from these offices. However, they still required the Jews to exploit and administer the wealth and concessions that had fallen to their lot. They borrowed money from the Jews and leased to them the management of their estates, forests, flour-mills, inns and especially the taverns, which constituted a not inconsiderable source of revenue.

As the burghers succeeded in driving the Jews outside the municipal bounds, the latter increasingly found protection on property owned by the nobility, either inside the towns or nearby. Many also went to live in the villages and hamlets owned by the magnates. Thus a number of new Jewish communities were established, and the Jewish population became diffused throughout the country. The full effect of this situation becomes evident in a communal statute of 1539, dividing the Jewish community into those who were subject to the jurisdiction of the Crown and those subject to the landed gentry.

Subsequently a similar process began to develop in the grand duchy of Lithuania, which from the 14th century extended over a wide area from the Baltic to the Black Seas. Here, too, the size and character of the ancient community was increased and modified with the infusion of Jewish immigrants from Central Europe and Poland.

JEWISH SETTLEMENT IN THE UKRAINE

From the mid-16th century, the Polish aristocracy rapidly began to acquire estates in the Ukraine. The Polish magnate was inevitably accompanied by his Jewish *arendar*—the lessee of the management of his estates. The leasing of concessions to manage the various branches of estate economy became a chief occupation of the Jews in the Ukraine. The large-scale *arendar* leased whole groups of villages, and the lesser *arendar*, single villages. Jews also leased, either directly or indirectly as second lessees, the concessions obtained by the nobility to own flour-mills, hostelries, and in particular taverns. The peasant was obliged to grind his corn in the Jewish mill, to drink his liquor in the Jewish tavern, and to work in the fields of the landlord under Jewish supervision. Besides the social antagonism existing between the nobility and peasantry in Poland, there was added in the Ukraine a national and religious tension, since the Ukrainian population was of the Greek-Orthodox faith. This opposition became all the more bitter as the Ukrainian peasants had been used to a tradition of independence. They did not take easily to the yoke imposed by the Polish squires; nor did they appreciate the way the nobility had delegated the responsibility for the implementation of this policy of subjugation to the Jews, which was viewed as a particular degradation. The Ukrainian peasants' hate of the Jews was no less intense than their hate of their Polish masters.

The Jewish *arendars* were the forerunners of numerous Jewish settlements in the Ukraine, both large and small. In their wake followed others to serve or assist them, such as secondary lessees and their families, teachers, cantors and rabbis. The papal legate Cardinal Commendoni, who traveled through the Ukraine in the 16th century, reports on 'masses of Jews' living there, 'who are not despised as in other countries. They do not gain their livelihood at all from contemptible professions, such as usury and other petty business, although there are some such among them. The Jews work the soil, engage in commerce, some concern themselves with letters, and in particular medicine and astrology. In nearly every place they farm the custom dues on exports and imports; they are in general wealthy. They wear no special sign on their clothing to distinguish them from Christians. They are permitted to wear swords and to arm themselves. In sum, they enjoy equal rights with the rest of the inhabitants.'

Conditions in the new regions were not secure. The lands across the Dnieper were inhabited by roving bands of Cossacks, who were not subject to the Polish Crown, and who used to make forays from time to time to the western side of the river. From the south, hordes of Tatars swooped down to plunder and carry off captives. The Jewish residents joined in defending the new towns, and they were granted permission to build fortified synagogues, which could be used as places of refuge and defense by members of the community in times of warfare or siege. Mainly, however, they relied for defense on their natural allies—the Polish rulers.

THE INTERNAL LIFE OF THE JEWS IN POLAND AND LITHUANIA

The political and economic conditions of the feudal Polish regime helped consolidate the Jewish population in the kingdom as an independent social class, a religious sect and a national entity. Socially, the Jews formed an intermediate class between the nobility and the peasants, which fitted admirably into the general structure of Polish society. Their religion separated them from their Christian neighbors and molded their daily lives, while their specific languages, Hebrew and Yiddish, served as an additional barrier and underlined their national specificity among the rest of the population of the state.

In these conditions the internal life of the Jews developed almost independently of that of their Christian neighbors. This independence found expression in the development of Jewish autonomy, which reached the same proportions in the kingdom of Poland as it had in the communities of Babylonia and Spain in their day.

The base of this autonomy was the organized Jewish community. It was recognized and given a special status by the secular authorities, along the same lines as the independent Christian burgher organization. The Jewish communal organization served as the official spokesman of the Jews in their relations with the authorities and was responsible for paying the taxes for which the Jews were liable to the government. Internally, the communal organization was responsible for apportioning the tax quota among the members of the community, levying special dues for its own requirements, and safeguarding the economic rights of the individual. The communal organization prevented unfair competition against its members from outsiders, Jews and non-Jews alike.

To carry this out effectively, the legal concept of *hazakah* (preemptive possession) developed, which stopped anyone from harming the means of livelihood or contract lease of a member of the community, either by unfair competition or by price cutting. The communal organization also saw to the upkeep and building of synagogues and cemeteries, as well as to the social welfare of the community, particularly through the many associations that operated under its supervision. Some of these associations were of a public character, such as the Hevrah Kaddisha (burial society), the Talmud Torah for religious study, the societies for 'visiting the sick,' 'clothing the naked', or 'ransoming of captives,' i.e. to obtain the release of Jewish debtors and war-captives. There were also professional or craft associations, caring for the material and spiritual welfare of their members. Furthermore, associations were formed for prayer and for study, such as the 'Reciters of Psalms', Talmud circles, and circles for the study of the Kabbalah.

Election to the communal body was restricted to a narrow circle of wealthy Jews or religious scholars. The committee was granted legal jurisdiction by the Polish authorities over the members of the community, and was able to impose punishment by fines, corporal punishment, imprisonment, or the stocks *(kune)*. The most severe category of punishment was the *herem* (ban of excommunication), generally imposed on those who refused to submit to communal authority.

Representatives of the communities in the various provinces in the country began to meet together from the beginning of the 16th century to ensure that the taxes for which Polish Jewry was liable were fairly distributed, and to discuss matters of mutual interest. These provincial assemblies became regular institutions, known as the 'Councils of the Lands'. After the Polish government decided to impose a roof tax on the Jewish population, the representatives of the Councils of the Lands used to meet at the great fairs held in Lublin and Yaroslav. By the end of the 16th century the assembly had developed into a central Polish-Jewish institution, known as the 'Council of the Four Lands'. (In 1623 the Lithuanian representatives separated from it, forming their own 'Council of Lithuania'.) The Polish government recognized the Council of the Four Lands as the Jewish representative body in Poland. The state conducted negotiations through the council's representatives *(shtadlanim)* on the amount of tax to be imposed, and other matters concerning Jewish life in the state. The Council of the Four Lands and the Council of Lithuania issued laws which were binding on all the Jewish communities.

The Jewish way of life in Poland was molded by the laws of the Bible and the Talmud. Religious study was the cornerstone of Jewish spiritual existence. In an age when to learn to read and write at all was the privilege of the few, the Jews set up a complete educational system of their own, that took in the education of children and the young as well as adults. Up to the age of thirteen all boys were obliged to attend *heder* (small schools) where they learned to read and write as well as their prayers, the Bible and the Talmud. Instruction was given by private teachers *(melammedim)*, who taught a limited number of children in their homes. For needy children the community maintained a 'Talmud Torah' Institution. The young learned independently, the more proficient leaving to attend the talmudical colleges *(yeshivot)*, which were supervised by local rabbis. *Yeshivah* students would often travel from town to town in order to hear the best teachers. The community supported *yeshivah* students, and its members were required to provide meals for them at the family table.

Until the end of the 15th century Polish Jewry looked for religious guidance to the *yeshivot* in the German area, which was also its source of rabbis. At the beginning of the 16th century, however, Jacob Pollak and his pupil Shalom Shachna founded the great *yeshivot* in Cracow and Lublin. They also laid the basis for a method of study that was to become unique to the *yeshivot* in Poland, the *pilpul* method which consisted primarily in comparing differing passages in the Talmud, attempting to point out the discrepancies between them, and reconciling them by means of dialectical explanations. Although many of the greatest rabbinic scholars in Poland criticized this method as casuistic, it remained firmly entrenched in the *yeshivot*.

In 1564 the first complete edition of Joseph Caro's *Shulhan Arukh* (The Prepared Table) was published in Venice and this code, comprising all the rabbinic decisions and Laws which a Jew should observe both in his public and his private life, had soon gained a wide circulation in Poland. It became evident, however, that the *Shulhan Arukh* contained a number of details and refinements that went against the accepted usages of Polish Jewry. R. Moses Isserles therefore undertook to adapt the *Shulhan Arukh* to the needs of Polish Jewry, and compiled his observations in a work entitled *Ha-Mappah* (The Tablecloth). Thanks to the authority of Isserles, the *Shulhan Arukh* together with *Ha-Mappah*

Torah Ark doors, Cracow, early seventeenth century. The motifs recall the Jerusalem Temple — on the left, the *menorah* (candelabrum); on the right the twelve loaves of shewbread, corresponding to the twelve tribes. Given by a husband and wife in honor of their son. Painted lead on wood. Jerusalem, Israel Museum.

became the accepted code for Jews throughout Europe.

Through these and other rabbis, Poland became a center of religious authority and learning for the whole of European Jewry. A major part of the activities and energies of successive generations of scholars was devoted to interpreting the *Shulhan Arukh* and providing ruling on religious and social questions.

The doctrines of Kabbalah also reached Poland from the East. The Zohar and its exponents won many adherents in Poland. The works of the kabbalists in Safed were also favorably received. A large body of popular literature, principally of an ethical and religious nature, was written for ordinary people, in particular for women. The most widely read was *Tz'enah u-Re'enah* (Go Forth and See), which contained a Yiddish translation of the Pentateuch interwoven with talmudic legend and ethical observations.

The first Hebrew printing press in Cracow was established in 1530. Subsequently, numerous presses were set up in many communities publishing various types of religious works. A book became a coveted possession in every Jewish home. It became the base upon which Polish Jewry created its unique national consciousness on alien soil.

THE YEARS OF THE DELUGE

In 1648 a mass Cossack revolt broke out against Polish rule in the Ukraine. It heralded a long series of violent disturbances which harassed the Polish state over the following decade. It was also a period of devastation and decline for Polish Jewry.

The Cossacks were a class formed partly of fighters, partly of

The synagogue in Luck (Volhynia), 1626. In seventeenth and eighteenth-century Poland, synagogues were built as fortresses so that Jews could find refuge there in times of attack. The synagogue at Luck, in Volhynia, was typical, with its thick walls and its watchtower. Photographed about 1920. Photo Radovan, Jerusalem.

Synagogue. The painter Solomon Yudowin (1892-1954) recaptures the spirit of the small Jewish town *(stetl)* — which no longer exists in Eastern Europe — with its low houses and its wooden synagogue. Jerusalem, National and University Library.

peasants. Some were subject to Polish rule and some, living beyond the last of the rapids of the Dnieper (Zaporozhe), were banded into a free association, led by an elected hetman. After allying themselves with the Tatars, the Cossacks penetrated into west Ukraine under the leadership of Bogdan Chmielnicki, and gave the signal for a general uprising. Both peasants and burghers helped them to destroy the mansions of the Polish landowners and to massacre the Jews. Those who accepted the Greek Orthodox faith were spared. Many of the Jews were handed over to the Tatars, who carried them back to Turkey. The Jews in Turkey and throughout Europe collected money to ransom the captives.

In several towns the Jews attempted to defend themselves from Cossack attacks. In Tulchin they made an agreement with the Polish citizens to man the fortifications. The Cossacks, however, negotiated secretly with the Poles, offering peace if they betrayed the Jews into their hands. The Poles opened the gates to the Cossacks, who slaughtered the Jewish inhabitants in their customary barbaric manner, afterward settling their account with the Poles. The Jews were massacred wholesale in the towns of Bar, Polonnoye, and Nemirov. Bands of the rebels then penetrated Belorussia and annihilated communities in Pinsk, Brest-Litovsk, Homel, and other cities. In September 1648 Chmielnicki reached the gates of Lvov, where the Jews had undertaken the burden of defense with the rest of the inhabitants. Chmielnicki's demand that the Jews were to be surrendered to him was rejected. Finally he was induced to lift the siege on payment of a huge indemnity.

The fighting against the Cossacks continued for several years. In 1654 the armies of the Muscovites came to their assistance, and butchered the Jews in every town that fell to them. The Jews of Vitebsk, who helped to defend the city, were sent to the Russian interior as captives. Those in Vilna fled as the Russian armies approached the city, and on their return found their entire property pillaged.

During the Swedish invasion of Poland in 1656, the Jews were accused by the Poles of helping the enemy. Thus it was now the turn of the Jews in west Poland to suffer. Polish irregulars, led by Stephan Chanetzky, wiped out large and ancient communities, such as Lissa, Plotsk and Kalish. In 1656 the Cossacks again invaded Poland, destroying among others the community of Lublin.

During the eight years between 1648 and 1656, about seven hundred Jewish communities in Poland were annihilated. The number of victims murdered in the period amounted to hundreds of thousands. In the part of Ukraine to the east of the Dnieper not a single Jew remained, while in the regions of Volhynia and Podolia the former Jewish population had been decimated. Hosts of Jewish refugees sought asylum in Turkey and West Europe. The tide of Jewish migration, which for centuries had flowed eastward from West Europe, now turned back to the west.

These tragic events left an indelible impression on Jews everywhere and the holocaust was commemorated by special days of fasting and prayer. To many Jews it seemed that the catastrophe could only herald the coming of the Messiah.

When, in 1665, Shabbetai Tzevi appeared in Turkey and announced that he was the Messiah of Israel, masses of Jews throughout the Diaspora believed his claim and he gained many adherents in Poland and the Ukraine. A contemporary anti-Jewish polemic relates that when the Jews heard of the appearance of Shabbetai Tzevi, 'they left their homes, abandoned their work and babbled that the Messiah would shortly convey them on a cloud to Jerusalem. The Jews regarded the Christians with arrogance, and threatened them with the advent of their Messiah: "Wait a little, we shall soon be your masters".'

Of the emissaries dispatched on behalf of the Polish communities to see the Messiah, some returned with enthusiastic accounts, while others were disillusioned. After Shabbetai's conversion to Islam (September 1666), the Polish Jews remained true to the faith and dissociated themselves from him. In 1670 the Council of the Four Lands pronounced the ban of excommunication on followers of the pseudo-Messiah. However, the eschatological ferment thus aroused continued to agitate many circles in Jewry and sought an active outlet.

Rimmon, probably Poland, seventeenth to eighteenth centuries. This *rimmon* is topped with a crown decorated with the signs of the zodiac. Paris, Kugel Collection.

THE ERA OF DECLINE IN POLAND

The last century of existence of the Polish kingdom was a period of political and economic disruption, which caused particular distress to the Jewish population. The central government became weaker, although occasionally a forceful monarch was to be found who gave the Jews protection. King Jan Sobieski (1674-96), for instance, severely punished perpetrators of attacks on the Jews, and frustrated their opponents' schemes to impose restrictions on them. But because of the state's economic difficulties, the burden of taxation increasingly fell on the Jews. While the power of the central government declined, the magnates gained in strength. Although they ousted the Jews from the most important

◀ *Hanukkah lamp,* Poland, seventeenth to eighteenth centuries. The *Hanukkah* lamp was often the object of Jewish folk art. This bronze lamp, with its branches decorated with rosettes, ends in an eagle with outspread wings. Haifa, Mané Katz Collection.

91

branches of the economy, they still required their services to manage their affairs. Thus, during the 18th century, the Jewish population tended to disperse to the estates of the gentry, subjected to their arbitrary whims and fancies. Contemporary annals record numerous incidents of the insolence with which the Jews were treated on these properties.

At the same time the burghers' hostility toward the Jews intensified, and they made efforts to expel them from the towns. This process culminated in a resolution of the Polish Sejm (parliament) in 1768, which made Jewish residence in the cities dependent on the municipality's consent. The Jews were increasingly forced to take up contracting in the villages; the keeping of inns and taverns now became the most common Jewish occupation in Poland.

The clergy intensified its anti-Jewish incitement and tried to force the Jews to convert. From time to time, too, the priests revived the blood libel and other false allegations against them. The Jesuits, in this period responsible for the education of the youth, encouraged their pupils to assault the Jews, who were obliged to pay special protection money to the rectors of the colleges to induce them to restrain their charges.

In the border areas to the east there were recurrent uprisings by the peasantry, or *Haidamaks,* the declared purpose of whose commanders was 'to exterminate the accursed Jewish race'. The most frightful of these insurrections took place in 1768. Among the communities then annihilated was that of Uman, where masses of fugitives had fled for safety. The *Haidamaks* penetrated into the town, and slaughtered about 20,000 people there, both Jews and Poles.

During this period the communal organization was also undermined. Enormous sums were required to defray the taxes and the expenses incurred for defense against blood libels and riots. The communities became heavily indebted to wealthy religious orders and Church authorities. In order to defray their debts and the high interest rates, the communal organizations increased the dues imposed on their members, putting a tariff on kosher meat among other taxes. This caused particular hardship to the poorer classes of the community. A tax was also imposed on the right of *hazakah* (preemptive possession). The heavy burden of taxation was an additional cause of Jewish exodus from the towns to the estates of the squires, where the communal officials were unable to enforce payment of the dues.

In line with this general deterioration, the power of the Council of the Four Lands also weakened. In 1764 the Polish administration decided to end these conventions, giving out as the reason that they constituted a pernicious political pressure group, influencing the course of the deliberations of the Polish Sejm behind the scenes. The central government now undertook to levy the taxes on Jews directly. For this purpose a general

Crown for Torah scroll, Poland, beginning of eighteenth century. Silver gilt with gems. Height: 17⅓", Diameter: 9½". Jerusalem, Sir Isaac and Lady Edith Wolfson Museum, Hechal Shlomo, 2237-315.

Torah Ark doors, Cracow. The doors were engraved by an unknown artist and decorated with pictures of birds, animals and plants topped by a crown representing the Torah Crown. The inscription reads: 'Be strong as a leopard, fleet as an eagle, quick as a hound and valiant as a lion.' Jerusalem, Israel Museum.

census of Polish and Lithuanian Jewry was held, showing the Jewish population to be about 620,000. This figure, however, is evidently about one-third less than the actual total, since the communal organizations did everything possible to hide the true number of their members. About one-third of the Jewish population resided in the villages, with one or two families to a village. The larger communities were Brody (7,200 Jews), Lvov (6,200), Lisse (5,000), Cracow (3,500), Vilna (3,400). Brest-Litovsk (3,200), and Grodno (2,400). The Jewish population on the eve of the downfall of the Polish kingdom constituted about 9 per cent of the total population of the state.

THE FRANKISTS

The economic and social decline in Jewish life was accompanied by spiritual decadence. The number of *yeshivot* decreased. Talmudic learning became the possession of the minority. On the other hand, a popular ethical literature flourished in Hebrew and Yiddish, typical of which were lurid accounts of the sinner's torment in hell. But the communal leadership was also criticized for misusing its authority over the public for ulterior motives and for enjoying the revenues from the communal funds.

Messianic hopes continued to agitate wide sectors of the Jewish public. They influenced groups and individuals who began to seek explanations for Jewish existence along new paths. One such sect was founded by the kabbalist Judah Hasid, whose members devoted themselves to penitence and prayer. When subjected to growing opposition from the communal authorities, who suspected them of connections with the Sabbetaian movement, many of the adherents of Judah left Poland for Palestine. About one thousand reached Jerusalem in 1700.

In 1755 Polish Jewry was thrown into confusion by the discovery of an extremist group of Sabbetaians in its midst. The group gained ground when it found a leader in the person of Jacob Frank, who used to visit Turkey for commercial purposes and came into contact with the Sabbetaians in Smyrna and Salonika. The main tenet of his doctrine was that the advent of the Messiah, of whom he supposedly was a reincarnation, abrogated all the practical religious precepts of Judaism. Instead, the followers of Frank substituted mystical rites which combined excesses of a sexual nature. The sect spread mainly in south-east Poland (Podolia). The communal authorities then began to take repressive measures against the sectarians, and in 1756 a rabbinical synod in Brody excommunicated the Frankists.

Thus persecuted, the Frankists turned for help to the bishop

◀ *Torah Ark,* Grodno Synagogue (Lithuania). Over the Ark are the Ten Commandments. The two columns on either side are inspired by the two columns at the entrance to Solomon's Temple, Boaz and Jachin. Jerusalem, Israel Museum.

Torah shield, 1736. Silver with gold. This decoration for the Scroll of the Law depicts two griffons who are holding a memorial tablet on which the donor's name is inscribed. Hamburg, Museum für Kunst und Gewerbe, Inv. No. 1893/80.

Hanukkah lamp, Poland, eighteenth century. Brass. A lion holds the servant lamp from which the other lights were kindled and rampant birds sit on the roof in this fanciful Polish *Hanukkah* lamp. Jerusalem, Israel Museum.

of Kamenetz-Podolsk. They informed him that they denied the authority of the Talmud and believed in the sacredness of the Zohar, and that the Messiah had already appeared. On their suggestion, the ecclesiastical authorities ordered the holding of a religious disputation between the Frankists and rabbinical representatives. One outcome of the debate was that the bishop ordered all copies of the Talmud to be surrendered and burnt. The Frankists, however, continued to be hampered by the Jewish authorities; their position became so difficult that they decided to become ostensibly converted to Christianity, as the Sabbetaians in Turkey had accepted Islam.

In 1759 a second disputation was held in Lvov, in which the Frankists asserted that Jesus was the real Messiah, as well as alleging that Jewish doctrine required the use of Christian blood for religious purposes. Afterward the Frankists were converted to Christianity in impressive baptismal ceremonies. Frank himself was baptized in Warsaw in the presence of the king. However, since the Church suspected the genuineness of the faith of the new Christians, Frank was imprisoned in Chenstokhov in order to lessen his influence over his disciples. From there he continued

to preach conversion to the 'religion of Edom'. In 1772 Frank was released from detention by the Russian army, which had then invaded Poland. He left for Austria, where he continued to hold 'court' until his death in 1791. The Frankists and their descendants, who had received on their baptism the titles of their aristocratic sponsors, became assimilated into Polish society. One of their descendants was the eminent Polish poet Adam Mickiewicz whose love for his Jewish origins permeated his poetry and influenced his political activities.

THE BEGINNINGS OF HASIDISM

If the appearance of the Frankists and their loss to Judaism was no more than an isolated incident, it was nevertheless a symptom of the serious spiritual crisis which had overtaken Polish Jewry.

Among the circles of the 'pious' (Hasidim) mystics, who studied Kabbalah and were seeking new outlets of expression in the spiritual sphere, a movement sprang up which was destined to be of the utmost significance and exert a decisive influence on the continuance of Judaism in East Europe. In the middle of the 18th century there appeared in the town of Medzibozh in Podolia, R. Israel Baal Shem Tov (known by the abbreviation Besht). He led a solitary life for many years in the Carpathian mountains, immersed in the study of Kabbalah. He gained a reputation for healing the sick, and giving advice to those who sought his help; at the same time he publicized his teaching which was essentially that the main point of religion is not solely theological study but intimate communion with God by means of active prayer. An important principle of his doctrine was that submission to the *tzaddik* (a man specially noted for his piety, saintliness as well as his miraculous powers) is the way in which divine communion may be accomplished. Baal Shem Tov soon acquired numerous devoted disciples. In one of his conversations with them he relates that in a dream he had seen the Messiah who told him that he

Bird's wing spicebox, Poland, late eighteenth century. The spicebox was used in the *Havdalah* service, marking the end of the Sabbath on Saturday evenings. Jerusalem, Israel Museum.

Hanukkah lamp, Poland, eighteenth century. Silver. The inscription is the last part of the blessing recited on the kindling of *Hanukkah* lights. Jerusalem, Sir Isaac and Lady Edith Wolfson Collection, Hechal Shlomo 5.26.2.

Synagogues, (above and opposite) Sidra and Piaski (Lithuania), end of eighteenth or early nineteenth century. Synagogues were built of wood, which was the most common material, and folk artists lovingly designed and decorated these simple buildings. Most such synagogues were destroyed in World War II.

would come to redeem the world when the doctrine of Baal Shem Tov had spread throughout it.

After the death of Baal Shem Tov in 1760, his disciples began to disseminate his teachings. In contrast to the talmudists of the old school, who shut themselves off and immersed themselves in study and looked down on the common people, the disciples of Baal Shem Tov, including notable religious scholars and talmudists, sought to gain the confidence of the simple folk and to bring them nearer to the worship of God, as far as it lay in their power. Each of Baal Shem Tov's disciples gained his own adherents, who originated their own methods and practice of Hasidism. They also popularized their teachings by the use of legends, parables, and tales of miracles. Hasidism spread rapidly throughout Poland and Lithuania. Its followers were recognizable by the ecstatic mode of prayer they adopted, having their own prayer halls *(klaus),* and dressing in white on the Sabbath. They adopted the liturgy of Isaac Luria, leader of the sixteenth-century kabbalists in Safed.

Hasidism soon met with opposition from the established rabbinical authorities, who were particularly powerful in

Lithuania. Its chief opponent was the greatest of the talmudists in Lithuania, R. Elijah, the *gaon* of Vilna. The ban of excommunication was eventually pronounced on all the followers of Hasidism at two large rabbinical assemblies representing numerous communities in 1772 and again in 1781, and their writings were condemned to be burnt. The head of the Hasidic movement in Lithuania, R. Zalman Shneour of Lyady, whose system became known as *Habad* (initials of *Hokhmah Binah va-Daat* or 'Wisdom, Understanding, Knowledge') introduced a more contemplative and intellectual basis to Hasidism, stressing the role of the *tzaddik* as a spiritual leader rather than a popular miracle-worker.

The controversy between Rabbinism and Hasidism continued after the abolition of the kingdom of Poland at the end of the 18th century. It drove thousands of Hasidim to settle in Palestine. Hasidism eventually became particularly popular in the Ukraine, Galicia and Poland, and introduced a new spirit into Judaism. At a time when the old-established Jewish autonomous organization in Poland was eroded by external pressures, and had become decayed within, Hasidism rallied the Jewish masses, gave life new

meaning to them and bound them to Judaism in new ways. It had enormous influence in shaping the features of East European Jewry in the last two centuries of its existence.

THE PERIOD OF THE PARTITION OF POLAND

The first partition of Poland took place in 1772 when about one-third of Polish Jewry was living in the areas that now passed to Austria, Russia, and Prussia. At the last minute, the Polish public became aware of the critical position of the country and sought to improve its position and salvage its continued existence. The Jewish question occupied a prominent place in the investigations made during this time in Polish official and intellectual circles. The censuses held showed the large and growing size of the Jewish population in Poland. Nearly all the internal trade was in Jewish hands, as was also a large part of the export trade. In many places the Jews formed nearly half the artisan class. On the other hand, no Jews engaged in agriculture in Poland, but one of their regular occupations was the management of taverns in the villages with everything this entailed (the granting of credit on interest to the peasants, purchase of their products at low prices, and so on).

The many recommendations and pamphlets that appeared at the time in Poland go to show on the one hand the number of attempts to strengthen economic pressure and restrictions on the Jews to the point of eliminating them from the country altogether; but there were, nevertheless, those who held other opinions, such as Butrymovich, a member of the Sejm (parliament) and author of a pamphlet called *A Means whereby to Transform the Polish Jews into Useful Citizens of the Country* (1791). These people advocated the promotion of agricultural occupations or crafts among the Jews, their removal from the liquor trade, the curtailment of the communal authority in order to lessen their isolation from the Polish environment, and substitution of Polish for Yiddish and Hebrew as the language of instruction in schools and for business transactions.

Times were not propitious, however, for making any radical changes in the status of Jews. In 1793 the second partition of Poland took place, and large areas were wrenched from the state.

A widespread popular uprising then broke out, headed by Kosciuszco, to fight Poland's perennial enemies, Russia and Prussia.

This time the Jews were called upon to join the defenders of Poland. The leader of the Jewish volunteers was Berek Yoselevich. Yoselevich appealed to Polish Jewry to put all its strength into defending Polish freedom: 'Help to redeem oppressed Poland,' Yoselvich wrote, 'Even if we ourselves do not attain it, at least our sons will live in tranquility and freedom.' A Jewish legion of some five hundred Jews was raised by Yoselevich, most of whom fell in the battle for Warsaw in November 1791.

In 1795 Poland was partitioned for a third time, and, with this, was wiped off the political map of Europe for the next one hundred and twenty years. The fate of East European Jewry now depended on the states which had taken over the former independent kingdom.

THE TSARIST GOVERNMENT AND THE JEWS

The partition of the kingdom of Poland brought the large majority of the Jews living there under the regime of tsarist Russia. For many centuries there had been a tradition of hatred and fear of the Jews in Russia. This tradition stemmed from dim memories of the Jewish Khazar kingdom, as well as the spread of religious sects which had based their rejection of Christianity on the Old Testament (the *Zhidovstvuyuschie* or Judaizing heresy at the end of the 15th century). The hostility was also founded on fear of Jewish competition on the part of the Russian merchant class and was nourished by the Greek Orthodox Church. When Ivan the Terrible annexed the town of Pskov (1563), he solved the problem of Jews living there who refused to be baptized by drowning them in the nearby river. When approached by the Senate to authorize Jews to enter Russia for trade, Tsarina Elizabeth summarily dismissed the request, saying: 'I desire no gain or benefit from the haters of Jesus.'

With the inclusion of thousands of Jews into the Russian empire at the first partition of Poland of 1772, and additional hundreds of thousands in 1793 and 1795, the tsarist regime was faced with the fact that the largest Jewish community in the world was now under its sovereignty.

The Russian government hesitated before settling the status of the Jews. As there had been formerly under the Polish kingdom, there was a general tendency to procrastinate, as well as to adjust the situation to suit the interests of the state. This consideration governed the imperial ukase (decree) issued in 1791, authorizing Jewish settlement in territory which had been annexed to Poland, and in addition permitting Jews to move to the empty steppes in the region of the Black Sea, which had been conquered at that time from the Turks and required further colonization. Jewish settlement was also permitted in the Ukraine, east of the Dnieper.

Thus originated the 'Pale of Settlement' or the area where Jews were permitted to live, a formulation that was to accompany the history of the Jews in Russia until the downfall of the tsarist regime. The Pale, as it finally developed in Russia, with the incorporation of Bessarabia (1812) and the kingdom of Poland (1815), extended from the Baltic to the Black Sea. This was a territory inhabited by a variety of different peoples, and the Russian regime made strenuous efforts to strengthen the Russian element, the Greek Orthodox faith, and the use of the Russian language.

One of the problems in the new territories that concerned the authorities was the depressed condition of the peasants, which reached catastrophic proportions during times of drought or famine. It was difficult for the government, which was dependent on the nobility, to fasten responsibility for the shocking condition of the peasants on the landowners who controlled peasant holdings and enslaved the people. It was easier to pin the blame on the Jews, who were living in the villages as lessees of the squirearchy. The separatism of the Jewish population and its specific communal organization also did not fit the Russian autocratic centralist framework.

These considerations and fears found their preliminary expression in the 'Jewish Constitution' of 1804. The first clause of the statute permitted Jews to enter all grades of elementary and secondary schools in Russia, as well as institutes of higher learning. Jews were also authorized to open their own schools on condition that they provided instruction in Russian, Polish, or German, in which languages Jews were also to conduct business. This clause took no account of the prevailing situation whereby Jewish education was built on the old religious system. Another clause in the statute impinged fundamentally on the means of subsistence of the majority of Jews living in the state. This provided that 'it is prohibited to any Jew to hold any lease or tavern in any village, either in his own name or in that of another, or to sell wine in them, or even to live in them under any pretext whatsoever, except in transit only.'

On the other hand Jews were authorized to take up agriculture on their own land or on the land granted to them by the state. The state also promised to give support to 'useful industrial enterprises'. Merchants and artisans were permitted to settle temporarily in the governments of inner Russia. The tsar also issued a rescript in 1817 forbidding allegations that the Jews murdered Christian children for ritual purposes.

Shortly afterward, both the expulsion of the Jews from the villages and Jewish settlement in south Russia began. However, it soon became apparent that agricultural settlement would be unable to absorb with sufficient rapidity the thousands of Jews who had been deprived of their livelihood in the villages. The expulsion order was therefore delayed, the Russian political and military situation during the Napoleonic Wars also contributing to the delay. Thus the systematic expulsion of the Jews from the villages, in particular from Belorussia, was not renewed until 1822.

NICHOLAS I

The reign of Nicholas I (1825-55) was a dark period for Russian Jewry. Nicholas, noted for his despotism in Russian history, also attempted to solve the Jewish problem by the most stringent methods of compulsion.

Holy book binding, Galicia, beginning of nineteenth century. A scene showing the binding of Isaac. Abraham can be seen, with the ram caught in the thicket bush and the angel halting the would-be sacrifice. Jerusalem, Israel Museum.

In particular his reign is linked to the memory of the 'cantonist legislation'. In 1827 compulsory military service was instituted for the Jews; its object was not only to recruit soldiers to defend the state, but also to use the army as a framework in which to assimilate part of the Jewish youth entirely. The ukase was designed to fit in with the general recruiting legislation. This imposed a military service quota on towns and villages, the recruits having to serve twenty-five years in the army. They belonged to the military 'estate' and their children also had to serve in the army. For this purpose special military training institutions were established, in which the harshest type of discipline was imposed. Trainees in these institutions were called 'cantonists'. Special regulations were provided for the Jews: a) the age of conscripts was fixed at between twelve and twenty-five; b) until the age of eighteen they were to be sent to the cantonist institutions. Responsibility for enlisting the recruits was imposed on the Jewish communal bodies, who were to elect 'trustees' for this purpose. If they failed to meet the recruitment quota the trustees could be impressed into the army.

This law completely demoralized the Jewish communities. No one wanted to serve in the army, and the trustees were forced to seek out recruits with the help of thugs, who were nicknamed 'snatchers'. A large number of the victims were children from the poorest sector, sometimes younger than the statutory age, who were snatched from their parents' homes and sent off to distant barracks in the heart of Russia. Not a few of them died on the way there or in the first few years of army service. The others underwent persecution and torture, primarily directed at making them renounce their faith. Very few held out and remained loyal to Judaism and Jewry. The older recruits also endured frightful hardship in the army ranks. Even a distinguished service record brought no benefit, since Jews could not be promoted unless they became converted. The sole advantage granted to the conscripts at a later date (1867) was the right to live outside the Pale. The 'soldiers of Nicholas' were therefore the forerunners and initiators of many Jewish settlements in the towns of the Russian interior.

Military service brought no general amelioration of the lot of Russian Jewry. The expulsions from the villages continued uninterruptedly. The Jews were also expelled from the city of Kiev, and Jewish settlement was prohibited in any town or village within an area of fifty versts from the Russian border. On the other hand, the government encouraged Jewish agricultural

Pins for head coverings, Russia, nineteenth or twentieth centuries. Top: *Sterntichl,* form of tiara decorating the head covering (bonnet, scarf, etc.) worn by the married Orthodox woman to hide her hair. Bottom: *Krone* or 'Diadem' also worn pinned onto the head covering. Garnets and pearls. Jerusalem, Sir Isaac and Lady Edith Wolfson Collection, Hechal Shlomo 1774-57.62/1775-57.63.

settlement, and colonists were freed from military service. Many Jewish colonies were established on state-owned or private land in south Russia and other areas within the Pale.

During the 1840s the government began to concern itself with Jewish 'Enlightenment'. Since the Jews had not taken advantage of their right to enter the general schools, the authorities decided to establish a special Jewish school system, maintained by an impost to be levied on the Jews (the 'candle tax'). In order to prepare the ground for these reforms, the government sent an emissary, Max Lilienthal, a German Jew, who had been a teacher in a Jewish school founded by Jewish adherents of the Enlightenment movement in Riga, to tour the Pale of Settlement. Lilienthal visited the large communities of the Pale, including Vilna, Minsk, Berdichev, Odessa, and Kiev. He was received warily by the majority of the Jews there. Among the reasons given for the

Jewish opposition to the idea of establishing modern schools, was that 'as long as the government does not grant full civic equality to the Jews, the acquisition of a general education will only be an impediment. The simple uneducated Jew does not flinch from the lowly occupation of agent or peddler, while the educated Jew who is unable to hold a respected position in the state will be driven out of despair or anger to renounce his religion, and no honorable father would educate his son for such an outcome.' In 1844 the order was issued establishing state schools for Jews, with both Jewish and Christian teachers. In a confidential appendage to this order, it was explicitly stated that 'the aim of educating the Jews is to bring them nearer to Christians and to eradicate the harmful ideas fostered by the Talmud.' When Lilienthal sensed that the authorities had ulterior motives, he left Russia. The government then began to establish a network of these schools; in the first

Goose market in Cracow, nineteenth century. The market-place was where the Jews met the farmers of the vicinity and conducted business with them. Etching after Alois Schönn, by Wilhelm Unger (1837-1932). Jerusalem, Israel Museum.

place, they opened rabbinical and teachers' training institutes in Vilna and Zhitomir, and relied on a nucleus of 'enlightened' Jews. Most Jews were apprehensive about sending their children to these institutes which served as a nursery for a class of 'enlightened' Jews, who knew Russian and were to play an important part in Jewish affairs in subsequent years.

In 1844 the government abrogated the Polish form of Jewish communal organization, but in practice was still forced to recognize it in a limited form. Its chief duty was to meet the requirements of military conscription, and to collect the special taxes levied on the Jews. In order to bring the Jews closer to their neighbors, a ukase was issued in 1844 forbidding them to grow sideburns and to wear their distinctive dress. The law was enforced in a grossly insulting manner by the Russian police.

The second stage in Nicholas I's program was classification of the Jews into 'useful' and 'useless' categories. The 'useful' category included the wealthier merchants, artisans, and agriculturalists. All the rest—the petty tradesmen and the poorest classes—were included in the 'useless' category and were subject to general military conscription, in which they would have to undergo training for other work or agriculture. This program was opposed by a number of Russian statesmen, and also led to the intercession of Jews from Western Europe on behalf of their brethren in Russia. In spite of this, an order for the classification to proceed was issued in 1851. The Crimean War delayed its implementation, but intensified the misery inflicted through military conscription. The quota of obligatory recruits was increased threefold, and the 'snatchers' were given a free hand to seize children or wayfarers indiscriminately, and turn them over to the army.

Silver plate, Galicia, beginning of nineteenth century. The scene of the binding of Isaac is depicted on this plate, surrounded by the signs of the zodiac. It was probably used at circumcision ceremonies. Paris, Klagsbald Collection.

ALEXANDER II

The reign of Alexander II (1855-81) is linked to the sweeping reforms in the Russian regime, the greatest of which was the liberation of the peasants from their serfdom to the landowners (1861). Toward the Jews, Alexander pursued a cautious policy, aimed at integrating them into the Russian environment. He abrogated the severest of the discriminatory legislation passed in his father's day, and permitted unrestricted residence in all parts of Russia to certain select groups among the Jewish population whom he regarded as useful for developing the country. These were (in 1859) the well-established merchants (merchants of the first guild), those who had received higher education (1861), and incorporated artisans (1865). Subsequently Jewish communities grew up rapidly beyond the Pale of Settlement. The largest, in St. Petersburg and Moscow, were to influence significantly the destiny of Russian Jewry.

In 1874 general compulsory military service was introduced. Hundreds of thousands of Jewish youths were now drafted to serve for four to six years in the tsarist army. Large concessions were granted to those with a higher education, and, as a result, the enactment stimulated the attendance of Jewish youth at the Russian secondary schools. However, Jews were not permitted to become officers.

The general feeling of the Jews in Russia was that the government was moving slowly but surely along the same path taken by the other West European states toward complete Emancipation for Russian Jewry. Jews began to penetrate the cultural and intellectual life of the country in journalism, literature, law,

The heder, East Europe. The *heder* was the first school of the East European child. Mané Katz (1894-1962), who knew the scene well from his own childhood in Kremenchug, depicts the typical clothes and posture of the *heder* students. Fribourg, Jean Nordmann Collection. ▶

theater and art. Among those who attained eminence were the composer Anton Rubinstein (1829-94—baptized during childhood), the sculptor Mark Antokolski (1843-1902), and the painter Isaac Levitan (1860-1900).

Jewish penetration into Russian economic, political and cultural life, however, immediately provoked an anti-Jewish movement among the Russian public. The anti-Jewish publicists included some of the greatest intellectuals in the country, such as the writer Sergei Aksakov and Feodor Dostoievsky. The liberal and revolutionary elements also treated the Jews with coolness. Jews were accused of various bizarre charges (the charge of ritual murder also serving as a weapon in the hands of agitators). But the principal argument of their opponents was that the Jews represented an alien element, invading the Russian precincts, controlling certain key economic and cultural positions, and exerting a highly destructive influence. The anti-Jewish movement grew particularly strong after the Balkan War (1877-8), which aroused a surge of nationalism in Russia.

DEMOGRAPHIC AND ECONOMIC DEVELOPMENTS AMONG THE JEWS IN THE 19TH CENTURY

The principal factor in determining Russian Jewish history in the 19th century was the rate of natural increase, which was much higher than that of the non-Jewish population. This was due to the early marriages (at the age of thirteen of fourteen) customary among Jews, to the high birthrate and comparatively low child mortality, thanks to the devoted care of the Jewish mother, and the advances made in medical knowledge at this time. The number of Jews, estimated in 1850 as 2,350,000, increased within fifty years to over 5,000,000, despite the by no means small emigration abroad.

The high natural increase brought growing competition in all branches of commerce. Many Jews were forced into the lowest rungs of trade, shopkeeping—and even lower—peddling and brokerage. Many were forced to go over to the artisan class, in those days considered of inferior social status.

Some mitigation was afforded by the large internal migration to southern Russia, a movement that continued throughout the 19th century. Large new communities grew up in this area, such as in Odessa (140,000), Ikatrinoslav, Kremenchug, Elizavetgrad, and others.

After the Russian annexation, a small but influential class began to form within the Jewish community, made up of wealthy Jews, who were able to adapt themselves to meet the requirements of the developing economy of the large empire and to establish contacts in official circles. These Jews were first the government contractors, who built roads and fortifications and supplied the bureaucracy and army. During the reign of Nicholas I many Jews took part in contracting for the manufacture and sale of liquor, which became a state monopoly, and in the 1860s they also had an important share in railroad construction and industrial development (in particular of foodstuffs and textiles), and the export trade (timber and grain). This type of businessman was prominent in the capital St. Petersburg, Moscow, and the large ports (Odessa). A number founded banks. The class of wealthy bourgeoisie, headed by the Günzburg and Poliakov families, regarded itself as the leaders of Russian Jewry. Verging on this category was another class of Jews with a Russian higher education, who penetrated the circles of the Russian intelligentsia and the liberal professions, such as law, medicine, engineering, journalism, and science.

In the reverse direction, forming the broad base of the social pyramid, was the increasing *lumpen* proletariat, made up of the masses of impoverished and unemployed Jews. Competition within the sphere of medium and petty commerce inside the Pale steadily increased. When, after the emancipation of the peasants, it became clear that there was a serious shortage of available land for the Russian peasants themselves, the government ceased to promote Jewish agricultural settlement. Many Jews remained without means of livelihood and were reduced to peddling, petty brokerage, and begging. Others earned a living as laborers, porters, and domestic servants. A steady stream of emigration began from Russia to Western Europe and overseas.

RABBINISM AND HASIDISM IN THE 19TH CENTURY

The inner life of Russian Jewry in the 19th century was marked by the fierce struggle between the massive forces of conservatism, the vigilant sentinels of Judaism, that had crystallized in the many centuries of its existence, and the no less powerful revolutionary forces calling for adaptation to modern conditions.

One of the most surprising developments in the spiritual annals of Russian Jewry was the regeneration of the traditional *yeshivah* and its transformation into a central educational institution for Orthodox Jewry. This innovation was the result of the efforts of the disciples of Elijah, the *Gaon* of Vilna. In 1802 Elijah's pupil R. Hayyim founded a *yeshivah* in the little town of Volozhin, which for ninety years was to serve as a center of talmudic learning and a potent influence in Russian Jewry. In its wake other important *yeshivot* were founded in Mir, Eisheshok, and Telz. These *yeshivot* flourished in the small towns to which in general modern ideas had not yet penetrated. They attracted the most promising youth, who had been educated in the *heder,* the *beth midrash* (school for higher rabbinic learning) and the smaller local *yeshivot*. (Over 80 per cent of Jewish children still attended *heder* at the end of the 19th century.) Learning in the *yeshivah* concentrated on the study of Talmud and its exegesis. The students, who studied independently under the guidance of the principal and teachers of the *yeshivah,* aimed at acquiring an exhaustive knowledge and understanding of the text, and at exercising their intellectual ingenuity. The ideal student of the *yeshivah* was the 'learned', the 'subtle-witted', and the 'diligent'

Talmud tractate, Warsaw, 1859. The title page of the first tractate of the Babylonian Talmud in one of the many editions which appeared in Eastern Europe in the 19th and first decades of the 20th century.

מסכת

ברכות

מן

תלמוד בבלי

עם כל המפרשים כאשר נדפס מקדם ועם הוספות הרשות

כמבואר בשער השני .

וואַרשא

שנה תרי״ט לפ״ק

בדפוס ר׳ שמואל ב״ר חיים ארגעלבראנד נ״י

TALMUD BABILOŃSKI,

TRAKTAT BERACHOT.

TOM I.

WARSZAWA,

W DRUKARNI S. ORGELBRANDA.

1859.

ГАБИМА הבימה

Б. АЛЬКАЗАР (Садовая-Триумфальная).

Телеф. 2-04-07, 5-22-16.   Трамваи 1, 5, 6, 13, Б.   Автобусы 1, 6, 9.

Понедельник 18-го Января

300 и ПОСЛЕДНИЙ 300 СПЕКТАКЛЬ

ГАДИБУК

Пьеса в 3-х действ., Анского, перев. X. Н. Бялика.

Вступительное слово — Н. Л. ЦЕМАХ.

Участвующие (по алфавиту): Баракс, Бен-Хаим, Бертонов, Брук, Варшавер, Виняр, Виняр-Кочур, Говинская, Голянд, Гробер, Гольдина, Иткин, Кинерет, Любич, Мескин, Падуит, Пудалова, Прудкин, Райкин-Бен-ари, Роввин, Роббинс Файнберг, Факторович, Фридлянд, Цемах Н., Цемах Вениамин, Чемеринский, Чечик-Эфрати, Шнейдер-Бенно, Эйдельман, Юделевич.

ПОСТАНОВКА
Евг. Вахтангова.

Художник Н. Альтман.   Музыка Ю. Энгеля.   Руководитель Н. Л. Цемах.

Начало в 8 час. вечера.

ЦЕНЫ МЕСТАМ от 1 р. до 10 руб.   Контрамарки не выдаются

Касса открыта ежедневно от 1 до 7 час. вечера.   Уполномоченный В. Шикул....

Ha-Bimah Theater poster, Moscow, 1925. The Ha-Bimah Hebrew Theater in Moscow announces the final performance of *The Dibbuk* on January 18 1925. Shortly thereafter the Ha-Bimah company left the USSR and eventually settled in Tel Aviv. Twenty-three years later the Yiddish theaters in Russia were also closed, leaving the Jews as the only nationality in the USSR without a theater of its own.

pupil, who devoted the whole of his day and most of the night to study, and above all there was the 'prodigy' who combined all three attributes. The youth who left the *yeshivah* was permeated with the spirit of Judaism, which accompanied him in everything he did and molded his way of life and opinions.

In the middle of the 19th century R. Israel Salanter initiated a new 'ethical system'. This was intended by Salanter and his school to replace worldly distractions by an aspiration to raise the individual in the spirit of Jewish ethics, by despising material achievements and secular values that constitute the main preoccupation of modern society. In the *yeshivot* founded by the school of Salanter, some time was dedicated to the study of ethical works, and students were required to pay attention to their moral improvement. The ethical system was adopted in many

yeshivot. An important center for this discipline was founded by R. Joseph Yessel in Novogrodek, Belorussia, in 1896. His pupils established *yeshivot* of this type in many places in Russia, Lithuania, and Poland.

The *yeshivot* produced generations of pupils impregnated with the knowledge and spirit of Judaism. Some of these continued to maintain the traditional life of their forefathers and endeavored to pass on the tradition to their children. A considerable number, however, influenced by modern ideas, left this tradition, although many of them were still influenced by the old *beth midrash*. The greatest modern Hebrew poet Hayyim Nahman Bialik was educated in the Volozhin *yeshivah,* and perpetuated his 'alma mater' in his poetry. The distinguished contemporary Hebrew novelist Shemuel Y. Agnon was educated in the old *yeshivah* of his little home town in Galicia.

Hasidism became a mass popular movement within East European Jewry in the 19th century. However it lost much of its originality in the course of its early development. The spiritual leaders of the movement, the *tzaddikim,* proliferated but never reached the heights of their predecessors. It became an accepted tradition in Hasidism that the holiness of the *tzaddik* was inherited by his descendants, and dynasties of *tzaddikim* were founded, whose disciples split up among their successors. Beside the leader of lofty spiritual caliber, there arose an inferior type of *tzaddik,* who throve on the ignorance of his adherents. But in general Hasidism became a powerful organizational force, which fostered devotion to the Jewish way of life and people. It consistently repelled any concession to modern ideas, but attracted its masses of followers by implicit faith in the *tzaddik,* and through him, in Judaism. The thousands of simple Jews and *yeshivah* students of the towns and villages became closely bound to their spiritual leader, and regulated their lives under his guidance and instruction. Hasidism was a tremendously powerful popular force, but a force without dynamism, which failed to guide the masses into constructive activity, and contented itself with stubborn guardianship of the established order.

The rapprochement between Hasidism and Rabbinism took place in the middle of the 19th century in face of the necessity to protect themselves from the ideology of the Enlightenment (see below), that had come to change and destroy traditional Judaism. The alliance was expressed in Hasidism by the restoration of religious study to its former place of honor, especially in Poland and Lithuania. In Poland the Hasidic rabbis enjoined their disciples to combine religious learning with prayer, and the small prayerhouses of the Hasidim were used as colleges (*batei midrashim*) for talmudic study. In Belorussia and the Ukraine the descendants of R. Shneour Zalman of Lyady succeeded in establishing an important Hasidic center in the town of Liubavitch, which had a wide influence on the whole area. They also founded *yeshivot* in which talmudic study was combined with study of Hasidic doctrine.

The social life of the masses of Hasidim centered round the 'courts' or seats of residence of the *tzaddikim*. Names such as Liubavitch and Stolin in Belorussia, Gur and Aleksander in Poland, and Belz in Galicia became proverbial in East European

Jewish musicians, Eastern Europe, 1830. Jewish musicians *(klezmerim)* were a familiar feature of Jewish folk-life in Eastern Europe, especially at family festivities, and even performed at similar occasions for Christians. Watercolor by J.S. Delaiewsky, 1830. Jerusalem, Israel Museum.

Jewry. Hasidism also penetrated beyond the Carpathians to Hungary, and beyond the Dniester to Bessarabia and Rumania.

The Russian government adopted a hostile attitude toward the *yeshivot* and centers of Hasidism. Attempts were made from time to time to close down the *heders* and abolish the *yeshivot.* Restrictive legislation was imposed on the *tzaddikim.* But none of these attempts bore fruit. The destructive forces which were to disturb this traditional conservative world came from within, and first and foremost from the Enlightenment movement.

ENLIGHTENMENT (*Haskalah*)

The movement for Enlightenment developed as a result of the social and economic changes affecting the Jewish people with the advent of the era of capitalism. The closed medieval class structure was replaced by the open society, in which each individual took his place on the basis of free competition. The Jew had to adapt himself to the new conditions. It became necessary to learn the languages of other nations, to acquire a different type of learning,

and to adopt the clothing and behavior of the environment. This was an objective process which had already at the beginning of the 19th century impelled many Jews in the large commercial centers such as Warsaw and Odessa to adopt the customs and way of life of their neighbors. On the other hand, the desire to preserve their Jewish faith and values, at least in some way, still existed. The idealists of the Enlightenment tried to create an outlook which would harmonize these changes with Jewish life, and facilitate their adoption by Jewry. The Enlightenment movement comprised a variety of tendencies. At one extreme were the complete assimilationists, formed in Poland of a thin layer of bourgeoisie and intellectuals, who regarded themselves as 'Poles of Mosaic persuasion', while at the other stood the nationalists. Prominent among the latter was the Hebrew writer Peretz Smolenskin, who in his monthly *Ha-Shahar* (Dawn), produced in Vienna from 1868 to 1886, urged the revival of the Hebrew language and national Jewish feeling.

The Enlightenment movement originated at the end of the 18th century in Germany. From there it spread to Galicia, and finally penetrated to Russian Jewry in the Pale of Settlement.

The herald of Enlightenment in Russia was the writer Isaac Ber Levinsohn, whose book *Te'udah be-Yisrael* (Instruction in Israel) (Vilna, 1828), formulated the objectives of the movement. Its main tenets were 1) Enlightenment, i.e., study of the Hebrew language by modern methods, the learning of a foreign language, and secular subjects; 2) work, i.e., the necessity of taking up crafts and especially agriculture.

The strength of the Enlightenment movement lay in its press and literature which became a powerful instrument of propaganda. The intellectual supporters of Enlightenment *(maskilim)* created a secularized neo-Hebrew literature, in externals following European literary models, but original in language and content. Prominent among the pioneers of this literature were the poet Judah Lieb Gordon (1831-92), and the writer Abraham Mapu (1807-67), father of the Hebrew novel. This literature was both critical and educational. An important medium for its development was the Hebrew press, beginning with *Ha-Maggid* in 1856. A more radical trend in Enlightenment stimulated the development of a Jewish literature in Russian, in recognition that Russian should replace Yiddish as the language spoken by Russian Jewry. However, their wish to use Yiddish as a means of propaganda among the masses prompted the intellectuals to develop a Yiddish press and literature. The most important of the exponents of the neo-Yiddish culture was Mendele Mocher Seforim (1837-1917), who wrote in both Hebrew and Yiddish, and was creator of a modern Hebrew style and progenitor of Yiddish modern literature.

The publications of the Enlightenment reached the *batei-ha-midrash* and *yeshivot,* calling upon the youth to emerge from their

◄ *Yom Kippur,* Poland, 1878. This depiction of the Day of Atonement, the most sacred day of the Jewish year, in a Polish synagogue, was the work of the artist Moritz Oppenheim, who was to die the following year at the age of twenty-three. The young man standing next to the Scroll of the Law is a self-portrait. Oil on canvas. Tel Aviv Museum, gift of Mr. S.J. Lamon, London.

Kiddush cup, Russia, mid-nineteenth century. This silver and niello cup, used for the wine drunk on the advent of the Sabbath, is inscribed with the word 'Jerusalem' according to the biblical verse 'If I set Jerusalem above my chiefest joy' (Psalms 137:6). Jerusalem, Sir Isaac and Lady Edith Wolfson Collection, Hechal Shlomo.

confines, to learn other languages and study general subjects, and to draw closer to the rest of the population by adopting their dress and behavior. The new ideas provoked violent conflicts in numerous towns and villages, sometimes dividing father and son or teacher and pupil.

Supporters of Enlightenment who were persecuted for their heretical convictions left for the cities to look for a way of pursuing the new learning, and were frequently assisted by the government. These intellectuals were particularly critical of Hasidism and the *tzaddikim,* whom they castigated in satirical or polemic literature.

The Jewish intellectuals of East Europe regarded their counterparts in the West as now having achieved their social dream; they had attained full emancipation and were now able to participate in the social and cultural life of their fellow-countrymen. These intellectuals were also aware that Jewish traditions and culture were disintegrating in the West, that the Hebrew language and values were being neglected, and that total assimilation was spreading there. Some gladly endorsed this situation; others regarded it as an inevitable process. Still others, however, opposed these tendencies, hoping to develop a Jewish nationalism, based on a revitalization of the Hebrew language and literature, on the links with the historic past and on the memory of Zion.

Torah breastplate, Nemirov (Ukraine), 1860. The theme of lions—here supporting the Two Tablets of Stone containing the Decalogue—was popular in many branches of Jewish folk art. Silver. Jerusalem, Sir Isaac and Lady Edith Wolfson Collection, Hechal Shlomo. 85-5-10.

THE CRISIS

In March 1881 Russian revolutionaries assassinated Tsar Alexander II, and the entire country was thrown into confusion. The revolutionaries called upon the people to rise up, and the old order was compelled to defend itself. Taking advantage of the atmosphere of a weakened regime, anti-Jewish riots broke out in a number of towns and villages in southern Russia. These generally took the form of mob pillaging, and there was little bloodshed. Similar pogroms again broke out in 1882 and 1883, until the regime became stronger and the pogroms ceased. The pogroms, however, provided the Russian government with a convenient scapegoat. It was found that the Jews were to blame for the misery of the people. The revolutionaries, who had hoped to fan the

disorders into a revolt against the landowners and state, also encouraged the rioters.

The result of the pogroms was a series of restrictive measures imposed on the Jews, limiting their participation in the political and economic life of the country. In May 1882 the 'Temporary Rules' were imposed, prohibiting Jews from settling in the villages and restricting their residence to the cities and towns. In 1886 measures were passed limiting Jewish admission to secondary schools and institutes of higher learning to a restrictive quota of 10 per cent within the Pale, and of 3 to 5 per cent outside it. Thus the same government that forty years earlier had ordered the Jews to receive a Russian education now did its best to seal

Warsaw Jew and Wife, Warsaw, 1846. A young couple in holiday clothes, similar to the clothes still worn by Hasidim. The Hasidim, in fact, merely traditionalized what was local costume. Engraving from *Les Israélites de Pologne* by L. Hollaenderski. Jerusalem, Israel Museum.

The young vagabonds. Pastel from the series 'The Tear Jug' by Abel Pann. Pann settled in Palestine in the early years of the 20th century and was one of the first teachers at the Bezalel Art School. Jerusalem, Israel Museum.

off the avenues to this education by every means. In 1891 the systematic expulsion of all the Jews from Moscow began. The new regulations were accompanied by oppressive bureaucratic measures. The tutor of the tsar and evil spirit of Russia, Pobyedonostzev, once disclosed the cynical aim of government policy toward the Jews: 'One-third will change their religion, one-third will die off, and one-third will flee the country'.

This policy was also continued during the reign of the last tsar, Nicholas II. A fresh outbreak of pogroms began in Kishinev during Passover in 1903, where large numbers of Jews were killed. The pogroms now became a tool of government policy, both to prevent Jews from participating in the national revolutionary movement and to divert popular hostility toward the Jews. The pogroms reached a climax in October 1905, when the tsar was forced to announce concessions in his autocratic form of government. During the pogroms the police and military sided openly with the mobs, and protected them from the Jews when they organized resistance to their attackers.

With the support of the government, an anti-Semitic monarchist party called the 'League of the Russian People' was

Adar folk calendar, Poland or Russia, end of nineteenth century. Folk calendar used for the month of *Adar.* The theme of fishes is based on the zodiac sign for the month (Pisces). The wine bottles recall that this is the month of the merry festival of Purim, and the Hebrew inscription records the traditional sign: 'When the month of *Adar* commences, merriment multiplies'. Basle, Jüdisches Museum der Schweiz, No. 107.

formed, which openly agitated for the annihilation of the Jews in Russia. Proclamations calling for pogroms were published by the printing office of the secret police.

The pogroms, restrictive legislation, and bureaucratic pressure were responsible for mass Jewish emigration from Russia to Western Europe, and in particular to the United States. Between 1881 and 1914 an estimated 2,000,000 Jews left Russia. This emigration had vital consequences for Jewish history, for it established the large Jewish communities outside Europe, notably in the United States. It also put new life into the communities in Western Europe. Even then the exodus did not actually lessen the number of Jews in Russia, since the high rate of natural increase made up for the decrease in population. However,

it did improve the economic lot of Russian Jewry, both by lessening the pressure on employment and because the emigrants soon began to send financial assistance to members of their families who had remained in Russia.

A number of attempts were made to direct and regulate this emigration. The most important was undertaken by the Jewish philanthropist Baron Maurice de Hirsch, who made an agreement with the Russian government to convey 3,000,000 Jews in the space of twenty-five years to Argentina. The ICA (Jewish Colonization Association) was established for this purpose. Although the project was never fully carried out, the ICA did much to settle Jews in the countries where they had emigrated, and in Russia itself.

THE REVOLUTIONARY AND NATIONAL MOVEMENTS

The pogroms and restrictive measures issued against the Jews engendered a tremendous upsurge of excitement within Russian Jewry, especially among the young. This was mainly due to their refusal to accept the inferior status to which they found themselves relegated, and their search for ways of changing the existing miserable situation and of acquiring for the Jewish people a respected status and normal life.

One reaction to the oppressive policy of the tsarist regime was that Jews joined all the various wings of the Russian liberation movement. Jewish youth joined the secret revolutionary organizations in the cities in Russia and abroad. The Russian student colonies in Western Europe, which played a significant role in the history of the Russian revolution, were largely composed of young Jews deprived of the right to study in Russian universities. The revolutionary movement dissociated itself from the stand taken by some of its early leaders, who had given the pogroms of 1881 their blessing, and instead condemned anti-Semitism as being a tsarist maneuver to mislead the masses. Its members helped defend the Jews during the pogroms, and many Jews were chosen as leaders by the revolutionaries. Jewish leaders of the Social Democratic Party included Julius Martov and Lev Trotsky. Among the founder members of the Social Revolutionary Party were Chaim Zhitlowsky and Gershuni.

Along with active participation of Jews in the general revolutionary movement, a revolutionary Jewish workers' movement was formed at the end of the 19th century. In 1897 the

Hanukkah lamp, Russia, 1858. Silver. Jerusalem, Sir Isaac and Lady Edith Wolfson Collection, Hechal Shlomo, 391-26-36.

various workingmen's and trade associations, first initiated by Jewish intellectuals, united into the 'Bund' (League). The Bund regarded itself as part of the All-Russian Socialist Revolutionary Party, but stood for certain national Jewish claims, including the right of national-cultural autonomy for the Jewish masses, the establishment of schools where instruction would be given in Yiddish, and promotion of a press and literature in this language.

Within a short time the Bund succeeded in instilling a spirit of human dignity and resistance in the workers and poor artisans against their employers and the tsarist regime. The party played an important role in the history of the Russian revolution within the Pale of Settlement.

A different reaction to the situation of Russian Jewry found expression in the Zionist movement. The hostility of the Russian authorities and Russian society in general toward the Jews made many realize that the root of the evil was the abnormal position in which the Jews found themselves as a people without a country. For this they could see no remedy other than mass settlement of the Jews on their own land in their own country, whether in Palestine or elsewhere. This view was clearly formulated in 1882 by Leon Pinsker in his pamphlet *Auto-Emancipation*. Pinsker's clarion call found a wide response among the Jewish masses. From the vast stream of emigration, a tiny rivulet was diverted toward Zion and provided the nucleus of Jewish agricultural settlement. The *Hovevei Zion* (Lovers of Zion) societies, which then formed throughout Russia, called upon Jews to colonize the land of Israel, and collected funds to support them. The movement gathered momentum after the First Zionist Congress in Basle in 1897 and the founding of the World Zionist Organization by Theodor Herzl.

In his article *Russian Jewry* Herzl writes: 'I must acknowledge that for me the appearance of the Russian Jews was the most important event in the Congress. How ashamed we were for imagining ourselves their superiors... They feel themselves Jewish nationals. They do not assimilate with other peoples, but try to learn the best from each. They thus succeed in remaining dignified and genuine, yet they are the Jews of the ghetto, the only ghetto-Jews still in existence. When we saw them we realized whence our forefathers had inherited the stubbornness that bore them up through their worst calamities. They seemed like the living embodiments of our past. I couldn't help recalling to mind the arguments of my early opponents: You will be able to win over only the Russian Jews to your cause. If the same argument were to be repeated today, I would reply "Then we are justified".'

Owing to the political conditions in Russia, the central institutions of the Zionist organization were established in Western Europe, but its greatest following and field of influence was among the Jews of Eastern Europe. Zionism won enthusiasts in every sphere, among the middle class, the proletariat, Orthodox Jews, educated Jews, the young, and the intelligentsia. It awakened nationalist aspirations among Jewry and linked them to their traditional cultures. A widely ramified press and literature emerged to serve the movement. Zionist meetings and assemblies were held openly or in secret. Herzl's efforts to procure a charter to enable speedy Jewish settlement in Palestine from the Turkish

Mezuzah, Russia, 1873. The container of a parchment scroll nailed to the doorposts in all Jewish buildings. It contains Deut. 6:4-9 and 11:13-21, and was often artistically decorated. Rabbis taught that the moral purpose of the *Mezuzah* is to teach that all man's material possessions are the gift of Heaven. Silver. Jerusalem, Israel Museum.

sultan were not successful. In 1903 Herzl conveyed to the Sixth Zionist Congress meeting in Basle a British government proposal for mass Jewish settlement in Uganda, Africa. He pointed out the merits of the scheme as offering an immediate solution for relieving the depressed plight of many thousands of Jews in Russia, and as an intermediate stage toward the goal of settlement in Palestine. His proposal to send a commission of inquiry to Uganda met with stormy opposition from the majority of the Russian delegates: after the proposal had been adopted they left the congress. The dissension within the Zionist movement over the Uganda project lasted for over two years, continuing even after Herzl's death in 1904. Heading the opposition to the project were the Russian Zionist leaders Menahem Mendel Ussishkin and Jehiel Tschlenow. The Seventh Congress (1905) decided on the principle that the Zionist movement should aim specifically at settling the Jews in their historic homeland. A few splinter groups seceded from the movement and formed 'territorialist' organizations, which cast around for a means of settling in other countries (Angola, Tripolitania, and Iraq were considered, among others), but the mainstream of the Zionist movement continued to move toward its historic destination.

The movement of emigration to Eretz Israel (Palestine), drawn almost entirely from Russia and Galicia, continued in the face of opposition from the Turkish government, and laid the foundation for the establishment of the future state of Israel.

The revolutionary and Zionist movements produced a tremendous upheaval among the Jewish youth. While the Orthodox wings—the rabbinical party and the Hasidim—kept strictly to their former positions, all the dynamism in Jewish society was chaneled into the new political trends.

When the new wave of pogroms broke out in 1903, Jewish youth responded by organizing a widespread system of self-defense. Defense corps of the Bund and the Zionists were formed in every city. The rioters were met with armed opposition. The authorities, who had been supporting the rioters in secret, were forced to appear openly to protect them. The main impulse for creating a defense movement was not merely the wish to protect life and property; the Jews also aspired to preserve Jewish honor.

The national revival found expression in a tremendous development of creative Jewish writing, in Hebrew, Yiddish and Russian. This literature, springing as it did directly from the Enlightenment movement, reached heights recalling the Golden Age of Spanish Jewry. Prominent writers of the generation preceding the Russian Revolution of 1917 were the thinker Ahad Ha'am (the pen-name of Asher Ginzburg), who formulated Jewish nationalism on a secular basis, the Hebrew poets Hayyim Nachman Bialik and Saul Tschernikovsky, and the Yiddish novelists Sholem Aleichem, Isaac Leib Peretz, and Shalom Asch.

The new generation of scholars and historians began the investigation of Russian Jewry and its history on scientific lines. The historian Simon Dubnow, who made an outstanding contribution to Russian-Jewish history, wrote his *History of the Jewish People* from an original viewpoint, with a more pronounced nationalist outlook than had been adopted by the German-born classic historian of Jewry, Heinrich Graetz. Moreover he took

The study of the Talmud, 1912. Heliogravure by Lazar Krestin. These Jews are seated in the back part of the synagogue which was known as *Beth Ha-Midrash* or 'place of study'. Jerusalem, Israel Museum.

into account social and economic factors to a far greater extent utilizing the newly developing social sciences as a tool of research. An important achievement was the publication in Russian of a *Jewish Encyclopedia*. Research was undertaken into Jewish folklore, poetry, folk tales, and folk art.

The Jewish press gained a vast circulation, selling hundreds of thousands of copies. For the mass readership there were daily newspapers in Yiddish, and for the intelligentsia they appeared in Hebrew and Russian. A modern Jewish school was inaugurated, and a start made in setting up a higher institute for Jewish studies

117

The Jews evacuated from a Polish town. The painter Abel Pann (1883-1963) drew a powerful series of drawings depicting the sufferings of Russian Jewish communities in the period during and immediately after World War I. Many Jewish communities near the front in Poland and Lithuania were expelled in their entirety. Pastel. Jerusalem, Israel Museum.

in St. Petersburg. In the specific conditions in Russia, public debate between the Zionists and their opponents became mainly centered on Jewish cultural questions.

The Bund and like-minded circles held that the Jews constituted a nation, like any of the other nations in Russia, and endeavored to break away from the religious tradition and all the nationalistic elements it entailed, and to launch a secular culture and to open Jewish schools where instruction would be given in the vernacular of the Jewish masses, i.e., Yiddish.

The Zionists and others of similar views regarded Hebrew as the national language, and the expression of the historic continuity and basic unity of world Jewry. They considered the spread of Hebrew to be essential for deepening Jewish nationalism and linking the masses with the national past and historic homeland—Eretz Israel.

The debate grew heated after the advocates of Yiddish (the 'Yiddishists') declared at their convention held at Czernowitz in 1908 that Yiddish was the accepted national language of the

Jewish people. The 'language schism' split the Jewish intelligentsia in Eastern Europe into two factions, and their campaigns took on a hostile and acrimonious tone.

In Galicia and Bukovina

In contrast to the 5,000,000 Jews in Russia, the 800,000 Jews living in Galicia and 100,000 Jews in neighboring Bukovina enjoyed a comparatively liberal rule under Emperor Franz Josef. From 1867 they enjoyed full legal rights of citizenship, and were formally permitted to develop their internal life in complete freedom. The Jews made up over 10 per cent of the total population in these regions of the Austro-Hungarian empire.

The most salient general feature of the Jewish community in these areas was its impoverished condition. Galicia was a poor agricultural region, populated mainly by peasants. In the former kingdom of Poland, before partition, the Jews had constituted the middle class of merchants and artisans. As their numbers increased, their scope of means of livelihood diminished. Many took up agricultural employment, and by the end of the 19th century, 14.3 per cent of the Jews in Galicia worked on the land (as compared to 3.5 per cent in Russia).

The second typical characteristic of the Jews was their conservatism. While there was a large group of 'enlightened' intellectuals *(maskilim)*, some with German cultural affiliations and others with Polish, the general Jewish proletariat clung to its ancestral patterns of living. Hasidism was a strong force in

Simhat Torah flag, Russia, c. 1920. The festival of the Rejoicing of the Law *Simhat Torah* is one of the most joyous in the Jewish calendar, marking the completion of the annual reading of the Pentateuch in the synagogue. The children carried specially prepared flags of which this is an example. Anonymous woodcut. Jerusalem, Israel Museum.

Galicia, and vast numbers of Jews lived in accordance with the injunctions of the *tzaddikim,* who held their 'courts' in Sadogora, Belz, and other centers.

The Socialist and Zionist movements also spread throughout Galicia and Bukovina, but did not take on there the violent revolutionary form they had assumed in Russia. Events in Russia had a strong impact in Galicia, and important among those influencing the young were emigrés and refugees from Russia. However, the Jewish youth in Galicia did not depart from their traditional way of life, and the new spirit reached the remoter parts of the country without any acute conflict accompanying it. Galicia also produced thinkers, writers and poets, who later won worldwide recognition, including the philosopher Martin Buber, and the Hebrew Nobel-prizewinning author Shemuel Yoseph Agnon.

A factor tending to preserve the Jewish national identity in Galicia was the struggle between German and Polish national influences there, and subsequently, in eastern Galicia, between Polish and Ukrainian influences. A small class of wealthy Jewish bourgeoisie identified its political fortunes with what was then the dominant element, the Poles. But many Galician Jews,

including Orthodox Jews and intellectuals, Zionists and Socialists, preferred to stand aside from the struggle.

WAR

World War I was the prelude to the decline and disintegration of East European Jewry. Between 1914 and 1918, the eastern front passed through the heart of a territory inhabited by millions of Jews. For the first time hundreds of thousands of Jewish conscripts on both sides of the front were despatched to fight in foreign armies. A typical situation showing the dilemma that faced the Jewish soldier can be seen in a story told in varying versions and in different places, of the Jewish infantryman who bayoneted a soldier in the enemy ranks, only to hear the dying man cry out the prayer 'Shema Israel'.

The victories of the Russian army and its invasion of Galicia at the beginning of the war were accompanied by looting and persecution of the Jews there. Many fled to the interior of the country, to Hungary and Vienna. Those who remained were crowded into refugee camps in different towns near the front.

In the zone of the Russian front and to its rear, martial law was imposed under a group of anti-Semitic generals. When a series of defeats followed the initial victories, culminating in the summer of 1915 in the retreat of the Russian armies eastward, the Russian high command found it convenient to pin responsibility for its failure onto the Jews. Jews were accused of treason and espionage for the Germans. A number of spy trials were staged and hostages seized and sent to the Russian interior. Subsequently mass expulsions of Jews from the towns near the front were instituted, ending in the mass expulsion of Jews from Lithuania in June 1915.

An additional restrictive measure prohibited the use of the Hebrew alphabet both for publication and for writing. The Hebrew and Yiddish press and literature were silenced, and even the use of the Hebrew alphabet for letter writing was debarred by the military censor. The victimization of the Jews aroused public opinion in Europe and America. However, the critical military and financial position in which Russia was then placed compelled the government to show some regard for these views, which were preventing countries in the West from providing loans. In the summer of 1915 the Pale of Settlement was practically abolished, and thousands of Jewish refugees from Poland and Lithuania streamed to inner Russia.

REVOLUTIONS

Revolution suddenly broke out in Russia in February 1917. The tsarist regime collapsed and with it went the repressive and discriminatory policy it had adopted against the Jews. One of the first steps taken by the provisional revolutionary government was the general abolition of the anti-Jewish legislation. The nine months following the February 1917 revolution form a brief spring in the history of Russian Jewry. At one stroke, unlimited

Jew carrying ducks in a basket, Russia. Etching by Issachar Ryback (1897-1935), who excelled in scenes of the small Russian Jewish communities which he portrayed in their period of decline. Jerusalem, Israel Museum.

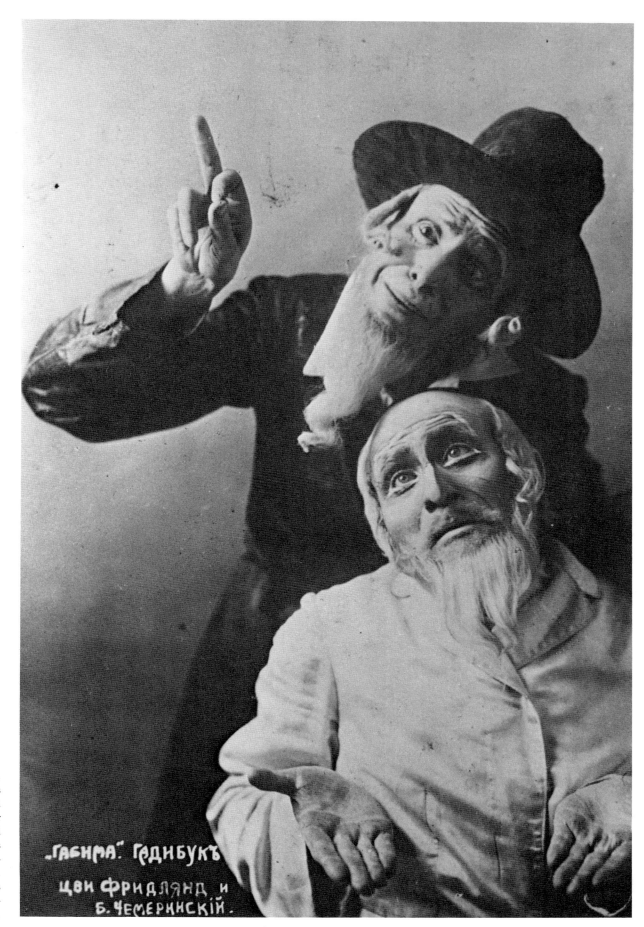

The Dibbuk, Moscow, 1922. An-Ski's *The Dibbuk* in Bialik's Hebrew translation, produced by the great Russian producer Vachtangov (an associate and disciple of Stanislavsky), was the greatest success of the Ha-Bimah Theater in Moscow. Shown here are two of its outstanding actors, Zvi Friedland and Baruch Chemerinsky.

„ГАБИМА". ГАДИБУКЪ
ЦВИ ФРИДЛЯНД и
Б. ЧЕМЕРИНСКІЙ.

possibilities of unhampered development opened up to the Jews in every aspect of their lives, both as citizens of the state and as a national entity. The hostility toward the Jews, that had served as a political weapon in the hands of the old regime, became not only a negation of revolutionary principles, but something of which every decent man was ashamed. Anti-Semitism itself did not cease, but was forced deeper underground.

It was natural that the Jews, as the most oppressed nation among the peoples of Russia before the Revolution, should wholeheartedly welcome it, and eagerly join in the excitement of political life that now began in the state. To name but a few examples of the most prominent Jews in politics, there were among the leaders of the Constitutional Democratic Party the jurist Maxim Vinaver; of the largest Socialist Party, the S.R., O. Minor and Abram Gotz; of the Mensheviks, their leader Julius Martov; and of the Bolsheviks, Lev Trotsky and Jacob Sverdlov. Many Jews led the revolutionaries in the rural centers, most of which were without intellectuals or men of education.

However, although so many Jews were to be found in the general revolutionary movement, they were still only a small proportion of the millions of Jews in Russia, who remained united as a whole and closely attached to their national-religious identity. The deepest expression of this attachment was in the tremendous gains achieved by the Zionist movement in the months following the democratic revolution. Thus the argument of the opponents of Zionism, that as soon as Jews had obtained equal rights Zionism would lose its appeal, was swiftly proved erroneous. Everywhere in the Jewish communities, from the Ukraine and Belorussia to remote Siberia, the Zionists came out first as the communal leaders. In May 1917, a short time after the outbreak of the Revolution, the Seventh Conference of Russian Zionists was held in Petrograd, at which 140,000 members were represented. At the opening session a message of greetings from the Russian Foreign Minister was read out, and the congress decided to strengthen the drive for the movement, and broaden the scope of its activities in all spheres of Jewish life.

Wartime conditions prevented immediate emigration to Eretz Israel, but in many towns and villages the young spontaneously organized groups, named *He-Halutz* (The Pioneer), to train for emigration there. The Zionists were paying particular attention at this time to the development of Hebrew culture, and for this purpose the Tarbut Society (Culture Society) was set up. Hebrew school and kindergarten teachers, seminaries, secondary and elementary schools were opened. A Hebrew daily *Ha-Am* (The People) was published in Moscow, and publication began of textbooks for learning and reading Hebrew. A particularly significant mark of the revival of Hebrew culture was the foundation of the Hebrew drama studio, the Ha-Bimah Theater in Moscow, which was the first step in initiating the Hebrew theater in other countries, and especially in Eretz Israel. In all the elections held in 1917 to both general and Jewish institutions, the Zionists and those near to them headed the Jewish lists, leaving the Bund and all the other Jewish parties far behind.

The historical significance of the short nine months separating the autocratic tsarist regime from the October revolution was that the Jews in Russia were given an opportunity of revealing their real national will and their loyalty to the historic Jewish traditions. These nine months, although revealing the existence of powerful national forces, were too brief a period to enable Russian Jewry to set itself up into a sufficiently solid organization to face up to the ordeals and disasters that were to follow.

The Bolshevik Revolution in November 1917 triggered off a civil war, which continued until 1920-1. Anarchy reigned in many parts of the country, and especially in the Ukraine and Belorussia, which became the battlegrounds for conflicting national groups and armies. This period was marked by the terrible brutalities against the Jews, which often took the form of pogroms and wholesale pillaging, and, during retreats and

The heder, Poland, 1938. In 1938, the photographer Roman Vishniac traveled extensively throughout Eastern Europe photographing Jewish life, unaware that this would be the last time it would be possible to record these scenes. Here he has 'caught' the teacher and pupils in the *heder*, the child's first Hebrew school.

defeats, of savage butchery as well. The Ukrainian and White Armies were particularly vicious, since they took revenge for their defeats by the Red Army on the Jews, using as their chief battle slogan 'Strike the Jews and save Russia!'

Words cannot describe the catastrophe that befell the Jews in the Ukraine and Belorussia in the three years of civil war. Bare statistics showing the hundreds of communities and the many thousands killed cannot convey the horror of this period, recalling the Nazi Holocaust in Europe that was to come twenty-five years later. In many places in East Europe self-defense organizations were formed, but the attempts remained local in character. They succeeded in several of the cities and a few smaller towns. In Odessa, for instance, 'Jewish fighting units' were formed at an early period in the Revolution led by a nucleus of demobilized officers and soldiers.

During the last two years of the civil war, as the Soviet government consolidated its position, the Jewish defense units received increasing assistance, either in the form of political support or in arms, and managed to deter the peasant mobs, and to cooperate with the Red Army in inflicting punishment. These units, in which the influence of Jewish national and Zionist elements were strong, were disbanded when the opponents of the Soviet regime were suppressed in 1920-1.

Between 1919 and 1921 the new pattern and division of East European Jewry between the different states established after World War I emerged. About three million Jews (including all the Jews in Galicia) found themselves within the republic of Poland. Some 2,500,000 remained in Soviet Russia. Approximately a quarter of a million passed to Lithuania and Latvia, and a similar number—the Jews of Bessarabia and Bukovina—found themselves in the enlarged Rumania. This division split East European Jewry into several components, each evolving under differing conditions in the twenty interwar years.

IN THE SOVIET MELTING POT

The fate of the Jews in the territory of the Soviet Union was largely determined by the theory and practice of the Communist Party, which wielded absolute authority in the state. The views of the party on the Jewish question had been formulated and crystallized in the decade preceding the Revolution. Like all the socialist and liberal parties in Russia, the Bolsheviks also rejected anti-Semitism. The principle of equal civic rights for Jews as individuals, along with the rest of the citizens in the state, was axiomatic with the Bolsheviks. More reserved, however, was the party attitude toward the postulate that the Jews constituted a separate nationality. In the pre-revolutionary period the Bolsheviks did not recognize the existence of the Jews as a nation. Influenced by the assimilated Jews, many of whom were to be found in the circles of the Socialist leadership, the Bolsheviks tended to regard assimilation as the most progressive means of solving the Jewish problem. Relying on Marx, Kautsky and Otto Bauer, Lenin declared that 'there is no justification for the concept of a separate Jewish people', and that 'national Jewish culture' is the slogan used by the rabbis and bourgeoisie, the slogan of our enemies'. Stalin stated in his pamphlet *Marxism and the Jewish Question* that a nation is a 'stable body of people, historically evolved, on the basis of community of language, territory and economic life'; since the Jews lack this common basis, they are only 'a nation on paper', while the development of human society leads inevitably to the assimilation of peoples into their environment. These assumptions of the founding fathers of Communism have had an important influence on Soviet policy toward the Jews up to the present day. If the Soviets on occasion had to deviate from it, when reality gave the lie to their theories, this was merely a temporary digression, and the pendulum swung back with renewed strength and vigor.

The opposition of the new regime to anti-Semitism and anti-Jewish terrorization won the warm support of the Jewish public, whose lives had depended on the Soviet victory. Jewish youth enthusiastically volunteered for the Red Army and took part in its organization. Some rose to a high rank, and their names figure among those of the founders of the Red Army (such as Yona Yakir and Yan Gamarnik). The Jews played a large part also in the reconstruction of the administrative machinery, which had broken down when a large part of the former Russian intelligentsia was exiled from Soviet Russia.

However, the new regime also ruined the livelihood of the majority of the Jewish population. The liquidation of the old economic system especially hit the Jews who had been mainly traders, shopkeepers and small artisans. The abolition of private trade, and of the status of the market town as the intermediary between the village and city, the confiscation of property and goods, and the imposition of heavy fines on the 'bourgeoisie', led to the total impoverishment of the Jewish community. Lenin's admission of the failure of his economic policy in spring 1921, and the introduction of the 'New Economic Policy' (NEP), as well as the termination of the civil war and restoration of order in the state, brought some benefit to the Jews, but their economic position remained broken and hopeless.

As well as bringing physical and economic ruin, the new regime also saw to the spiritual destruction of Russian Jewry. After the Bolsheviks had seized power, they were forced to recognize, even if only as a passing phenomenon, the existence of millions of Jews adhering to their national language and traditions. In order to deal with the Jewish question, special 'Jewish Sections' (*Yevsektsii*) were established in Communist Party branches. Here were organized Jewish party members to work actively among Jewry. The function of the 'Yevsektsii' was 'to install the dictatorship of the proletariat in the Jewish street'. A large number of those active in the 'Yevsektsii' were drawn from the Bund and other Jewish socialist parties, some even from the left-wing Zionists. These brought with them their ideas of developing a secular national Jewish culture in the Yiddish language. The existing conditions in the Jewish 'street' compelled the Communist Party to accept these views, with the reservation that it regarded the use of Yiddish as a practical means of conducting party activities among the Jews only as long as they were still dependent upon it.

Synagogue, Russia, early twentieth century. This is a rare photograph taken during prayers in a synagogue in Russia early in the century. The Jews looking toward the camera are facing along the Eastern wall which was regarded as a place of special honor. Jerusalem, Photo archives of the Israel Museum.

The first act of the 'Yevsektsii' was to dissolve the religious and national organization of Russian Jewry, to eradicate the use of Hebrew, and to suppress the Zionist movement. In August 1919 the Jewish communities were wound up and all communal property confiscated. The repression of religion was implemented by prohibiting religious instruction to children, closure of the *heder* and *yeshivot,* and sequestration of the synagogues, which were converted into clubs, workshops, and warehouses. A powerful anti-religious offensive was launched against Judaism and its leaders, and heavy taxes were imposed on the rabbis and the rest of the 'servants of religion', in order to force them to resign their offices. In doing so the 'Yevsektsii' encountered opposition from the mass of religious Jews, who invoked the promised right to freedom of religious worship included in the Soviet constitution, and struggled for the right to continue in their customary way of life. The arrest and expulsion from the Soviet

Union of R. Joseph Isaac Shneersohn, head of 'Habad' Hasidism in 1927, marked a certain stage in the struggle, but religious observance also continued clandestinely, the scope of which was revealed as soon as the hundreds of Hasidic families who had left the Soviet Union reached Palestine after World War II.

Learning the Hebrew language was debarred in practice in the Soviet Union, and Hebrew publications ceased to appear. The end of the war on Hebrew culture was signified by the emigration from the Soviet Union in June 1921 of a group of Hebrew writers headed by Hayyim N. Bialik. A few years later the Hebrew theater Ha-Bimah which had attained a high artistic standard, followed suit. For a long time a number of prominent Russian intellectuals had defended it from the 'Yevsektsii', foremost among whom was Maxim Gorki. The remaining Hebrew writers were fiercely persecuted, and many sent to forced labor camps.

The dynamism running through the Zionist movement was viewed by the Soviets as a threefold danger: it strengthened on the one hand the force of the Jewish national movements; it was diverting the talents of the Jewish intelligentsia, an important asset of the Soviet regime, into activities outside the country; and it had links with the World Zionist Organization, then closely associated with Great Britain, considered among the countries most hostile to the Soviet Union.

The Zionist movement continued to function underground. The majority of its members were younger people and youths active in youth movements or within the framework of the 'He-Halutz' (Pioneer) organization, which was preparing its members for emigration to and for work in Palestine. Many of them were arrested and exiled to detention camps in Soviet Asia.

For a few years the Soviets permitted the 'He-Halutz' organization to continue in certain areas in the state, but this permission was withdrawn in 1928. In practice, any organized Zionist activity was silenced by the end of the 1920s. At this time, too, all surviving Jewish scholarly or social associations were dissolved. In 1930 the Jewish Sections were liquidated. The first stage in eliminating Jewish national life in Soviet Russia was completed.

To replace the shattered Jewish culture, the Jewish Communist Party workers tried to foster a 'Jewish proletariat culture', based on the establishment of Yiddish-language schools and institutions. A Yiddish Soviet press came into being, its main organ being the Moscow daily *Emes* (1920-38). Hundreds of Yiddish books and pamphlets were published yearly. Much effort was expended on developing the Yiddish theater, notably the Jewish State Theater in Moscow, directed by Solomon Mikhoels, which owed its principal success to the presentation of the works of the classic Yiddish authors Mendele Mocher Seforim, Sholem Aleichem, and Isaac Leib Peretz. 'Jewish Cultural Departments' were established in Minsk and Kiev, mainly to promote research into Yiddish language and literature. In the short period between the mid-1920s and the mid-1930s while this Jewish Communist-orientated culture flourished, it seemed to many faithful supporters of Yiddish elsewhere that new avenues were opening up before them, and that with the support of the Soviet government a new Yiddish culture would emerge. Writers and scholars who had left the country in the early years of the revolution began to return to take part in its development, among them the author David Bergelson and the poet Peretz Markish.

The chances of success for this cultural activity depended on the establishment of a Yiddish-language school system, to which the Yiddishists devoted much effort. Yiddish schools were opened in a number of towns and cities. The parents began by sending their children to these schools, and the peak annual total was reached in 1932 with a school attendance of some one hundred and sixty thousand pupils (over one-third of the number of Jewish children of elementary school age). But subsequently the number began to decline. Parents preferred to send their children to non-Jewish schools, either because there were few Yiddish-language secondary schools and a shortage of such institutes of higher learning, or because of the nature of this type of school, where the teaching of Jewish values was limited to the study of a few chapters in Yiddish literature, which supplied explanations derogatory to Jewish religious and national values. Religious Jews and Zionists refrained from sending their children to these schools, and along with the assimilationists of various categories, sent their children to the ordinary state schools. By the end of the 1930s the Yiddish-language schools had been closed down throughout nearly the whole of the Soviet Union.

On the other hand, the process of assimilation gathered momentum as Jews became integrated into the new Soviet society. The young were attracted to the cities, where the facilities for Yiddish were lacking. National Jewish-Russian language media, i.e. a Jewish-Russian press or literature, were practically non-existent. Intermarriage became a frequent occurrence. Over sixty thousand Jews attended Soviet institutes of higher learning in 1935 (over 10 per cent of the total number of students). By the end of the 1930s Russian Jewry had already reached an advanced stage of national disintegration, both spiritually and culturally.

However, the most decisive factor affecting Jewish history in the Soviet Union was the economic disruption of the 1920s and 1930s. The destruction of the former economic basis of the mass of Jewry after the revolution has already been mentioned. A vast class of people without any means of livelihood or work was created and, because of their social condition, they were also deprived of their civic rights; the right to work, to public medical assistance, and, for their children, the right to attend secondary schools, vocational schools or institutes of higher learning.

The solution to this problem developed in three ways in this period: 1) by the migration of thousands of Jews to the Russian interior, formerly closed to them under the tsarist regime, and their entry into the ranks of Soviet administrators and factory workers. This movement accounted for about five hundred thousand people, a large number of whom reached Moscow and Leningrad; 2) by their concentration in the cities and industrial areas in the Ukraine and Belorussia, in which new classes of state officials and industrial workers were developing; and finally 3) by agricultural settlement.

Agricultural Settlement and the Birobijan Project

During the 1920s many of the Soviet leaders looked upon agricultural settlement as the key to the solution of the Jewish problem. This was a revival of the tsarist government's program of the beginning of the 19th century, but it was now put into practice on a larger scale. In 1924 the government established a 'Commission for the Rural Placement of Jewish Toilers' (Komzet), and in the following year the 'Association for the Rural Placement of Jewish Toilers' (Ozet). A group of Communist officials, headed by Mikhail I. Kalinin, regarded the settlement project not merely as an economic solution, but also as a means of preserving Jewish national existence for those who did not wish or were unable to assimilate with their neighbors. They began concentration of this settlement in a series of groups that would constitute independent national units.

At first the project was concentrated in southern Russia, which had been the center of Jewish agricultural settlement from the tsarist period, and in the Crimean peninsula, where the northern areas were mainly uninhabited. Within several years five Jewish agricultural autonomous districts had been founded (Kalinindorf, Novo-Zlatopolye, and Stalindorf in the Ukraine; Freidorf and Larindorf in the Crimea). Settlement was carried out with active assistance from Jewish organizations in the West —the 'Joint', ICA (Jewish Colonization Association) and ORT (*Obshtchestvo Remeslenovo Truda*). But it was clear that there was no space in southern Russia for Jewish settlement on a sufficiently large scale to enable the establishment of an autonomous Jewish state.

In 1928 the government decided to direct Jewish settlement toward a remote, barely inhabited area, the region of Birobijan in the extreme east, on the banks of the river Amur and on the Russo-Chinese border. To encourage Jewish migration to this isolated territory, it was decided to give the project something of a national character, a Soviet-type Zionism. Jews throughout the world were urged to help in establishing a Jewish republic within the framework of the Soviet Union, and in May 1934 Birobijan was declared an 'autonomous Jewish province' with an area of 16,000 square miles, and whose official language was Yiddish. However, there was soon a shift in the attitude of the Soviet government regarding the Birobijan project. In 1936 the administration of the autonomous region was liquidated, and from that year on the Jewish participation in the region began to decline, even if formally Birobijan retained its status as a Jewish province. Today Birobijan has no more than symbolic significance in Soviet-Jewish life. The 1959 census registered 14,269 Jewish inhabitants there, constituting 8.8 per cent of the total population. Of these less than 10 per cent declared Yiddish to be their mother tongue.

In practice, the problem of Jewish integration into the economic structure of the Soviet Union was solved by their absorption into Soviet administration and industry, which totally revived in the first two five-year plans. In 1939 the division of Jews according to social status could be broken down in the following way:

Officials	40.5%
Manual workers	30.5%
Skilled workers in cooperatives	16%
Agricultural workers in kolkhozes	6%
Independent skilled workers	4%
Others	3%

In the new Soviet society the Jews retained an exceptional social structure. The place of commerce, which had occupied a predominant position in the Jewish economic structure before the Revolution, was taken by the administrative services and the technical and academic professions. As far as is known, this trend has increased since the 1939 census.

By the end of the 1930s the Jews already formed an organic part of the new Soviet society. They occupied respected positions in the administration, in the army, in the sciences and arts. During the purges at the end of the 1930s, which were principally directed against the veteran Communist administration, many of the members of the 'Yevsektziya' were liquidated, and the main Jewish daily *Emes* and the *Ozet* were closed down. However, the purges were not anti-Semitic in character, being part of general party policy. Assimilation made gigantic strides, the Communist-Yiddish cultural institutions were in the process of extinction, although a group of several thousand communal leaders, writers, artists, and teachers, still stood firm in face of the prevailing atmosphere of disintegration. Small groups of Jews, mainly elderly persons, kept up their links with the Jewish faith. The remaining Zionists found themselves in labor camps and prisons.

In the first stage of World War II, until the German invasion of Russia in June 1941, the Jews in the Soviet Union enjoyed a comparative respite. The annexation of the territories in the Ukraine and western Belorussia (in September 1939), and of Lithuania, Latvia, Estonia, Bessarabia and northern Bukovina (in the summer of 1940) by the Soviet Union, brought in over two million more Jews into Soviet Jewry, and the number was swollen by the hundreds of thousands of refugees from Nazi-occupied Poland. These masses of Jews, who were imbued with a profound national Jewish spirit, might well have exerted a profound influence on Soviet Jewry. However, the Soviet regime took immediate measures to suppress the Zionist movement, liquidate the Jewish religious and communal institutions, and close down the Hebrew school system. In addition, they arrested Jewish businessmen, industrialists, religious functionaries, Zionists and others, who were sent to detention camps or to forced labor camps in the north. It was clear that Soviet policy was aimed at 'denationalizing' the new Jewish citizens, just as it had 'denationalized' the Jews in the Soviet Union over the previous twenty years.

On the whole the Jews reconciled themselves to their position, realizing that this could only be regarded as a minor evil in comparison with what was happening in the Nazi-occupied territories. Their ties with Jews in the outside world were almost entirely severed; in fact, Soviet Jewry was not informed of the frightful fate of their coreligionists in the countries belonging to the Soviet Union's new ally. They were unprepared for the Nazi invasion in June 1941 with all its implications for the Jews.

POLAND BETWEEN THE TWO WORLD WARS

In the period between the two World Wars, Poland had the largest Jewish concentration in Europe. This new state, established in consequence of the collapse of its two powerful neighbors, Russia and Germany, harbored a number of ethnic minorities within its extensive borders, including Ukrainians, Belorussians, Lithuanians, Germans, and Jews. But while the other minorities generally occupied areas where they formed the majority of the population, the Jews were dispersed throughout the country. They numbered over three million, forming one-tenth of the total population. Since many were living in cities and towns, where they formed from a third to half of the inhabitants, the Jews were a particularly noticeable alien element, distinguished by their dress, their appearance, and their language. The Jews in Poland formed the majority in the business sector and a good proportion of the artisan class, as well as figuring largely in the professions (medicine, law, etc.).

In theory, Jewish citizens had equal rights with non-Jews in the new Poland. Moreover, the peace treaty by which the state was established in 1919, bound Poland to guarantee national rights to its ethnic minorities in which the Jews were included. However, these guarantees were not honored.

The economic position of the new Poland was far from satisfactory. It had lost its large markets in the east, and, worse still—the country being overpopulated—the gates of emigration to the West began to close. While all the inhabitants of Poland suffered from these two primary factors, the Jews did so in particular. Hundreds of thousands of people from the countryside flocked to the towns, where they had to compete for sources of livelihood with the Jews.

Generally speaking, all the governments in Poland in the interwar period followed a policy of ousting the Jews from the various branches of the economy and replacing them by Poles. Entry to the civil and municipal administration was obviously going to be closed to Jews, but this was not deemed sufficient. The government periodically increased taxation and exacted it more rigorously from the Jews. The state began to take over various branches of industry and commerce, and subsequently the Jewish businessmen and office workers employed in these sectors were dismissed.

The pressure increased in the 1930s, and rightist-Fascist circles in Poland, drawing encouragement from the Nazi successes in Germany, urged more drastic measures against the Jews. Acts of terrorization occurred. Jews were attacked in the universities, in the market places, in the villages. Periodic anti-Jewish riots broke out.

At the same time the Polish government was prevented from taking extreme measures. The Jews occupied too important a place in the Polish economy. Jewish businessmen and manufacturers played a significant role in pioneering and extending many

Entrance to Old Ghetto, Cracow, 1938. For centuries Jews in Eastern Europe lived in their own quarters where they were able to preserve their way of life. This picture shows the entrance to the old ghetto in Cracow—one of the most ancient and distinguished of the East European communities. This picture was also taken by Roman Vishniac.

branches of commerce and industry. The government also had to take into account public opinion in Europe and America.

Jewish political life found expression in this period in Jewish party organizations, the most important being the various Zionist parties, which considered that the future of Polish Jewry lay in emigration to Palestine, but at the same time the Zionists defended Jewish civic and national rights, so long as Jews remained on Polish soil. There was also the Bund, which pinned its hopes on alliance with the progressive and Socialist elements in Poland. Orthodox Jews were mainly attached to the Agudat Israel Party, supported by many of the leaders *(tzaddikim)* of the Hasidic movement in Poland, which used the traditional system of political negotiations *(shtadlanut)* with the authorities in their struggle for Jewish rights. The illegal Communist Party was active among the Jewish youth and workers. Each party had its own youth movement, mutual assistance and professional associations, and school and educational systems.

Despite the immigration restrictions in other countries, hundreds of thousands of Jews left Poland, some for Palestine and others for South America and elsewhere. But this emigration was still insufficient to relax the political and economic tensions harassing the Jews living in Poland, and which were getting worse year by year.

In the discouraging conditions of economic depression and political pressure, Polish Jewry showed an astonishing vitality in its national and cultural life. This made itself evident in the establishment of a Jewish educational network, which met the needs of some one hundred and eighty thousand pupils. Contrary to the provisions of the treaty guaranteeing national rights, it received no assistance from the state. The educational system was also divided on party lines. The Orthodox Jews supported *hederim* and *yeshivot,* many of whose pupils completed their education in Polish schools. In addition to the old-time *yeshivah,* modern-type *yeshivot* were established. Among these was the 'Yeshivat Hakhmei Lublin', the Lublin *yeshivah,* which instituted a program for daily study by Orthodox Jews throughout the world of a designated page in the Talmud. A special school network, 'Beth Yaakov', was established for Orthodox girls, whose education had previously been neglected. The Zionists supported a secular Hebrew school system, the 'Tarbut', maintaining also three teachers' training seminaries. Beside giving instruction in Hebrew language and literature, the 'Tarbut'

schools imbued their pupils with the love of Zion. The intensive educational activities conducted within the Zionist youth movements also drew youngsters from all sectors of the Jewish public to Zionism, knowledge of Hebrew, and the wish to settle in Palestine. The largest Zionist youth organizations were 'Ha-Shomer Ha-Tzair', 'Gordonia,' and 'Dror', which encouraged the young to join the 'He-Halutz' organization, trained them for pioneer settlement in Palestine as laborers or *Kibbutz* members, and the right wing (revisionist) 'Brit Trumpeldor' youth movement ('Betar').

The Yiddishists, who were the principal supporters of the Bund, established a Yiddish secular school system. This movement remained limited, even though Yiddish was the spoken language of the great majority of Polish Jewry. A diversified Yiddish press and literature appeared in Warsaw, Vilna, and other places. Several attempts were made to start a modern Yiddish theater (the Vilna Troupe). It is interesting to note that the Yiddish theater achieved its greatest success, as did its Hebrew counterpart in Moscow, with the production of An-Ski's *The Dibbuk.*

Jewish scholarship flourished and a central academic institute for research into Jewish history and the Yiddish language, the 'Yidisher Visenshaftlikher Institut' (Yivo), was founded. The Jewish contribution to the Polish revival was less spectacular than the part played by Jews in Germany or even in Russia. However certain Jews achieved prominence such as Julian Tuwim, one of the great Polish poets of the modern era.

The continuing poverty and despair with the situation in Poland led a number of Jewish writers and poets to emigrate to Palestine, Russia, and America. However, there still remained a considerable group of Jewish intelligentsia and Yiddish writers in Poland, which included the poet Isaac Manger, the novelists Israel Singer, Alter Katzina, and others, as well as the 'Young Vilna' group (Abraham Sutzkever and Hayyim Grade). The poet-playwright Mattathias Shoham, who composed his monumental biblical dramas in Hebrew, remained in Poland until his death.

The position and fortunes of the Jews in Lithuania and Latvia were in general similar to those of Polish Jewry, but as the Jewish proportion in the population was smaller and the level of national culture of the surrounding peoples lower than in Poland, the pressure on the Jews was less.

It is worth mentioning that the majority of Jewish children in Lithuania and Latvia attended the various types of Jewish schools, which provided instruction in Hebrew and Yiddish.

The Holocaust

However bad the position of East European Jewry may have been after World War I, and despite the threats of annihilation by enemies from without, and the warnings of well-intentioned persons from within, no one could have foreseen what awaited the Jews with the Nazi invasion of Poland and Russia.

A clique of assassins now led a nation that had reached a high standard of civilization. Commanding all the resources of

Outside the Ghetto. The Nazis herded all the Jewish communities into inhuman conditions in special ghettos in many East European towns. Inside one, a young girl expresses her dream of what it is like outside the ghetto... in freedom, symbolized by the butterfly. Jerusalem, Yad Vashem, Central Archives for the Disaster and the Heroism.

Polish wedding. The young couple are under the wedding canopy, surrounded by their families. Painting by Mané Katz, who lived in France after 1921. At first he concentrated principally on biblical and ghetto scenes. There is a museum of his works at Haifa. Fribourg, Jean Nordmann Collection.

its science and technology, they could exploit the abilities of the German people to organize the systematic annihilation of one of the ancient historic nations of the world.

The Nazis were determined to establish their domination throughout the world and to enslave all other nations to the 'master race'. In every detail their doctrine was directly opposed to the spirit of Judaism and the values Judaism had bequeathed to the world. It was necessary, therefore, to extirpate the progenitors of this spirit, the Jewish people.

The Nazis embarked on the series of anti-Jewish persecutions immediately after their accession to power in 1933. However, the scientists in their service insistently drew their attention to the fact that the vital nerve center of the Jewish people was East European Jewry, and it was this that would have to be destroyed for the complete annihilation of Jewry to be achieved. With the conquest of Poland in 1939, and the western part of Soviet Russia in 1941, the Nazis realized that they held the fate of the Jewish nation in their hands.

During the first stage, up until the invasion of Russia, the Nazis isolated the Jews from the rest of the population, first by forcing them to wear a distinguishing mark, the 'yellow badge', and later by imprisoning them in ghettos in a number of the large towns. These were generally established in slum neighborhoods, and surrounded by walls or wire fences. To leave the ghetto was prohibited without a permit, which was usually granted for working in factories or workshops run on behalf of the Nazis. The ghettos were heavily overcrowded, while the Jews were allocated mere starvation rations. Individuals or groups of Jews were being murdered all the time. A 'Jewish Council' *(Judenrat)* was set over the ghetto, and a 'Jewish guard' maintained order within it. These institutions generally became the servants of the Germans and carried out their orders.

At this stage the Jews imprisoned in the ghettos believed that despite the frightful ordeal they were going through and the toll of victims claimed, they should hold out until the enemy had been defeated. So that notwithstanding the terrible ghetto conditions, they organized self-help, clandestinely ran schools for the youth, kept synagogues and *yeshivot* running, and organized full cultural activities and programs. They regarded their position as yet another disaster visited upon the Jewish people.

This changed entirely after the Nazi invasion of Soviet Russia. Four special units *(Einsatzgruppen)* followed in the wake of the German Army in the Ukraine, Belorussia, Lithuania, and Latvia. Numbering some three thousand men, they embarked upon the mass murder of the Jews with the help of the German army and units of militia conscripted from local collaborators. The first wholesale massacres took place in September 1941: in Berdychev, Vinniza, Uman, and Kiev. Several tens of thousands of Jews were killed at the close of September in Babi Yar, a valley near Kiev. The Nazis commemorated November 7 1941, the anniversary of the October revolution, by mass slaughters of Jews in many towns.

Monument to the Warsaw Ghetto uprising. A memorial erected after World War II on the site of the desperate uprising in 1943 which marked the final liquidation by the Nazis of the Warsaw Ghetto. By the sculptor Nathan Rappaport. Jerusalem, Yad Vashem, Central Archives for the Disaster and the Heroism.

Synagogue, Leningrad, 1893. Few synagogues are left today in the Soviet Union. One of these is the building in Leningrad, put up in 1893 in the Moorish style. It has room for 1,200 worshipers. In recent years, young Russian Jews have congregated in their thousands every year on the festival of the Rejoicing of the Law outside this synagogue in Leningrad, and others in Moscow and elsewhere, to dance throughout the night and demonstrate their attachment to the Jewish people.

It was in Soviet Russia that the Nazis made their first attempts at mass murder, with the transportation of men, women, and children, young and old, to places outside the towns, to forests, anti-tank trenches and wells, to be mown down by machine-guns or suffocated in gas vans and other ways. The areas of Odessa and Podolia, which were handed over to the Rumanian authorities (Transnistria), served as detention centers for hundreds of thousands of Jews from Bessarabia, Bukovina, and other areas in Rumania. While they were there, a large number were removed and killed or died from sickness or hunger.

The 'success' of the murder campaign in the east encouraged the Nazis, and on January 2 1942, at a meeting of those responsible for the occupied territories convened in Berlin, it was decided to embark on the systematic annihilation of the whole of European Jewry. All Jews were to be assembled for this purpose in ghettos and concentration and death camps in East Europe. Implementation of this decision was assigned to the chief of the S.S., Heinrich Himmler. Heading the special department for carrying out this program was S.S. Captain Adolf Eichmann.

The principal death camps were established on Polish soil. Their names have become infamous throughout the world: Auschwitz, Chelmno, Treblinka, Belzec, Maidanek, Sobibor, and others. Special apparatus were installed in these camps to carry out mass murder by suffocation in gas chambers. The Jews were sent to the camps by rail. Once there, those suitable were separated from the rest and sent to work in plants run for the German army, where they were forced to do hard labor on the most meager rations. Many died in these conditions. When the others had also become too debilitated, they were sent to the gas chambers. The majority of the deportees, especially women, children, and old people were sent straight to the gas chambers. On July 22, 'action' began in the largest ghetto, that in Warsaw. Within two and a half months, three hundred thousand Jews had been despatched to their deaths. Along with the Jews from Eastern Europe, hundreds of thousands of Jews from Germany, France, Holland, Belgium, and Greece perished in the death camps, and in 1944 those from Hungary as well. In addition, Soviet prisoners-of-war, gypsies, and people who had not adapted themselves to the Nazi regime were also sent there to be murdered. In all, some six million Jews in Europe met their deaths in Nazi camps.

The Struggle against the Nazis

There is little point in debating whether the millions who were sent to their deaths might have risen against the Nazis in revolt. The attempts made by certain historical investigators and authors to shift the blame for this monstrous crime in history onto its victims are misguided. Far stronger and better organized nations submitted to the Nazi yoke, and passed over the atrocities they committed in silence. If the record of Jewish resistance to the Nazis has been submerged in that of the general struggle, it still holds a most honorable place in the annals of the fighters against Nazism. Jewish resistance took three forms: uprisings in the ghettos and death camps, membership of the partisan movement, and participation in the armed forces fighting against the Nazis, particularly in the Soviet Army.

Jewish underground organizations were formed by Zionist and Communist youth movements and other bodies in many of the ghettos. Their anti-Nazi activities were extremely limited, owing principally to their sense of responsibility to the thousands of their coreligionists who would have had to pay heavily in executions and hangings at the first sight of Jewish resistance. The Nazis managed to conceal their program of extermination from the Jews for a long time, and cleverly kept alive the delusion among the prisoners of the ghetto that if they worked for the Nazis they would remain alive. Only after it had become clear to the Jews that there was no possibility of survival did they actively rebel. Sometimes the revolt was quite spontaneous, other times it was planned by groups of the underground. The Warsaw ghetto uprising, which made a tremendous impression throughout the world, began on April 19 1943, and was led by Zionist youth groups, who were joined by Communists and Bundists. It continued for several weeks and ended in the complete annihilation of the ghetto by the Germans.

Occasionally uprisings also broke out in the labor and death camps, when the German guards were killed and the prisoners managed to escape. A Jewish partisan movement developed in various parts of Poland and Russia, and was especially active in the forests of Belorussia and Lithuania. Some of the Jewish resistance fighters joined the general underground movement, while others formed special Jewish units. Unlike the non-Jewish partisan groups, who were mainly concerned with military actions, the Jewish units also looked after the 'family camps' consisting of refugees unable to fight, women, children, and old people, who had sought refuge in the forests. The Jewish partisans also took part in the war of demoralization in the rear of the German forces, attacking the German pickets, blowing up railroads and bridges, and punishing collaborators.

The young Jews who joined the Red Army had good opportunity for avenging the murder of their people. Hundreds of thousands of Jews served in the Red Army with unquestioned loyalty. Many distinguished themselves in action, and about one hundred and sixty thousand Jews were awarded military honors. Jews served in the anti-tank units in the Volga and the Dniester regions, in the air force in flights over Berlin, and in the naval and submarine crews.

It was to a Jewish lieutenant-colonel, Leonard Winocour, that the Nazi Field-Marshal Pauls surrendered and handed over his revolver. The commander of the first tank corps to enter Berlin was a Jewish lieutenant-general, Krivoshein. Over half the members of the Lithuanian Division in the Red Army were Jewish.

During the war the Soviet government permitted the formation of a 'Jewish anti-Fascist Committee', headed by the Russian-Jewish writer Ilya Ehrenburg, the actor Solomon Mikhoels, and General Jacob Kreiser, a 'Hero of the Soviet Union'. The committee established contact with Jews throughout the world to coordinate action against the Nazis.

The Jewish soldier in the Soviet Army, as in the rest of the Allied forces, knew that he was not only fighting to defend the land of his birth, but also to save the Jews throughout the world. In general the story of Jewish resistance and—where possible—participation in the war against the Nazis is an integral aspect of the growth of a new attitude among the Jews in the course of the 20th century—from what is called the 'Diaspora mentality' to a stance of proud independence illustrated by the stand of Israel, the proud refusal of Soviet Jews to surrender their identity—and by the many heroic events that occurred during World War II.

THE POSTWAR PERIOD

After the end of the war, the Jews with Polish citizenship began the process of leaving the Soviet Union. Mingling with them were a number of groups of Jews from the Soviet Union itself, such as the 'Habad' Hasidim, who had preserved their religious life through the years under Soviet rule. The majority joined the survivors of the Holocaust in Poland, but after an overtly hostile reception from the Poles, they left Poland for the refugee camps in Central Europe, and from there many found their way to Palestine. Several thousand Jews remained in Poland, mainly those who wished to assimilate, Communists, or elderly people dependent on state pensions. Although the Communist regime in Poland officially opposed anti-Semitism, a number of anti-Semitic outbreaks occurred, which prompted

further Jewish emigration from the country. In the late 1960s the dissension between the conservative and liberal wing in the Polish Communist Party inaugurated a fresh wave of anti-Semitism leading to further emigration, pointing to the complete liquidation of the remaining Jewish community in Poland.

On the other hand, about 2,300,000 Jews remained in the Soviet Union. According to official statistics, about 250,000 live in Moscow, 162,000 in Leningrad, and about 154,000 in Kiev. In the first few years after the war, national feeling began to revive among the Soviet Jews under the influence of the emotion aroused during the war, which reached a climax at the establishment of the State of Israel (to which the Soviet government initially gave its political support). The manifestations of national revival angered Stalin, and at the end of 1948 a violent anti-Jewish campaign was launched, directed against the remnants of Jewish nationalism. Distinguished Jewish writers and actors were arrested, accused of conspiracy with Zionism and American imperialism, and secretly executed, most of them on August 12 1952. A few months later the government accused a group of doctors (mainly Jews) of a plot to poison the Soviet leaders. Anti-Jewish propaganda commenced, and it was rumored the Jews were to be sent to remote parts of Soviet Asia. The death of Stalin in March 1953 ended the period of nightmare, although periodically there have been fresh manifestations of anti-Semitism.

Soviet policy toward the Jews since the death of Stalin has not changed in principle. Although the persecution of Jews as private individuals has ceased, and many hold important positions in Soviet literary and academic circles, including two Nobel prizewinners, Boris Pasternak (Literature) and Lev Landau

Coins, Poland, thirteenth century. Coins with Hebrew inscriptions minted in Poland by Jewish officials.

(Physics), any manifestations of a religious or cultural nature are suppressed. Although in the 1959 census, 18 per cent of the Jews declared Yiddish their mother tongue, the establishment of Yiddish schools has not been permitted, and publication of a Yiddish literary monthly *Sovietish Heimland* was only licensed in 1961. Synagogues are systematically closed, and the publication of religious works is in practice prohibited as previously.

In the Soviet Union the attitude toward Jews is one of suspicion. They are considered an alien element, linked by family ties, by history and sentiment to Jews in the State of Israel, the United States, and other foreign countries. The process of assimilation and absorption is making strides, progressively strengthened by increasing intermarriage. However, in this advanced stage of assimilation, the Jews have preserved sufficient traces of their national identity to label them at any time as foreigners, and single them out as a scapegoat and target for popular vindictiveness.

Despite the official policy of cultural deprivation, the Jews have stubbornly maintained their identity and strengthened their identification with the Jewish people and with Israel. The full extent of this phenomenon is hard to assess but it appears to be widespread and takes in wide circles of youth who demonstrate their Jewishness despite the intense Soviet indoctrination to which they have been subjected. Jewish identification reaches a powerful expression in the mass appearance of Jewish youth in the vicinity of synagogues each *Simhat Torah*. More recently it has expressed itself in the determination to leave the USSR for Israel. Specific cultural expression has been drastically and unnaturally curtailed—the Yiddish journal and a few itinerant theatrical troupes are all that are permitted. Jews are also not permitted openly to study their own history and culture. But none of these curtailments have succeeded in putting out the basic Jewish spark.

CHAPTER XI

United States of America

by Rabbi Abraham Karp

In early September 1654, twenty-three Jews arrived in the town of New Amsterdam to found the first Jewish community in what is now the United States. The twenty-three came from Recife in Brazil, having been forced to leave that city when it was recaptured by the Portuguese from the Dutch.

The immigration of Jews to America in the 17th and 18th centuries was part of the general movement of the center of the Western world from the Mediterranean to the Atlantic. The discoveries of the 16th century turned the attention of nations and men to the promise of the Americas.

Tales and evidence of the great wealth of the new continents in commodities and in land filled the dreams of the daring and raised the hopes of the hungry: for hungry they were in increasing numbers, with the population of Europe growing at an unprecedented rate and rapidly becoming urbanized. New frontiers were needed to support the poor, that could be exploited by the enterprising. America became the goal and destination, and the Atlantic, a route to new hope and new life.

It is estimated that the Jewish population of the United States at the time of the first Federal Census in 1790 was between 1,300 and 1,500. Small as it was in number, the Jewish community felt itself an important and integral part of the new nation. The western world, nurtured on the Bible, knew and lived with the Hebrews and 'seed of Abraham' without ever having met a Jew. In Colonial America, the works of Josephus were second only to the Bible itself. Though numerically few, the Jews of Colonial America nevertheless constituted distinct figures on the landscape.

In the first three decades of the republic, the Jewish population increased from fewer than two thousand to fewer than three thousand, while the general population trebled. In the next three decades, 1820-50, the general population doubled, but the Jewish population soared to some fifty thousand—a seventeenfold increase! The difference is attributable to one factor: immigration.

America was open for immigration, and the condition of the Jew in Europe was such as to make the enterprise most attractive.

The Congress of Vienna, convened in 1815 to restore Europe to its pre-Napoleonic ways, set off a wave of reaction in which the Jews suffered greatly. Newly granted rights were revoked and new oppressive measures enacted and enforced. The unsuc-

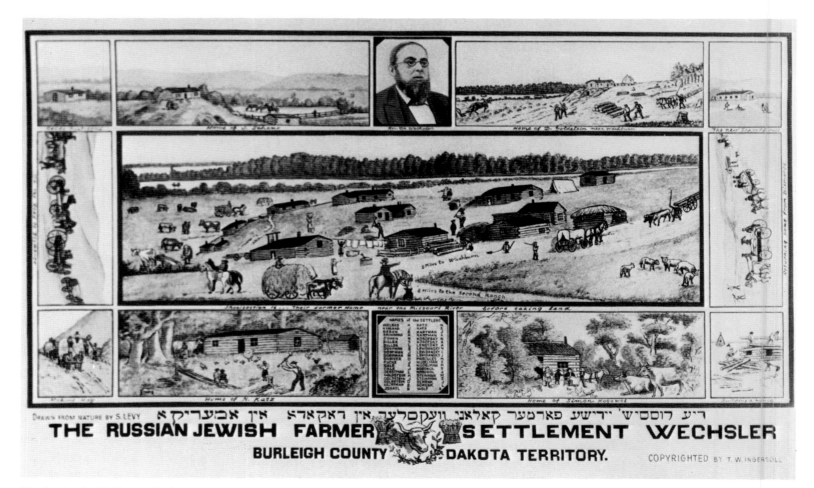

The Russian Jewish Farmer, Settlement Wechsler, 1865. The paper was founded in 1865 by Dr. Judah Wechsler in Burleigh County, Dakota Territory, and the illustrations drawn from nature by S. Levy. Jewish agricultural colonies were founded in the mid-west and far-west in the second half of the 19th century; all were short-lived. American Jewish Archives.

THE OCCIDENT,

AND

AMERICAN JEWISH ADVOCATE.

Vol. I.]   NISSAN 5603, APRIL 1843.   [No. 1.

INTRODUCTORY REMARKS.

It is a time-honoured custom, that when an Editor appears for the first time before the public, he is to state something of the course he means to pursue, and of the subjects he intends laying before his readers. In our case, this is hardly necessary, since the name of "Jewish Advocate" amply shadows forth that we mean to devote our pages to the spread of whatever can advance the cause of our religion, and of promoting the true interest of that people which has made this religion its profession ever since the days of the great lawgiver, through whom it was handed down to the nation descended from the stock of Abraham. But this general view may, perhaps, not be sufficiently detailed for many whom we would gladly number among our readers; and we will therefore briefly state our object in assuming the editorship of this new periodical, and of the course it is our firm determination to pursue.

With regard to our object, we state candidly, that the plan of a religious periodical did not originate with ourself, nor did we approve of it when it was first suggested to us. We thought then, and still think, that newspaper knowledge is at best but superficial; for, to make a paper or magazine really interesting to the general public, (and for such a one it is our duty to labour in our present vocation,) much matter must be admitted which is more pleasing in its nature than instructive, and the variety, which is to be constantly furnished, will naturally prevent long and continuous articles being given, although they might be extremely rich in information, even such as the people stand most in need of. We dreaded, moreover, that despite of the greatest care which we could bestow, articles might at times gain admission which

VOL. I.   1

The Occident, April 1843. Page 1, volume 1 of *The Occident,* edited by Isaac Leeser. For a quarter of a century, the remarkable Isaac Leeser (1806-68), minister, editor, translator of the Bible and prayer-book, textbook editor and communal architect, ran the high-quality magazine *The Occident* (from 1843-68). He was the first to introduce English sermons in the American synagogue. American Jewish Historical Society.

cessful revolutions of 1830 and 1848 and the reaction which followed gave further cause for Jewish uneasiness. Add the despair which ensues when hopes become shattered, and all the conditions were ripe for migration.

In the 1830s and particularly in the 1840s Jews arrived in significant numbers, mainly from Bavaria. They founded congregations in the existing communities and established communities in such cities as Boston, Hartford, New Haven, Albany, Syracuse, Rochester, Buffalo, in the northeast; Baltimore, Columbia, Augusta, Columbus, Mobile, New Orleans, and Galveston in

the south; and Cincinnati, Cleveland, Chicago, Louisville, Milwaukee, Pittsburgh, Columbus and Indianapolis in the midwest. The De Sola-Lyons Calendar of 1854 listed ten congregations in the new state, California.

In 1820, the American Jewish community was largely native-born, English-speaking, small in number and rapidly assimilating. By 1850, it was largely a German-speaking, immigrant community beginning to establish those institutions and organizations which would give it structure and identity.

Jewish immigration from Germany to the United States showed a dramatic increase during the period of political and civic reaction in the central European countries affected by the Revolution of 1848. The Jewish population of the United States increased in the decade 1850 to 1860 from some fifty thousand to one hundred and fifty thousand.

Among the new immigrants were a growing number of Jews from Eastern Europe. American Jewry, in the three decades which followed the mid-century, was made up chiefly of immigrants from the 'German' countries of Central Europe, with a significant admixture of East European Jews from Russia, Poland and Rumania.

As the Jews of Europe joined their neighbors in flight to the New World, so the American Jew joined fellow Americans in moving westward. Individual Jews could be found in many pioneer settlements, and Jewish communities dotted the entire map of expanding America.

In the decades of the Civil War and Reconstruction, Jewish immigration greatly decreased. The first attempt at a Jewish population survey, undertaken by the Board of Delegates of

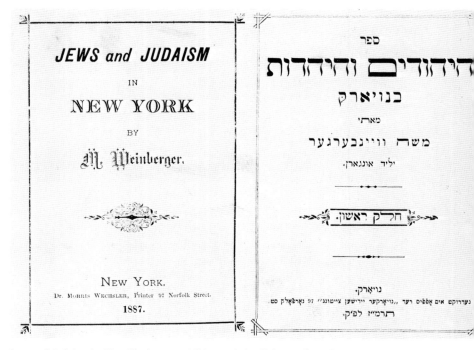

Jews and Judaism in New York, 1887. This work in Hebrew describes Jewish religious and cultural life in the New York immigrant community by the Hungarian-born rabbi Moses Weinberger, 1887. American Jewish Historical Society.

Weighing and Delivering Matzot, New York, 1870. Leslie's *Popular Monthly* carried a series of pictures depicting the method of baking *matzot* (unleavened bread for Passover) and its weighing and distribution in New York in 1870. American Jewish Historical Society.

American Israelites in 1877, placed the number of Jews in the United States at 230,257.

Few events had greater influence on the course of American Jewish history than the assassination of Alexander II, 'Tsar of all the Russians', in March 1881. This assassination touched off pogroms in more than a hundred Jewish communities (see chapter on Eastern Europe). Physical persecution, political oppression, and economic disabilities set in motion a wave of immigration which brought two and a half million Jews from Eastern Europe to American shores in the half-century from 1880 to 1930. The mass migration began in the 1880s and was brought to an end for the Russian Jew by the Revolution of 1917 and for the Polish Jew by the restrictive American immigration law of 1924.

In the decade 1880-90, some two hundred thousand Jews emigrated from Eastern Europe; in the following decade the number doubled. The very great majority came from Russia-Poland, but an appreciable number also arrived from Galicia, Hungary and Rumania.

Economically, America was ready to receive them. The depression of the early seventies had come to an end, and the country was again expanding, geographically and economically. The industries needed new labor, and the new laboring class needed purveyors of food and clothing. The Jewish immigrant became the small merchant and clothing worker to supply this need. In small towns across the country he opened stores; in the large cities he entered the shops.

Well into the 20th century immigration continued to be the single most important factor in the American Jewish historic experience. Some six hundred thousand Jews came to the United States in the last two decades of the 19th century. Three times that number arrived in the first two decades of the 20th.

Some 95 per cent of the immigrants originated in Eastern Europe. Most came directly to America; some had remained for shorter or longer periods in West European countries. The rise of Hitler in 1933 precipitated a migration of German Jews to America in significant numbers, and some one hundred and fifty thousand arrived in the years which followed World War II.

The fifty thousand Jews of America in 1850 constituted 1 per cent of world Jewry. The million Jews in 1900 were 10 per cent of the world's Jews. Today America's six million Jews constitute almost half of world Jewry.

AN OLD FAITH IN THE NEW WORLD

The Jews of New Amsterdam, while yet petitioning for rights of domicile and trade, established a congregation, 'Shearith Israel', in 1655. A century later, the Newport, Rhode Island, Jewish community of some fifteen persons, turned to the established New York congregation for help in erecting its own synagogue. The beautiful building, now a national shrine, still stands in that seaport city. By the end of the Colonial period congregations had been established in New York; Newport; Philadelphia and Lancaster, Pennsylvania; Richmond, Virginia; Charleston, South Carolina; and Savannah, Georgia. Religious functionaries were imported, trained and maintained. Kosher meat was provided, burial grounds were consecrated, marriages solemnized. All things considered, there was a flourishing religious life in Colonial America, including the publication of the prayer-book in an English translation by Isaac Pinto in 1766 in New York.

Jewish religious development was fostered in the general atmosphere of Colonial America, where religion pervaded all of life. Many of the colonies were founded by religious groups, some for religious purposes.

A busy street on the old East Side. The pushcart was the open-air store of the Lower East Side of New York. This district was the first area of residence for most East European Jewish immigrants, who were poor and skilled in no craft. Because many of them had been petty traders at home, they carried on the same type of business in New York. American Jewish Archives.

There were, then, observant Jews and those who had thrown off the 'yoke of Commandments'. In formal public manner the faith was maintained. Congregations were organized, synagogues built, boys circumcised. The early minute books of New York's Congregation 'Shearith Israel' give evidence of serious and far-reaching congregational activities. At the same time we derive a picture of waning personal religious observance. Public religious institutions were founded and maintained but personal piety fell victim to the atmosphere of the free frontier which was Colonial America.

Immigrants. A New York East Side street scene. The order of economic ascent for many Jewish merchants was from peddler to pushcart to store to department store. American Jewish Archives.

Although Jews most often married other Jews, intermarriage was common, if officially condemned. The necessities of life made it acceptable in deed if not formally approved by the community. There was considerable social integration in the frontier communities and Jews became, through marriage, members of some of America's socially elite families. Most often it was a choice between religious loyalty and bachelorhood as against the married bliss that an intermarriage promised. Many remained Jews, some practicing, participating Jews in their lifetime, but their children entered the majority society.

IN THE EARLY REPUBLIC

The *Savannah Republican* of April 21 1820 reports:

> 'On Wednesday the Grand Lodge of Georgia, and the subordinate Lodges of this city, assembled in Solomon's room, for the purpose of making the necessary arrangements for the laying of the cornerstone of a Hebrew Synagogue, about to be erected in this city.'

The assembly then proceeded to consecrate the ground and lay the stone. After an 'Anthem from a band of music', Thomas P. Charlton, Grand Master of Georgia spoke:

> 'This ceremony is a beautiful illustration of our happy, tolerant and free government. Everyone here is permitted to adore the eternal after the dictates of his conscience...'

The erection of a synagogue became an event of public celebration. The synagogue, as it were, gave to the Jewish community a place of worth and equality in the general community. The Constitution guaranteed freedom of religion for all. The Jew, whose history taught him to cherish rights more than most, accepted this right as a mandate. The American Jew established and maintained a synagogue in answer to his spiritual needs as a Jew. He also did so as an American, for a synagogue was also part of the American religious landscape.

In Colonial America religion held sway. Toward the latter part of the 18th century deism and atheism gained acceptance and respectability. The decades which followed the American Revolution saw a vast decline in the prestige of the religious establishment and in the place of religion in the life of the people. But in the early 19th century there was a great religious revival throughout the country. De Tocqueville was struck by the vast power religion had over the lives of the American people. Churches were built and filled. Religious concerns like salvation, the state of one's soul, the power of grace, the need of baptism were topics of conversation and controversy. The clergy was esteemed, and newspapers, magazines and countless books and pamphlets recorded their words and views. Laws were enacted to preserve the sanctity of the Sabbath. Religion was a chief American concern.

The Jews could not help being influenced by this atmosphere. Believers founded congregations and erected synagogues for their own spiritual needs; nonbelievers helped maintain them because it was the American thing to do. In city after city, a small group of Jews would establish the Jewish community by

Immigrants and immigration. The view of the Statue of Liberty in New York harbor brought a surge of hope for a new life to some two million Jewish immigrants, arriving mostly from Eastern Europe following pogroms and anti-Semitic persecutions in their countries of origin. American Jewish Archives.

organizing a congregation. Mrs. L. Maria Child writes in her *Letters From New York* (New York and Boston, 1843):

> 'Last week (September 1841) a new synagogue was consecrated in Attorney Street, making, I believe, five Jewish synagogues in this city, comprising in all about ten thousand of this ancient people. The congregation of the new synagogue are German emigrants, driven from Bavaria, the duchy of Baden, and other lands by oppressive laws. One of these laws forbade Jews to marry; and among the emigrants were many betrothed couples, who married as soon as they landed on our shores... If not as "rich as Jews", they are now most of them doing well in the world, and one of the first proofs they gave of prosperity, was the erection of a place of worship.'

The Touro Synagogue, Newport, 1763. An architectural masterpiece, the Touro synagogue of Newport, Rhode Island, has been designated a national shrine. The building was consecrated in 1763, and its architect was Peter Harrison. American Jewish Historical Society.

An event of prime significance to Jewish religious life was the founding of the Reformed Society of Israelites in Charleston, South Carolina, in 1825 'for promoting true principles of Judaism according to its purity and spirit'. Five years later it published its own prayer-book. Isaac Harby, the moving spirit of the Society, describes its purposes in the *North American Review,* 1826:

> 'The principal points aimed at by the reformers, are order and decency in worship, harmony and beauty in chanting, the inculcation of morality and charitable sentiments upon individuals, and the promotion of piety toward the Deity. In these things, the Society believes, consist religion, virtue, and happiness; in these, the salvation of every rational and immortal being.'

The Society did not long survive Harby's departure from Charleston. Thus ended a native American attempt to establish Reform Judaism. In retrospect, the Society did triumph when Beth Elohim, the mother congregation from which its adherents had seceded and which they later rejoined, itself became a Reform congregation.

Viable Reform Judaism was an importation from Germany. The American atmosphere was hospitable to it and it flourished on American soil as nowhere else in the world. Reform had its American beginnings in the religious societies Emanuel in New York and Har Sinai in Baltimore, organized by German immigrants in the early 1840s. The Baltimore congregation brought to its pulpit the eminent rabbi, David Einhorn, whose ideology dominated American Reform Judaism throughout the 19th century. In 1846 a young Hebrew teacher from Bohemia, Isaac Mayer Wise, arrived in America and began a rabbinical career which in time bestowed upon him the deserved tribute of 'architect and builder of Reform Judaism in America'.

The traditional forces were not idle. In 1826, the first prayer-book with English translation was published in America. The Hebrew text was 'Carefully Revised and Corrected by E.S. Lazarus and Translated into English from the Hebrew by Solomon Henry Jackson.' Both were American Jews. A decade later Isaac Leeser translated and published the Daily, Sabbath and Holy Days and Festivals Prayer-book in six volumes; the Pentateuch with translation in 1845, and a *Book of Daily Prayers... according to the custom of the German and Polish Jews* in 1848.

It should also be recorded that in 1840 the first ordained rabbi to serve in America, Abraham Rice, arrived in Baltimore where for many years he was a spokesman for Orthodox Judaism.

TRADITIONALISTS AND REFORMERS

The growing self-awareness of mid-nineteenth century America had its Jewish expression in the desire to establish an American Judaism. Its chief exponents were Isaac Leeser and Isaac Mayer Wise. The former, a German immigrant who became *hazzan*-minister of Sephardi congregations in America, was a traditionalist and expressed his 'Americanism' by introducing the English sermon and inspiring the first Sunday school. He had faith that America would be hospitable to a traditionally religious and highly cultured Jewish community, if only the Jews willed it and matched will with enterprise and accomplishment. He set out to establish the institutions which would fashion such a community.

Isaac Mayer Wise, an enormously energetic and optimistic newcomer from Bohemia, believed that Judaism would in time become the religion of enlightened modern man. But first it had to be modernized and democratized, or better still, 'Americanized'. He thus became the exponent of a moderate pragmatic Reform Judaism, based on the pressures and practicalities of modern, democratic living. Thus for example, the prayer-book which he prepared and vigorously promoted was a modified traditional order of services with Hebrew text and facing German or English translations. Modernity ordered the elimination of hopes for the restoration of sacrifices. References to a Messiah

The Touro synagogue, Newport, 18th century. The interior of the same synagogue as above, built in 1763, as it looks today. The design of this interior is reminiscent of the Sephardi synagogue in Amsterdam. American Jewish Historical Society.

and return to a homeland were eliminated, for America was Zion, 'Washington our Jerusalem'. Appropriately, he titled this prayer-book, *Minhag America* (The American Rite).

Overriding any individual differences and preferences was the conviction that American Jewry needed unity, and American Judaism, some kind of central authority. Reform and Traditionalist elements were brought together at a conference convened in Cleveland in 1855. Unity demanded compromise. Leeser's compromise consisted in attending a conference planned and dominated by Reform Jews; Wise's in accepting the Talmud as the authoritative interpretation of the Bible.

The conference did not lead to unity. It strengthened division and led to subdivision. Leeser and Wise dissolved their 'partnership' with recriminations which grew progressively more acrimonious as the years went on. The Reform group of the East, led by Rabbi David Einhorn of Baltimore, attacked the conference and dissociated itself from the Reform movement of Wise, rejecting it as puerile and retrograde, and accusing its chief proponent of opportunism. The rift between the moderate, practical Reform of the West and the radical, ideological Reform of the East divided the movement for three decades. Whatever chance Leeser had of giving leadership to, or exerting influence on, the East European Orthodox immigrant, he lost by consorting with the enemy, Reform.

In Philadelphia in the late 1860s, Reform and Traditionalist elements each marshaled their forces and undertook enterprises which would foster their interests. Isaac Leeser, supported by the Board of Delegates of American Israelites and the Hebrew Education Society of Philadelphia, organized and served as provost of Maimonides College, the first Jewish seminary in America. It opened its doors to four students in 1867 and died for lack of support four years later. In an attempt to heal the rift between the Reform parties of East and West, a conference was called in November 1869. It was convened and dominated by the triumvirate of the East: Rabbis David Einhorn and Samuel Hirsch of Philadelphia and Samuel Adler of New York. Wise and Max Lilienthal came from Cincinnati. A set of principles prepared by Einhorn was accepted. The conference concluded, the rabbis went their separate ways, having failed to bring their points of view any closer.

Religious practice and ideology were being fashioned not in conferences or seminaries, but in the individual congregations. The congregations of Colonial America were all Sephardi and continued their distinctive ritual even after a majority of their membership was Ashkenazi. The new immigrants from Western and Eastern Europe alike were pleased and proud to become associated with the existing Spanish-Portuguese synagogues, which in their eyes had the twin virtue of being 'native American' and aristocratic to boot. Not until the beginning of the 19th century was the first Ashkenazi synagogue founded, Rodeph Shalom of Philadelphia; and it was only in 1825 that a group of English Jews left Shearith Israel to organize B'nai Jeshurun in New York. With increased immigration, congregations proliferated. By 1860 there were perhaps two hundred congregations, permanent and temporary (meeting for the High Holy Days only), in more than one hundred cities and towns. There were the old Sephardi synagogues, traditional synagogues of the Western European type, and Reform congregations. The first East European synagogue, the Beth Hamidrash, was founded in New York in 1852. A contemporary report in *The Occident* states:

'Its founders were few, and they established it in poverty... in affliction, deprivation and straightness they watched over its early rise... Now (1857) it is supported by about eighty men in Israel...'

As a typical East European synagogue:

'It is open all the day... There is daily a portion of the law expounded publicly... every evening, when the people rest from their daily task... there are persons who study the law

Hebrew synagogue, Charleston, South Carolina, 18th century. Founded in 1795, the Hebrew synagogue was designed by Solomon Carvalho. Owing to the town's liberal constitution, Charleston in South Carolina became a leading Jewish community in the US through the first quarter of the 19th century. The synagogue was destroyed by fire in 1838. American Jewish Historical Society.

Rebecca Gratz (1781-1869), by Thomas Sully. Rebecca Gratz was a noted and beloved member of the Philadelphia Jewish community through the first half of the 19th century, and is said to have been the prototype for Scott's characterization of Rebecca in *Ivanhoe*. She is credited with having founded the first Jewish Sunday school. American Jewish Historical Society.

for themselves, either in pairs or singly... it is filled with all sorts of holy books... on Sabbaths and festivals, in the evening and morning... the house is full to overflowing...'

Even on the remotest frontier, Jews gathered for prayer. In *The Occident* of December 22 1859 is the report:

'...In this town and county of San Diego, there number some twelve or fourteen Israelites. These scattered few of God's chosen people agreed to unite in the observance of the sacred festival of the New Year, as well as in the solemnities of the Day of Atonement... On the eve of that memorable day, a worthy citizen, named M. Manasse, journeyed fifty miles to be with us, and complete the number designated and requisite to form a congregation.'

A small number of the congregations were served by rabbis, many of them former teachers or minor religious functionaries, who, in the freedom of America, took the liberty of conferring ordination upon themselves; and some added the degree and title 'Dr.' as well. Wise, whom we have already met, Lilienthal and Rice came to America to seek opportunity to serve. Others, like David Einhorn, Samuel Adler, and Benjamin Szold, were brought by their congregations. The desirability of American-

born and American-trained rabbis was felt by thoughtful and concerned leaders of the community. Simon Tuska, a graduate of the university of Rochester, went to Breslau in 1858 to study in its seminary. Temple Emanuel sent some young men to Germany for rabbinic training. Of these, Bernard Drachman returned to serve as an Orthodox rabbi, and Felix Adler to found the Ethical Culture movement. The first viable seminary was established by that master builder, Isaac M. Wise. He first fashioned a lay organization, the Union of American Hebrew Congregations, as a base for support, in 1873.

The 'Call for Convention' which called the Union into being stated its purpose:

'To establish a Jewish Theological Institute... in order that some of our youth, conversant with the language of the land, should be educated for the Jewish ministry...'

'On the third of October 1875, the college was formally and solemnly opened in the city of Cincinnati...,' the college's president, Isaac M. Wise, reported. 'The class consists of seventeen students...,' he continued, one being a college freshman, thirteen high school students, three due to enter high school. 'Twelve of these students are American-born and five European.'

The American Jewish community was beginning to stabilize its institutions and to establish its own forms of religious education.

ORTHODOX, CONSERVATIVE, REFORM

'Perhaps one third of the Jews in the United States are still Orthodox, another third neglect religion except on the greatest days of the religious year... another third are in various stages of Reform...,' wrote James Parton in 1870. The East European immigration which followed added to the first two groups, and introduced a new phenomenon in Jewish religious life in America: the active anti-religionists. The latter, consisting of Socialists, anarchists and a variety of freethinkers, launched all manner of anti-religious projects. Periodicals in Yiddish and Hebrew (such as *HoEmes,* edited by Chaim Enowitz) launched regular and sustained attacks, and books and pamphlets were published to argue the falsity of religious doctrine and to portray organized religion as a retrograde, reactionary force. Religious laws and customs were scoffed at and religious leaders attacked in spoken and written word. Perhaps the most dramatic anti-religious projects were the *Yom Kippur* balls, held on *Kol Nidre* night, 'to eat, drink and make merry,' while other Jews were observing the day in prayer and fasting.

Within organized religious life there was heightened strife and contention which led to the current divisions into Orthodox, Conservative and Reform. To be sure, there were those who pleaded for one uniform American Judaism. Jacob Goldman, who had traveled widely in the United States, argued in his *The Voice of Truth* (Philadelphia, 1870):

'The *Jehudim* of the different parts of Europe, etc. have brought into this country their different *minhagim*... Our Rabbis, D.D.'s, Reverends, Preachers... are holding on to

The Hebrew Purim Ball at the Academy of Music, New York, 1865. The Purim Ball illustrated was held in New York on March 14 1865. Charity balls were popular in mid-nineteenth-century America. The Hebrew Purim Ball was a highlight of the New York Jewish social season. One of the guests has come disguised as a *Hanukkah* top or *dreidel*. American Jewish Historical Society.

their various *minhagim*... In the name of God, in the name of all Israelites whose hearts are still accessible... in the name of all Jewish American citizens, prepare... a code of *minhagim* common to all, and to be adopted by all of us survivors of the year 1870! Look upon our posterity! They are no longer Polander, German, Russian, English, Portuguese; they are Americans, and will and can have nothing more useful than "a *minhag* of America"...'

The Union of American Hebrew Congregations established in 1873 and its Hebrew Union College, founded two years later, were intended to serve all of American Israel. Indeed, the traditionalist Sabato Morais, minister of the Mikveh Israel Congregation of Philadelphia, served as a college examiner. But the issues which divided American Jewry were stronger than the wish to establish an American Judaism. Which prayer-book was to be used for an 'American Judaism': the traditional, the moderate reform *Minhag America* of Isaac Mayer Wise, or the radical

Olat Tamid of David Einhorn? An increasing number of leading congregations were holding their main religious service of the week on Sunday morning. Others denounced this as the rankest apostasy. There were those who were most meticulous in their observance of the laws of *Kashrut,* while others termed it a remnant of an ancient barbaric cult and poked fun at 'kitchen Judaism'. Some congregations left the Union (now becoming more pronouncedly Reform) on this issue. The conflict came to a dramatic head at the banquet celebrating the First Commencement of the Hebrew Union College in 1884. The first course served caused the observant Jews present to leave the dinner and the movement. Visible insult had been added to the long-standing verbal attack on Jewish traditional usage. Such disparity of views on religion, law and custom inevitably led to division.

The break was long in the making. For three decades there had been division between Reform Jews and Traditionalists.

Within the group there was further division, between moderate and radical reform, and between West European and East European traditionalists. The ever-increasing immigration of Jews from Eastern Europe caused a restructuring: the Reform groups drew closer to one another in their desire for separation from the new immigrants. It has been suggested that radical reform gained the victory over moderate reform, because the 'native' Jew was convinced that its form of religious life and worship would keep the new immigrant out of the Temple.

All the elements of Reform Judaism joined in a conference held in Pittsburgh in November 1885 'for the purpose of discussing the present state of American Judaism... and of uniting upon... plans and practical measures...' Nineteen rabbis deliberated for three days. Isaac Mayer Wise presided, but the leading spirit was Kaufmann Kohler, a son-in-law of David Einhorn. The radical Reform of Einhorn dominated the proceedings. The eight-point platform was a forthright and succinct statement of an extreme Reform viewpoint on God, the Bible, *Kashrut,* priesthood, nationalism, Jewish mission, immortality, and social justice. It remained the most authoritative statement of Reform Judaism for half a century.

The East European immigration had its effect on the Traditionalist camp as well. The West Europeans were not at ease with the East European Orthodox Jew, and he in turn would

The Temple at Atlanta (exterior). Colonial, Byzantine, Romanesque, Gothic, neo-classical — American synagogical architecture often reflected the architect's and building committee's views of the nature of Judaism. Note here the Ionic portico. American Jewish Archives.

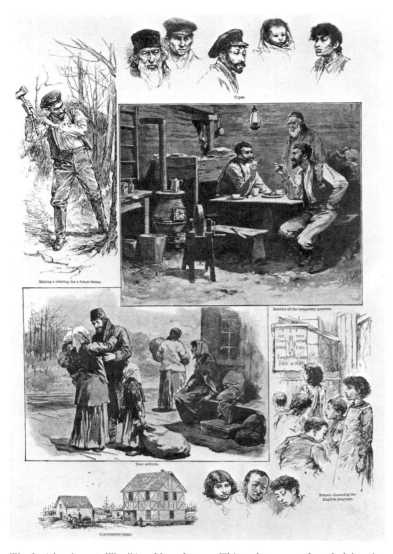

The Jewish colony at Woodbine, New Jersey. This colony was founded by the Baron Hirsch Colony Society. The New Jersey agricultural colonies established by the Baron Hirsch Fund were the most successful Jewish agricultural settlements in America. American Jewish Historical Society.

intelligent Orthodoxy'. This task was to be entrusted to a chief rabbi, who would 'be the leader in the battle which must be waged to keep the next generation faithful to Judaism in spite of the educational, social and business influences, which in America are so powerful as to make our sons and daughters forget their duty to... (their) religion...' Rabbi Jacob Joseph of Vilna came as chief rabbi to a community fired with great hopes and high enthusiasm. It proved to be an ill-fated undertaking in all ways. Ill-conceived and utterly mismanaged, it aroused antagonisms and rivalries in the community and brought personal tragedy to the rabbi. But it also marked Orthodoxy in America as an independent, self-conscious force.

In the three years 1885, 1886 and 1887, three events took place which concretized the division of American religious Jewry into Orthodox, Reform and Conservative movements. Each group had made its decision to strike out on its own, and undertook an endeavor from which there was no turning back. Each enterprise was also in accordance with the nature and particular brand of the movement.

Reform Judaism, which had rejected the binding authority of a received tradition, had to meet in conference and adopt a platform which would state its ideological position and commitment. Orthodoxy, accepting the authority of the received legal tradition, needed a rabbinic figure of such stature as to become accepted as the symbol, transmitter and executor of that authority. The Historical School (called Conservative Judaism), committed to the relevance of the entire Jewish historical experience and the evolutionary character of Jewish Law, established a school for the scientific study of Judaism by its rabbinical students.

The tripartite division of the American Jewish religious community into Orthodox, Reform and Conservative Judaism continued and became formally institutionalized in the 20th century. Each group had its rabbinical seminary, lay and rabbinical organizations. Each movement also underwent change. Reform continued its drift away from tradition for the first two decades of the 20th century. A return to traditionalism then began, at first hardly perceptible, then slowly developing, and finally bursting into great activity in the years which followed World War II. An increasing number of rabbis who were ordained by the Reform seminary, the Hebrew Union College, came from an East European Traditionalist background. A significant number came under the influence of Zionism, which turned their attention and interest to Jewish peoplehood and Jewish culture. This interest became a commitment that they brought to their movement and their individual congregations. A comparison between the Pittsburgh Platform of 1886 and the Columbus Platform of 1936 shows up the new trends in Judaism which transferred the emphasis from the credal formulation to the ongoing historic spiritual experience of the Jewish people. The mass influx of sons and daughters of East European immigrants into the Reform congregations permitted and stimulated a return to traditional forms in the temple and a reintroduction of ritual into the home. The Sabbath eve service on Friday night replaced the Sunday service as the main service of worship. The use of Hebrew in the liturgy increased. *Bar* and *Bat Mitzvah, Kiddush,*

not look for religious leadership to a Sephardi *hazzan,* such as Sabato Morais, or a moderate reformer like Alexander Kohut. The West European traditionalists and the moderate reformers of the 'historical school' (spiritual disciples of Zacharias Frankel, principal of the Jewish Theological Seminary of Breslau), repelled by the ever-increasing radicalism of American Reform, now joined together in common endeavor to found a Jewish Theological Seminary. Its purpose would be to assure 'the preservation in America of the knowledge and practice of historical Judaism as ordained in the Law of Moses and expounded by the prophets and sages of Israel in biblical and talmudical writings...' It began instruction in 1886.

The East European Orthodox Jewish community was growing in size and self-awareness. For a quarter of a century, since 1860, its leading rabbinical figure had been R. Joseph Asch. With his death in 1887, an Association of the American Orthodox Hebrew Congregations was organized 'in order to create an

and even *Havdalah* became part of Reform practice. The formerly proscribed head-covering for men was made optional in many congregations, and some reintroduced a form of the *tallit* for pulpit wear. The return to tradition continued, with committees and commissions now charged with the responsibilities of revitalizing the Sabbath, and preparing new prayer-books and a new *Haggadah,* with all indications that they will be far more traditional in form and content than those currently in use.

Conservative Judaism in the era of Solomon Schechter, 1902-15, was an ideological reaction to Reform. It was a reaffirmation of the autority of Halakhah, as a living, albeit changing, system of laws, usage, customs and traditions. It placed emphasis on the total historic religious experience of the Jewish people, and held

precious all Jewish cultural and spiritual creations. In later decades, it came into competitive confrontation with Orthodoxy. Many Orthodox congregations turned Conservative in the hope of retaining the interest and loyalty of the rising generation. Graduates of the Jewish Theological Seminary founded Conservative congregations which drew their membership from the Orthodox camp.

The Conservative emphasis on Zionism and Jewish culture won for it the adherence of elements of the Jewish community which so far had been content to be accounted part of Orthodoxy. The chief influence on the movement in the years between the wars when it stood in ideological and practical contention with Orthodoxy was Mordecai M. Kaplan, who espoused a liberal

The Temple Ohalei Sholom, Brookline (Mass.). American synagogue architecture followed no single design or pattern. All modes and all styles were reflected in its architecture. American Jewish Archives.

theology, urged a reinterpretation of traditional belief and a reconstruction of traditional forms. His definition of Judaism as a total civilization—'the evolving religious civilization of the Jewish people'—became the basic position of his Reconstructionist movement. In consequence, Jewish culture in its totality, language, literature, art, music were stressed. The synagogue was turned from a House of Worship into a spiritual, cultural, educational, social center for congregation and community.

The earliest experiences of East European Orthodoxy in America were a complete disaster. The immigrant transplanted Old World synagogal forms to the New World. They answered his own spiritual needs, but could not win the interest or allegiance of his children. The reaction was a withdrawal from the American scene, into self-contained communities and spiritual and cultural isolation. Forward-looking leaders, taking example from the neo-Orthodoxy of Samson Raphael Hirsch of Frankfurt-am-Main, launched an attempt at making the traditional faith at home in the modern world. It took the form of a *yeshivah*-university, where young men would receive modern high school and college training while studying the sacred texts in the traditional manner in an Orthodox religious atmosphere.

The Yeshiva University and Rabbi Isaac Elchanan Theological Seminary has now put forth a generation of rabbis, teachers and lay leaders who have given great vitality to Orthodoxy. Orthodox Jews were to be found on college faculties, in the laboratories and in communal and cultural life. The Orthodox congregations took on new life, though the price has sometimes been the adoption of new forms borrowed from coreligionists on the left: mixed seating, English prayers and readings at services, the *Bat Mitzvah* ceremony and others. In the years since World War II there has been a growth of a re-emphasis on traditionalism in certain sectors of Orthodoxy, occasioned by the immigration of Hasidim from Central Europe, and a new militancy on the part of native-born Orthodox leaders as they stand in con-

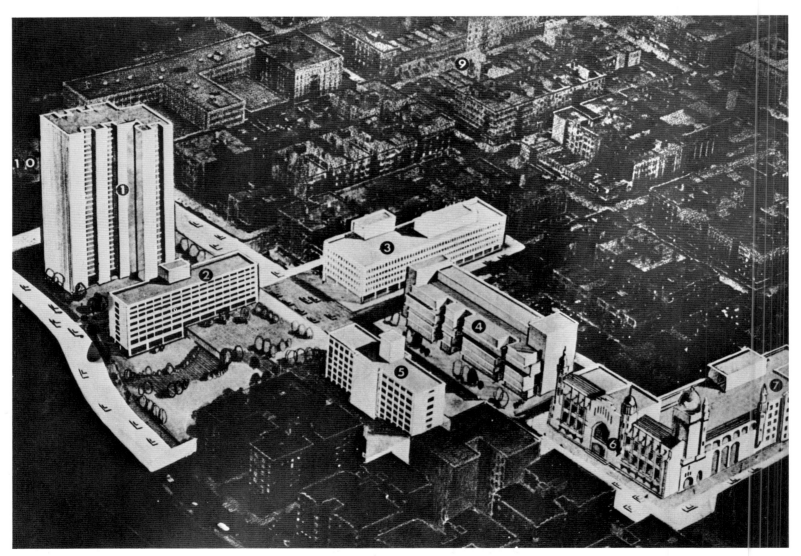

Plan of the main center of Yeshiva University. Yeshiva University, New York City, was the first American University under Jewish auspices. It traces its origins to 1886, before merging and being elevated to a university in 1945. It combines rabbinical and secular studies and among its many branches particularly notable is perhaps the Albert Einstein College of Medicine.

Modern Jewish-American tapestries. Stone, metal, wood, glass, cloth are all used in synagogue art. Samuel Wiener Jr.'s woven tapestries adorn the vestibule of Temple Beth El, South Orange, New Jersey. Hebrew letters and symbols are used: tablets, Torah, *shophar*, star and lyre. *Contemporary Synagogue Art.*

frontation to what they term the 'deviationist' movements of Conservative and Reform Judaism.

In recent decades Reform has been characterized by an attempt to rediscover tradition and to tackle the challenge it presents. The majority of rabbis and laymen are committed to the ever-widening influence of Traditionalism, but a few have sounded the alarm that this is a reactionary and retrogressive tendency. Orthodoxy has discovered the world outside, and most leaders and committed laymen are grappling with its implications and demands—with a small but significant number advocating great caution or actual withdrawal. Conservative Judaism continues to stress the total Jewish civilization, placing its em-

phasis on Jewish cultural creativity, educational enterprise, and communal activity.

The American Jew, having viewed America as a 'melting pot', then as a land of 'cultural pluralism', is now beginning to react to a new image of America: America as a land of 'ethnic assimilation and religious differentiation'. America as a nation demands political unity and civic concern, but it also fosters religious diversity. The Jew, sensing this, has made synagogue affiliation his expression of Jewish association. Salo Baron points out: 'In Western Europe and America, the religious factor has retained its preeminent position in the scale of communal values... the religious congregation has continued to attract the relatively

◄ *Ark*. Wood carving in synagogue art, Temple Israel, Charleston, West Virginia. Milton Horn's door for the Ark of Temple Israel, Charleston, West Virginia. Left: Moses receiving the Torah. Right: Bezalel carving the Cherubim (Exodus 35). Photo Estelle Horn, *Contemporary Synagogue Art*.

most constant and active participation of a large membership... total congregational membership in the United States vastly exceeds, numerically, Jewish membership in purely philanthropic undertakings.'

America considers the Jews to be members of a religious community, a view shared equally by the Jews themselves.

CULTURE AND EDUCATION

In the religious revival which swept through early nineteenth-century America, missionary activity played a central role. There were missionaries to the Indians and missions to the peoples of Asia, Africa, and the Islands. Nor were the Jews forsaken. The 'American Society for Ameliorating the Condition of the Jews' by converting them to Christianity was founded in 1819, when there were hardly three thousand Jews in the country. The next year *Israel Vindicated; Being a Refutation of the Calumnies Propagated Respecting the Jewish Nation: In which the Objects and Views of the American Society for Ameliorating etc... are investigated. By an Israelite* was published in New York.

Congregation Israel, North Shore, Glencoe (Ill.). The graceful, stately, ethereal synagogue that the architect Minoru Yamasaki fashioned of concrete and glass for Congregation Israel, standing on the shores of Lake Michigan in the Chicago suburb of Glencoe. *Contemporary Synagogue Art.*

Menorah. The use of metal in synagogue art. A stylized *menorah* of nickel, silver and steel by Seymour Lipton for Temple Beth El, Gary, Indiana. Photo Oliver Baker, *Contemporary Synagogue Art.*

In 1823 *Israel's Advocate or The Restoration of the Jew Contemplated and Urged,* a missionary journal, began publication. Within a year Samuel H. Jackson began the publication of *The Jew, Being A Defense of Judaism Against All Adversaries and Particularly Against the Insidious Attacks of ISRAEL'S ADVOCATE.*

For two years, this first Jewish periodical in America was published monthly, engaging in vigorous polemic and argument.

The generation of the 1820s through the 1840s had grown up in freedom and seized the opportunities it provided. Jews entered the arts, professions and public service, a few with modest success. Daniel L. M. Peixotto became president of the Medical Society of the City and County of New York, while Dr. Jacob De La Motta served as secretary of the Medical Society of South Carolina. Samuel B. H. Judah and Jonas Phillips were playwrights and literary figures of some distinction. Isaac Harby was a newspaper writer and editor. Naphtali Phillips published *The National Advocate,* edited by Mordecai M. Noah.

Mordecai Manuel Noah was the most fascinating American Jew of the first half of the 19th century. A famed playwright and

a founder of native American drama, he edited a number of newspapers, and attained considerable political influence as a leader of the Tammany Society. He was a man of pronounced opinion and forceful character; he apparently delighted in controversy. His public service included the offices of Surveyor of the port of New York, high sheriff, and consul to Tunis. He was the first to advocate the establishment of a Jewish agricultural settlement and a Jewish college in America and his dedication of Grand Island as a refuge for persecuted Jews is well known. He was indeed a man of many parts.

Rosa Mordecai reminisced about the first Hebrew Sunday School organized by her great aunt, Rebecca Gratz, in 1837:

> 'On the table was a much worn Bible containing both the Old and New Testaments... Watt's Hymns, and a penny contribution box "for the poor of Jerusalem..." The "Scripture Lessons" were taught from a little illustrated work published by the Christian Sunday School Union. Many a long summer's day have I spent pasting pieces of paper over answers unsuitable for Jewish children...'

The Sunday School idea, like its textbooks, was borrowed from the Protestant neighbors and adapted for Jewish use.

In the 1840s and 1850s congregations and individuals opened schools for Jewish children where a full curriculum of general and Jewish subjects was taught. A typical curriculum would include in Hebrew studies: Hebrew reading, translation of the prayers and the Pentateuch, some Hebrew grammar, Jewish religion taught through a Catechism, and biblical history. The secular studies might include: reading, writing, arithmetic, grammar, geography, spelling, composition, rhetoric, music, and language instruction in German or French. The outstanding private all-day schools (which boarded students as well, at a fee of about $200 for board and tuition) were the Misses Palache's school for girls, and Dr. Max Lilienthal's school for boys. Hyman B. Grinstein, in his *The Rise of the Jewish Community in New York,* states:

> 'Lilienthal's students wore a special uniform; they used German and French in everyday conversations... It became the outstanding Jewish school in New York City.'

There was sharp division in the Jewish community on the question of all-day schools. Some maintained that they alone provided an adequate education for the Jewish child. Others opposed them as being separatist and divisive of the community. With the secularization of the free public schools beginning in the late fifties, and the removal of specifically Christian readings and practices from many of them, the enrollment in the all-day schools declined. By the 1860s economics and a desire for full integration had their effect. The Jewish child now received his education in

Mordecai Manuel Noah (1785-1851), by John Wesley Jarvis. Newspaper editor, ▶ playwright, politician, communal leader, Mordecai Manuel Noah was the leading American Jew during the first half of the nineteenth century. He was United States Consul to Tunis 1813-15, sheriff of New York County, and even planned to settle a Jewish city of refuge on the Grand Island in the Niagara River.

Mural. The mosaic mural 'The Call of the Shophar' by Ben Shahn (1898-1969), one of America's leading artists, in the vestibule of the Temple Oheb Sholom, Nashville, Tess. The call of the shophar turns everybody's attention to the *menorah* which is kindled by God's spirit. Ben Shahn was born in Russia and settled in the United States in 1906. Photo Bill Preston.

the public school. Attempts at congregational afternoon and evening schools were, with some notable exceptions, sporadic and haphazard. Some private schools carried on, but Jewish education was and remained at a low level, until the communal institutions and agencies took on the job decades later.

The creation and promotion of Jewish literature in mid-century and in the decades which followed was largely the enterprise of two men, Isaac Leeser and Isaac Mayer Wise. In 1843 Leeser established—and for twenty-five years edited—the first Jewish periodical in America, *The Occident.* (Jackson's *The Jew* had been devoted almost wholly to anti-missionary polemics.) He also prepared and published children's textbooks; translated and published the Sephardi and Ashkenazi prayer-books; translated the Bible into English: organized the first Jewish Publication Society in 1845, which published fourteen little volumes of popular literature as *The Jewish Miscellany* series; and published ten volumes of his own sermons and addresses. Wise founded the weekly, *The Israelite,* in 1854, edited and wrote most of it for many years; a year later he began the publication of *Die Deborah* in German; he wrote historical and polemical works as well as popular novels; he helped establish the first publishing house devoted to Jewish literature, Bloch and Company; and began the practice of publishing the *Annual Proceedings of the Union of American Hebrew Congregations.*

In addition to *The Occident* and *The Israelite,* other papers, the *Asmonean* and *The Jewish Messenger* in New York, *Sinai* in Baltimore, and *The Gleaner* in San Francisco, had readers and influence. The Hebrew and Yiddish press in America began their activity in this period as well. Joshua Falk's *Avnei Yehoshua,* homiletical commentary on the Ethics of the Fathers, the first Hebrew book written and printed in America, was published in 1860. *Shir Zahav Likhvod Yisrael ha-Zaken* (1877) contains three poems in Yiddish, and is therefore acclaimed as the first Yiddish book printed in America.

YIDDISH IN AMERICA

Among the earliest Jews to come to America were Yiddish-speaking Ashkenazim. It is even suggested that the very first Jew to reach the new continent, Jacob Barsimson, was an Ashkenazi Jew. Since Yiddish remained the language of German Jews until the middle of the 19th century, the language was heard already with the arrival of the first Jews.

There are extant a considerable number of Yiddish letters written by and to Jews in Colonial America. The famous Gratz brothers, Bernard and Michael, who lived in Philadelphia in the latter half of the 18th century, wrote in Yiddish, as did their townsman, Jonas Phillips. Yiddish words and phrases dot the correspondence of the New York merchant Uriah Hendricks and the well-known patriot and financier, Haym Salomon.

The first large Jewish immigration wave, in the middle of the 19th century, consisted of residents of towns and villages of the German states, mainly Bavaria. They sought consciously to use the German language and suppress Yiddish, first to establish their credentials as devotees and practitioners of German culture, then in high esteem in America, and later to distinguish themselves and be distinguished by others from the Jewish immigrants from Eastern Europe.

Yiddish cultural activity and creativity in America begins with the first 'wave' of East European immigrants who came in the wake of the Polish uprising of 1863.

THE YIDDISH PRESS

Interest in the Franco-Prussian War of 1870 and the Russo-Turkish War in 1877 became the impetus for the establishment of the Yiddish press in America. The lithographed *Yiddische Zeitung* began to appear in 1870, and *Die Post* a year later. A half-dozen years later the *Israelitische Presse* of Chicago began its brief career. The language of the early press was a Germanized Yiddish; their social view, conservative, and favorable to religion. Their existence was precarious, their appearance, weekly, monthly or 'on occasion'.

Ezekiel Sarasohn, who with his father Kasriel Zvi Sarasohn established the Yiddish press on a firm foundation, described their early struggles:

Park synagogue, Cleveland (Ohio). The Park Synagogue of Cleveland, Ohio, by the German architect, Eric Mendelsohn (1887-1953), opened a new and exciting chapter in American synagogue architecture. It welded building with landscape and placed a house of worship in a park setting. Mendelsohn was a noted architect in Germany before having to leave when the Nazis came to power. After a spell in England and Palestine, he settled in the United States. Photo Hastings and Willinger, *Contemporary Synagogue Art.*

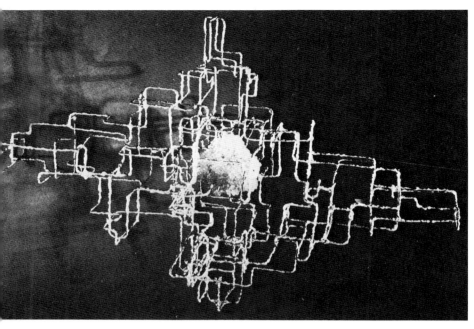

Eternal light. The architect, Percival Goodman, was a pioneer in commissioning works by contemporary artists for his synagogue buildings. Ibram Lassaw's Eternal Light of bronze and calcite crystal (hung before the Ark of the Law) is in the Beth El Synagogue, Springfield, Mass. *Contemporary Synagogue Art.*

'Most Polish and Lithuanian Jews came from small towns. The older ones among them did not have the slightest need for a newspaper... The younger ones, those who had some education, read German newspapers and gradually English newspapers... The very young were ashamed of a newspaper with Hebrew characters.'

The East European immigration, which was but a trickle in the 1870s, turned into a stream in the 1880s as a result of the restrictive May Laws. It enabled the Sarasohns to establish the daily *Yiddisches Tageblatt* in 1885, which attained wide readership and influence and was published till 1928 when it merged with the *Morgen-Journal.* The newspapers of the day were also journals of opinion. The *Tageblatt* represented the Orthodox viewpoint; its competitors, *Der Volksadvocat* and *Die Volkzeitung* were critical of the religious 'establishment'. The *New Yorker Yiddische Folkzeitung* attempted to speak for both Socialism and the nascent Jewish nationalism represented by the *Hibbat Zion* movement. Morris Rosenfeld, the 'poet of the ghetto', began his literary career in this paper in 1886. Indeed, the newspapers were also literary journals and represent the first blossoming of Yiddish literary activity in America. The 1890s saw the beginning of the famed Jewish daily, *Forward (Forverts)* which in time, under the editorship of Abe Cahan, became the largest Yiddish newspaper in the world, and still appears daily. The outstanding Yiddish journal of literature and thought, *Die Zukunft* (still appearing monthly) began its life in 1892. Its most distinguished editor was the poet, Abraham Liessin. The Socialist *Zukunft* was preceded by two years by the anarchist *Freie Arbeter Shtimme,* which also continues to appear.

Periodicals began to proliferate in the early years of the century. In time the leading journals were the *Zukunft,* and Chaim Zhitlowski's literary journal *Dos Naie Leben* (1908). The editorial goal of Liessin for his *Zukunft* reflected the mood of much of the periodical press of the time. The goal of Yiddish literature would be not only 'to combine the pleasant with the useful' but to place before the reader 'the entire radiant world of science and progress, as well as the intellectual world of art and esthetic enjoyment.'

The Yiddish press, dailies and periodicals, attained the widest circulation and greatest influence in the 1920s and 1930s. The 1924 restrictive immigration laws, which brought Jewish immigration to a virtual end, dealt a heavy blow to the Yiddish press. The young American Jew today is no longer ashamed of 'Hebrew characters', but very few are able to read Yiddish.

Today, the *Forverts* appears daily in New York, as does the *Freiheit.* Canada's Jews can read the *Kanader Adler* of Montreal and the Toronto weeklies, *Daily Hebrew Journal* and the *Vochenblatt.* Some two dozen Yiddish periodicals representing a variety of Jewish ideological positions and cultural interests are now published in the United States and Canada.

THE YIDDISH THEATER

Hutchins Hapgood wrote at the turn of the century:

'In the three Yiddish theaters on the Bowery is expressed the world of the Ghetto—that New York City of Russian Jews, large, complex, with a full life and civilization. In the midst of the frivolous Bowery, devoted to tinsel variety shows, 'dive' music halls, fake museums... the theaters of the chosen people alone present the serious as well as the trivial interests of an entire community.'

The Yiddish theater in America had its beginnings in the early 1880s when members of Abraham Goldfaden's troupe arrived as immigrants and presented some of the plays of 'The Father of Yiddish Theater'. In 1891 a gifted playwright, Jacob Gordin, and the leading actor of the Yiddish stage, Jacob P. Adler, joined forces to present the first play 'worthy of serious consideration', *Siberia.* The early theater was dominated by the folk operettas of Goldfaden and by Gordin's serious plays.

The theater began to attract literary figures of high talent who made the Yiddish state a cultural force in the Jewish community. Among them were Leon Kobrin who wrote realistic plays on American themes; and David Pinsky whose plays expressed his Labor Zionist orientation, a passion for social justice and a love for the Jewish people. The works of Sholem Aleichem and Isaac L. Peretz attracted large audiences. Outstandingly popular were

The Asmonean, 1849. Volume I, No. 1, page 1 of *The Asmonean,* appeared on October 2 1849. The periodical press of nineteenth century America was greatly enriched by *The Asmonean* of New York which was its first weekly and was founded by Robert Lyon. American Jewish Historical Society.

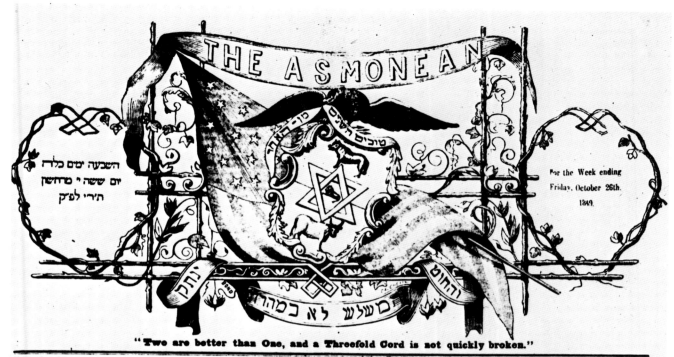

THE ASMONEAN

For the Week ending Friday, October 26th. 1849.

"Two are better than One, and a Threefold Cord is not quickly broken."

VOL. I.—No. 1.   "KNOWLEDGE IS POWER."   { ROBERT LYON, PUBLISHER, 140 Nassau St., New York. }

The Asmonean

HAS THE PATRONAGE AND SUPPORT OF THE MINISTERS AND PRESIDING OFFICERS OF THE FOLLOWING CONGREGATIONS IN THE CITY OF NEW YORK:

שארית ישראל Crosby St.   בני ישרון Elm Street,
שערי תפלה Wooster St.   אנשי חסד Henry Street,
שער השמם Attorney St.   רודף שלום Attorney St.
שערי צדק White St.   עמנו אל Chrystie Street.
בני ישראל Pearl Street.

Subscribers Names received by the following gentlemen:

NEW YORK.

THE REV. DR. LILLIENTHALL.
THE REV. S. M. ISAACS.
BACH, J. L., 146 William Street.
DITTENHOEFER, I., 44 Beaver Street,
GOLDSMITH, H., 4 West Broadway Place,
HART, H. E., 137 William Street,
HABER, ISAAC, 134 William Street.
ISAACS & SOLOMON, 53 Nassau Street.
LEVY MARK, 49 Maiden Lane.
LEVETT, Dr. M., 628 Broadway.
MAWSON, BROTHERS, 161 Water Street.
MORRISON & LEVY, 134 William Street.
SIMONS, E. & H., 33 Maiden Lane.
SOLOMON & HART, 243 Broadway.
WOOLF, M. 61 Maiden Lane.
WALTER, I. D., 40 Beaver Street.

SYRACUSE.

LEVY SYLVESTER.

PHILADELPHIA.

LYON, SAMUEL, Bookseller, Chestnut Street.
MAWSON, E. S., North Third Street.

ST. LOUIS.

LEVY, LEWIS M.

NEW ORLEANS.

BARNET, MICHAEL, Camp Street,
GOLDSMITH, HABER & CO.
HART, ISAAC.

MOBILE, ALA.

MORRISON, JOS.

☞ Agents are wanted in every City of the Union.

NOTICE.

The Asmonean is sent to various persons not at present on the Subscription List, with a view to canvass for their patronage.

Trustees of Synagogues, Congregational and Society Officers are solicited to lend their co-operation.

Booksellers and Agents will be allowed twenty per cent. on all Subscriptions canvassed for and remitted.

Agents are wanted in all sections.

TO OUR SUBSCRIBERS.

In the circular announcing our intention to publish this Journal, we set forth that the Asmonean would be devoted to the advocacy of a congregational Union of the Israelites of the United States, and the general dissemination of information relating to the people. That its columns would be open to all and every communication appertaining to our Societies, our Congregations, our Literature, and our Religion. That all Foreign and Domestic News would be collected up to the latest moment prior to going to press, and that all matters of public interest, would be temperately commented on. At the commencement of our labors, we deem it necessary to repeat this statement, in order that there may be no misconception of the purpose and intention of the proprietors of this Journal. Emanating from a zealous desire to incite the cultivation of a *Unity of action* between the learned and the philanthropic of Israel, and of diffusing amongst our brethren, a better knowledge of the principles of the Jewish Faith, the paper comes into existence perfectly unfettered and unpledged. Free from the trammels of the schools of casuistry, we are disposed to act according to the maxims of our sages דרוש וקבל שכר "Investigate and acquire merit," this we hope to do soberly and humbly, craving at the hands of our co-religionists, who are better qualified, every aid and assistance which it is in the power of eminent talent to grant to those less gifted than themselves, for it is the duty of all Israelites to further every undertaking having a tendency to dissipate existing prejudices, and induce a better understanding of the true interests of Israel as a religious brotherhood. What is the value of ambition which seeks distinctions in the pursuits of commerce, the labors of the bar, or the senate, compared with that which seeks the elevation not merely of the individual, but of the Jewish people! "No man can hope to attain eminence as a Jew, or glory in remaining one, until he has done his share in removing the prejudices of darker times." It is with these sentiments, and not in a spirit of arrogance, that we have assumed the grave responsibility of directors of a public Journal. As journalists, we may lack experience, but we are not deficient of zeal in our desire of preserving our national integrity, and averting the curse of infidelity from our people.

Our arrangements for obtaining intelligence respecting country congregations are at present incomplete. We shall at the earliest moment appoint correspondents in every section of the States, and by the exercise of unremitting enterprise, make our paper the means of concentrating the energies and resources of the believers in Israel.

Whenever the subscription list of the Journal warrants it, or the demands of our Advertisers encroach on our Columns, we will increase the size of our paper. Correspondence from all parts of America and Europe relating to our people, may be transmitted at the Editors charge. Communications appertaining to private interests must necessarily be post-paid.

SPEEDY JUSTICE.

Our State Legislature with a host of legal empyrics, have been for many sessions, the former actively, the latter for themselves, profitably employed in pruning and training, extirpating and replanting the prolific vine called the CODE, exhibiting at various times certain portions as plants of extraordinary vigour, capable of resisting the insidious action of the many caterpillars crawling about the Courts, and of affording shelter and protection when necessary, yet, were a stranger to enter several of the Courts, and observe the mode in which the business is conducted, he would conclude that *speedy justice* was a term without meaning, and that there were many places to dispel *ennui* in the city, besides those enumerated in the published lists of amusements of the day. The San Francisco method, with its rough and ready call on the posse commitatus, its instanter election of judges, and impanneling of juries, with all the passions strong upon them, is far better worthy of adoption than New York's retinue of enquiring justices, investigating and petty juries, and sentencing judges; if the proceedings upon all the late trials of importance are to be considered fair specimens of the administration of justice. Witness the late reports of the mode of obtaining a juror in the cause of the people against Judson and others. Now, was it possible to find a citizen with a gleam of intelligence beyond a beast of burthen, who had not heard of the Astor Place disturbance, of the slaughter of many persons on the eventful night in May, yet the admission of such knowledge, made by calling things by their proper term, and a public tumult is a riot, if riot have any meaning, was held to be a ground of incompetency in a juryman, and in the case of the people against John Price, for the murder of G. W. Campbell, at Baltimore, where the Court decided that no man who had read the accounts of the murder as published in the newspapers, could be competent to sit as a juror, as his reading must have created an impression of the guilt of the prisoner, and therefore, after calling 500 talesmen, and spending three days at an enormous expense to the county, they were obliged to remand the prisoner, and change the venue.

We will suppose, (which was the fact) a man to be found dead, under such circumstances as leave no doubt that his death proceeded from the violence of others, would a man be morally incompetent to sit as a juror, because a grand jury had returned a true bill, or the proposed juryman had read an account of the murder, and believed that it had been perpetrated. What has his reading to do with the evidence to be offered in the case, for on that, and that only, is the verdict to be founded. We refrain from offering all that occurs to us upon the ruling of the judges in these cases, but we cannot resist calling the judges attention to the fact, that many of the decisions tend to lower public estimation of common law instead of the legal authorities we instance one point which strikes us as particularly rich. In re Judson, "The court suggested to the triers

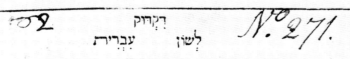

DICKDOOK LESHON GNEBREET.

A

GRAMMAR

OF THE

𝕳𝖊𝖇𝖗𝖊𝖜 𝕿𝖔𝖓𝖌𝖚𝖊,

BEING

An ESSAY

To bring the 𝕳𝖊𝖇𝖗𝖊𝖜 𝕲𝖗𝖆𝖒𝖒𝖆𝖗 into 𝕰𝖓𝖌𝖑𝖎𝖘𝖍,

to Facilitate the

INSTRUCTION

Of all thofe who are defirous of acquiring a clear Idea of this

Primitive Tongue

by their own Studies ;

In order to their more diftinct Acquaintance with the SACRED ORACLES of
the Old Teftament, according to the Original.   And

Publifhed more efpecially for the Ufe of the STUDENTS of *HARVARD-COLLEGE*
at *Cambridge*, in NEW-ENGLAND.

נֶחְבַּר וְהוּגַת בְּעִיּוּן נִמְרָץ עַל יְדֵי
יְהוּדָה מוֹנִישׁ

Compofed and accurately Corrected,

By J U D A H   M O N I S,   M. A.

B O S T O N, N.E.

Printed by JONAS GREEN, and are to be Sold by the AUTHOR
at his Houfe in *Cambridge*.   MDCCXXXV.

The first Hebrew grammar in America, 1735. There was great interest in early Jewish history and in the Hebrew language in Colonial America during the first decades of the 19th century and many editions of Josephus and Hebrew grammars were published: Judah Monis' was the first to appear in America. Judah Monis was probably born in Algiers and left for New York in 1716 and Boston in 1720. He was instructor in Hebrew at Harvard until 1760. American Jewish Historical Society.

a staff of distinguished scholars and has an enviable list of scholarly publications in the field of Jewish history and language study. It carries on the great scholarly tradition begun by YIVO in Vilna. In a sense it is a symbol of the transplanting of Yiddish culture from the Old World to the New.

HEBREW LITERARY CREATIVITY

The typesetter of the above-mentioned little Hebrew volume *Avnei Yehoshua*, which was published in New York in 1860, recorded the historic importance of this publication:

'I give thanks that it is my good fortune to be the typesetter for this scholarly book, the first of its kind in America...'

To be sure, books in Hebrew had appeared in America since 1735 when Judah Monis published his *A Grammar of the Hebrew Tongue... for the Use of the STUDENTS of HARVARD-COLLEGE at Cambridge, in NEW-ENGLAND*. Those which followed were grammars, lexicons, prayer-books, and editions of classic texts. Many were meant for Christian divines and their more scholarly congregants.

The first printing of the prayer-book in Hebrew occurred in 1826, 'The Hebrew Text carefully Revised and Corrected by E. S. Lazarus'. A decade later Isaac Leeser began the publication of his six-volume edition of *The Form of Prayer According to the Custom of the Spanish and Portuguese Jews* (Philadelphia 1837-8), with his own translation into English. He did the same for the Ashkenazi prayer-book in 1848. A number of editions of the traditional *Siddur* and the holiday *Mahzorim* were put out by the publisher and printer W. L. Frank of New York.

Various Reform prayer-books appeared in the mid-19th century, containing more or less Hebrew. *Minhag America* (1857) of Isaac M. Wise; *The Order of Prayer* (1855) by L. Merzbacher; *Olat Tamid* (1858) of David Einhorn, and a series of prayer-books by Benjamin Szold (beginning in 1861) were the best known and most widely used.

The first Hebrew Bible in America was published in Philadelphia in 1814. With a Latin introduction and notes and with vowel points it was intended for the Christian Bible student and reader. The subsequent edition in 1848 already took the Jewish reader into account for it boasted the editorial supervision of Isaac Leeser. Three years earlier Leeser put out a Pentateuch for Jewish congregational use with Hebrew text and his own English translation.

Beginning with the 1860s, contributions by American Jews began to appear in European Hebrew periodicals. The *Ha-Maggid* (published in Lyck) of 1864, for example, contains reports and articles from San Francisco, St Louis, Detroit, Chicago and New York.

The second and third Hebrew books published in America were of greater interest and significance than the first, for they dealt with the American-Jewish scene. *Emek Rephaim* (1865) by M. E. Holzman is a vigorous and at times vitriolic attack against American Reform rabbis, notably Max Lilienthal and Isaac M. Wise. 'A sect has arisen in Israel who attempt to form a code of worship... men who call themselves Doctors, and who are in fact destroyers of all that is sacred.' *Tuv Taani* (1875) by Aaron Zevi Friedman was a 'vindication of the Jewish mode of slaughtering animals for food called *Shechitah*.' It was in response to an accusation by the Society for the Prevention of Cruelty to Animals that the Jewish method of slaughtering was 'cruelty, needlessly inflicted'.

the dramas of Sholem Asch. The best products of European dramatists were also adapted for the Yiddish stage.

The stars of the Yiddish stage were the cultural heroes of the ghetto and each had his adherents and advocates who formed loyal, spirited, partisan claques.

In 1918 there were twenty-four Yiddish theaters in America, no less than eleven in New York City. Maurice Schwartz, through his Yiddish Art Theater, brought the Jewish stage to its triumphant heights. He gathered about him a gifted group, but it was his vision, enterprise and will that welded the Yiddish Art Theater into one of the greatest of repertory companies. From this group Muni Weisenfreind went on to become an outstanding movie star under the name of Paul Muni, and Joseph Bulow to be a prominent actor of the American stage.

Of the beloved stars of the Yiddish theater perhaps none had more devoted 'fans' than Boris Tomashefsky, the idol of the working girl, and Molly Picon, the *gamine* musical comedy star.

The theater reached its heights in the 1920s and early thirties. Its decline since has been rapid, although there has been a limited revived interest in the Yiddish stage in recent years.

YIDDISH POETS AND NOVELISTS

American Yiddish poetry had its origins in complaint and protest. The immigrant's golden dreams turned to bitter dross when he reached the shores of the Promised Land. Freedom and wealth were the promise America held out; reality offered a dingy tenement, back-breaking sweatshop labor, a grinding poverty which enslaved body and soul. Morris Rosenfeld expressed the plight and plaint of the immigrant in a series of simple, sentimental, bitter poems like the descriptive *I Am a Millionaire of Tears,* and *My Little Boy* which became the anthem of the sweatshop worker. 'I have a little boy... who is my whole life... but seldom, seldom do I see him... I leave for work when he's still asleep... and return from my labor after he's gone to bed...' His songs of immigrant life became the folksong of the immigrant. A contemporary, David Edelstadt, was the poet of angry protests and cry of rebellion. He died at at tender age of the immigrant affliction, tuberculosis. Morris Winchefsky's poetic cry is classic: 'You can kill only our body, our flesh, but not our holy spirit.'

The most gifted of American Jewish poets was Yehoash (Solomon Bloomgarden). His poetry, universal in theme, draws upon Jewish sources and uses Jewish images. A man of spiritual tendency, his poems breathe deep national feelings and some rise to psalm-like feeling and expression. His major life's work was the translation of the Bible into Yiddish 'in a style that purified and enriched the Yiddish language itself.'

Die Yunge was a name given to a group of writers whose work began to appear before World War I. One of the group, Joseph

◄ *The Jewish press in America,* 1917-18. A montage of banners of the Jewish press of New York City—Yiddish, English, Ladino and Hebrew newspapers and periodicals—which was the most widely varied in the world. American Jewish Historical Society.

Title page of Yiddish translation of Bible by Yehoash, 1941. One of the great works of literary scholarship in America was the translation of the Bible by the American Jewish poet Yehoash (Solomon Bloomgarten) into a poetic and contemporary Yiddish. Yiddish was the major language among the Jews of America up to World War I, but its use has been declining since. American Jewish Historical Society.

Opatoshu, described its creed: 'Yiddish literature ceased to be an educational tool and became an end in itself. It assumed artistic standards...' It was a kind of 'art for art's sake' movement, and the poets and writers turned from themes of tears and struggle, of social protest and upheaval, in toward impressionism, mysticism, individualism.

The famed and beloved Sholem Aleichem spent his last years in America and incorporated his views and experiences in his works. Sholem Asch lived for many years in America and wrote of American Jewish life. Israel Singer was a novelist and playwright of rare power. His brother, Isaac Bashevis Singer, writes in Yiddish, though he has attained his fame through English translations. Hayyim Grade is considered the outstanding Yiddish novelist today.

Yiddish scholarship is fostered by YIVO, the Yiddish Scientific Institute, which boasts an outstanding library and archives. It has

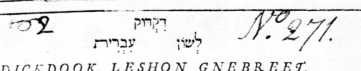

DICKDOOK LESHON GNEBREET.

A

GRAMMAR

OF THE

Hebrew Tongue,

BEING

An ESSAY

To bring the Hebrew Grammar into English,

to Facilitate the

INSTRUCTION

Of all thofe who are defirous of acquiring a clear Idea of this

Primitive Tongue

by their own Studies ;

In order to their more diftinct Acquaintance with the SACRED ORACLES of the Old Teftament, according to the Original. And

Publifhed more efpecially for the Ufe of the STUDENTS of *HARVARD-COLLEGE* at *Cambridge*, in NEW-ENGLAND.

נֶחְבַּר וְהוּגַת בְּעִיוּן נִמְרָץ עַל יְדֵי
יְהוּדָה מוֹנִיש

Compofed and accurately Corrected,

By JUDAH MONIS, M. A.

BOSTON, N. E.

Printed by JONAS GREEN, and are to be Sold by the AUTHOR at his Houfe in *Cambridge*. MDCCXXXV.

The first Hebrew grammar in America, 1735. There was great interest in early Jewish history and in the Hebrew language in Colonial America during the first decades of the 19th century and many editions of Josephus and Hebrew grammars were published: Judah Monis' was the first to appear in America. Judah Monis was probably born in Algiers and left for New York in 1716 and Boston in 1720. He was instructor in Hebrew at Harvard until 1760. American Jewish Historical Society.

a staff of distinguished scholars and has an enviable list of scholarly publications in the field of Jewish history and language study. It carries on the great scholarly tradition begun by YIVO in Vilna. In a sense it is a symbol of the transplanting of Yiddish culture from the Old World to the New.

The typesetter of the above-mentioned little Hebrew volume *Avnei Yehoshua,* which was published in New York in 1860, recorded the historic importance of this publication:

'I give thanks that it is my good fortune to be the typesetter for this scholarly book, the first of its kind in America...'

To be sure, books in Hebrew had appeared in America since 1735 when Judah Monis published his *A Grammar of the Hebrew Tongue... for the Use of the STUDENTS of HARVARD-COLLEGE at Cambridge, in NEW-ENGLAND*. Those which followed were grammars, lexicons, prayer-books, and editions of classic texts. Many were meant for Christian divines and their more scholarly congregants.

The first printing of the prayer-book in Hebrew occurred in 1826, 'The Hebrew Text carefully Revised and Corrected by E. S. Lazarus'. A decade later Isaac Leeser began the publication of his six-volume edition of *The Form of Prayer According to the Custom of the Spanish and Portuguese Jews* (Philadelphia 1837-8), with his own translation into English. He did the same for the Ashkenazi prayer-book in 1848. A number of editions of the traditional *Siddur* and the holiday *Mahzorim* were put out by the publisher and printer W. L. Frank of New York.

Various Reform prayer-books appeared in the mid-19th century, containing more or less Hebrew. *Minhag America* (1857) of Isaac M. Wise; *The Order of Prayer* (1855) by L. Merzbacher; *Olat Tamid* (1858) of David Einhorn, and a series of prayer-books by Benjamin Szold (beginning in 1861) were the best known and most widely used.

The first Hebrew Bible in America was published in Philadelphia in 1814. With a Latin introduction and notes and with vowel points it was intended for the Christian Bible student and reader. The subsequent edition in 1848 already took the Jewish reader into account for it boasted the editorial supervision of Isaac Leeser. Three years earlier Leeser put out a Pentateuch for Jewish congregational use with Hebrew text and his own English translation.

Beginning with the 1860s, contributions by American Jews began to appear in European Hebrew periodicals. The *Ha-Maggid* (published in Lyck) of 1864, for example, contains reports and articles from San Francisco, St Louis, Detroit, Chicago and New York.

The second and third Hebrew books published in America were of greater interest and significance than the first, for they dealt with the American-Jewish scene. *Emek Rephaim* (1865) by M. E. Holzman is a vigorous and at times vitriolic attack against American Reform rabbis, notably Max Lilienthal and Isaac M. Wise. 'A sect has arisen in Israel who attempt to form a code of worship... men who call themselves Doctors, and who are in fact destroyers of all that is sacred.' *Tuv Taani* (1875) by Aaron Zevi Friedman was a 'vindication of the Jewish mode of slaughtering animals for food called *Shechitah*.' It was in response to an accusation by the Society for the Prevention of Cruelty to Animals that the Jewish method of slaughtering was 'cruelty, needlessly inflicted'.

In the wake of the abortive Polish uprising of 1863 an immigration from Eastern Europe began. Though small in number, it brought to America readers of Hebrew and some Hebrew writers. Among these was Zvi Hirsch Bernstein, a pioneer of both the Yiddish and Hebrew press in America. In 1871 and for some five years he published the first Hebrew newspaper, *Ha-Zofeh ba-Arez ha-Chadashah*. The periodical served the new immigrants as a tie to the Old World, and helped introduce them to the New. Thus, for example, the reader became acquainted with Henry Wadsworth Longfellow, whose poem *Excelsior* was translated by Henry Gersoni.

The second East European immigration, that of the 1880s, produced a Hebrew reading public of such size as to encourage the establishment of three Hebrew weeklies in New York. Michael L. Rodkinson, who later translated the Talmud into English, published *Ha-Kol*; Ephraim Deinard, bibliographer and polemicist, whose bibliographical acumen and enterprise helped establish the major Jewish libraries in America, put out thirty-two issues of *Ha-Leumi*; and Wolf Schur began the publication of *Ha-Pisgah*. The last-named continued his publication efforts in Chicago, Boston and Baltimore, undaunted by financial difficulties and undiscouraged by indifference and rebuff. He was active in promoting early Zionism and combating assimilatory tendencies in American Jewish life.

The Society for the Advancement of Hebrew Literature in America published the Hebrew literary monthly, *Ner Ma-aravi* (1895-7). The Society's president was K. Z. Sarasohn, who established the first successful Yiddish daily in America; its treasurer was J. D. Eisenstein, author, anthologist, and encyclopedist, whose ten volume *Ozar Yisrael* encyclopedia in Hebrew is a landmark of Jewish scholarship in America.

The new century witnessed a rebirth of Hebrew literary creativity in America. The annual East European Jewish immigration, which had numbered in the thousands, now was counted in the hundred thousands. Among them were men of literary achievement and enterprise. The new Hebrew literary society bore the name of *Mefizei Sfat Ever* (Disseminators of the Hebrew Language). The mood was more optimistic, the goal more elevated, not merely to preserve a bit of Hebrew, but to establish Hebrew creativity. In 1909 and again in 1913 a Hebrew daily, appropriately titled *Ha-Yom* ("The Day"), was launched. Though short-lived, it is evidence of the mood of optimism.

The young Hebrew writers were in and of America. They received their general cultural education in America. In turn, many took American themes for their poetry. The first among them was Benjamin N. Silkiner, who in 1910 published an epic poem of Indian life, *Mul Ohel Timorah* (Facing Timorah's Tent). Ephraim E. Lisitsky's *Medurot Doakhot* (Dying Campfires) deals with the same theme. The American Negro as well as the Indian provided Lisitsky with material. Negro folklore and the suffering of the American Negro is found in his *Be'Ohalei Kush* (In Negro Tents). The poet and philosopher Israel Efros writes of the tragedy of the Red Indian and treated another American theme, the California gold rush, in an epic poem *Zahav* (Gold). In the writings of Simon Ginsburg, Hillel Bavli, Simon Halkin we find

American themes; the last-named translated Walt Whitman's *Leaves of Grass*. As an indication of how much at home they felt in America and how much they appreciated the English language and its literature, Silkiner, Lisitsky, Efros, Bavli, and Halkin each undertook to translate plays of Shakespeare.

Why the preoccupation with the experience of the American Indian and Negro? The poets express a sense of identification of the American Jew fighting for spiritual survival on American soil with the plight of the Indian who struggled to preserve life on his soil and the Negro struggling to preserve a sense of proud identity. The fine student of Hebrew literary creativity in America, Jacob Kabaloff, states:

'They felt at home in the natural beauties of America and in its literature. And they wished to transmit their appreciation of the American spirit as their contribution to modern Hebrew letters. In so doing, they helped free American

Hatzofeh B'Eretz Hachadashah, 1871. The first page of *Hatzofeh B'eretz Hachadashah*, appearing on June 11 1871. It was the first Hebrew periodical founded in America, and edited by Tzevi Hirsch Bernstein. The Hebrew periodical press reached its height in the 1920s, and the number of periodicals and readers has been declining since. American Jewish Historical Society.

Hebrew writing from the dominance of the Russian Jewish center and to give it character of its own.'

The leading Hebrew periodical in America today is the weekly, *Hadoar*. For many years it was edited by Menahem Ribalow who made it the central organ of American Jewish literature. He added supplements for the younger readers, edited the annual *Sepher Hashanah Li-Yhudei Amerika*, and founded the *Ogen* publishing house. The central body promoting Hebrew culture and literature is the *Histadrut Ivrit* (Organization for Hebrew Culture). The *Massad* Hebrew summer camps inspired the Hebraically-oriented Ramah camps of the Conservative Movement and Camps Yavneh and Sharon.

The cultural dependency of American Jewry on Europe came to an end with the Holocaust. The establishment of the State of Israel has revived interest in the Hebrew language. Israelis who have settled in the United States brought the Hebrew language with them and many serve as its most zealous advocates. The growth of the day school movement is producing a goodly number of Hebrew-reading and Hebrew-speaking American Jews. The increasing number of American Jewish youth who visit Israel, and students who spend a year or more there, are all sources of encouragement to those who espouse Hebrew cultural creativity in America.

The American Jewish community must look to its own resources for its spiritual life even though it can receive inspiration and strength from the cultural forces and institutions in the State of Israel. In the end, however, it is a question of will and enterprise in the American community. In the field of Hebrew cultural and literary creativity, American Jewry can look to a past of achievement but a future of uncertainty.

SCHOLARS AND SCHOLARSHIP

In 1901 a work which boasted of itself that 'for the first time the claims to recognition of a whole race and its ancient religion are put forth in a form approaching completeness,' was published in New York City. The boast was not an overstatement, for the twelve-volume *Jewish Encyclopedia* remains a landmark of Jewish scholarship. It speaks well of the state of Jewish scholarship in America at the turn of the century that it felt secure enough to undertake as monumental a project as the first Jewish encyclopedia. It speaks well, too, of the cultural interest of the Jewish community that the publishing firm Funk & Wagnalls had sufficient confidence in it to sponsor the venture.

The preparation and publication of the Encyclopedia stimulated scholarly activity in America and turned the attention of world Jewish scholarship to America. Though leading Jewish scholars of the world were joined in the enterprise, the great bulk of the work fell on American Jewish scholars. To be sure, almost all of these were European-born and European-trained, but it is important to note that scholarship accompanied Jewish immigration to the New World.

On the editorial board one finds such names as Cyrus Adler, American-born, first recipient of a doctorate in Semitics in America, an important scholar, who in a distinguished career in service of American Jewry, served as president of both Dropsie College and The Jewish Theological Seminary of America; Richard Gottheil, Professor of Semitic Languages, Columbia University, and President of the Federation of American Zionists; Marcus Jastrow, distinguished rabbi and author of the ever-useful and scholarly *A Dictionary of the Targumim, the Talmud Babli and Yerushalmi, and the Midrashic Literature* (1886-1903); and Kaufmann Kohler, later to serve as president of the Hebrew Union College, whose works on various aspects of Jewish thought and theology are lasting contributions to the field.

The youngest member on the editorial board was Louis Ginzberg who in the next half-century became the acknowledged leader of American Jewish scholarship. Trained in the *yeshivot* of Eastern Europe and in German universities, he became a master in virtually every area of Jewish learning. His *The Legends of the Jews* brings the reader a multi-volume collection of the *aggadic* material on biblical personalities and incidents. He brought to his studies of law, liturgy, ritual and custom, not only full knowledge of Jewish sources but a mastery of cognate material and disciplines. The three-volume *Perushim ve-Hiddushim bi-Yerushalmi* (A Commentary on the Jerusalem Talmud) deals only with the first four chapters of the tractate *Berakhot*, but in so broad a manner as to constitute a work on Jewish law, theology, history and culture.

A year after the publication of the *Encyclopedia*, Solomon Schechter was brought from Cambridge University to head the Jewish Theological Seminary. A scholar in theology, *aggadah* and liturgy, and a scholarly popularizer, he became a masterly statesman of scholarship. He brought to the faculty of the Seminary a body of scholars unsurpassed by any institution of Jewish learning. Chief among them was the aforementioned Louis Ginzberg. His colleagues were Alexander Marx, historian and bibliographer, who made the Seminary library the greatest repository of books and manuscripts ever assembled; Israel Friedlaender, scholar of the Bible and Judeo-Arabic, whose untimely martyr's death while on a mission to Eastern Europe brought to an end a career of infinite promise; Israel Davidson whose *Otzar ha-Shirah ra-ha-Piyyut* (Thesaurus of Medieval Hebrew Poetry, four volumes, 1924-33) is the basic work of medieval Hebrew poetry and liturgy; and Mordecai M. Kaplan, American-trained rabbi, educator, theologian, and religious leader, who has been the single most important influence on American Jewish religious life and thought. His emphasis on the total Jewish cultural experience as the necessary spiritual expression of Judaism, his radical theology and his espousal of Zionism and Jewish cultural activity and creativity have had wide influence beyond the Reconstructionist Movement which he founded and heads.

The faculty of the Seminary has continued in this distinguished tradition. Louis Finkelstein has made distinguished contributions to the field of Rabbinics; Professor H. L. Ginsberg and Robert Gordis are biblical scholars of note; Shalom Spiegel has continued the faculty's contributions to medieval Hebrew literature; Abraham Joshua Heschel, scion of Hasidic aristocracy, by birth and spirit, is the most widely read and highly regarded Jewish theologian in America. The faculty is headed by Professor Saul

Lieberman. His works on the Palestinian Talmud, the *Tosefta,* and the influence of the Hellenistic civilization on Jewish life and thought in talmudic times, mark him as the preeminent scholar of Rabbinics in the world today.

In 1917, the Jewish Publication Society issued a new translation of the Bible done by a group of American Jewish scholars. Although the preface states that the board of editors contained 'an equal representation of the Jewish Theological Seminary... the Hebrew Union College... and Dropsie College...,' most of the translations were done by men associated with the Hebrew Union College.

The College's faculty has made a signal contribution to Jewish scholarship. Jacob Z. Lauterbach wrote with authority on the talmudic age; David Neumark's has been a distinguished contribution to the history of Jewish philosophy; Max L. Margolis, Julian Morgenstern and Harry M. Orlinsky have enriched biblical study; Jacob R. Marcus has done pioneering work in American Jewish history and founded and heads the American Jewish Archives; the president of the College, Nelson Glueck, was a distinguished archaeologist.

Talmudical study and scholarship in the East European tradition is carried on in the third great institution of higher Jewish learning, Yeshiva University. Its most influential faculty member is Dr. Joseph B. Soloveitchik, scion of a distinguished family of talmudic scholars, who is a world-renowned authority on Jewish Law and philosophy. Dr. Bernard Revel, its first president, succeeded in fashioning a school which blended sacred and secular studies. Under the imaginative and energetic leadership of his successor, Dr. Samuel Belkin, it has branched out into a multi-school institution, ranging from high school through medical school.

Scholars of originality and accomplishment have abounded. Brilliant linguistic insight and daring conjecture mark the wotk of the biblical scholar, Arnold B. Ehrlich, author of *Mikra ki-Peshuto* (The Bible in its Plain Meaning). Originality and daring is also the hallmark of the historian, Solomon Zeitlin, of Dropsie University, the Philadelphia institution for graduate studies in Hebrew and cognate subjects. One must also mention Alexander Kohut's monumental *Aruch Hashhalem*, completed in America, as well as Meyer Waxman's five-volume *History of Jewish Literature*, and Menahem M. Kasher's twenty-volume compendium of *midrashim* on the Bible, *Torah Shelemah.*

Two universities, Harvard and Columbia, have made great contributions to Jewish scholarship through their eminent faculty members: Harry A. Wolfson and Salo W. Baron. Wolfson undertook a rewriting of Western philosophy. He presents Philo as the seminal thinker whose philosophic concerns and concepts dominated European philosophy until Spinoza. Salo W. Baron is a preeminent historian, who has mastered the entire Jewish historical experience. He sees Jewish history against the background and in the setting of world history. His three-volume *The Jewish Community* is the first study of the Jewish community as an institution considered chronologically and topically. He attributes its viability to its ability to accommodate itself to new political conditions and social challenges, while remaining steadfast in its values and preserving its inner patterns. *A Social and Religious History* (now fourteen volumes up to 1650) is a complete reassessment of Jewish history stressing its uniqueness in its emphasis on social patterns and relationships, and spiritual goals. Baron's influence is exerted not only through the written word but also through the works of many young historians who trained under him.

It should be noted that American Jewry and its institutions of higher learning are now producing its own scholars. Professors of various aspects of Jewish studies, born and trained in America, now grace the faculties of such leading universities as Harvard, Yale, Chicago, California, Pennsylvania, Brown, Brandeis, and Columbia as well as the Jewish institutions of higher learning. There is a justifiable mood of optimism about the future of Jewish scholarship in America.

EDUCATION IN THE AMERICAN SETTING

The history of American Jewish education is one of the accommodation of traditional Jewish forms to the needs of the American scene. In broad terms, this means that the strong influence of individual congregations in the United States has had some effect on weakening the community structure of traditional Jewish education.

Democracy itself can be responsible both for strengthening and weakening an educational program. To the extent that democratization means lack of centralization, educational programs in the United States tend to be directed by the local community, or in the case of religious education, by the local parish or congregation. In certain cases this allows for freedom, creativity, and strong educational programs. But just as frequently this lack of centralization can be the cause of low standards and indeed a complete breakdown in educational programming.

Programs of Jewish education can come under various forms of sponsorship. In certain countries the organized Jewish community has taken on this responsibility. In others there is an arrangement or accommodation with the public school system whereby funds are chaneled into Jewish-sponsored and Jewish-oriented schools. In America Jewish education is largely congregation-oriented.

The American environment encouraged the growth of congregations. Indeed, early American public education was largely parochial, that is, church or parish sponsored. Jews followed suit and the early congregations were quick to organize such services as cemeteries and schools that had till then been communal. These were all-day schools where the student was exposed to the whole gamut of curricular interests, secular as well as religious. In the mid-19th century, Jewish boys and girls also received their total education in private all-day schools conducted by rabbis and Jewish 'educators'.

With the expansion of the American community in the second half of the 19th century, public education gained a foothold and was rapidly dissociated from the churches. The early synagogue-sponsored Jewish schools and the private schools began to dissolve as Jews sent their children to the nascent public school system. As the free and universal public school grew to dominate the American scene, Jews began to conduct their programs of Jewish education in supplementary fashion with children attending either congregational or community-sponsored religious schools on Sunday morning and/or on weekday afternoons after public school. A small minority of Jewish parents rejected this arrangement and sent their children to all-day Jewish schools, the first of which was the Yeshivat Etz Haim, established in 1886.

It was the supplementary type school, most notably the afternoon religious school, which gained the strongest foothold in the United States during the late 19th and early 20th centuries. Initially, these schools, the Talmud Torahs, were sponsored by communities. However as the national religious movements grew, Reform, Conservative and Orthodox synagogues established their own schools. During the fifty years from World War I to the present, the sponsorship of Jewish education changed radically from approximately 90 per cent of schools under communal organization to the same percentage today being under congregational sponsorship.

One of the effects of this has been to create a large number of small and unviable school units. While there may be as many as two thousand different Jewish schools in the United States today, the great majority of them are quite small with enrollments ranging from thirty to a hundred. There are, however, a significant number of large congregational schools, with adequate funds and enrollments of above five hundred.

Following the end of World War II there has been a significant rise in enrollments in Jewish all-day schools. Previously they had tended to be concentrated in the greater New York area and attracted children only from Orthodox homes. Currently enrollment in day schools is well in excess of fifty thousand pupils. Almost one in every ten Jewish students enrolled in any sort of Jewish school is enrolled in a day school. The figure is even higher in the large metropolitan areas where the motivation for day-school enrollment is not only religious or cultural, but results from the difficulties facing the urban public school systems.

Almost half of the Jewish school population at any one time is enrolled in Sunday school programs. These are deemed inadequate by all three religious movements. The Conservative movement has all but eliminated the Sunday school for the middle grades. The greatest strength of the Sunday school lies in the Reform movement. Reform congregations however are more and more turning to the afternoon supplementary school which is strongest in the Conservative movement. Orthodox weekday afternoon education has been weakened to some extent by the loss of a considerable number of pupils to the day-school movement. Day schools tend to be community-sponsored or inter-congregational while afternoon and Sunday schools are almost exclusively congregationally oriented.

The curricula of the afternoon schools sponsored by the three movements tend to be remarkably alike and the areas of difference are more structural than ideological. That is, Conservative and Orthodox schools usually require more hours and more years of attendance than Reform congregational schools. The emphasis on Hebrew in each of the schools is considerable, though achievement does not always match emphasis. The greatest level of achievement takes place in the day-school setting both because of the amount of time devoted to Jewish studies during the course of the week and also because pupils tend to react with more seriousness and greater motivation toward a school which is not supplemental to their general schooling.

There are eleven accredited Jewish teacher-training institutions in the United States, which do not, however, graduate sufficient teachers to meet the needs of the schools. Many graduates gravitate to other fields. Some use teacher-training as the first step toward the rabbinate. As often as not, the student of a teacher-training college in the United States is studying simply for the sake of the knowledge gained and has no professional aspirations in the field of Jewish education.

Significant strides have been made in supplementing programs of Jewish education through the use of summer camps. Hebrew is the spoken language of some of these camps and the educational personnel has full control over the atmosphere they establish. Significant numbers of Jewish teenagers and college students visit Israel for short periods and an increasing number study in the various universities in Israel.

Despite many false starts and often blind gropings, significant advance has been made in the field of Jewish education. These have benefited as yet only a small number of Jewish children. Valiant efforts are now being made to make available to significant numbers of American Jewish children the successful educational experiences pioneered and advanced by the progressive day schools and the imaginative supplementary educational endeavors.

In American Literature

'If the statistics are right,' wrote Mark Twain in 1896, 'the Jews constitute but 1 per cent of the human race... Properly the Jew ought hardly to be heard of; but his contributions to the world's list of great names in literature, science, art, music, finance, medicine and abstruse learning are way out of proportion to the weakness of his numbers.'

Nowhere in the Diaspora has the Jewish contribution to general culture been more remarked upon than in twentieth-century America. In the late 1950s and the sixties, Jewish writers were widely considered to form the dominant 'school' in literature and criticism. Any best-seller list throughout this period contained one or more books written by Jews and usually concerning Jews.

This eminence was achieved after the great mass of East European immigrants, or their children, had learned the language and found themselves at home in the new land; and after writers, publishers and the reading public, horrified by the Holocaust and enchanted by the establishment of Israel, found a new interest in Jews as a subject.

In the 19th century the poetry of Emma Lazarus (1849-87) gained depth when she turned from classical themes to her own people's heritage and promise. She spoke of past glories and a restored Zion, urging 'Let but an Ezra rise anew, To lift the banner of the Jew'. It is her verses that are inscribed in the base of the Statue of Liberty, inviting:

'Send these, the homeless, tempest-tost to me.
I lift my lamp beside the golden door.'

'It is from the Russian Jews, who are the mass of poor Jews in America, that the real contribution to American life is likely to come, because their aspirations are spiritual, their imagination alive,' wrote the editor of *Harper's Weekly* in 1916. In 1917 appeared *The Rise of David Levinsky,* the best novel of Abraham Cahan, founder and editor of the influential Jewish Daily *Forward, (Forverts).* This classic describes the coming of the penniless *yeshiva bachur* from the Russian *stetl* to New York in the 1880s, as Abe Cahan himself had come. The book tells of the 'rise' of its hero to multi-millionaire clothing manufacturer, sacrificing along the way the piety, the love of learning, the ideals of social justice, and even the hope for simple family joys that might have been his heritage as a Jew.

The Promised Land was the name given by Mary Antin to the new country, and the title she chose for her paean of praise in 1912 to the freedom of America in contrast to the repressions of the Old World. She decided to discard Jewish ties and assimilate into the beckoning new society.

The lot of the immigrant was treated by others with less starry-eyed optimism. Anzia Yezierska found poverty and near-desperation, as told in *Hungry Hearts* in 1920; yet she was sustained, as she reiterated thirty years later in her autobiographical *Red Ribbon on a White Horse,* by loyalty to Jewish ideals and the hope that America might yet become the golden land of justice the immigrants had envisioned.

Problems and disillusionments of the newcomers, and the defections of the second generation to the ephemeral lures of American society, were treated sympathetically by Myron Brinig in *Singermann* (which takes place in Montana); by Sholem Asch in *East River;* by David Pinski in *The House of Noah Eden,* Charles Reznikoff in *By the Waters of Manhattan,* Louis Zara in *Blessed is the Man.*

Negative aspects of ghetto life, its poverty, narrowness and ugliness, and the purported desperate greed of its offspring, were made much of by writers such as Ben Hecht, Samuel Ornitz, Budd Schulberg, Jerome Weidmann; and by leftist writers of 'proletarian' literature like Michael Gold in the thirties.

The bewilderment of a Jewish immigrant child whose parents were having their own struggle to find their place in the new world is feelingly evoked by Henry Roth in *Call It Sleep.* Terrified by his sordid surroundings and by his paranoiac father, the boy clings to his mother. He almost meets death while striving to find the glory that he has somehow glimpsed as hiding in the heart of the rote Judaism he is being forced to learn at *heder.*

A masterly, panoramic novel of second-generation Jews growing to young adulthood in the Chicago of the thirties is *The Old Bunch,* written by Meyer Levin in 1937. The relationship of child to foreign-born parents, the conflict of traditional ideals with youthful drives for success or freedom, the love of learning and the desire to serve humanity that characterize several of the 'bunch'—all ring true in this superb picture of American life.

That the Jews were not accepted in the American intellectual world until the 1940s was made most clear by the experience and report of Ludwig Lewisohn. This erudite young man found in graduate school in the early part of the century that a Jew had no place on an English department faculty.

'We boast of equality and freedom,' he said bitterly; but the disappointment opened his mind to new self-awareness as a Jew. His novel *The Island Within* and autobiographical works such as *Upstream* tell of the hopelessness of trying to find fulfilment through intermarriage and assimilation. 'To rise from my lack and confusion into a truly human life,' he concluded, 'it was necessary for me to affirm the reintegration of my entire consciousness with the historic and ethnic tradition of which I was a part.' It was as a loyal member of his own group that a Jew could make his greatest contribution to the pluralistic American society.

Most brilliant of the analysts of the place of the Jew in history and in the modern world was Maurice Samuel, who upheld the peculiar virtues of his people with a pride born of deep knowledge. This graduate of Manchester University never ceased educating himself. He taught himself Yiddish so that he could better understand his people's tradition, and became the great popularizer of Peretz *(Prince of the Ghetto)* and Sholem Aleichem *(The World of Sholem Aleichem).* In later years, he taught himself Russian to be able to write profoundly on the Mendel Beilis case in *Blood Accusation.*

With keen insight and mastery of polemic, Maurice Samuel put forth challenging hypotheses. He found, in *The Great Hatred,* the basis for anti-Semitism in amoral man's rage against the group which imposed moral restraints on his pagan passions. Reading *The Gentleman and the Jew* convinces one that the world suffers through its idealization of the Gentleman's role, who fights, kills, and admires power and honor; while the Jewish ideal, that of the peace-loving, moral, cooperative human being, is the one that might yet save the world.

Following World War II, one novel after another dealt with the Jew as pitiable victim of anti-Semitism. Arthur Miller's *Focus* and Laura Hobson's *Gentleman's Agreement* treated the question through gimmicks, in each case having as hero one who is really a Christian mistakenly regarded as a Jew, and who thereby has his eyes opened to the wrongs being perpetrated. Two of the three young men in Irwin Shaw's *The Young Lions* are Jews; Noah, who is a victim of barracks anti-Semitism, has no Jewish background at all, since he has been raised in foster homes. Norman Mailer's powerful novel of the war in the Pacific and the many American types who fought it, *The Naked and the Dead,* contains two Jewish characters, Goldstein and Roth, who are marked only by their 'authentic' and 'unauthentic' acceptances of the predicament of being a Jew.

Portraying the shallowness of upper-middle-class Jews of New York, Herman Wouk in his best-selling *Marjorie Morningstar* shows a college girl pursuing the American dream of stardom and success, but eventually becoming a Westchester matron who sends her children to Hebrew day school. Unlike the more negative writers whose knowledge of Judaism is sketchy, Wouk is a learned and committed Jew, whose *This Is My God* well expresses that commitment.

Charles Angoff's multi-volume saga beginning with *Journey to the Dawn,* of the life of a literate, sensitive American Jew, David Polonsky, is probably the most comprehensive fictional study of American Jewry since the turn of the century. As he describes it, it is 'multi-generation in structure and takes in every aspect of Jewish life in the United States: Americanization, assimilation, Zionism, secularism, the various religious denominations, Jews in industry and the professions, anti-Semitism and intermarriage.'

The Holocaust and the founding of the State of Israel were of course reflected in many of the postwar books. Leon Uris's *Exodus* became a popular source of knowledge about the events leading up to and following the establishment of the state. Meyer Levin wrote *Eva,* about a survivor of Nazi persecution, and *The Stronghold,* about a distinguished group of Europeans and the moral questions that plague them at the time of the Nazi surrender.

The greater literature on the Nazi experience has been written in Yiddish or Hebrew, or one of the European languages. Elie Wiesel, survivor of Auschwitz, whose works are in the main translated from French into English, can be counted among American writers. *Night* is his greatest single statement; while *Dawn, The Accident, The Town Beyond the Wall,* and *The Gates of the Forest* all speak to the conscience of the survivors of Nazism—not only those who were actually in the camps, but all men.

DRAMA AND POETRY

In drama and in poetry, Jews continued in the 20th century to make their contribution. Socially conscious Jewish playwrights of the thirties and forties like Clifford Odets and Elmer Rice showed the shortcomings of American life sometimes through the medium of Jewish characters. Lillian Hellman in a serious vein and such well-known lighter playwrights as Samuel N. Behrman, George S. Kaufman, and Neil Simon were mainstays of Broadway. In musicals, up to the point where Sholem Aleichem's *Tevya* stories became the basis for the smash hit *Fiddler on the Roof* in the sixties, and in the movie and television industries from their very beginnings, Jews have been singularly prominent.

Arthur Miller in the sixties was considered by many the foremost American playwright. His works, such as *Death of a Salesman, All My Sons, The Crucible,* deal not with overtly Jewish characters but with what might be called Judeo-Christian ethical questions of man's duty to family, self and society.

Poets of earlier stock, such as Louis Untermeyer and Babette Deutsch, both known also as critics and anthologizers, contributed much to American poetry in the first half of the century. After World War II, others rose into prominence. Karl Shapiro, champion of a more humane and emotional style against the leading

Saul Bellow (1915-). Saul Bellow is an outstanding representative of a group of Jewish novelists which dominated the American literary scene in the 1960s. His novels are rich in Jewish themes and expression. American Jewish Archives.

school of 'cerebral' (and often anti-Semitic) poets led by Pound and Eliot, gathered his best works into *Poems of a Jew.* In it he speaks of the Jew as 'man essentially himself, the primitive ego of the human race... absolutely committed to the world.' On the liberation of Israel, he writes, echoing Judah Halevi:

'When I think of the battle for Zion I hear
The drop of chains, the starting forth of feet,
And I remain chained in a Western chair.'

Others whose Jewishness added depth and furnished subject matter for their poetry include Howard Nemerov, Hyam Plutzik, Delmore Schwartz and Muriel Rukeyser, who writes:

'To be a Jew in the twentieth century
Is to be offered a gift. If you refuse,
Wishing to be invisible, you choose
Death of the spirit, the stone insanity.'

Charles Reznikoff wrote lovingly of Judaism in such poetic lines as these in praise of Hebrew:

'*Like Solomon,*
I have married and married the speech of strangers;
None are like you, Shulamite.'

The most brilliant expression of love and understanding of Jewish tradition is that of Abraham M. Klein, a Canadian, whose masterpiece of prose-poetry, *The Second Scroll,* sums up the entire range of Jewish history, wandering, suffering, longing and glory. A brief love poem reads:

'*How shall I cherish thee?*
How shall I praise
Thee, make thee lovelier than is the case?
One does not don phylacteries
On Sabbath days.'

The leader of a cult of outspoken, free-living 'beat' poets of the fifties and sixties, many of them young Jews, is Allen Ginsberg. His howls against society's infringement on the individual soul include *Kaddish,* an unmodulated lament for the warping of his youth by the presence of his psychotic mother.

With the coming into dominance of the 'Jewish school' in American literature in the 1950s, the number of writers' names becomes overwhelming. Jewish critics also multiplied in numbers and in influence. Norman Podhoretz (editor of *Commentary,* the monthly sponsored by the American Jewish Committee), Leslie Fiedler, Irving Howe, Alfred Kazin and Theodore Solotaroff were among the leading arbiters of literary taste.

Isaac Bashevis Singer, like Sholem Asch before him, is a Yiddish writer living in New York, who, in translation, has been adopted as a favorite by the American reading public. Singer's *The Slave,* telling of a survivor of the Chmielnicki massacres (see chapter on Poland and Russia) and his forbidden love for a Polish woman, is, like his many other works, a haunting tale, emphasizing the mystical and offbeat elements in Jewish folk tradition.

The most revered writer for some years, especially among the young, was John D. Salinger, whose characters in *The Catcher in the Rye* and in the Glass family saga exemplify alienation, sensitivity, and the search for meaning. These characteristics, considered by many to be at least 'half-Jewish' (as are the Glass family), in the nuclear age seem typical of young people.

In his incisive stories collected in *Goodbye, Columbus* and in his novel of academic intermarriage, *Letting Go,* Philip Roth astutely comments on the bourgeois failings, spiritual insufficiency, and loss of identity of the American Jew. Charles Angoff once characterized one type of Jewish novel as being 'racked with self-degradation and obsessed with various aberrations, sexual and otherwise.' Exactly fulfilling this earlier description was Roth's best-selling novel *Portnoy's Complaint.* In its self-pitying ridicule of monstrous Jewish mother and sex-obsessed son, it has been said to 'cap—or put a yarmulke on—the American-Jewish genre.' In the literature of Jewish self-hatred, this can be said to be true.

Often named as the two top Jewish writers in America are Bernard Malamud and Saul Bellow. Both portray modern man seeking fulfilment or salvation. A difference pointed out by Joseph C. Landis is that in Malamud's parables, 'reluctant, less-than-ordinary men, seeking only to survive, unlikely candidates for moral greatness, grow into heroes that illustrate his theme of the ability of any man to redeem himself by acquiring moral identity,' while 'Bellow's heroes are more often conscious seekers of fulfilment, in essence intellectuals, driven like Henderson by a persistent "I want, I want, I want".'

In Malamud's *The Assistant,* Frank Alpine, amoral drifter, through his association with the good Jewish grocer, rises to the discipline of moral law and becomes a Jew. In *A New Life,* and in many of his short stories, the battered, well-meaning *schlemihl* gains a kind of nobility in failure. *The Fixer* again reveals the pattern: a little man, attacked by fate (the blood accusation against

Norman Mailer (1923-). Novelist, social critic, literary fashion-setter, creator of a new genre in literary expression, Norman Mailer is a major force in the contemporary American literary scene. American Jewish Archives.

Ernest Bloch (1880-1959). Ernest Bloch brought Jewish themes and nuances to his musical compositions in such works as the *Israel* symphony, *America* symphony and the *Shelomoh* rhapsody. His example inspired and encouraged a host of young Jewish composers to do the same. Born in Switzerland, he studied at the Geneva Conservatory in 1911-5. In 1917, he settled in the United States. American Jewish Archives.

Mendel Beilis is the prototype for the plot), gains greatness as he seeks only to survive.

Saul Bellow, better versed in Jewish as well as in general culture than most men, brings vitality and intellectual power to his works. Augie March seeks fulfilment by following adventure wherever it leads him, longing to become a better person than he is; Henderson, the rich and powerful, is driven to darkest Africa to seek purpose.

'The pay-off Jewish novel', as it was called upon its appearance in 1965, is *Herzog,* which details a neurotic, twice-divorced intellectual's musings and searchings as he seeks to improve the world and recapture his identity—finally concluding

that, when there is nothing left to say, the best first step is to set one's own house in order, as well as one can. A later novel of Bellow's, *Mr. Sammler's Planet,* received much critical acclaim and seems to be a more positive statement in Bellow's quest for meaning.

The popular fiction of today has even embraced the rabbi as a protagonist. The writing of Herbert Tarr, Harry Kemelman and Chaim Potok, among others, are entertaining and have given insights into the inner workings of Jewish life in the US. The Jewish contribution to and coloration of the current American literary scene is stated in a lead article in the *New York Times* book review (May 30, 1965), titled 'Some of Our Best Writers':

> 'There seems to be a dominant school at any given time in American fiction: in the 1920s it was realist-naturalist; in the 1930s it was proletarian; in the 1940s and early 1950s it was southern. We live now in the time of Bellow, Malamud, Mailer, Salinger, Roth.'

MUSIC

Music is an integral ingredient of the Jew's life. It accompanies him as he prays, studies, celebrates and mourns. It is therefore not surprising that Jewish music in America is as old as the Jewish community. The chief function of the Sephardi *hazzan* was to chant the service, and services were held as early as 1655.

In the early decades of the 19th century more varied and complex musical activity was begun. In 1818 Shearith Israel of New York, the oldest congregation in America, organized a synagogue choir. The practice quickly spread to New York's other leading congregations, Anshe Chesed and Temple Emmanu-El. By 1849 the choir of Temple Anshe Chesed, under the direction of Cantor Leon Sternberger, was regularly performing the very popular choral synagogue music of Sulzer and Lewandowsky. At a concert given by Temple Emmanu-El in 1853 to raise funds for a new organ a program of sacred music was performed by its choir accompanied by a concert orchestra.

Among the first volumes of Jewish music to be published in America is a work entitled *Principal Melodies of the Synagogue from Ancient Times to the Present.* It was issued by the Jewish Women's Section of the 'Parliament of Religions' held in Chicago in 1893 in conjunction with the Columbian Exposition. Alois Kaiser of Temple Ohev Shalom in Baltimore and William Sparger, of Temple Emmanu-El in New York, two leading cantors of the day, acted as editors for this first attempt to document the development of Jewish music. In addition to the historical material, the volume contains an anthology of the traditional modes, a collection of melodies used on the Sabbaths and festivals, and compositions by a number of European and American composers of the day.

Rimmonim by Myer Myers, 18th century. Myer Myers was a leading silversmith ▶ of Colonial America. The Shearit Israel synagogue of New York and Mikveh Israel of Philadelphia contain examples of his artistry. American Jewish Archives, Courtesy of Mikveh Israel Congregation, Philadelphia.

Torah crown. Ilya Schor recreated the world of East European Jewry in his own stylized fashion. His artistic creations abound with men, women and children of the Hasidic *stetl* (small town). The crown is at the Oheb Sholom Synagogue, Nashville. Photo J.J. Breit, *Contemporary Synagogue Art.*

With the arrival of great numbers of immigrants from Eastern Europe in the late 19th and early 20th centuries, East European *hazzanut,* which had by then reached its pinnacle in Europe, was introduced to America. Many of the cantors who had created the Golden Age of *hazzanut* in Eastern Europe began to find their way to America, and soon after a procession of talented choir directors followed. The cantors and choir directors brought with them the music of the 'old country'. With the exception of the number of hymnals produced for use mainly in Reform congregations, no Jewish music of any consequence was published in America until after World War I.

In the late 1920s a small group of talented composers began to create a new musical literature which reflected the cultural, social and artistic realities of the time. By 1930 the names of Abraham W. Binder, Jacob Beimel, Jacob Weinberg, Herbert Fromm and others were already well known as composers of music for the American synagogues.

The most significant new work to be created for the American synagogue was *Avodat Kodesh* by Ernest Bloch. It was a work for cantor, chorus and orchestra. Ernest Bloch arrived in America in 1916 already established as a composer of first rank. Among his works are the beautiful violin suite, *The Baal Shem Suite,* and the moving *Schelomo,* a Rhapsody for cello and orchestra.

Bloch's contributions were many. He was a particularly gifted composer who was able to combine the nuances of the musical impressionism of the day with the romanticism of an earlier period in an especially appealing amalgam. He was an inspiration to a whole generation of young composers, allowing and even encouraging his Jewishness to permeate all of his creative works. He showed the world that Jewish music could be accepted within the sacred temples of classical music on an equal footing with the music of other peoples.

In the years immediately following World War II such great names in European music as Darius Milhaud and Mario Castelnuovo-Tedesco turned to writing serious Jewish art and synagogue music.

More recently, a crop of young composers has emerged who are as closely related to American cultural life as to the synagogue. One example would be Samuel Adler who occupies the influential chair of composition at the Eastern School of Music and has more than a hundred published compositions to his credit.

While the list of composers who devoted themselves to Jewish creativity is a respectable one, a much larger list of Jewish composers turned their attention to the creation of classical music. Among their works are many on specifically Jewish themes. The multi-talented Leonard Bernstein, for example, created first the *Jeremiah Symphony* followed later on by his massive work, *Kaddish,* and still later by a new setting to a number of psalms entitled the *Chichester Psalms.*

In the performance of music, Jews far outnumber, proportionately, the instrumentalists of any other people. The roster of the leading instrumentalists of the first half of the 20th century is filled with names like Heifetz, Menuhin, Elman, Milstein, Rubinstein, Feuermann, and Stern. A number of great Jewish singers achieved world prominence. Among these are the tenors Jan Peerce and Richard Tucker; the soprano, Roberta Peters, and the baritone, Robert Merrill.

Jews have made a signal contribution to the American musical theater. Jewish names abound among composers of music for the American theater: Leonard Bernstein, Richard Rogers, Irving Berlin, Jerry Herman, Sheldon Harnick are but a few of the most successful. The breakthrough of jazz as a serious musical form was due almost entirely to the genius of George Gershwin who began as an apprentice composer in the Yiddish theater and turned to Broadway's Tin Pan Alley to realize his great musical ambitions. His was the first jazz composition to receive a performance in Carnegie Hall.

One must also add the names of Mark Blitzstein, who achieved fame in the thirties as a composer of music dramas on the social issues of the day; Aaron Copland, whose music for the ballet, opera and symphony hall are among the finest of its kind; Jerome Kern who became one of the masters of the early Broad-

Stained-glass window. Leading American artists received commissions to fashion stained-glass windows, arks, eternal lights, *menorot,* ark curtains and other items for the synagogues built in the post-World War II era. This window by William Gropper is a notable example in the West Suburban Temple, Har Zion, River Forest, Illinois. Photo Gerald Hardy.

Memorial window, 1909. This memorial window was designed by American-born sculptor, Moses Jacob Ezekiel, a leading artist of the 19th century, for the Temple Keneseth Israel, Philadelphia. He studied and had studios in Berlin and Rome. The window was erected in memory of Isaac M. Wise, father of Reform Judaism in the United States. American Jewish Archives.

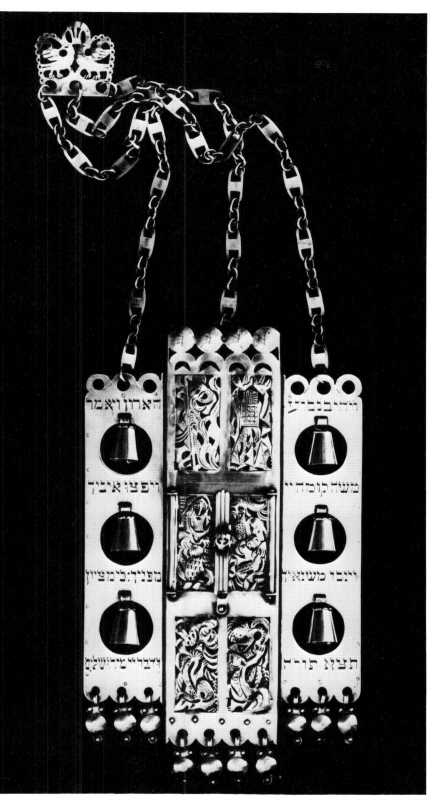

Torah shield. The Torah shield contains the traditional bells. The Hebrew inscription is the words chanted by the congregation as the Torah is taken from the Ark. 'When the ark journeyed ... For out of Zion shall go forth the Law, and the word of the Lord from Jerusalem'. The shield was made by Ilya Schor, the Polish-born artist who settled in the US in 1941 and gained a great reputation for his outstanding work on religious objects made in silver. The shield is in the Temple Beth El, Great Neck, New York. *Contemporary Synagogue Art.*

way musical period; Arnold Schoenberg who revitalized the whole field of musical composition with his twelve-tone scale; and Kurt Weill who came from Nazi Germany to continue a distinguished musical career.

IN ART

Philanthropic patrons of the arts such as the Guggenheim and Lewisohn families have long been well-known in America. In the second half of the century, other Jews have emerged in disproportionately large numbers as benefactors, patrons and fosterers of art in every sizable community throughout the country. The fact that they are particularly known as collectors of modern art may in part be due to the fact that the art of previous centuries has largely been bought up by 'older' families and museums. Openness to new forms, however, seems typical not only of the patrons but also of the many American Jewish artists themselves, whose number increases each year.

Jewish artists born in Eastern Europe and coming to America around the turn of the century, many of them studying for some time in Paris, brought modern European influences with them. Max Weber, whose work included nostalgic and gently humorous evocations of East European life, went from Cubism to what has been called the style of 'New York Expressionism'.

In a more realistic style, tending toward the romantic, the brothers Moses and Raphael Soyer portrayed sympathetic human figures, often scenes of Jewish or immigrant life.

During the Depression and Roosevelt years, Jewish artists, among others, often subsidized by WPA commissions, expressed strong social consciousness through their work. William Gropper, a Marxist from the Lower East Side, used the medium of violent caricature to great effect. Others whose work tends toward caricature and moral comment are Joseph Hirsch and Jack Levine, whose detailed, agitated paintings evoke the effect of hallucination.

The work of many of the artists, while not forming any 'Jewish school', expresses elements of Jewish background, such as the biblical themes of Ben Zion, and the Byzantine or Persian effects of the primitive, Morris Hirschfeld. David Bekker and Hyman Bloom often painted or drew scenes of the *stetl,* or ghetto, as does the younger Leonard Baskin, whose sculptures also continue to explore Jewish themes.

Todros Geller's strong feeling for Jewish culture came into full evidence when he was asked to create synagogue windows and other Jewish functional art. Ben Shahn, basically a lithographer and lover of letters, used his dramatic artistic gifts to further social causes in which he believed, and to add to Jewish ritual art as well.

The Jewish Museum in New York, under the auspices of the Jewish Theological Seminary, with Stephen Kayser as its first director, presents Jewish ritual and historical art, as well as shows of current and often controversial artists.

Jewish sculptors, beginning with Antokolski of Russia, have emerged to prominence in the past century. In America, Moses Jacob Ezekiel, born in Richmond in 1844, was well known in his lifetime as a good portrait sculptor. A large group of American Jewish sculptors were born in Eastern Europe, many of them spending parts of their lives in Rome, Paris or London as well as New York. Enrico Glicenstein's many-sided realistic and expressive talent is seen in wood and terra-cotta moldings and in marble forms, including busts of Rabbi David Einhorn and Lincoln, done in the United States.

William Zorach, master worker in structural forms in stone and wood, living most of his life in Cleveland, taught and influenced a large school, including the outstanding Chaim Gross, Maurice Glickman, Nat Werner, Berta Margoulies, and Minna Harkavy. The 'classic antique' style in American sculpture has been represented by Saul Baizerman and Maurice Stern.

Temple Beth El, Rochester, N.Y. The Temple was designed by Percival Goodman, the leading synagogue architect in the U.S. The ark is of marble from Israel and the stained-glass windows are by Samuel Wiener, Jr. ▶

A leading sculptor, Jacques Lipchitz, whose themes of struggle and emotion are often illustrated through Jewish subjects such as the rebirth of Israel, is said to be the first to translate concepts of abstract painting into sculpture. Jo Davidson, whose activity centered in Paris, sculpted busts of many outstanding personalities.

As revealed in Avram Kampf's *Contemporary Synagogue Art,* congregations in the United States have been attempting to utilize

Temple Mount Sinai (exterior), El Paso (Texas). Architect Sidney Eisenshtat's Temple Mount Sinai, El Paso, Texas, soars out to its desert setting and to the hills beyond. The site becomes an integral part of the artistic expression. Photo Julius Schulman, *Contemporary Synagogue Art.*

◄ *Temple Mount Sinai* (interior), El Paso (Texas). The vaulted ceiling, the white interior, the dominant chandeliers echo El Paso's Spanish-Mexican heritage. The culture of the community is thus incorporated into the structure. Photo Julius Schulman, *Contemporary Synagogue Art.*

contemporary art forms to add to the beauty of their new buildings and to 'awaken an intrinsically religious feeling'. Boris Aronson, Ilya Schor, A. Raymond Katz, Nathaniel Katz, Abraham Rattner and Adolf Gottlieb are a few of the many artists who have designed stained glass and sculpture, doors and pulpits, to aid Jews to 'worship the Lord in the beauty of holiness'.

Jewish architects who have designed synagogue buildings include Erich Mendelsohn, Fritz Nathan and Percival Goodman; of these, Goodman has best achieved total synthesis between art and architecture on the one hand and the specific needs and functions of the sanctuary on the other.

TODAY

The six million Jews in America today constitute 3 per cent of the American population. Almost all live in the large urban centers. They belong almost entirely to the middle class. Increasingly they are concentrated in the professions. Education remains a top priority, with some three out of every four Jews of college age on campus. The dream of the immigrant has been realized. His sons are not in a shop or factory, but in an office or laboratory, his grandchildren in college classrooms. Almost all professions are fully open to the Jew. Settlement houses have become community centers. Synagogues are architectural landmarks on the American landscape and have taken their place in American religious life. The community remains divided into the three religious groupings, Orthodox, Conservative, Reform, but most congregants view these as institutional distinctions rather than as religious schisms. Although there is no overall American Jewish representative body, American Jewry is largely united in sentiment. Common concerns and joint efforts unite, where institutional differences and organizational competitiveness tend to divide.

The American Jew has entered the cultural life in all its aspects, has made important contributions and exerts signal influence. Initially, the Jewish participation and contribution was in the field of entertainment. More recently and increasingly it has been in the arts and literature. Jews are now prominent on university faculties. A good deal of American culture today has taken on a kind of Jewish coloration. Being Jewish is no handicap today in American cultural life or in American life in general. The Jews seem vividly, firmly and permanently incorporated into the American landscape.

But problems there are, and they are serious.

Sociologists point with concern to the low Jewish birthrate, a rate below the survival level. Religious leaders speak with alarm of the rising rate of intermarriage, particularly among the intellectually gifted and the economically favored. Integration is good and desirable. But at what point does integration become assimilation? In sum, the central question facing the American Jew is: can a minority group survive in a free and open democratic society? More pointedly, can Jew and Judaism survive and flourish in America?

The Jew has exerted vast energies and expended great sums in fashioning institutions to assure his survival and foster his faith, but the question of survival nevertheless remains. In a land torn by violence but aware of its potential and its dreams, Jewish survival is bound up with the future of other minorities who seek to flourish in America. The question asked, then, addresses itself not only to the Jew but also to his neighbors.

CHAPTER XII

South and Central America

by Dr. Haïm Avni

While Columbus was busy with the final plans for his voyage to discover the short route to India, the time granted to the Jews by the Spanish monarchs Ferdinand and Isabella to leave their country or convert to Catholicism was also running short. July 31 1492 was the deadline, and after that date those few Jews who had not been baptized or had not yet left were compelled to convert or were forcibly expelled across the border to Portugal. Two days later, on August 2, the ships *Santa Maria, Pinta* and *Niña* set out on their historic voyage.

This proximity of the two sets of circumstances—a catastrophic event in Jewish history, and the beginning of an era in the history of mankind—was not accidental and its consequences for Jewish history were decisive. Whether or not Columbus himself was a Marrano (as has been suggested and quite plausibly argued), there is no doubt that he availed himself of the help of Jews and Marranos within the Spanish royal court and elsewhere, in the preparation and financing of his voyage. We know with certainty of the Jewish identity of at least one member of his crew—Luis de Torres, who converted to Christianity only a few days before the voyage, and whom Columbus took along to serve him as Hebrew and Arabic interpreter once he reached 'the farthest East'. It was the fate of this Jew to be the first Spaniard to disembark on the shores of the New World on October 12 1492, on the island of Guanahani.

Thus new horizons were opened for Spain—as for all of Europe—while new possibilities for evading their plight opened up before those Jews of Spain, who had outwardly converted and had been labeled '*Marranos*' (pigs) by the people. During the first years following the discovery, there were apparently a number of Marranos in the group of Spaniards who reached 'Hispaniola'; the tendency of others to follow in their footsteps is apparent from the decrees forbidding them. Queen Isabella the Catholic's first edict, issued in 1501, forbade the traveling of 'Moors, Jews, heretics, the reconciled, persons recently converted to our Holy Faith.' Even though this edict appeared again after her death in 1508, her husband, Ferdinand, in 1511 permitted 'all natives, neighbors, and residents of these kingdoms who wish to go to pass to the Indies, islands, and land of the oceanic sea'. This permission—whether dictated by the needs of the new colonies or granted in return for high payment—testified to the existence of many 'New Christians' interested in settling in the New World; and even though it was annulled by Charles V in 1518, there was a natural increase in the number of Marranos on the 'Spanish Island' and in other Spanish territories. The prohibition on all Marranos, their sons and their grandchildren, and all those whose blood was not 'clean' of Jewish origin, to go to the colonies was continuously repeated for hundreds of years in the Spanish laws pertaining to the American colonies, but this very repetition in itself demonstrates the inability of the Spanish authorities to prevent the influx of descendants of the 'New Christian' to America, as well as the actual tendency of many of the Marranos to move there.

Thus, in spite of prohibitions, many 'new Christians' went to the Spanish colonies throughout the Colonial period, and there held key posts in all branches of the economy, international trade (which was against the Colonial laws), as well as in administration. A great part of them—but by no means all—secretly kept up Jewish ritual or vestiges of it.

During the same period, a greater Marrano presence grew up in the Portuguese colonies of the New World. We already find the Jew, Gaspar da Gama, in the expedition of the Portuguese discoverer Pedro Alvares Cabral (1500); but here, in the wake of the discovery, came the activity of the 'New Christian' Fernando de Noronha who already in 1502 leased the right to exploit the 'Pau Brasil' (the redwood tree used for dyeing) and to discover and settle the new areas. This commercial operation—behind which apparently stood other 'New Christians'—was carried out against the background of hardship and despair which at that time was the lot of the Jews of Portugal where their hopes of settlement had been cruelly dashed (see chapter on Christian Spain). Fernando de Noronha's enterprise—which continued until 1515 in great areas of the new territories, to which Portugal attached very limited importance—served, for the more daring ones, as a solution to their situation. Others arrived shortly afterward when Portugal began sending people, condemned for various offenses, to Brazil as a land of exile.

In 1533 Portugal decided to consolidate her rule in Brazil and organized it into fifteen *capitanias* ('captaincies') granted to *donatarios* ('donees') who were granted the privilege of developing and settling the areas allotted to each of them. The interest the donees had in increasing the Portuguese population made the continued emigration of 'New Christians' possible; their distance from the center of Portuguese government allowed them to keep up their Jewish traditions relatively undisturbed. This situation did not change essentially when in 1548 Brazil passed over to a more centralized administration under a governor-general whose seat was in Bahia. During this period the Jews helped actively in the development of sugar plantations; they held central positions in trade, import and export, while secretly—but in relative security—practicing their faith. This security came to an end in the last quarter of the 16th century, particularly when Philip II in 1580 forced Portugal to unite with Spain.

THE INQUISITION

In contrast to the Portuguese territories in America, which were secondary in importance, the Spanish territories served as the primary source of wealth for the mother-country, and here the power of the Monarchy and the Church was greater. Catholic priests already accompanied Columbus on his second voyage, and in the first part of the 16th century, as the conquests expanded, the heads of the Church in America were delegated as representatives of the Inquisition. Thus empowered, they already arranged an auto-da-fé in Cuba in 1523, and in 1528 they condemned Hernando Alonso—one of the men of Cortés (the conqueror of New Spain, later Mexico)—to death at the stake. In 1570-1, inquisitional tribunals were established in Mexico and Lima, the capital of Peru, but inquisitorial action was not limited to them; it was based on the cooperation of heads of the local churches, in every town and village of the empire, who were delegated to investigate and report anyone suspected of heresy and Judaism. The result of this system of the Inquisition could be seen in the extent of its control and persecution of 'unbelievers'. Before the end of the 16th century, the courts had judged some of the most notable cases in their history: like that of Luís de Carvajal y de la Cueva—a 'new Christian' who, despite the prohibitions, was the first governor of the 'New Kingdom of León' and who, despite his Jewish origin, remained faithful to Christianity; and especially the case of his nephew, who was intended to succeed him, and who bore the same name, although he called himself Iosef Lumbroso and was faithful to Judaism (1590; 1596).

At the end of the 16th century, the alertness and activity of the Inquisition intensified. One reason for this was the increase in the number of Portuguese Marranos in the Spanish colonies in America as a result of the union with Portugal. In 1610 a High Court of the Inquisition was established in Cartagena (present-day Colombia). In 1631 an inquisitorial decree established a special festive ceremony, to be held once every three years in each city and village, the purpose of which was to strengthen the alertness of the inhabitants in all matters concerning religious deviations, and particularly, signs of Judaism.

The activity of the Spanish Inquisition in America reached its peak during the second quarter of the 17th century, owing to the strengthening of Holland's position in the New World, Portugal's secession from the union with Spain, and the key positions held by many of the Portuguese 'New Christians' in the colonial economy and society. A large group of Marranos—mostly Portuguese—were discovered in Lima in 1634 and the following year. Among them were leading merchants who had agencies and representations in cities throughout the Viceroyalty of Peru. This investigation raised what the historians call the 'Great Complicity' of Peru, ending in one of the most gruesome auto-da-fés. In 1639, eleven people were burnt at the stake, fifty-one were sentenced to lengthy prison terms, and many others imprisoned on suspicion. Because of the economic importance of the condemned and imprisoned, the confiscation of their properties caused a crisis on the money market of Lima until, to save the situation, the Inquisition was forced to release some of the property it had frozen. In the course of investigating the economic ties of the Jews, an additional group of Portuguese Marranos was discovered in Cartagena, and twenty-one suspects were detained, nine of whom were given severe penalties.

Some three years later, the Inquisition won an even greater and more impressive victory, this time in Mexico. About one hundred and ninety suspects fell into its snare; their questioning and punishment continued throughout the 1640s, reaching a climax in a huge auto-da-fé in 1649. Thirteen Marranos were condemned to death, another forty sentenced to prison terms and other heavy 'repentance' sentences. Some fifty suspects who had by then died in the cellars of the Inquisition were judged for their 'sins' together with those prisoners still alive, and their bones were disinterred from their graves and burnt at the stake.

Despite the large number of condemned persons in each of the mass trials, we have no proof of organized Jewish life in the Spanish colonies of America during that period. It is true that the documents of the Inquisition named Manuel Bautista Pérez, who was burnt at the stake in Lima in 1639, as the 'Great Captain' of the Marranos, apparently signifying their spiritual leader. Even though we do not have the details of the trial—which were destroyed in Lima, together with a large part of the archives of the Inquisition—this appellation suggests religious activity which went beyond the narrow confines of the family. Again in Mexico, during the same period, there might have been an assembly for prayers; and in the course of their affairs, principally commercial, many of the Marranos must have come into frequent contact with each other. But even so, the daily Jewish life of the Marranos was seemingly confined to the most intimate family group.

The Judaism of the Marranos of Spanish America expressed itself primarily in the maintenance of rules and regulations to be observed by the individual. An indirect testimony to this is also the edict which called upon the inhabitants to inform on suspects; as previously has been mentioned, it was called out in public, and with much ceremony, once every three years. This enumerates obvious signs to be watched for in the behavior of a 'Judaizer'—the Marrano—all of which were taken from his personal and daily manner of life. Isolated with his God and his conscience, the Marrano fought for his Jewish existence. He alone weighed up and decided whether or not to circumcise himself, whether and how to keep the Passover, how to avoid eating pig's meat, and with what symbols to celebrate his Sabbath. He alone decided if and when to inform his children of their Jewishness, always fearful of their reactions and the dangers awaiting them and him. When caught, he stood alone before his Inquisitors, denying his 'guilt' or admitting it openly, betraying his relatives and 'repenting', or suffering his tortures and burning at the stake.

INTERLUDE IN BRAZIL

Contrasting sharply with this form of Marrano life in the Spanish and Portuguese areas, another way of Jewish life was possible in Latin America for a short, unique period: that of an open and organized congregation in an autonomous and traditional community. This was during the brief period of Dutch rule on the north-eastern fringes of Brazil. The first manifestation of this legal Jewish existence already occurred in 1624-5, when for a short time Bahia was taken; but it was only fully realized from 1630 onward, with the conquest of Pernambuco.

'The liberty of the Spaniards, Portuguese and natives, whether they be Roman Catholics or Jews, will be respected...,' ran the tenth paragraph of the regulations for the Dutch Colonies in the West Indies, ratified in 1629 by the States General in the Hague. On this basis, Jews participated actively in the conquest and the subsequent colonization. Once the conquerors established

Isaac Aboab da Fonseca, Brazil, 1842. The first rabbi in the Americas: Isaac Aboab da Fonseca (1605-93) came in 1642 from Amsterdam to Dutch Brazil and served as the spiritual leader of the Zur Israel Community in Recife—the only organized Jewish Community to exist in Continental Latin America during the Colonial era. After the expulsion of the Dutch in 1654, he went back to Amsterdam.

themselves in Pernambuco, the number of Jews there increased greatly as a result of the arrival of new immigrants from Holland; and also, to a certain extent, because of the open return to Judaism of many Marranos in Brazil. Since they were all from Portugal, the Jews of Pernambuco founded communities based on those existing in Lisbon before the conversion edict. The regulation and minute books of two of these communities still exist today, enabling us to study the communal life of the Jewish community in Brazil. They are the minute books of congregations Tzur Israel in Recife and Maguen Abraham in Mauricia, covering the period 1648-53.

The authority of the community was vested in the *Mahamad* —an executive committee consisting of five members, which was partially renewed through elections every six months. Marranos who returned to their Judaism after spending only one year in completing their knowledge of Judaism could also be elected as members of the *Mahamad*. The regulations determined the organization of prayers and Bible readings as well as the education system and maintenance: first and second grades for small children and classes in the Talmud for the older ones were taught by the rabbi of the community himself—the *hakham* Isaac Aboab da Fonseca, one of the young Amsterdam rabbis who went to Recife in 1642 and became the first rabbi in America. Charity for the poor was also organized: a central fund—the '*Sedaca*'—financed assistance and special needs; but, in addition, there existed special financial officials *(gabbaim)* who were responsible for paying ransoms for prisoners, particularly those who were likely to fall into the hands of the Inquisition. On New Year, other *gabbaim* were elected to administer the money intended for the Holy Land and for the support of its community, and a special regulation adjured that 'the gentlemen of the *Mahamad* shall be very careful to remit the money of Eretz Israel.' Other regulations prescribed the relationships of the Jews to the Gentiles. It was forbidden to argue about religious problems in order not to offend Christianity; a woman or a slave may not be converted to Judaism without the agreement of the *Mahamad*; recourse should not be had to a Gentile court in matters between one Jew and another, nor should one Jew testify against another without the agreement of the *Mahamad*. Thus, while in Lima, Cartagena, and Mexico, the Inquisition celebrated its victory over oppressed Jewish cells, at another end of the continent Jews lived within a community, free to teach their children Judaism and firmly bound both to the Jewish center in Holland and to Eretz Israel.

THE PORTUGUESE RECONQUEST

But this tranquil state of affairs did not last. Already in 1645— when the Jewish community had reached its greatest proportion and comprised about 50 per cent of the 1,500 white inhabitants of Dutch Brazil—the war between the Portuguese and the Brazilian patriots was renewed. In 1646 the Portuguese succeeded in besieging Recife and starving it. Two supply ships followed by reinforcements arrived in the city and saved the besieged,

moving Rabbi Isaac Aboab to compose a poem of praise as 'a memorial of the wonders of God and of the great kindness which He in His compassion and great mercy showed to the house of Israel in Brazil...' But the guerrilla warfare continued for a period of years, until in 1654 the Dutch were forced to capitulate and evacuate the area. According to the capitulation agreement, the Jews also were permitted to leave with their possessions: some returned to Holland, twenty-three went to New Amsterdam where they founded the Jewish community of New York, others settled on those Caribbean islands which were not under Iberian rule, and a few returned to their previous state as Marranos dispersing over south Brazil and even reaching areas ruled by Spain.

The activities of the Inquisition continued throughout the 17th and 18th centuries, as did suspicions and legislation discriminating against the 'New Christians'—who by then had already been converted to Christianity for one and even two hundred years. At the beginning of the 18th century many Marranos were imprisoned in Brazil and sent to be judged by the Inquisition in Portugal. In 1726, one of the most famous of them —the playwright Antonio Jose da Silva, called 'The Jew'—was burned at the stake in Lisbon. During the same period the activities of the Inquisition in the Spanish areas were much more limited. In the course of the 18th century the remnants of the Marranos disappeared completely because of their final absorption in the pattern of Colonial life, leaving only a dim memory in the consciousness of many families all over the continent, and sometimes even in whole regions such as Antioquia in Colombia. Here and there remained some vestigial customs whose origins lay in Judaism and whose significance was unknown and meaningless to those who kept them.

THE CARIBBEAN ISLANDS

Against the background of the withering and ultimate disappearance of the Jews of the Latin American continent, the founding of new communities on the Caribbean Islands—on the fringes of this continent—stood out notably. The rule of the powers competing with Spain and Portugal attracted many of the refugees from Brazil—and also other Jews from Europe—to seek refuge there. Even on the islands of Martinique and Guadeloupe, possessions of Catholic France, the Jews of Recife were welcomed in 1654, although already in 1683, for religious reasons, restrictive legislation and even an expulsion decree were applied to them. England agreed even more readily to the petitions from Jews to settle in its Caribbean islands. New Jewish settlers supplemented the few living in Jamaica before its conquest by the British in 1655; and Barbados—which became a British possession in 1627 —also received its first group of Jewish immigrants in 1655. Organized Jewish communities were soon formed on both islands; and after some time an additional community, an Ashkenazi one, was founded in Kingston, Jamaica. Large numbers of Jews were attracted by the possibilities of developing the sugar industry, by commerce with continental Latin American

Tombstone, Curaçao, 1656. Reliefs on tombstones in the old Jewish graveyard in Curaçao; shown above the tomb of Abigail Cardozo. Many similar reliefs, most of which depict biblical scenes, are to be found in this cemetery which was first established by the founders of the Jewish community in 1656. These pieces of funerary art from an obvious deviation from the traditional opposition to human figures in Jewish religious art.

centers—in spite of the Spanish monopolistic laws—and by the monopolistic trade with England whose development received a special impetus owing to the Navigation Acts. Despite attempts made in 1680-1 by local traders to limit the rights of the Jews and even to expel them, the Jews of Jamaica and Barbados established their position, and their communities continued to develop during the 18th century.

Even more than on the French and British islands, Jewish life developed in the Dutch areas of the New World, particu-larly on the island of Curaçao and the colony of Surinam on the northern part of the continent. Here, as in Recife, Jews began to arrive with the Dutch conquest expeditions, and in the 1630s began their organized existence which was strengthened after the Dutch defeat in Brazil. The central Jewish community of Mikveh-Israel was founded in Curaçao in 1654 and thereafter the number of Jews, as well as their organizations, increased until, in the first quarter of the 18th century, they made up half of the white population of the island, occupying key positions in economic affairs and administration. In Surinam, some parts of which for a time passed from Dutch to British control, there existed a Jewish community in Paramaribo as well as in other places. Here Jews also founded a rural settlement in the interior, which to this day is called Joden Savanne. An attempt, which had been made ten years earlier, to establish an agricultural settlement in Cayenne —for which purpose a large group of Jews had been brought from Leghorn in Italy—was canceled when the area was con-quered by the French, and the settlers joined the Surinam and Curaçao communities. During the 18th century, German Jews also came to the Caribbean, adding variety and strength to the Jewish community in these areas.

Thus, on a small part of the Caribbean Islands and on the northern fringes of the Latin American continent, a substantial Jewish community was concentrated, living in complete religious freedom and to a great extent enjoying equal rights. This con-centration of Jewish communities is the only living legacy which the colonial period in the history of Latin American Jewry has bequeathed to modern times.

First Steps in Modern Times

During the last quarter of the 18th century the ideas of the Enlightenment and Rationalism slowly but surely seeped into Latin America. When the historic moment was ripe, this spread of ideas ripened into wars of independence all over the continent. The victory of the ideas of the French and American revolutions also brought in its wake new possibilities of Jewish existence. This was symbolized by the abolition of the Inquisition in all the states during the first quarter of the 19th century. The constitutions, then in the making, were based mostly on the precepts of freedom of religion, while anticlerical pressures at times even brought about demands for a separation of Church and State. This created a special situation in the history of Jewish emancipation in the 19th century whereby the basis for emancipation was laid in the absence of Jews to claim it.

The first Jewish immigrants to Latin America came from the Caribbean communities found on the fringes of the continent

Mikve-Israel, Curaçao, 1732. Mikve-Israel Synagogue, Curaçao (Netherlands ▶ Antilles), 1732. The oldest in the New World, consecrated in 1732, it is now called Mikve-Israel-Emmanuel and is still in active use. Its floor is strewn with sand—possibly a relic of Marrano days when worshipers sought to muffle their sounds. By courtesy of Dr. I.S. Emmanuel, Cincinnati.

Rimmonim, Curaçao, early eighteenth century. Silver *Rimmonim* (Torah ornaments) at the Mikve-Israel synagogue, Curaçao, made between 1700 and 1740. By courtesy of Dr. I.S. Emmanuel, Cincinnati.

Maria (1867), became famous as a writer even beyond the borders of Latin America.

North Africa was another source of immigrants who founded organized communities in the first half of the 19th century. Hundreds of Jews from there, particularly Morocco, settled in Latin America. These Jews founded their community in Belém, in the state of Parà, in 1824, and during the following decades spread out also into the state of Amazonas. Others, who went to Rio de Janeiro, joined together in 1848 to found the first synagogue there.

From the mid-19th century onward, the first Jews from Western Europe, particularly from France and Germany, began to arrive. Some of them were driven to leave Europe by political events—such as the unsuccessful Revolutions of 1848, and later the conquest of Alsace-Lorraine—while others came for business reasons, or, as in the case of Colombia, Venezuela and Peru, as professionals and engineers. Even though their religious heritage was sparse, it was they, together with Jews from North Africa who had settled in these countries, who were forced to work for the application of religious freedom and equality to the Jewish community.

In Brazil, the laws of the empire prevented this equality and freedom since Catholicism was established as the state religion and other religions were permitted to be practiced only in private houses whose appearance would not indicate that they were houses of prayer. The organization here could not, then, exceed the limits of private synagogues and accompanying charity institutions. Only after the declaration of the republic and the establishment of its Constitution in 1891, were conditions established for a Jewish existence with full rights. In Argentina, where the Constitution of 1853 gave equal religious rights to all inhabitants of the country—although it prevented non-Catholics from being elected to the offices of president and vice-president—the Jews needed the intervention of the court to have the legal validity of the Jewish marriage contract recognized. In Peru, the Central European Jews founded a community organization, acquired a large cemetery and enjoyed equal rights; but in other Andean countries similar Jewish immigrants did not establish an organized, consolidated Jewish presence.

In the history of Latin American Jewry, this layer of West European Jews played an important—even if rather sad—part: in spite of their success in obtaining equal rights and establishing institutions which constituted a pattern for Jewish communities in several countries, the founding generation had almost no continuation within the Jewish public on the continent. Since most of them were bachelors, even the most traditional among them were forced to marry women of other faiths, and their limited knowledge of Judaism was not sufficient to enable them to educate their sons as Jews, while, according to Jewish tradition, the children were considered to be non-Jews.

Jewish immigration to Latin America underwent a change from 1881 as a result of the wave of pogroms which stirred up the Jews of Eastern Europe. The systematic persecutions coming in their wake during the 1880s and 1890s, increased the flood of immigrants to the New World, including South America.

during Colonial times, particularly from Jamaica, St. Thomas and Curaçao. From the time of his exile there, Simon Bolivar, the Liberator, had strong ties with the Jews of Curaçao of whose help he availed himself. The first organized community in former Spanish territories was founded in Coro, Venezuela, in about 1820. The cemetery it acquired is still used by the small community existing in that city today. Other Jews of the same origin, acting individually, settled also in Colombia, Panama and Costa Rica. After a time, some of them reached distinguished positions and one of their sons, Jorge Isaac, the author of

In view of the pogroms, the government of Argentina during the presidency of Julio A. Roca decided in 1881 to encourage immigration, and to authorize a special representative in Europe to direct Jewish immigration toward Buenos Aires. Although this appointment did not bear very great fruit, individual Jews began trickling in, particularly in the second half of the 1880s, some of them no doubt attracted by the hope of getting rich quick. A rumor of the discovery of gold in the south of Argentina brought in 1885 to the southern tip of the continent one of the outstanding Jewish adventurers—the engineer Julio (Iulio) Popper, who later became one of the explorers of Tierra del Fuego, and the *de facto* ruler of enormous territories. Popper even minted his own coins, printed his own stamps, and clashed with the authority of the duly appointed governors of the territory, until ultimately his conflicts with them became the subject of a governmental investigation and the intervention of the president of the republic.

AGRICULTURAL SETTLEMENT

Only at the end of the 1880s did Argentina become the target for immigration of larger groups of Jews, who linked their future to agricultural settlement. In August 1889, 824 souls arrived in Buenos Aires aboard the ship *Weser*. Some of them subsequently established the colony of Mosesville, in the province of Santa Fé. One year later, in view of the steady deterioration of the situation of the Jews in Russia, the European philanthropist Baron Maurice de Hirsch decided to devote fifty million francs to organizing the emigration of the persecuted Jews of Russia,

Torah crowns, Curaçao, eighteenth century. Three crowns of gold (center) and of silver (left and right) donated to the Mikve-Israel synagogue, made in Curaçao in 1711, 1716 and around 1750 respectively. By courtesy of Dr. I.S. Emmanuel, Cincinnati.

and settling them in agricultural settlements in the countries of the New World. As soon as his intentions became publicly known—with the establishment of the Jewish Colonization Association—a stream of proposals reached him from Latin America, particularly from Mexico, Honduras, Paraguay, Peru and Brazil; but at that time he preferred to locate his agricultural undertaking in Argentina. Although his agricultural enterprise never reached the proportions nor had the success which its founder had envisaged, it did put Argentina on the map of mass Jewish immigration, and moreover as an objective which was linked with the ideals of social and economic transformation—from urban middlemen to productive occupations. These ideals of 'productivization' formed an integral part of the national Jewish thought at that time; and, therefore, at least some of the settlers considered immigration to Argentina as the implementation of a national mission.

At first, the Jewish colonies were concentrated in three provinces—Buenos Aires, Santa Fé, and Entre Ríos—and only later were others added in Santiago del Estero, Chaco, La Pampa and Río Negro. The colonies in Argentina were formed of concentrations with Jewish majorities, which sometimes were an organic continuation of the traditional way of life of the small towns and villages of Russia. A graphic illustration is the minute book of the burial society in one of the colonies close to the city of Basavilbaso in the province of Entre Ríos, whose settlers had come in 1894 from a Jewish village in the Kherson region of Russia. In the first pages, we find the regulations of the burial society copied from the *pinkas* (register) of Novopoltavka: 'Everything correct with nothing missing'. On the following page the *gabbaim* of the Russian village testify that they were entrusting to those emigrating to Argentina a Scroll of the Law written in Jerusalem, and they determine the details of its ownership; immediately thereafter, we come upon the entries concerning the colony in Argentina.

During the first generation of the colonies' existence, most of them preserved a religious way of life. In the second generation, however, secular currents increased and cultural life was focused on the library—which for all practical purposes constituted a cultural club—more than on the synagogue. There was an increased influence of the environment, at first noticeable mainly in the change of dress; and in the personality of the 'Jewish gauchos of the Pampas', (described in a series of lyric stories by Alberto Gerchunoff, one of the sons of the colonies who became famous as an Argentinian writer), the gaucho features gradually increased at the expense of the Jewish ones. After some time, some of the colonies evidenced a tendency for complete 'Argentinization'. However, the majority of the Jewish society gave this development the character of an internal Jewish struggle rather than a complete break with the Jewish community.

In view of the hitherto unknown environment, the strangeness of Argentinian agriculture, and the absence of real agricultural experience, there was a growing tendency among the Jewish settlers toward mutual help. The I.C.A. Corporation also encouraged them in this direction, and so the cooperative movement came into being in the Jewish settlements. From 1900, when the first cooperative nucleus was created—it was the first or perhaps the second in the whole of Argentina—this movement grew until it came to include the vast majority of Jewish settlers. In addition to cooperation in purchasing and marketing, its activities initially included also cultural activities, welfare, and medical aid. Later they also developed enterprises for processing agricultural produce. The network of cooperatives in the colonies was soon united under a roof organization—the Fraternidad Agraria (Agrarian Fraternity)—which purchased and marketed jointly a good deal of the necessities and products, at the same time constituting one of the cornerstones of Argentinian cooperatives in general.

Although at the time of its maximum expansion in 1925 the population of the Jewish colonies numbered only 34,250, their demographic contribution to the Jewish community was great. The difficulties of absorption and agriculture, and the attraction exerted by the city—particularly in the 1940s and 1950s—led to a situation in which the number of Jews leaving Argentinian agriculture for the cities or for neighboring countries was many times larger than that of those who remained in agriculture. In many cases those who left the colonies brought with them a social experience which constituted an important contribution to public life in the cities.

In Brazil, also, in the state of Rio Grande do Sul, I.C.A. established two agricultural colonies in the early 20th century, attempting to base them on mixed small farms. Their extent was small, with the one not numbering more than forty families. The difficult agricultural conditions, the isolation on lands still to a large extent covered with forests, and the more attractive economic and social opportunities offered by small towns and cities, explains why these colonies did not surive. In Uruguay a small group of Jews tried to establish an agricultural settlement on government land in 1914, but in spite of their efforts and idealistic approach, their experiment failed.

COMMUNAL URBAN CONSOLIDATION

Subsequent to the agricultural settlement, Argentina and other countries witnessed an urban Jewish immigration numerically much greater than that of the farmers. The worse the situation became in Eastern Europe at the beginning of the 20th century, the greater the immigration, which—after a certain interval during World War I—reached its peak in the 1920s. The preferred target for immigration was Argentina, with Brazil in second place. However, many thousands of immigrants also turned to Mexico and Cuba, with the thought that from there it might be easier for them to reach the even more preferable objective—the United States of America. Once the first limitations on immigration to Argentina were imposed, the influx into Brazil and Uruguay increased. At the same time thousands of Jews also went to Chile, some of them after having spent some time in Argentina, and also to Peru, Colombia and Venezuela.

Tombstone, Curaçao, 1762. The Jews of Curaçao owned over one thousand boats, and at least two hundred of the owners were captains. Among them was Mosseh Henriquez Cotiño, who died in Curaçao on October 11 1762. His family engraved a ship on his tombstone at the Old Jewish Cemetery of Curaçao. If there were sufficient Jews aboard ship, they took along their own ritual slaughterer to kill poultry on the journey. By courtesy of Dr. I.S. Emmanuel, Cincinnati.

Ketubbah, Curaçao, 1782. The oldest marriage contract (*Ketubbah*) extant in the Mikve-Israel-Emanuel synagogue, Curaçao, dated May 29 1782, signed by Haham Jacob Lopez Fonseca, by the bridegroom Samuel de Casseres, married to Lea, daughter of Abraham Henriquez Melhado, and by two *parnassim,* David Morales and Mordechay Motta. The bridegroom received a dowry of 9,050 pesos. By courtesy of Dr. I.S. Emmanuel, Cincinnati.

Parallel with the Ashkenazi immigration, and without any organic link to it, every one of these Latin American countries was also reached by Sephardi Jews. Some of them were the victims of the Balkan Wars and the Turkish-Greek conflict; others were fleeing the miserable poverty which they had known in the Jewish communities in Turkey, Syria, and North Africa. Up to the beginning of the 1930s there were sizable concentrations of Jews in almost all Latin America—some 260,000 in Argentina, 50,000 in Brazil, 10,000 in Uruguay, in Chile, and in Mexico, and 2,500 in Peru and Colombia. Their size in proportion to the general population was small and—aside from Argentina, where they reached 2.2 per cent of the population, and Uruguay, where they numbered 1.2 per cent—their number in the remaining countries did not even reach .05 per cent of the general population. But as against this, the Jews were concentrated geographically mainly in the big cities, and this heightened the impression of their presence.

In the economic field the Jews were concentrated in particular occupations. Already at the beginning of the century some Jews in Argentina were to be found in major commercial enterprises, as well as among the leading industrialists of the textile and wood industries; isolated Jews were in similar trade and industrial classes also in Brazil, Bolivia and Chile, as well as other countries. But up to the 1930s, the great majority of Latin American Jews belonged to the lower, urban strata whose character was determined by the lack of industrialization, typical of Latin America during that period. In Argentina, and to a lesser extent in some other countries, there was a Jewish proletariat of journeymen (workers earning a daily wage) in all crafts, but particularly in the needlework, woodwork, and food branches. In all countries, without exception, there was a wide layer which engaged in the peddling of personal consumer goods, on an installment basis. The economic progress of these two layers of breadwinners normally led them to the two layers directly above: independent tradesmen employing salaried workers in their workshops on the one hand, and shop owners on the other. The most successful ones graduated to industry and wholesale commerce. Parallel with these developed the stratum of professionals, particularly from among the younger generation who had been born or educated in Latin America. Among the Jews of Argentina, where this process began earlier because of the greater seniority of that community, there were already in 1934 no less than 1,175 Jews in the medical and pharmaceutical professions, and about 190 in engineering and law, in addition to a long list of writers, journalists, artists and university lecturers. At the same time the majority of the Jewish population was characterized by a low standard of living, crowded living conditions, and the desire to make a major effort to save in order to progress, as well as to bring over relatives left behind in Europe.

The geographical and professional concentration made it possible for Jews in every one of the countries to satisfy their religious, cultural, and social needs in spite of the relatively small numbers. The first generation, particularly those from Western Europe, were satisfied with establishing synagogues, where they met primarily during the High Holidays and other attempts to resolve the problem of Jewish funerals—attempts which often resulted in the leasing of plots in Protestant cemeteries. Immigrants from North Africa, the Balkans, and Turkey, who were often more firmly rooted in Jewish religious tradition, required the synagogues and the other religious institutions much more intensely, finding their full satisfaction in religious frameworks, except for those few who also organized for Zionist or social ends. On the other hand, the immigrants from Eastern Europe, with their varied secular Jewish heritage, required a much wider network of organizations and institutions. The strangeness felt by these Jews in their contact with the Latin Catholic culture, which remained dominant even in cosmopolitan immigration cities such as Buenos Aires and São Paolo until the 1930s, no doubt contributed to this phenomenon. In the establishment of religious, and some philanthropic, organizations, the East Europeans were assisted by the initiative and the leadership of those leaders from Western Europe who had preceded them. With their help and sometimes with their initiative, they established philanthropic institutions, such as a Jewish hospital, an anti-tuberculosis league, an orphanage, a home for the aged, and particularly, aid organizations for new immigrants. In addition they established libraries, which in fact also constituted clubs, in which a very intensive social and cultural daily life found its expression. Particular attention was paid to dramatic circles, which in some places became Yiddish theaters, where some of the major figures of the Jewish stage in the United States and Eastern Europe appeared. Before even the Jews numbered many thousands, the first big Yiddish newspapers made their appearance, becoming a foremost factor in daily life, and also constituting a platform for the growth of a local literature. The Yiddish language became a badge of Judaism, and sometimes even a principal hallmark. A considerable effort was therefore made to cultivate the language among the younger generation.

There was widespread organization also in the economic field: Jewish professional societies were founded as special branches of Jewish trade unions; cooperative depots where organized by peddlers, credit institutions for mutual help were instituted, and manufacturers in various branches were also organized. All this was done in the most concentrated manner in Argentina, and in different forms and in varying measures also in other countries.

The intensiveness of social life among those who originated from Eastern Europe was characterized by deep party divisions, which had been imported from the 'old country'. Zionists of different shades on the one hand, and leftists of varying degrees of extremeness on the other, were also represented in every one of the Jewish communities of Latin America as they had been in the communities in Poland and Russia. When a bitter struggle took place between Zionists and Communists over the Palestine problem, and later, on the question of an autonomous Jewish district which the Soviet Union had decided to estabish in Birobijan, a struggle no less bitter was waged between the handful of partisans of each side, even in small communities. On the basis of these divisions, the education network which was established in the 1930s was usually divided between the religious and secular, the leftists and Zionists.

In this wide gamut of opinions and organizations, the two dominant tendencies were those of secularism and nationalism, with secularism being supported by the leftists and the majority of the Zionists, and nationalism being opposed by the majority of the leftists but shared by the religious elements. These two tendencies determined that the identity of the Jewish community in Latin America was based first and foremost on ethnic, national, and cultural definitions, and only to a lesser extent—and for limited sectors—on a definition which was basically religious. This definition was also accepted by the youth and the intelligentsia, who established their literary outlets and cultural organizations in the Spanish and Portuguese languages, in which they cultivated Jewish values, attempting to establish a bridge between them and the local culture.

In spite of the existence, on a limited scale, of tendencies toward absolute assimilation and escape from Jewish identity, the Jewish community until the 1930s was crystallized in tight social frameworks whose power reached, when necessary, even to complete ostracism of negative elements which seemed to threaten them.

DAYS OF CRISIS

The 1930s witnessed a change in the status and organizational methods of Latin American Jewry when in many countries there emerged national movements advocating a complete cultural and ethnic monolithism, and deriving their inspiration from the victories of fascism and nationalism in Europe. Furthered by the worldwide economic crisis, this movement undermined the constitutional regime in Argentina, and overthrew the old republic in Brazil. At the same time security was undermined in a number of other countries, such as Uruguay, Peru, Chile, and Venezuela, and the democratic liberal base on which Jewish existence had been founded was jeopardized. A vociferous anti-Semitic movement, aided by the agents of the Third Reich, came into being. The Nazi Party formed cells among the considerable number of settlers from Germany. When the political danger inherent in them caused a reaction—and this manifested itself in Argentina by the imposition of limitations on immigrant organizations, and in Brazil by the limitation of the use of foreign languages in education and journalism—the institutions and newspapers of the Jewish community also suffered. Hostility toward Jews brought about the limitation of Jewish immigration, which gradually became more severe even within the framework of the strict immigration statutes operating in the older immigration countries of Latin America.

The external attack led to the internal consolidation of the Jewish communities. Under the influence of the World Jewish Congress, local roof organizations were gradually established and represented the entire community, Sephardi and Ashkenazi (with the exception of the small Communist groups) in its dealings with the outside world. At the same time, international Jewish organizations attempted to thaw the rigidity of the immigration restrictions. Programs for agricultural settlements were suggested for various countries. Some of them, particularly one for the Dominican Republic, was even realized on a reduced scale. A considerable number of the countries in which colonization projects were being planned, agreed to absorb thousands of Jewish refugees; and others arrived in countries like Cuba, Peru, and even Brazil and Argentina—slipping through loopholes in existing immigration laws. Thus, in the course of the 1930s and the early 1940s, a new layer was established in Latin American Jewry, consisting mainly of persons originating from Central Europe.

This new group of Jews broadened and enriched the life of Latin American Jewry. In the economic field, these immigrants brought with them experience and know-how which made the development of new urban branches possible, and their penetration into others; they were also attracted in some countries by the growing industrialization which had resulted from the isolation forced upon them by the World War. From the cultural and religious viewpoint, immigrants from Germany brought with them the traditions of Conservative Jewry, and also of Reform Judaism in its German version. In addition to synagogues, the new immigrants developed welfare organizations for themselves, which from the outset combined social and cultural aspects. A press came into being, and entertainment forms in the German language were established. The lack of affinity with the majority Latin group, and with Jewish societies of Eastern European or oriental origin, contributed to the intensiveness of their cultural life and the preservation of the independence of German Jewish communities. However, German Jews joined the roof organizations which were being established.

THE LAST TWENTY YEARS

The European Holocaust and the establishment of the State of Israel on the one hand, and the socio-economic processes in Latin America on the other, were factors which shook the personal and collective image of Jews in the period following World War II.

The Holocaust directly involved practically every individual among the Jews of the American continent, who had left behind considerable parts of their families in the 'Valley of Death'. Thus, for the immigrant generation, the Warsaw Ghetto Anniversary became a personal and collective 'Yahrzeit' (Day of Remembrance). The Holocaust also enhanced the relative weight of Latin American Jewry within the sum total of the Diaspora, and its representatives were now being given a greater opportunity than before to operate within the framework of international Jewish organizations on central issues.

The establishment of the State of Israel broadened and strengthened the ethnic and national identity of the Jews of the continent. Central institutions became more efficient. Zionist parties, which had already to a large extent influenced the texture of the communities, now were dominant in community institutions, whereas their previous rivals—particularly the Communists and the Bundists—either joined them or continued to voice their reservations and their criticism of Zionism from the sidelines of the organized community. Without joining Zionist parties —which for all practical purposes were structured like branches of Israel parties in the Diaspora—a vast majority of the Jews of the continent supported the State of Israel materially. Jewish education, which was controlled by central institutions, was now broadened in every one of the countries. It was based to a large extent on emotional identification with the State, and symptomized by the great increase in the proportion of Hebrew instruction within the curriculum.

The Zionist movement also had direct influence in the field of education as a result of new budgets, books, and particularly teachers active on its behalf in local educational networks.

The two central events in the Jewish history of our time thus contributed to a more positive Jewish identification of Latin American Jewry with the Jewish people and its tradition. The social and economic processes in their countries, on the other hand, at least partially operate in the opposite direction. The accelerated industrialization, during World War II and the following years, opened broad new economic possibilities for many Jews. As a result, important changes occurred in their professional stratification and in their economic situation. Many of the agricultural settlers in Argentina left their farms, leasing them to others or working them with hired labor; the proletariat and the peddlers who sold on a credit basis disappeared gradually, while at the same time the number of those engaged in major com-

merce, in production and the marketing of new items—such as the products of the electronics and plastics industries—is on the increase. The number of Jewish academicians is also growing, particularly in the fields of medicine, psychology, sociology, engineering, and the exact sciences—and with it the number of Jews engaged in teaching, administration and communications. Thus, in most countries, the Jews advanced considerably within the middle class, parallel with the growth of that middle class itself.

Alongside economic progress, there is a tendency toward broader cultural and social absorption. This affects, first and foremost, the university graduates who have completed their studies, and have been aroused to the challenge which is presented by the social and class problems of Latin America. The inadequate Jewish background of many of them, their remoteness from the Yiddish language and from the Jewish 'Establishment', and the absence of a traditional way of life, facilitate their integration in an open and anticlerical society, which they find particularly in the leftist wings of the student body. The number of assimilationists who part completely from the Jewish community is increasing. For many of them the resistance of the Jewish home to mixed marriages is nothing but the remnant of a fossilized culture. Those who are more faithful to their Jewishness find an organizational outlet in the established cultural Jewish frameworks which foster a general and Jewish culture in

Purim bowls, Curaçao, late eighteenth century and 1801. One of these two was donated in the eighteenth century and the other in 1801 by Mordechay de Crasto and Haïm Gabriel da Costa Gomez. By courtesy of Dr. I.S. Emmanuel, Cincinnati.

the language of the land. At the same time the emphasis of these frameworks is now being shifted to social and sports activities; in the field of cultural activity, general culture is taking a more prominent place at the expense of Jewish culture. In the main countries, where many of the general population are the sons of immigrants, there is an increasing tendency among these circles to consider themselves an integral and legitimate part of the society in general, which is normally considered by them from the ethnic and cultural viewpoints as a pluralistic society.

However, as against this consideration of the general society, nationalistic forces—among which anti-Semitic groups have constituted an active and vociferous part—have in recent decades been demanding a monolithic society. These groups were reinforced to a certain extent after World War II by Nazi officers and officials, who found refuge in Latin American countries, and more recently have enjoyed material support from Arab countries. In Argentina they have even attempted—not without success—to penetrate the broad labor strata.

This anti-Semitism becomes particularly dangerous when seen against the background of the social tensions which result from the underdeveloped economy. Class polarization, which characterizes the majority of Latin American countries, constitutes a breeding ground for the extension of different revolutionary trends. With the increase in tension, many countries are often faced with the choice between a leftist evolution or a military coup supported by the right. Although there are Jews, particularly students, who are active in revolutionary circles, they do not belong to the leadership of the trade unions, while Jews in general are not part of the proletariat. On the other hand, Jews are not represented in the oligarchic strata who are mostly Catholics and clerics. The political importance of the liberal middle class, to which they tend to belong, has increased under these circumstances.

An example of the situation in which a Jewish community may find itself as a result of the revolution from the left, although not accompanied by any active hostility toward Jews, can be found in the fate of Cuban Jewry. When the revolution of Fidel Castro began, Cuba had about ten thousand Jews, the majority in the capital Havana, who were integrated in the economy of the country, particularly in the services, light industries, and commerce. They had been organized in a long series of philanthropic, educational, and communal institutions. The nature of the Cuban revolution destroyed the economic basis for the existence of the majority of the Jews. They took advantage of the regime's willingness to let them emigrate, and thus—in 1969—there were only about two thousand Jews, mainly elderly, left in Cuba. Though synagogues and communal institutions have not been expropriated—the community is even being assisted by the government in the maintenance of its social life—most of the institutions have been left empty and with little prospect for Jewish life in the long run.

Against the background of dangers from the left and from the right, and in spite of the undermining processes of internal assimilation, Latin American Jewry continues its daily life within the frameworks it has constructed. The Ashkenazi community in Buenos Aires, the largest and best organized community on the continent, has the deep consciousness of being the continuation of the communities which were destroyed in Eastern Europe. It has broadened the framework of schools under its care, its religious and welfare services, and cultural activities, both in Yiddish and in Spanish. The relatively small Sephardi communities in Argentina are also increasing their educational and communal activity, and the same is true of São Paulo (Brazil) and Mexico. The Conservative and Reform synagogues throughout the continent are broadening their attempts to create a new religious challenge for the youth and for its parents. The B'nai B'rith lodges in all countries are increasing their membership. The main communal institutions, such as Hebraica in Buenos Aires and the Centro Deportivo Israelita in Mexico City, which are among the largest of their kind even in relation to similar non-Jewish organizations, continue to constitute a social focus point for Jews from all countries of origin.

The social and cultural life of about 750,000 Jews who, according to estimate, live in Latin America today has, then, the characteristics of Jewish life in developed countries. However at the same time, this life is instituted in societies of countries defined as 'developing', with all the social tensions that characterize them. This fact creates the necessity for conscious self-defense which finds its expression in the activities of the political roof organizations representing the Jewish community vis-a-vis its environment. This factor strengthens the identification of the Jews of the Latin American continent with the State of Israel.

CHAPTER XIII

Israel Today

by Yaakov Tsur

At the turn of the century, Palestine—the present State of Israel —was of only secondary importance in the broader complex of Jewish life. A mere fifty thousand Jews lived in this impoverished, far-away province of the crumbling Ottoman empire. Most of them were concentrated in Jerusalem and in the other holy cities: Hebron, Tiberias, Safed. There were, certainly, already some tangible signs of a national revival: a thin network of agricultural settlements spread over the whole country, from Metullah in the north, to Ruhama on the Negev border. Palestinian Jews, however, did not represent, either quantitatively, or in any other form, an important factor in the general structure of Jewry— except for the militants of the new movement which, a short while previously, had styled itself 'Zionism'. At that time, as now, world Jewry numbered approximately thirteen million; but then, the overwhelming majority (more than nine million) lived in Europe, being mostly concentrated in the two giant empires of Eastern Europe, the Russian and the Austro-Hungarian.

Seventy years later, at the end of a period which witnessed the

First Zionist Congress in Basle, 1897. Theodor Herzl delivering the opening speech at the First Zionist Congress. The Viennese journalist and playwright Herzl was the founder of the modern political Zionist movement. He convened a gathering of representatives of Zionist groups from throughout the world in 1897 in Basle at which the basic program for the Zionist movement was adopted. To Herzl's right is the philosopher Max Nordau, also one of the leaders of the Zionist movement. Central Zionist Archives, Jerusalem.

horrors and destructions of two world wars, the State of Israel has revived Jewish independence lost in 70 A.D. With its two and a half million inhabitants it constitutes today the third largest Jewish community in the world and is outnumbered only by those of the US and possibly the USSR. Over 17 per cent of the Jewish world population lives in Israel.

The rise of Israel coincides with a total change in the face of Jewish dispersion. The communities of Eastern Europe which once constituted the very heart of Judaism have disappeared, wiped out by the Holocaust or cut off from the outside world by an impenetrable wall. Conversely, a new dispersion has come into being, spreading from Canada in the north, to Argentina and Australia in the southern hemisphere. Territorial and cultural cohesion which, in former times, had been the mainstay of Jewish survival, exists no more. On the other hand, the struggles, misfortunes and achievements of the Jewish State focus the permanent attention of this Diaspora and constitute a source of constant inspiration.

To a modern observer, the idea of Israel conjures up pictures of a Middle East on the brink of war and evokes the tragic clash between Arab and Jewish nationalisms. Discerning historians, however, had long previously pointed out that the present state of affairs is the outcome of a slow process, the origins of which are to be found in nineteenth-century liberal Europe. No one could then foresee the overwhelming changes that were to come over the world following the tragic pistol shot at Sarajevo in the summer of 1914. And certainly no one was concerned over the fate in store for millions of human beings condemned to lead lives of second-class citizens on the periphery of enlightened Europe. The only people who thought about the fate of the Jews were the Jews themselves.

The Birth of Zionism

The idea of Zionism took shape against the dismal grey backdrop of the seemingly endless misery in which the Jewish masses were sunk, apparently without hope of redemption. They were oppressed by an autocratic regime and forcibly crammed into the immense ghetto formed by the southern and western provinces of tsarist Russia, which included, at that time, the Russian-held part of Poland. Beyond the Austrian border, the Jewish population lived in the squalor of former Polish Galicia; alternatively, across the river Dniester, they eked out a miserable living in Rumania, a comparatively new kingdom which shared with its Russian neighbor a common hostile and contemptuous attitude toward the Jews.

The Jewish masses were mainly concentrated in small towns, the *stetl*, where they led a wretched existence behind the protective barrier of their religion. But the Haskalah, the lay doctrine of liberal enlightenment promoted by emancipated German Jewry, had already made breaches in the ghetto wall. Overcoming legal restrictions and the reluctance of their families, who were terrified at the mere thought of innovation, increasingly large groups left the houses of their fathers to go abroad and quench their thirst at the sources of Science, especially in German and Swiss universities. Although they spoke Yiddish, their *langue savante* was Hebrew which they had been taught in the *heder* and in the *yeshivah* of their youth. As the 19th century drew to a close, thousands of them had already acquired a command of Russian, sometimes of German, which enabled them to associate with their emancipated brothers over the frontiers.

On their return, this new educated élite passionately absorbed the ideas which had begun to agitate Russia since the liberal reign of Alexander II. Jewish newspapers and literary reviews unleashed a crusade against Jewish obscurantism and the exclusive domination of rabbis. They were in favor of merging the Jewish masses into the great Russian nation. As far as censorship allowed them, the young Jewish intellectuals preached emancipation of the Jews, the abolition of restrictive laws and equality of rights with the other nationalities that went to make up the Russian empire.

It was in this environment, completely devoted to the idea of progress, freedom, equality and human brotherhood, dreaming of a cosmopolitan society in which the Jews, like the others, would have the rights and prerogatives of a free people, that the movement advocating the taking of practical steps to implement a return to Palestine was born. This was an unexpected turn, and not in keeping with the popular ideas of the period. It was the result of bitter disillusionment, of a sudden and tragic awakening from the sweet daydream entertained by progressive circles in the 19th century, which seemed so fraught with promise.

The 'Lovers of Zion' movement (*Hovevei Zion*) came into being around 1881. It was in that year that for the first time since the beginning of the century, a wave of pogroms swept over the 'Pale of Settlement'. In one fell swoop, all the illusions of liberal Jewry were destroyed including those of Jewish youths who had given their souls to the revolutionary ideals of the time and had possessed a seemingly unshakable faith in the humanitarian virtues of the Russian people. In their eyes, once they had overtly shown the moral beauty of Judaism to their non-Jewish environment, they would without further ado be admitted to their rightful place in this great civilization. Now, suddenly, without warning, the *muzhik*, idealized by Turgeniev and Tolstoy, glorified by the poetic fervor of Nekrassov, the idyllic peasant of the great poets slaughtered thousands of innocent Jews, men, women and children, whose only crime was to be different.

Liberal Russian opinion stood silently by; not a word was uttered in condemnation of these dastardly acts. Worse still, among the revolutionary circles, which were quietly preparing their revolt against absolutist power, pogroms were considered mere symptoms of the decay of the hated regime. As these fateful events were taking place, one of the theoreticians of the revolutionary movement is reported to have said: 'Jewish blood is the oil that lubricates the wheels of revolution'.

In the face of bitter reality, the ideology of assimilation lost a good deal of its appeal. From now on, the question which Jewish youth asked itself was: 'Is it only our religion that separates us from the Russian people? Is it not legitimate for us to live a free life according to our own customs, and follow our national destiny?' The answer was contained in the tragic revelation that they had just lived through. A Jewish national doctrine came into being. This was clearly formulated in a frank and penetrating pamphlet written in German and published in Odessa under the title *Auto-Emancipation*. Its author, Judah L. Pinsker, a middle-aged physician who was far from being a dreamer, soon became the head of the 'Lovers of Zion' movement which began to propagate itself in the towns and villages of Eastern Europe. In the meantime, a small group of university students who had joined the movement from the very beginning decided to get down to concrete action and formed a society which set out to prepare the return of the Jews to Palestine by promoting the reconstruction of their new homeland. The first group of pioneers belonging to the *Bilu* movement, as it was called, landed at Jaffa in 1882. This was the first stage in a chain reaction that was to culminate with the creation of a Jewish state in Palestine.

THE ZIONIST MOVEMENT

'Auto-Emancipation', or more simply 'self-liberation', is the keyword to this agitated period of the 1880s. The Jewish people, whether looked upon as a nation or as a demographic and cultural entity, had to wage its own battle and thereby decide its own fate. Fifteen years later, Theodor Herzl, with his astonishing intuitive capacity, his creative imagination and an acute sense of organization, was to give final shape to this theory.

Unlike the 'Lovers of Zion', Herzl came of emancipated Jewry and was steeped in Western culture. He created a Zionist organization the aims of which were expounded at the Basle Zionist Congress in 1897. The 'Lovers of Zion' became, then, Zionists and the movement took on an essentially political character. From then on, the Jewish problem was brought forcibly to the attention of world opinion. Anti-Semitism was no longer condemned as a passing ephemeral aberration of misled public opinion, but as the logical consequence of the abnormal, unbearable situation of the world Jewish masses. The doctrine expounded was the following: 'The Jews are a people. They are different from the others in their way of life and their ways of thought. They are heirs to a common heritage, to a great civilization which belongs to them alone. But everywhere they are a minority, dispersed throughout the world. This causes their very existence to be unnatural and distorted. They do not constitute a normal society because the conditions of national life are refused them. Their very qualities, stemming as they do from a long process of forced adjustment, doom them to remain a foreign body in the midst of their European environment. Although they are a people, they lack the main element that makes a nation: a territory in which they, like the other nations, might organize their life according to their own image of themselves. The only territory to which they have a natural right must be the cradle of their own culture—and no other—the land to which they are bound by their past, by their tongue and by the civilization which they gave to the world and to which they have remained faithful for nineteen centuries: the Land of Israel.'

The dream of a return to the Holy Land was, of course, nothing new: the longing for the lost homeland was deeply rooted in Jewish tradition. The constant expectation of divine redemption, the faith in the coming of the Messiah and the restoration of former glory are an essential part of the Jewish faith. These themes are present in all the pages of the prayer-book which a pious Jew reads with complete devotion three times a day. In the same way, the nature festivals, in whichever clime Jews celebrate them, remain closely related to the four seasons of the lost paradise in the Land of Israel. Throughout the centuries, all the mystical revivals that the Jews experienced and all the scourges that were visited upon them, from the darkest periods of the Middle Ages to the beginning of modern times, were accompanied by messianic movements that promised a miraculous return to the Holy Land. If such movements never actually brought about a true national revolt, this is to be attributed to the very conditions of Jewish existence which was subjected to relentless oppression.

This metamorphosis of religious dogma into an ideology of national revival, essentially non-religious in character, at first raised the fierce opposition of the ultra-Orthodox circles of world Jewry. Their opposition was not without some effect on the subsequent history of Palestine and, to some extent, on that of the State of Israel. The movement was also bound to encounter the opposition of the Jewish upper class, which was numerically important and powerful in the emancipated communities of the West. This upper class categorically rejected a doctrine which stressed the particular character of the Jew for it saw a panacea in the total assimilation and adjustment of the Jews to their environment. Later, the movement found another irreconcilable adversary in the Jewish Socialists of the *Bund* (which at the time enjoyed vast popularity in Russia and Poland) who accused Zionism of being a retrograde movement, preaching a backward and reactionary brand of nationalism and diverting the Jewish proletariat from the more essential task of class struggle.

The Zionist movement, which was to change the face of world Jewry, was thus from the outset up against hostility and slander and stood in isolation. For a long period, it had to face its detractors with the only weapon it had at hand: its faith in the righteousness of its cause and in the correctness of its historical analysis of Jewish past and present. But the isolation and the bitterness that followed only succeeded in whetting the movement's thirst for action.

This national awakening must be put in the context of other contemporary doctrines of national awakening abroad at the same time which were based on a longing for independence and a return of lost freedom. It had a different inspiration from the modern nationalistic currents in which the independence of the new nations was based on the domination of a territory and on demographic unity. Like the nationalist movements in the Balkans, especially in Greece, Bulgaria and Serbia, which strongly influenced it, Zionism was surrounded with a romantic aura, with the nostalgia of a lost Golden Age. The young Jew turned away from his unhappy present to contemplate his remote past, bathed in its distant glory. The nineteen intervening centuries of exile had no appeal to him because, beyond their rich literary heritage, he could not avoid thinking of the accompanying suffering, persecution, and humiliation. The Bible nourished his dream of liberty. Not only did it appeal to him as divine revelation; it was also the written record of an age when the Jews lived free on their own land, like the other nations of the world. It was in the familiar pages of his Bible, which he had studied in his youth and which he now discovered in a new light, that he found the lost kingdom he longed for and would some day link to the future kingdom of his dreams.

The Hebrew Revival

Long before the Bible had become the inspiration behind the national revival, its language, its poetic style, its imagery and landscapes had nourished the writings of a multitude of writers,

The Western Wall, c. 1900. The Western Wall is one of the last surviving walls of the Herodian Temple compound. The bottom layers of stones are from the original Temple times, the upper layers of a later period. The wall reaches down very deep, twenty or so layers. The top part was added in the 19th century to stop stones being thrown over it. On the other side is the courtyard of the Mosque of Omar. Central Zionist Archives, Jerusalem.

novelists and poets. In the course of their everyday life, ghetto Jews seldom read the Bible, with the exception of those extracts included in the prayer-book and in the weekly portion read on the Sabbath. The Talmud, that gigantic creation of Jewish thinking during the first centuries of exile, was more central to their spiritual life. Rabbinic style, shaped by centuries of religious studies and casuistics, dominated epistolar and intellectual exchanges. And now, suddenly, without warning, the young emancipated rebels, reacting violently against the restrictive traditional teaching of the synagogue, turned toward the light of ancient sources.

Love of Zion, the famous novel by Abraham Mapu, written in a romantic style and drawing upon the purity of biblical language, revived the idealized picture of Judeans during the period of the Kings. In the same way, the nostalgic poems of Micha Joseph Lebenson and the heroic epics of Judah Leib Gordon, the prince of poets of the Haskalah period, gave new life to the Hebrew language and made it the perfect symbol of this renewal which the youth of that time so ardently longed for. All three writers shared the brilliant expectations of a generation that burned to shake loose its shackles.

However, Hebrew had always, in fact, remained the medium of Jewish literary creation. From Russia to Galicia, from Italy to Morocco, it was used as a *lingua franca* in scholarly and business letters and transactions. Because it was the language of the Bible, however, it had been kept in a sort of bondage; people wrote and read it but did not speak it in their everyday lives. In Eastern Europe, the vernacular was Yiddish, while Judeo-Spanish or Ladino was the idiom of Sephardi communities dispersed over the immense Ottoman empire after their exodus from Spain. The awakening of Jewish national consciousness implied, almost simultaneously, endeavors to turn Hebrew into a living language. This was done timidly at first, then more and more systematically. The language of the Bible thus became a national language; it was to become the basis and unique quality of Israel culture and of its influence throughout the Jewish world.

At about the same time that the idea of the return to Zion was gaining favor among the Russian Jews, Eliezer Ben-Yehuda wrote a sensational article in which he suggested turning Hebrew into a living language and thereby ensuring the unity of the Jewish people. As a young student in Paris, he used to consort with Bulgarian, Czech, and Serbian revolutionaries and dream with them of the rebirth of national cultures. Resolved to put his ideas into practice, he settled in Jerusalem with his family, with the intention of devoting himself to a revival of Hebrew.

Hebrew was actually already used at that time, as a vernacular, among the pious circles of the Holy City. Jerusalem was probably the only place in the whole of the Jewish world where Jews from Western and Eastern countries had the opportunity to meet. A never-ending stream of Jews flowed toward Jerusalem and constantly increased its Jewish population. They massed in the narrow streets of the old city and in the first quarters built outside the walls, representing all the different sectors of the dispersion. Emissaries were sent by institutions of sacred learning in Jerusalem, Hebron, and Safed to the remotest corners of the

Jewish world to whom they brought the message of Zion. Clad in the traditional garb of their communities, they would speak Hebrew with the Jews they met in the course of their travels.

This beehive of Jerusalem Jewry was a miniature model of the future Israel society. Down the narrow, dingy streets leading to the Western Wall, a picturesque crowd ebbed and flowed: Persian Jews who spoke their old Judeo-Persian dialect; Jews from North Africa talking in Judeo-Arabic or Judeo-Berber; Ashkenazi children, shouting in all the various accents of Eastern European Yiddish; rabbis from Salonika or Izmir discussing in Judeo-Spanish; bearded Kurds conversing in an old Aramaic dialect of which they alone knew the secret; and Bukharians in colorful dress went about their daily business using an idiom derived from one of the numerous vernaculars of Central Asia.

More and more frequently, these communities used Hebrew as a common language in their dealings with each other and thus, Hebrew increasingly acquired the qualities of a spoken language. Moreover, Hebrew sounded more natural when spoken by Oriental Jews who had continued to use it in the course of their travels within the immense Ottoman empire. This probably explains why Sephardi pronunciation prevailed over Ashkenazi and became the accepted phonetics of current modern Hebrew.

But Ben-Yehuda, who was soon joined by a circle of young disciples, set himself a higher, long-term task. In his mind, Jewish revival and the creation of a new Jewish society could not take place unless Hebrew became not only a *lingua franca* but also the mother tongue of the new generation. He began speaking Hebrew at home and with his friends. He taught it to his children. Soon his example was followed by schoolteachers resolved to teach 'living Hebrew' without translating it first into the mother tongue of the pupils, a method which was fairly revolutionary at that time.

In everyday use, the language gradually became simpler and more versatile. It shed the rigidity of its former 'bookishness', that it had acquired as a result of drawing on the elevated style of the Bible. Everyday life demanded an exact terminology that would allow it to designate technical things. Such a terminology was created either by resorting to the inexhaustible talmudic literature, or the philosophical works of the Middle Ages, or by using analogies with other Semitic tongues, especially Arabic.

The result was a flood of neologisms which were often rejected by the European purists, for, at that time, Europe still remained the main center of Hebrew literature. If the younger generation of writers was prepared to give up the purity of biblical style in favor of a more flexible and concise tongue derived from the logical and wonderful simplicity of the Mishnah, the new terminology and bizarre coinages of the Jerusalem linguists were

Moses, tapestry by Chagall. Part of the tapestry triptych by Marc Chagall (1887-) in the main hall of the Knesset (Israel's parliament), Jerusalem. Chagall left Russia in 1922 and settled in Paris but his work nevertheless has drawn much inspiration from scenes of life among the East European Hasidim and village communities near his native Vitebsk. Photo Harris, Jerusalem.

rejected by connoisseurs who ridiculed them. Some of the new terms that were naïve and sometimes artificial have, indeed, completely vanished; but most of the new coinages have survived and added to the richness of modern spoken and written Hebrew.

The first generation of Jews whose mother tongue was Hebrew was brought up by an admirable generation of school-teachers in Jerusalem, Jaffa, and in the new agricultural settlements of the coastal plain and the Galilee Hills. Young women teachers brought to the country by new waves of immigration, who adhered to the theories of Pestalozzi and Froebel, opened the first kindergarten in which young children got used to the sound of Hebrew. Nevertheless, the schools created by the Alliance Israélite Universelle kept teaching in French, those of the Hilfsverein propagated German, while the Anglo-Jewish Association of London taught in English. In secondary school programs, however, subjects related to Hebrew study played an increasingly important part. Furthermore the children spoke Hebrew among themselves.

On the eve of World War I, a few secondary schools already taught in Hebrew. The first among these was the Herzlia school in Tel Aviv, the construction of which was responsible for the creation of the first Jewish city in 1909. It was followed by other schools in Jerusalem and in Haifa, as well as by teachers' training colleges capable of supplying the teachers who, so far, had come from abroad.

In 1913, after a general strike of teachers and pupils at the German Hilfsverein, Hebrew was finally established as a teaching language—a demonstration of popular feeling that caused a great

stir in the whole Jewish world. The cause of this strike was the establishment by the German-Jewish association of an Institute of Higher Polytechnical Studies on the slope of Mount Carmel in Haifa. After prolonged discussions, the governing board of the school had decided that the teaching language of the Institute should be German, Hebrew being thought unsuitable for the teaching of technical and mathematical sciences. This led to the immediate resignation of all the representatives of Russian Zionism on the committee whose example was followed by all the teachers and pupils of the Hilfsverein schools throughout the country. Thousands of pupils left their classes. A general boycott was decided against those schools using German as a teaching language. The strikers (teachers and pupils) opened temporary schools in private buildings, with Hebrew as a teaching language. This strike had the enthusiastic character of a popular rebellion although the immediate issue at stake was the education of a few thousand children of a rather small community.

After the war, when Palestine Jewry was about to enter the new period of the National Home with universally recognized rights, the position of Hebrew as a national language was no longer in jeopardy. Soon it was recognized as one of the official tongues of the Mandate and became the medium of communication of modern Israel society.

THE RETURN TO ZION

It is customary to divide the formative years of Israel into five distinct periods corresponding to the five waves of immigration (called *Aliyah* or plural, *Aliyot*). These waves represent clear-cut periods, each of which had its own character and contributed in its own way to the evolution of the image of Palestinian society before the birth of the Jewish state. When the first Jewish pioneer set foot on the Holy Land, he intended to settle there and cultivate its soil. At that time, the idea of returning to the land was much in the air and had already caused some young Jerusalem and Safed Jews to leave the shelter of the walls of their Holy Cities and acquire land in the open plains and hills where they created villages and lived off the land.

In this way the village of Petah Tikvah was created among the swamps of the coastal plain which, at that time, bordered the site of the future Tel Aviv. Soon afterward, it was followed by Rosh Pinnah in the Galilee Hills and by Rishon le Zion and Gederah, founded by the *Biluim*, those pioneers of the 1880s. Nobody could conceive of a Jewish Homeland that was not an agricultural homeland, so that the aim was to change the Jew and have him return to the biblical ideal of 'every man under his vine and under his fig-tree'.

These idealistic farmers had nothing in common with the peasant class. They were the sons of quiet middle-class towns-people from Russia or Rumania, students who had left their universities to engage upon a bizarre adventure; university students who had never handled a spade or hitched up a mule-cart. They knew nothing about the rainfall and the soil properties of their new country. They had never suspected that it had been

Pioneers, pre-1914. A typical group of young pioneers of the pre-World War I Second Aliyah (wave of immigration). The members of *Ha-Shomer* (The Watchmen) defense organization carry rifles and some wear Bedouin *Keffieh* headdress. Many of Israel's leaders today are to be found among those who came with the Second Aliyah. Central Zionist Archives, Jerusalem.

David, tapestry by Chagall. Part of the tapestry triptych by Marc Chagall in the main hall of the Knesset, Jerusalem. Chagall made his reputation as one of the initiators of the Surrealist school. His use of color and wild fantasy give his work its particular quality, quite apart from his superb technical mastery. Photo Harris, Jerusalem.

devastated by centuries of destruction. However, they clung to their work which they regarded as a sacred mission. Their aim was to change the social structure of the Jewish nation and to recreate the missing peasant class. They also hoped that through their endeavors they would be able to dominate the land which, they felt, was theirs by right. Soon, however, they were beset by poverty and loneliness. The First Aliyah gradually lost its impetus, in spite of a short comeback in 1890. These proud pioneers had to have recourse to the philanthropic aid of a generous donor: Baron Edmond de Rothschild of Paris, a man of visionary imagination, who became their protector. In return, they had to accept direct administration and the inconvenience it implied. Strikes and revolts occasionally broke out. The more prosperous of the settlers hired Arab labor and became gentlemen-farmers who merely administered their plantations while the Arab hands did the hard work. Faced by reality, the generous impulse of the first period gave way; the idealism of their own early pioneering was forgotten.

However, these forefathers of Jewish agricultural reconstruction who, at the turn of the century, numbered barely five thousand, played a decisive role in the evolution of the national revival. Beyond the seas, Jewish public opinion became aware of the existence of a new type of Jew who was bound to the soil and led a peasant life. In Odessa and Warsaw, poets sang with nostalgia of the Jewish villages, of the cornfields and vineyards in the Land of Israel. Hayyim N. Bialik, who was to become the king of Hebrew poets, became known through his poem *To the Bird* in which he spoke of the beauty of the sunny fields that illuminated the gloom of his exile. At the same time, literary reviews in Russia received from Palestine the first naïve stories describing in idyllic tones the life of Jewish farmers driving their plows in the ground of the distant homeland.

It was there, in small lonely villages, at the far end of winding dusty paths, that the seeds of a new way of life were sown; a way of life that was truly Jewish, even though this term was completely different from its former meaning. Nothing, indeed, seemed farther removed from life in the *stetl* or the traditional Russian ghetto. In schools, Jewish children in a natural way learnt a Hebrew that was becoming more and more a living language. Life on the land and in the open gave birth to a proud, strong race that felt bound to the country which, only yesterday, had been unknown to their parents. From an early age, Jewish boys practiced riding and shooting. They rode further and further into the empty plains and barren hills.

As a result of their close contact with the land, the Bible acquired a new significance. The Arab names of localities were often recognized as biblical Hebrew names. The fauna and flora of the Scriptures became overnight a concrete reality.

In the villages, such as Rishon le-Zion, Rehovot, Rosh Pinnah and Zikhron Yaakov, a new way of life came into being. Young men and women used to gather in the village barn during the warm summer nights and sing Jewish songs. At first, it was Russian or Ukrainian ones that they had heard from their parents; but soon Hebrew words crept into—and were adapted to—the familiar tunes or to the Oriental melodies which they heard from

their Arab neighbors. Thus, Naphtali Imber, an itinerant poet who was to die in poverty in the New York East Side, adapted new words to a popular East European melody that he called *Ha-Tikvah* (Hope). This song became the national anthem of the Zionist movement and later the national anthem of the State of Israel.

It was in these *moshavot* or 'colonies' as they were called in the vocabulary of the time, that the first popular orchestras and choirs (which were often organized by amateur schoolteachers) came into being. It was there that the first circulating libraries and the first people's clubs were established. But these villages also served as experimental laboratories for the young agronomists who had gone to study abroad in foreign universities. They made a great many experiments and published the results in the early journals appearing in Jerusalem and Jaffa.

Thus, as the years passed, a tiny New World grew among the vineyards and orange groves of the sandy Judean plains.

THE SECOND ALIYAH

The meteor-like career of Theodor Herzl, whose Zionist mission began in 1896 and ended with his premature death in 1904, completely changed the context of Zionist action in Europe. The idea of a national Jewish revival which until then had been popular with only a few scattered groups who felt the urge to support the struggle of their brothers in Palestine now infected the masses. Zionism became an ideological issue which in the feverish atmosphere of the time was passionately discussed. Even influential circles of emancipated Jewry were won over to this idea, especially in Germany and Austria, but also in Great Britain and in the United States. The outside world, for its part, did not remain indifferent: Herzl began negotiating with British statesmen, with the German Kaiser, and even with the inaccessible ministers of the tsar. The idea of a return of the Jews to Palestine was seriously discussed by European governments although these negotiations did not lead to any concrete political results.

After Herzl's death, the World Zionist Organization, disillusioned by its political setbacks, decided to create its own financial institutions in order to speed up the development projects of the Jews in Palestine. The Jewish National Fund came into being to provide the financial means of buying the land, as did a bank for the encouragement of economic initiatives, called the Jewish Colonial Trust. It opened branches in Jaffa, Jerusalem and Beirut, under the name of the Anglo-Palestinian Company. A few years later, a society for land development was created. Its Palestinian office was directed by a young economist of German birth, Dr. Arthur Ruppin, who soon became the soul of Zionist agricultural efforts. Although these institutions had few means, they represented the embryo of an administrative body as well as an organization to which newcomers could turn for aid.

Another characteristic of this period was that the young immigrants were motivated by a clearly defined ideal, and not by vague longings like those who came with the preceding *aliyot*. To them, this was the beginning in Palestine of a new Jewish society which foreshadowed the autonomous territory planned by the Basle Zionist Program of 1897. This program actually spoke of a 'home', a transitory stage before total independence which was not to be expected until the Ottoman empire had reached the last stages of its disintegration.

The number of immigrants that came to Palestine between 1906 and 1914 is estimated at about twenty thousand. Many of them were discouraged and disenchanted and went back to their home countries, while others emigrated overseas. However, this handful of men left its mark on the future development of the country. From their ranks came the leaders that created the Jewish State and a great many of the statesmen who formed its political élite when it came into existence (among them, three prime ministers: David Ben-Gurion, Moshe Sharett and Levi Eshkol, and two of its future presidents, Yitzhak Ben-Zvi and Zalman Shazar).

They were young men, the oldest among them being scarcely over twenty, and came from mostly poor or middle class families of Russian Jewry. Others came from the masses of Jewish youth that stagnated in Russian towns, waiting endlessly for changes that would grant them the right to study. Sometimes their families had provided them with the money for their passage on Russian ships carrying *muzhiks* and monks on pilgrimage to the Holy Land. But, in the majority of cases, they came without asking their father's blessing and paid their fare out of their own pocket or with borrowed money. As often as not, they landed in Palestine with no more than a bundle containing a change of clothing.

The Second Aliyah came straight from the whirlpool of the 1905 Russian Revolution. It bore the scars of its ideological struggle and of its bitter defeat, and those that came had witnessed shameful pogroms and had had the same bitter experience as their older brethren of the 1881 generation. They had watched the Russian people, for whom they had been ready to give their lives, slaughtering, looting, and raping in the Jewish streets of Bialystok, Kishinev and Kiev. They were deeply shaken and felt that they belonged to a people which had let itself be massacred without even attempting to defend itself. In their new homeland, they meant to create a new society and a new kind of Jewish life and were determined never again to put their fate into the hands of alien protectors.

Austerity and devotion to work were the characteristics of this wave of immigrants and for a long time these ideals continued to inspire Palestinian society. They scattered round the less prosperous villages of Galilee and volunteered for the hardest work: plowing the barren hill slopes like Beduin, for mere board and lodging. They were determined to create a Jewish working class; they themselves would therefore be the initiators and flag-bearers of this new class. Physical work was the basis of their ideology and they found their theoretician in the person of a middle-aged, pious Jew, Aharon D. Gordon, the one exception among this group of young men. He had left his European home town and given up an easy job and the small fortune he had there in order to wander from village to village, an eternal optimist who preached to his younger comrades the theory of the purifying value of work. According to Gordon, creating a Jewish working class and teaching Jews to admire physical work were the only means of redeeming the Jewish people and working for its rebirth. Tolstoy's theories of renunciation and his cult of simplicity were the *leitmotifs* of the interminable discussions that took place in the huts or in the tents of the workers. For these pioneers, the 'religion of work', as people started calling it, was the path to the creation of a new Jewish society.

The young workers lived in small groups that scattered among the villages. They were often distrusted by the farmers who misunderstood them and accordingly they developed a strong sense of cooperation among themselves. Toward the end of this period, some of them, out of discouragement, went to the P.I.C.A., the society for land colonization which had succeeded the Rothschild administration. They were given farms, for the most part in Lower Galilee. Others continued to work as farmhands, either on plantations or on the experimental farms which had been created by the Zionist authorities.

At that period, a great decisive event took place. It is difficult to say whether it was a natural development or a consequence of ideological planning, but in 1909, following a strike in one of the experimental farms, a small group of farmhands was granted the right by the Palestinian office of the Zionist Organization to settle in the Jordan Valley on the basis of common responsibility and common lease of the land. The first communal settlement, the *kevutzah* of Deganiah was founded, thus initiating the era of the collectivist movement with its *kibbutzim* which, in turn, gave Israel society its specific character.

Not long before the outbreak of World War I, the labor leaders had decided to encourage the immigration of a small community of Jews who led an obscure existence in the southern-most corner of Arabia. This ancient branch of Oriental Jewry had been living for many centuries in a primitive kingdom where they had suffered persecutions and humiliations from their Muslim masters. Although they were completely cut off from the centers of Judaism, the Yemenite Jews had remained true to their ancestral faith and had kept the traditions of Judaism. They had also preserved their holy language, Hebrew, which they transmitted from generation to generation, and spoke in the course of their everyday lives.

An emissary of the workers' movement, disguised as a rabbi succeeded in entering Yemen at the risk of his life. He wandered on foot from one village to another telling the wonderstruck Jews about the miracle of the return to Zion. Everywhere he raised messianic hopes, and families, sometimes whole communities, set out for the Promised Land. They crossed deserts on foot, eventually reaching Aden from where, after a great many tribulations, they sailed for Jaffa. Soon these swarthy Jews, with their goatees and sidelocks, appeared in Judean villages and in the poorer districts of Jaffa and Jerusalem.

With their arrival, Hebrew gained in popularity because Yemen Jews spoke the holy tongue fluently while the vernaculars of European Jewry were completely unknown to them. Thus Hebrew became the necessary means of communication of labor circles that, otherwise, had little or no contact with the Oriental communities of Jerusalem.

Underpopulated and badly governed by the corrupt and lethargic Ottoman administration, Palestine was far from being a safe country. Brigandage was a normal and an almost officially recognized phenomenon. Beduin 'razzias' were frequent and did not spare the Jewish villages. According to custom the Jewish farmers employed the prospective robbers as watchmen over their cattle and crops. The thought that they depended on Arabs and on the Turkish police for their security was unbearable to the new elements that came with the Second Aliyah, who were forever haunted by the pogroms they had witnessed and the defenselessness and passivity of the Jewish victims. Many of them had organized units of self-defense armed with revolvers or with knives in their native towns and villages and these had often succeeded in saving whole communities. Unable, then, to accept that in their new homeland the Jews had to resort to foreign protection, they created a semi-clandestine organization, *Ha-Shomer* (The Watchman), that took in hand the protection of Jewish villages. It was organized as a secret order whose members were subject to strict discipline. Armed with rifles and wearing Beduin *keffieh* headdresses, they rode purebred mares and stood watch during the night around the basalt walls that surrounded Galilee villages. They not only drove the thieves away but sometimes chased them as far as their camps beyond the Jordan river. Taken aback by this unexpected turn of events, the Arabs began to respect these fearless riders. *Ha-Shomer* became a legendary corps that fired the imaginations of young people. Their feats evoked the admiration and longing of young Zionists in Eastern European countries.

The creation of *Ha-Shomer* is an important stage in the history of Jewish Palestine. Self-defense became a basic principle and similar groups were formed in the older settlements. When World War I broke out, the oppressive measures of the Turkish government became unbearable and another secret organization came into being in Zikhron Yaakov, in Samaria. This was *Nili*, set up to help the British armies take Palestine. Contact was made at an early date with British intelligence in Cairo, but the spy ring was clumsily organized and the number of its agents was too small. It was soon discovered by the Turks and wiped out. Nevertheless, it played an important role in establishing the first contacts between Palestine Jewry and Great Britain.

Ha-Shomer can be regarded as the forerunner of the underground army which made Israel's independence possible. It was this unshakable resolution never to be unprepared in case of surprise attack, and never to rely on the good will of the authorities for protection that led to the creation of the *Haganah,* the secret defense force. The same principle also inspired the formation of regiments of Jewish volunteers that fought in the ranks of the Allies during the two World Wars.

This was an important stage. Although they remained numerically weak, the Palestinian Jews from then on acquired a specific national physiognomy. Instead of being resigned to their fate or fleeing from it, they felt they were capable of taking their future into their own hands. The same spirit of initiative and taste for innovation soon came to infect urban development which had begun to expand before the outbreak of World War I. In Jerusalem, the majority of the population was Orthodox Jews who gave the city its very special character. New districts now began to rise outside the walls of the Old City. The number of modern schools constantly increased; the short-lived 'gazettes' were superseded by a modern daily press; banking institutions sprung up. Haifa, which according to Theodor Herzl's prophetic vision was to become the country's main industrial center, reached the first stage of its development with the building of the first modern districts on the slopes of Mount Carmel.

But it was principally in Jaffa that the newcomers concentrated. For the wave of immigration was made up not only of pioneers bent on tilling the soil, but also a large number of families who had been won over to the Zionist ideal or who merely wanted their children to receive a Hebrew education. They came at a period when the country was far from thriving. Yet enterprising men succeeded in setting up shops and even developing small industry. They were followed by young schoolteachers who took up their lodgings in the neighborhood of the Hebrew schools. Young Hebrew writers began to cater for a new reading public; intellectuals were drawn to Jaffa by its picturesque and stimulating atmosphere. Besides these, a new class of civil servants appeared in the city, as a consequence of the Palestinian Office's decision to establish its headquarters in Jaffa.

But the narrow, foul-smelling streets of the Arab city of Jaffa were not always to the taste of the new citizens accustomed to European housing conditions. Thus in 1909, a large plot of land was bought in the nearby dunes, reaching down as far as the sea coast. Presently, a new garden-city sprang up from the sandy dunes around the new high school (incidentally, this was to be the first secondary school in the world in which the teaching was entirely in Hebrew).

This new district was called Tel Aviv (an attempt to render in biblical Hebrew the title of Herzl's prophetic novel *Altneuland*). This large city with its gardens, its wide streets and modern buildings was entirely built by Jewish workers—something that at the time was absolutely novel. From its very beginning, it had an autonomous local council and was inhabited and administered exclusively by Jews. Its schools were attended by young people who had come to Palestine from all the corners of Russia. Young workers, who landed in the port of Jaffa, had no trouble finding employment there in building houses or streets. Long before Zion had become a reality, Tel Aviv was already 'the Gate to Zion'.

In this small society, intellectual life was very intense. It had many publishing houses, magazines and weeklies, which, although up against great financial difficulties, attracted a circle of assiduous readers and kept Hebrew literary life in Palestine and abroad alive and flourishing. They opened their columns to Hebrew poets

The Tribe of Dan, stained-glass window by Chagall. One of the stained-glass ▶ windows by Marc Chagall in the synagogue of the Hadassah Hospital, En Kerem, Jerusalem. This comes from a series of twelve depicting the twelve tribes. The inscription on top is from Genesis 49:16. Photo Sandak Inc., New York.

and novelists and soon Palestinians began to take great interest in the new Hebrew literature.

But the man who influenced the readers of this time more than any other was Joseph Hayyim Brenner, a writer of some reputation abroad who had come to settle in Tel Aviv. Brenner was an original writer and a rebel who had left London, where he had edited a small literary review, and had come to Palestine despite his misgivings. The helplessness of the Russian Jews on the one hand had driven him to despair, but on the other he also rejected the rootlessness of the young intellectuals and artists whom he describes in his novels. Palestine appealed to him despite the fact that he was disgusted by its oppressively provincial atmosphere. The small Palestinian working class listened to him, although he constantly attacked its shortcomings and its false poses; at the same time he condemned the hypocrisy and ineffectiveness of Zionist leaders abroad. He put all the ardor of his faith and all the bitterness of his tormented soul into his stories, which told of the blind gropings, illusions, and mistakes of a world struggling to come to life. He was to die shortly after his arrival, knifed by an Arab during the bloody clashes of May 1921.

THE JEWISH NATIONAL HOME

The Great War almost put an end to the fragile structure which the pioneers of Israel had so painfully set up. The oppression of

Tel Aviv — early days, 1909. The first inhabitants-to-be of Tel Aviv visit the site of the future city as the building plots for the first houses are distributed. Tel Aviv, named after the Hebrew translation of Theodor Herzl's *Altneuland* started as a suburb of Jaffa. Within a few years these sand dunes had become a thriving little town. By now Tel Aviv is the hub of a conurbation of 388,000 inhabitants. Central Zionist Archives, Jerusalem.

Jewish soldiers in World War I. Soldiers of the first Jewish battalions of the British Army during World War I march to their barracks in the Southern Plain. At first, the British allowed only the Zion Mule Corps to be formed; despite opposition from various quarters, they decided in 1917, however, to raise a Jewish battalion, and in fact three (one coming from America and one from the liberated areas of South Palestine) were formed, comprising some 5,000 men. They participated in a number of campaigns against the Turkish army and in the crossing of the Jordan. Central Zionist Archives, Jerusalem.

the Turkish military regime, the deportations of foreign citizens, the famines and epidemics, took a heavy toll of the Jewish population. But when General Allenby made his triumphal entry into Jerusalem and British administration took over from the tyrannical Turkish rulers, new horizons opened before the Jewish inhabitants of Palestine. The future was full of promise. The 1917 Balfour Declaration recognized the historical bond between the Jewish people and Palestine, and the name of Great Britain was linked with the creation of a Jewish National Home in Palestine. This recognition became an international obligation when the British Mandate over Palestine was ratified by the League of Nations. Jewish battalions formed in Great Britain and in the United States had helped the British troops liberate the land, and volunteers from Palestine had joined the British army under their own blue and white flag, among them several distinguished leaders of the *Yishuv,* the Jewish community. A Zionist Commission, which had been given wide powers by the British government, arrived in the country, headed by Chaim Weizmann,

the man really behind the Balfour Declaration. Weizmann was to hold the reins of the Zionist government during the coming thirty years.

A dream had become reality. There was every reason to think that the sufferings and the sacrifices of two generations of pioneers had not been in vain. But the painful awakening was not long in coming. Palestinian Jews soon realized that a National Home was not a state. British administration, first military, then civilian, was far from convinced of the value of British commitment toward Zionism. It was pervaded with pan-Arab and pan-Islamic ideas nurtured by influential circles connected with the British embassy in Cairo.

The Arab world was in ferment. The creation of semi-independent states in Syria, Lebanon and Iraq, and the support given to pro-Arab circles in the British administration encouraged active opposition among the Arab population of Palestine. As early as 1920, riots broke out in Jerusalem. These outbreaks of hatred, fanned by unrelenting religious and racialist agitation, very soon became chronic, and caused the Palestine Jews to close their ranks for active defense and be in a permanent state of readiness.

The enthusiasm had been short-lived. Now, the Jewish community realized that the British Mandate, far from putting an end to its difficulties, was only the beginning of a long struggle on two fronts: on the one hand, against the reserved attitude of the mandatory administration; on the other, against the increasing hostility of Arab nationalists.

There were, however, yet further difficulties to be faced. The toll on the Jewish population in World War I had been high and Palestine's Jewish community needed to grow to strengthen the fragile structure now in place. Worse still was the question of Russia; it was there that the Zionist ideal was born and from there came the first waves of immigration to Palestine. Furthermore the financial contributions that enabled the Palestinian Jewish community to survive came largely from Russian Zionists. Now, quite suddenly and unexpectedly, Russian Jewry was cut off from the rest of the world. Toward the end of the 1920s, an 'iron curtain', the first of its kind in modern times, had fallen over millions of Russian Jews. At first, the February revolution of 1917 had been enthusiastically followed by the Jews who shared in the general elation of the newly won liberty of the Russians. At that time, the Jewish national revival experienced a renewal of popularity. The Balfour Declaration was seen by the Jewish masses as a messianic event. Zionism which, at the outset had been the doctrine of restricted circles, now became a mass movement with tens of thousands of young followers. A new pioneer organization came into existence called *He-Halutz* (the Pioneer),

which was headed by Captain Joseph Trumpeldor, a war hero who had lost an arm in the Russo-Japanese war and was to find a hero's death in defending an outpost in the Galilee Hills against Arab aggressors. Groups of young pioneers set out to join their brothers in the Land of Israel.

But these great hopes were shattered by the attitude of the new regime in Moscow. As the Soviet regime grew stronger, its attitude toward Zionism became more and more intolerant. The Jewish Communists had played an important part in the Revolution. They came for the most part from the Bund, the Socialist party that had always been bitterly hostile to Zionism. These militants now became the most active persecutors of their Zionist opponents. Hebrew papers and Hebrew schools were closed. Zionist circles were forced underground and their militants began to fill the Russian prisons and the Siberian camps.

Worse still, the borders were closed, shutting off three million Russian Jews from Palestine. At the beginning of the 1920s, certain isolated groups still succeeded in escaping, and prisoners deported to Siberia were sometimes allowed to exchange their prison terms for an emigration visa to Palestine, but as the years passed, these forms of escape became increasingly rare; Russian Jewry was now beyond reach.

The Third and Fourth Aliyot

The time was ripe for the Third Aliyah, the first mass immigration to Palestine. Ships cast anchor off Jaffa and crowded trains arrived from Egypt. They were loaded with Zionist families who

Third Aliyah, 1920-3. Pioneers of the Third Aliyah (1920-3) engaged in agricultural work near a new settlement. The wooden huts served as housing in the early days of the settlements in the Jezreel Valley. Much of the work was in draining swamps and the pioneers suffered terribly from malaria and other diseases. Central Zionist Archives, Jerusalem.

at the last moment had succeeded in leaving a Russia in the throes of civil war. Among the new arrivals were a number of Hebrew writers, most belonging to the Odessa school. But the great majority of the new immigrants were young pioneers, members of the new *He-Halutz* movement who had been infected with the enthusiasm of East European Jewish youths. Russian *halutzim* left their country via all imaginable routes: the Caucasian mountains, Persia, even Siberia and the Far East. Legally or illegally, they crossed the Polish or Rumanian borders where they were joined by thousands of young members of local organizations. They then made their way in organized groups to Trieste and Constanza whence they sailed for Palestine.

These young men were exultant with new ideas gleaned from the storm of the Revolution or from the ideological agitation which shook postwar Europe. They were apostles of renewal. Their aim was to live in *kibbutzim* and most of them could not imagine their future except in terms of collective action. Others preferred the *moshavim,* the cooperative villages which were being created for the first time. They launched themselves into the political turmoil of Palestinian Jewry which they inspired with a new ardor.

The Zionist authorities who had encouraged this movement were now overwhelmed by the task facing them: the country had barely emerged from the war and everything had to be rebuilt— with no money on hand. Russian Jewry could no longer be reached and America had not yet taken over, so that vital financial contributions from abroad simply failed to come. This money was desperately needed to create farming settlements and to develop the cities. The meager budgets of the Zionist institutions were hardly sufficient to maintain welcoming centers for the immigrants and the essential services, especially schools, which were now compelled to expand drastically under the demographic pressure of the new *aliyah*. But the most urgent task was to find work for the masses of newcomers. At first this was provided by public works undertaken by the mandatory administration to fill the vacuum left by the Ottoman powers. Groups of immigrants in this way found an occupation building roads. Government wages, though very low, were sufficient for the needs of the Arab workers, but inadequate to meet those of the new immigrants. However, the Jewish workers joined together and created collective companies. Living in tents, underpaid and underfed, they pitched their camps in every corner of the land and started building roads or breaking up stones for the paving. At night, after the day's exhausting work under the scorching sun of Palestinian summers, these camps resounded with songs and with the rhythms of the *Hora,* the Balkan folk-dance that became the national dance of Israel. The tents were the scene of passionate discussions, clashes between members of different parties; groups were formed and dissolved all the time.

The *Histadrut*—the Labor Federation created by the political parties in 1920—was strengthened by this wave of new immigrants. It played an increasingly important part in promoting the initiatives taken by the workers of the new *aliyah*. The enormous influence of this Labor Federation on the political life and economic structure of the country dates from that time.

Characteristic of this first postwar period was the purchase of a large expanse of land in the Jezreel Valley. From then on, the systematic agricultural settlement of the Jews in Palestine struck deep roots. This valley which people grew accustomed to call the *Emek* (the Valley) had been the granary of ancient Israel. In its present abandoned state, it was a desolate expanse of fallow land interspersed with swamps. The purchase of this valley was made by the Jewish National Fund, the agricultural fund of the Zionist Organization, which bought it from an Arab family in Beirut.

The valley became the center of Zionist agricultural efforts. All the different forms of settlements were represented there, ranging from the *kibbutzim* (or from their smaller models named *kevutzot*).The *moshavim*.The *Emek* became the symbol of the new era. Owing to the lack of financial means, life in the new villages was a permanent struggle against poverty. The young farmers barely had enough to eat and their miserable huts were damp with rain during the rainy season. For all these hardships, the glamor of the *Emek* inspired thousands of would-be pioneers who ardently awaited their turn to come and settle in Palestine. Agricultural expansion in the valley was a model for future agricultural development for it was a testing-ground for agricultural theory and practice. It was there that the *kibbutz* and the *moshav* became crystallized institutions.

Simultaneously, the political direction of the Jewish community changed. The new wave of immigration with its organized groups, its insistence on economic planning and its ideal of fast economic growth and social justice, took over from the traditional élite of the prewar period. Conversely, the men from the Second Aliyah merged into the working class and integrated into the unions side by side with the new politicians that the new wave had brought to the fore.

As often happened in the history of Palestinian society, the Third Aliyah period was brought to a close by an economic crisis which did not, however, last very long. In 1924, a new type of immigrant, totally different from the preceding ones, appeared on the Palestinian scene. This new wave arrived from Poland, the European country with the most Jews.

The Fourth Aliyah was mixed in character: young enthusiastic pioneers rubbed shoulders with middle-class families. Small shopkeepers from Warsaw or from the provincial towns, businessmen, factory owners and artisans, all came together. These people had brought their children with them as well as their furniture, their stocks of merchandise or their work tools. In Jaffa harbor, small family chests replaced the bundles of clothing of former times.

A period of prosperity began. Hundreds of houses sprang up overnight on the sandy beaches of Tel Aviv. The price of plots soared in the cities. Industry, which so far had been practically non-existent in the economic structure of Palestine, was introduced into the country. Capital streamed in and unemployment was no longer a nightmare haunting workers. Apparently the Jewish National Home had overcome the dangerous period of its infancy and could look forward to a bright future.

In April 1925, the dream of Chaim Weizmann (President of the Zionist Organization who was also a chemist of international eminence) at last came true: on top of Mount Scopus, he presided over the opening ceremony of the first Hebrew university in the world. Zionism seemed to be on its way to success. Speeches were delivered by Lord Balfour, Lord Allenby, and by representatives of the foremost universities in the world. This forgotten corner of the Orient again became a center of interest for international scientific circles. The Jewish population was constantly on the increase. Tel Aviv was growing into a big city. In the agricultural domain, citrus-growing was in full swing. Everything seemed to be headed for success. But this period of euphoria was short-lived. In Poland, new restrictive measures were taken against the Jews, which represented a severe blow to the Palestinian economy and, what with land speculation as well, a financial crisis rapidly ensued. Several years later, this crisis worsened with the terrible crash on the New York Stock Exchange. Many immigrants returned to their former homelands. A long period of stagnation and unemployment followed, with all the political repercussions that such a crisis usually implies.

Thus the Fourth Aliyah, which had been so full of promise, eventually proved, in fact, a failure. It nevertheless left an enduring mark on the economy of the country. From that period on dates systematic town planning and development, as well as the first timid beginnings of Israel's industry which was later to become one of the fundamental elements of the economy. At the same time, many middle-class immigrants took to citrus-growing in the Sharon Valley, north of Tel Aviv, which presently became a densely populated zone, and even today the effects of this new direction taken by agriculture are to be felt: citrus-growing holds an important place in Israel's exports.

But, first and foremost, this wave of immigration proved to the world that Palestine was not only a center of attraction for young idealists ready for every sacrifice, but that it was also a shelter for the persecuted Jewish masses. The new immigrants of the Fourth Aliyah, peaceful families from small Polish towns, foreshadowed the 'rescue operations' to come.

Refugees from Germany

As far back as the early 1930s, there were discernible signs of the storm gathering over Europe. In Eastern European countries, anti-Semitism grew worse and racial discrimination became a principle of government. Hitler at that moment came to power. In one of the most enlightened countries in the world, hatred for the Jews was not only accepted as legitimate, it was made compulsory at all levels of political life. The indifference of the world and the cowardice of public opinion which was increasingly paralyzed by its desire for peace at all costs encouraged Nazi cruelty. But as long as the gates remained open, the European Jews sought to escape. First, there was the exodus from Germany, followed by that from Austria and Czechoslovakia. The roads of Europe began to fill with long columns of refugees.

Countries that could have opened their borders to the thousands of Jews who looked for a haven remained hermetically closed. The Evian Conference (which remains a sinister memory in world history) was convened to find a solution to this intolerable situation, but ended as a macaber farce. The Jewish refugees were not wanted. Living in perpetual fear, German Jews ran from one closed border to another. They raised their eyes toward Palestine. But at that time, access to the Holy Land was strictly limited. The Jewish Agency tried every possible means and a number of entrance visas were eventually obtained. Tens of thousands of Central European Jews crowded into the country. From 1933 till the outbreak of World War II, Jews in the Diaspora no longer had any illusions: even in such countries where Jews led a free existence and had a certain influence on the economic and political life of the nation, they were unable to change the attitude of their governments. The only country where, despite the mandatory administration, the Jews had the right to raise their voices and could successfully demand admittance for their persecuted brothers, was Palestine. In Palestine, the Jews could afford to ignore the official policy and did not hesitate to violate laws which, in their eyes, were iniquitous, in order to rescue the European Jews. As early as 1934, the first clandestine refugee ships began arriving in Palestine despite the close watch maintained by British patrol boats. Young *Haganah* fighters guided them from the coast and later took charge of the passengers.

The Jewish masses of the threatened countries of Europe looked toward this last haven. Political discussions had by now come to a stop, for there was no longer any point in bandying arguments for or against a Jewish national ideology. The racist threat menaced the whole Jewish people and Palestine was the only ray of light in the universal gloom.

The arrival of the German Jews of the Fifth Aliyah, the last before the outbreak of World War II, brought a completely new type of immigrant into the country. Although the contribution of German Jewry to the movement had been far from negligible, only a small minority had adhered to Zionism. As a rule, the German Jews were among the most assimilated in Europe. They had obtained Emancipation around the middle of the 19th century and had quickly merged into the life of the country with whose culture they had completely identified themselves.

The blow to the German Jews was heart-breaking, as, in many cases, they had been genuine German patriots that racialist laws had turned overnight into outcasts, whatever their social position or political opinions. Nevertheless, in spite of this dreadful trauma, the reaction of German Jewry did not fall short of its long tradition. The refugees who set out for Palestine engaged upon their new life with energy and determination. Although they were far less steeped in Jewish knowledge and tradition than their East European brothers of the preceding *aliyot*, they brought into the Israel melting pot new qualities which considerably enriched it and profoundly marked its character.

As soon as they had set foot in the land, they did their utmost to adjust themselves rapidly to their new and totally unfamiliar environment. They set aside for the time being their university degrees and professional experience and accepted any kind of work. This was a time when doctors raised chickens and lawyers became taxidrivers, when opera singers went to work on *kibbutzim*. The German immigrants also had a hard time learning their new and mysterious language, Hebrew, of which they had not had the slightest notion. Progressively, they managed to tear themselves loose from German culture in which they had been so steeped.

They introduced unfamiliar habits into Palestinian society and to some degree shattered the austerity which the Second Aliyah had imposed upon the country. These new immigrants had been accustomed to a high standard of comfort. They introduced modern architecture, habits of cleanliness and order into the appearance of the cities, a taste for luxurious window dressing and suchlike improvements. Palestine, which up to then had borne the stamp of the East European ghetto, took a step toward being more 'European'.

The coming of the German Jews had a lasting effect on the planning of the economy as well as on industrial development, science and art. The research institutes of the Hebrew University opened their doors to a great number of distinguished scientists from Germany, Austria and Czechoslovakia. After the anti-Semitic turn taken by the Mussolini regime, they were joined by scientists from the Jewish élite of Italy.

During World War II, Jewish Palestine happened to be part of one of the decisive fronts. As it was cut off from European harbors it had to mobilize all its scientific and industrial resources to contribute to the Allied war effort. This was made possible by the changes which had taken place in its economy during the years that had preceded the outbreak of the war. At the same time, war emphasized the progressive character of Israel society, its capacity for new initiative, and its Western bias.

Development of Jewish Autonomy

Before attaining political independence, Jewish Palestinian society had almost acquired *de facto* autonomy. This achievement was a consequence of the specific conditions in Palestine and of the policy of the British administration compelling the Jews to create their own institutions and administrative services.

With a few exceptions, British rule in Palestine presented all the characteristics of a colonial regime. The civil servants of the Mandate considered it their duty to ensure that the services functioned properly. But, when it came to developing the country, they showed an utter lack of imagination. Their first care was the welfare of the Arab population who fitted better into their concept of 'natives'. The Jews they considered pretentious and restless romantics, pursuing an aim which seemed to them totally unreal. Moreover, at a very early stage, they saw the rapid progress of the Jewish National Home as a threat to British policy in the Middle East based, as it was, on winning the support of the Arab world.

The only solution left for the Zionist Executive and the National Jewish Council which democratically represented the Jews of Palestine, was to create their own executive institutions and establish a parallel administrative system, and thanks to the self-discipline of the Jewish population, they eventually succeeded in doing so. An independent educational system thus came into being. In a very short time, this parallel schooling system was attended by the majority of the Jewish children, though at that time education had not been made compulsory. Pedagogical methods constantly improved and kindergarten, elementary and secondary schools were set up in all the important settlements. Modern medical services, hospitals and social security won the battle against endemic diseases (such as malaria, which had been one of the main scourges of the country and had taken a heavy toll on the first pioneer settlements).

The executive institutions took advantage of this new liberty to emphasize the Jewish character of their administration. The *Histadrut* and its *kibbutzim* and *moshavim* constituted a 'ready-made' network for overt or clandestine action.

The creation of an independent economy was encouraged by the permanent Arab threat which forced the Jews into unrelenting vigilance, a vigilance made further necessary by the restrictive steps taken by the authorities to limit immigration and the purchase of land from the Arabs.

Conflict with the Arabs

After the 1920 and 1921 disturbances in Jerusalem and Jaffa, the year 1929 saw new massacres of Jews by fanatical Arab crowds. Many were slaughtered in Hebron and Safed, although the *Haganah,* the self-defense organization, with its old rifles and rusty pistols, succeeded in protecting many isolated Jewish quarters. These riots were a warning which the *Haganah* never forgot. It systematically set out to purchase weapons and train men. In April 1936, new Arab rioting broke out. This new period of disturbances lasted almost three years and security became a crucial problem for the Jews.

This period of great danger in which thousands of defenders were killed (as well as many innocent victims), had a decisive effect on the formation of the nation. The Arab revolt spread quickly; it had won the support of the Nazi-Fascist axis which, in anticipation of the coming war, sought to infiltrate into the Middle East. It was encouraged in this aim by armed bands which crossed into the country from the neighboring Arab states with impunity. The British reaction was slow and weak. The Supreme Arab Committee, led by the Jerusalem Mufti, Hadj Amin el-Husseini (who a few years later proclaimed himself the friend and agent of the Berlin regime) led a general strike against the Jews and a total boycott of Jewish life. Isolated Jewish settlements and Jewish quarters situated near the Arab districts of towns with a mixed population were subjected to constant attacks. The lines of communication between cities were cut, buses were attacked by armed gangs. The Jewish population lived in an atmosphere of siege. One of the inevitable consequences of such a situation was the final separation between Jewish and Arab economies. Arab workers left their jobs on the plantations and were replaced by Jewish manpower while Arab products were withdrawn from the Jewish markets, causing Jewish agricultural production to improve in quantity and quality.

This was no longer rioting; this was war, on the issue of which depended the survival or total annihilation of the whole Jewish

Palmah soldiers. A group of *Palmah* (Shock Companies) soldiers attacking an Arab village during the Israel War of Independence (1948), followed by a few primitive armored cars. No uniform was worn until the companies were integrated into the Israel Defense Army. Originally formed to assist the British against the Germans, it continued to exist as an underground, permanently mobilized, force. Its units were dispersed throughout Palestinian labor settlements and their time was divided between work and training. Central Zionist Archives, Jerusalem.

community. But the nation rose in arms against its attackers. The *Haganah* mobilized all available men while the majority of the women and schoolchildren stood by ready for any emergency. Weapons which had been secretly purchased or had been made in clandestine factories piled up in their caches. Not a single village was allowed to remain isolated and a system of convoys kept the roads open. Presently, Jewish units left their purely defensive role and began attacking the concentrations of armed Arab bands.

It soon became necessary to organize regular troops. The *Palmah* (abbreviation of *Paluggot mahatz*—'assault units') was therefore formed. The young soldiers received a hard military training in camps which were usually located in *kibbutzim*. Their time was spent in cultivating the fields, training, and taking part in military actions. This élite corps was mainly composed of young people born in Palestine; most of the top people in Israel's army today, men who later achieved fame during the wars forced upon their country, emerged from this hard school of war. This is the case of Moshe Dayan, Yigal Allon, Yitzhak Rabin and many others. But the *Palmah* also bred a multitude of writers, poets and administrators who played a leading role after the independence of the country.

This period also saw the creation of dissenting organizations: first came the *Irgun Tzevai Leumi,* followed by the *Lohame Herut Yisrael* (also known as the Stern group). Both movements grew out of the Revisionist Zionist Party, an activist and overtly anti-British group, founded by Vladimir Jabotinsky. These groups did not recognize the authority of the *Haganah* and were in favor of direct offensive action both against the Arabs and the British administration.

This split with the underground organizations considerably hindered the unity of action of the Jewish community which could only be sporadically maintained. Under the leadership of David Ben-Gurion, the *Haganah* prepared to become a regular army, while, during the last years of the Mandate, bold terrorist actions committed by the dissenting groups drew the attention of world opinion to the situation in Palestine and helped to precipitate the withdrawal of the British.

The government of Great Britain did not resist the pressure of Arab terrorism very long. Its policy toward the Jews, which had always been reserved, became openly hostile. It made public its decision to restrict the number of Jews in Palestine in order to keep the Jewish community from becoming the majority since, at the outbreak of World War II, there were about half a million Jews and one million Arabs in Palestine. While the Arab revolt exhausted itself, the Jews had to face a new struggle. They now had to fight for their right to open the gates to the refugees and to settle on the lands which they had legally purchased from their former Arab owners.

Creating new villages in remote areas became a heroic feat. It had been decided from the very beginning of the Arab disturbances that settlements were to be established on every plot of land owned by Jews, even if it meant isolation in the midst of territories which were practically under the control of Arab bands. In order to keep the surprise element on their sides, the builders adhered to the so-called 'Tower and Stockade' system. Prefabricated elements were brought to the site of the future settlement and put together in the course of a day. The village consisted of a wooden palisade, a watchtower, and a few wooden huts. The epic of the 'Tower and Stockade' period reached its climax with the simultaneous creation, during one autumn night, of eleven settlements in the Negev desert.

WORLD WAR II

The events of the tragic years 1939 to 1949, the decade which preceded the birth of the State of Israel, are still vivid memories to many. War; the invasion of Poland; the last and desperate efforts to save the Jewish refugees that flocked to Balkan harbors and Danubian ports; then the hermetic closing of the gates; the invasion of Western Europe; the Nazi butchers masters of the fate of millions of Jews; the lightning thrust of Rommel's armies to the suburbs of Alexandria; the threat hanging over Palestine and the British plans for withdrawal. Mercifully, the El Alamein victory crushed the Nazi menace to the Middle East. Then there began to emerge the first incomplete rumors of horrors in ghettos and death camps. Following these events, the revolts broke out in ghettos and desperate efforts were made to help the Jewish partisans. The Jews now felt their terrible isolation and world indifference; the horrible truth concerning the fate of six million European Jews came out ... and, at last, peace, that came too late....

When the guns fell silent, there remained, however, the tremendous hope of saving the survivors, of welcoming to Palestine the pitiful remnants of the once prosperous communities of European Jewry. But what bitterness when, months after the end of the war, hundreds of thousands of 'displaced persons', ('D.Ps' as they were called), were still kept in German camps to serve the ends of a brutal policy and prevented from joining their brothers in Palestine. Then came open revolt and its repression. Dozens of refugee ships defied the might of the British fleet in the Mediterranean, highlighted by the tragedy of the *Exodus* in 1947. Argument raged in the United Nations until the resolution of November 29 1947, advocating the creation of a Jewish state in Palestine. The Arabs issued threats, but failed to prevent the proclamation of the State of Israel on May 14 1948. Israel found itself invaded by seven Arab armies. Bloody battles of the Independence War took place against tremendous odds, ending in the victory of the Jewish State. The first Truce Agreements were then signed and the new state entered into the family of nations.

From the very start of World War II, the Palestine Jews had spontaneously offered their services to Great Britain to contribute to the struggle of the Allies against the Germans who were the sworn enemies of the Jewish people. Tens of thousands of men volunteered for the Palestinian Jewish units of the British armies once the Jewish authorities had managed to overcome the prolonged hesitations of the British government, wary of Arab reactions. This success was largely due to the tenaciousness

David Ben-Gurion (1886-). David Ben-Gurion who led the struggle for the State during and after World War II and who became Israel's first Prime Minister and Minister of Defense. Born in Plonsk (Poland), he joined the Zionist movement at an early date and settled in Israel in 1906, since when he has played an active role in a multitude of different spheres. Government Press Office, Tel Aviv.

of Chaim Weizmann and to the indefatigable activity of Moshe Sharett, later to became the first Foreign Minister of Israel. Over thirty thousand Palestinian Jewish volunteers took part in the Desert War and in the operations in Greece and Ethiopia. Subsequently, a Jewish brigade helped in the invasion of Italy, Austria, Germany, Holland and Belgium.

As they proceeded along the North African coast, the Palestinian soldiers came into contact for the first time with the Jewish communities of Cyrenaica, Tripolitania and Tunisia. Other units, especially the engineers and the signal corps, as well as specialists in public works directing projects for the army, associated with Syrian, Iraqi, and Iranian Jews.

The encounter between Oriental Jews and the young Palestinian soldiers who came to them as liberators in the ranks of the British army had a tremendous effect on both groups. For the first time, Oriental Jews became really aware of the existence of a Jewish political center established in the land of Israel, where

people spoke the holy tongue, enjoyed complete freedom, and led Jewish lives. The Palestinians, for their part, discovered a distinctly and deeply Jewish world in which the remembrance of Zion was alive; a world both very close to them and at the same time very different, utterly unlike the Europe from which they and their parents derived their Jewish heritage. This encounter marked the reuniting of the two branches of Judaism which had been separated by centuries of parallel development; a reuniting which had already been prepared by the recent history of Palestine. During their stay in the countries of the Orient as well as in Libya, Tunisia, and Iraq, the soldiers organized courses for the Jewish population. Emissaries were sent from Palestine under the cover of the Jewish units, whose task was to constitute the nuclei of a pioneer youth movement.

These seeds were not long in bearing fruit: when the State of Israel came into being (at a period when life in Muslim countries

Chaim Weizmann (1874-1952). Chaim Weizmann, president of the Zionist organization, who became first president of the State of Israel. Born at Motel near Pinsk, he moved to England where he was largely responsible for winning the support of England's leaders and obtaining the Balfour Declaration. Government Press Office, Tel Aviv.

had become unbearable) masses of Oriental Jews left the lands they had lived in for hundreds, sometimes even for thousands, of years. Syrian Jews had only to cross the mountains which served as northern border to the State. The majority of Iraq's Jews who had suffered terribly during the 1941 Nazi coup of Rashid Ali Keilani, were brought to Israel a few years after Independence, an exodus made possible through the intervention of the great European powers. In the following years, the majority of Tunisian, Moroccan, and Egyptian Jews came to settle in Israel. Mere vestiges of a once densely populated Diaspora were left in Islamic countries, after centuries of enslavement and decadence.

The encounter between the Palestinian brigade and refugees from the death camps in Europe was infinitely more tragic. These men and women had just emerged from long years of torture in the ghettos and concentration camps. Suddenly, before these skeletal figures loomed the unimaginable and unimagined sight of uniformed Jews of all grades and ranks, proudly sporting the Shield of David on their sleeves. For the Palestinians, it was a heart-breaking experience. Here they found their lost brothers, survivors from their own families whom they had given up prematurely for dead, neighbors from their native European towns and villages whose Jewish streets were now plunged in the everlasting silence of death.

'Illegal' immigration boat. An 'illegal' immigration boat arrives somewhere off the coast of Palestine. The passengers disembark with the help of a rope thrown into the sea by hundreds of volunteers coming from neighboring settlements. During the later part of the Mandate, the British authorities severely limited Jewish immigration to Palestine. Tension ran high as this was the Nazi- and immediately post-Nazi period when many Jews were struggling to get to Palestine. To get round the immigration quotas, 'illegal' immigration was organized which brought immigrants to Palestine without the knowledge of the British authorities. Those captured were deported to internment camps in Cyprus and elsewhere. Central Zionist Archives, Jerusalem.

These Palestinian units were largely responsible for rescuing the *Sheerit Ha-Pletah* (The Last Remnants), a biblical term used to designate the survivors of the death camps. It was they who organized, with the complicity of superior authorities in the Allied armies, the sending of the 'D.Ps' across chaotic postwar Europe, toward harbors in Italy, France, and Greece. There, the men in charge of the clandestine *aliyah* crowded them into dilapidated boats bound for the coast of Palestine. Many of these vessels were caught by the British patrol boats and their pas-

sengers put into camps in Palestine or in Cyprus. But, despite the repressive measures, the stream of immigrants kept flowing.

The annihilation of European Jewry left an indelible mark on the people of Israel, including the younger generations and Oriental Jews who had not lived through the same experience. Later the capture and trial of Adolf Eichmann was to give further intensity to their feelings. The young Israelis were proud of the act of justice accomplished by their State and realized how imperishable for them was the memory of this exterminated world.

Maabarah (tent camps), post-1948. New immigrants arriving at a *Maabarah* (transit immigration camp). From its establishment Israel received a mass immigration and many Jews from all parts of the world welcomed the foundation of a Jewish State, and went there in their hundreds of thousands. Especially during the early years of the State, it proved impossible to provide immediate housing for all the newcomers and tents, tin huts, and wooden barracks were put up throughout the country to house the immigrants until some more permanent home could be built. Central Zionist Archives, Jerusalem

Haifa. The city of Haifa has been built up the slopes of Mount Carmel. The area became a major industrial zone partly as a result of the extensive port and harbor facilities in the nearby Kishon river. The view here is of the lower city in the neighborhood of the port. The residential quarters are built on the slopes and on the top of Mount Carmel. Photo Harris, Jerusalem.

The Ingathering of the Exiles

Because of its heterogeneous composition, the Israel nation is, demographically, like a tapestry, and woven with the multiple threads of the various Jewish communities dispersed throughout the world, whether now extinct or still alive in some remote corner. It was the first time in the course of Israel's 'long march' that such an 'Ingathering of the Exiles'— *Kibbutz Galuyyot*—had been achieved.

At the turn of the third decade of its existence, Israel had a Jewish population of almost two and a half millions (apart from 400,000 Muslims, Christians and Druze). Between 1882 and its independence, nearly 600,000 Jews came as immigrants; this figure doubled in the first twenty years following the creation of the State. During the latter period, the majority of the immigrants (about 700,000) came from Asian and African countries where the population was largely Muslim; the remainder (about 600,000) came from America and Europe, especially from countries beyond the Iron Curtain and from the European refugee camps.

But this very general statistical data can only give an abstract picture of the situation. In concrete terms, this meant that Israel had to absorb whole communities which, as a result of this emigration from their homelands, simply disappeared from the map of the Jewish dispersion. Such is the case of the Oriental communities as well as the remnants of formerly prosperous and influential groups of European Jewry. There remain practically no Jews in Yemen, Libya, Syria, Iraq, and Egypt any longer.

The North African communities have decreased by nine-tenths. The majority of Balkan Jews, especially the Bulgarian Jews, and the remnants of Greek and Yugoslav Jewry, have been absorbed into Israel. The exodus from Rumania brought hundreds of thousands of Jews to the country. Most of the survivors from Poland are now living in Israel; so, too, are tens of thousands of German, Austrian and Czech Jews. More recently and remarkably, Jews have begun to arrive from Soviet Russia.

Tel Aviv. Founded in 1909, the city developed rapidly under the British Mandate, mainly as Arab riots forced the Jews to abandon Jaffa. On the eve of Independence, Jaffa was abandoned and the two cities united in 1949 under the name Tel Aviv-Jaffa. The city houses Israel's main theaters and newspapers, and is the hub of national life. Shown here is the central part of Tel Aviv, seen from the air. In the foreground, left, Dizengoff Circle, main entertainment center of the city, named after the city's first mayor. On the seashore, the Dan Hotel, the first big hotel built in Tel Aviv. Government Press Office, Tel Aviv.

It is not an easy task to define the respective share of each of these communities in the building of the nation. As the years go by and new generations born or raised in the country take over, a new type of Jew has come to the fore. This is the native Israeli, the *sabra,* completely free from the outlandish heritage of the older generation and from their idiosyncrasies and national particularisms; for the older generation had absorbed so many elements from its non-Jewish environment that, until today, numerous communities have kept their own individual ways of life. These older people are bound together by their customs, by common memories and by the sentimental or linguistic contacts which they have maintained. Though it is too early to define the new type of Jew created in the Israeli melting pot, a general

Modern Israel coins. After the 1948 War of Independence, Israel's coinage remained denominationally the same as under the British Mandate (copper and nickel coinage up to 100 *perutot*), as well as 25 and 250 *perutot* nickel coins; 1,000 *perutot* = £I 1. In 1960, the *perutah* was abandoned in favour of the *agorah* (100 *agorot* = £I 1) and a new coinage adopted.
a) 25 *agorot* coin (reverse)
  Three-stringed lyre, inspired from silver dinars and bronze coins of the Bar Kokhba revolt.
b) 5 *agorot* coin (reverse)
  Three ripe pomegranates as a motif appear on coins of the Bar Kokhba revolt (132-5 A.D.).
c) 10 *agorot* coin (reverse)
  Seven-branched palm-tree, symbol of Judea in ancient times.
d) 1 *agorah* coin
  Three ears of barley, as on the ancient coins of Agrippa I (10 B.C.-44 A.D.)
All the coins are inscribed in Hebrew and Arabic. Photo Goldberg, Jerusalem, Israel Government Coins and Medals Corporation Ltd.

Postmarks, postage stamps. Israel's postage stamps are much sought after for their striking graphic qualities and vividness. Philatelic Service, Tel Aviv.
a) stamp commemorating the 400th anniversary of the publication of *Shulhan Arukh,* the authoritative code of Jewish Law, by Joseph Caro in 1565.
b) Stamp commemorating the Eighth Maccabiah World Jewish Sport Rally. The torches are carried from Modiin, the burial place of the ancient Maccabees.
c) Stamp commemorating the 20th anniversary of Israel's independence.
d) Stamp commemorating the 1969 national stamp exhibition and showing a carving above the Lion Gate (St. Stephen's Gate) in Jerusalem.
e) From a series of stamps representing Israel's main items of export.

appreciation of the share of each community in the building of the nation can at least be attempted.

The general direction and ideological trend was given by East European Jews (Russian, Polish, and Rumanian). Even today, the men who hold political power come largely from these countries (although many of them arrived before World War I). Immediately behind, comes the group of those born in the country, some of whom grew up on *kibbutzim* or *moshavim.* These men also form the majority in the leadership of the *Histadrut* (Israel Labor Federation) and of the *kibbutz* movements whose influence goes far beyond its rather restricted numerical importance. At the level of government administration, a field of foremost importance in the modern era of economic planning, the largest and most influential group is that of the *sabras.* The *sabras* also hold dominant positions in the army and in the defense ministry where, on David Ben-Gurion's insistence, young leadership has always been stressed. Officers retire from active service at a relatively early age and are then available as the executive class for the administration and the economy.

We have already mentioned the changes in structure introduced by the immigrants from Eastern Europe, Austria, and Czechoslovakia. The influence of these immigrants is still ubiquitous in the field of science (although the *sabras* are increasingly numerous there, especially in the provinces of nuclear and exact sciences) and art, particularly music. The banking sector of the economy also profited greatly from their contribution. In the field of literature, Hungarian Jews followed the tradition of their country of origin, contributing much to the development of humor and satire. Bulgarian Jewry gave many actors and directors to the Israel stage. The merchant navy was largely created through the initiative of Greek Jews, especially from Salonika

Hadassah Hospital. Hadassah Hospital and Medical School of the Hebrew University of Jerusalem built on a hill facing En Kerem in the south-western outskirts of the city. The hospital replaced that on Mount Scopus which was inaccessible between 1948 and 1967. Photo Harris, Jerusalem.

Meah Shearim. Main center of the extreme Orthodox Jewish community in the new city of Jerusalem, and the Jews here continue to lead an ultra-religious life. The notice in front is a warning to women not to dress immodestly (which would include the wearing of short sleeves). Photo Harris, Jerusalem.

where, for many decades, Jews practically controlled all the activities of this Balkan harbor, either as workers in the shipyards or as shipowners. The medical profession owes a great debt to the small but very active wave of immigration from South America.

Apart from the group of Sephardi Jews long established in the Holy Land, who quickly merged in the general stream, the first important group of Oriental Jews to settle in Eretz Israel were the Yemenites. They deeply influenced Israel society, for they clung to their original customs and introduced Oriental themes into the folklore and music of Jewish Palestine which thus lost their exclusively Slavonic character. Very noteworthy is the fact that the first popular girl singers were for the most part of Yemenite origin.

Like the Sephardi Jews of Jerusalem, Iraqi Jews played an active role in developing the financial system of the country and its network of banks. The Egyptians, who came from a cosmopolitan environment, were quickly absorbed by the administration, the banks, and the municipalities.

It is still too early to give any final appreciation of the role

of the North African Jewish masses, one of the latest to come. Their élite, though numerically fairly small, contributed to expanding French cultural influence, which was further strengthened when Israel and France struck closer links of friendship. This mass of Jews from the Orient, North Africa, Iraq, Iran, and Yemen, also constituted the backbone of agricultural expansion at a time when the State had just come into existence, and hundreds of villages and small towns sprang up everywhere, from the borders of Upper Galilee to the outskirts of the Negev desert. These settlements owe their present prosperity largely to the Oriental immigrants and to their capacity for adjusting quickly to a totally new kind of work. Abruptly transplanted into a completely new environment, these families of newcomers overcame their initial setbacks with rare tenaciousness and became surprisingly successful.

Thanks to these successive layers of immigrants and to the varied influences of their respective communities, Israel was able to develop a unique culture, bearing little resemblance to that of the first pioneers. Today, the merging of the various elements is accelerated by the pursuit of a common aim and by the continuance of a mortal threat beyond the borders, a threat forcing Israel to live in a constant state of alert.

RELIGION IN ISRAEL

Is the national identity of the Israeli based on national consciousness or on his common religion? Since Israel's creation, this problem has never ceased to haunt the young state. The first law passed by the Israel parliament was the 'Law of the Return' which grants free entry into the country to every Jew wishing to settle there. But who is to be considered a Jew? Anyone who is conscious of being Jewish or someone whose Jewish identity is defined by the religious laws based on the Halakhah (the talmudic code)? How should the State be ruled? According to a modern legislation established by the elected bodies, or according to the religious code which had ruled the Jewish communities in ancient times?

A sensational verdict was returned by Israel's Supreme Court in the case of a Roman Catholic priest, Brother Daniel, who, on the grounds of his Jewish origin, claimed the status of Jew and the benefit of the 'Law of the Return'. The judgment did not enter into the definition of a Jew but established that a man who converts to another faith can no longer be regarded as Jewish. Of course, this case did not for a moment question the legitimacy of the fundamental assumption, accepted by all, according to which every citizen of the state, whether Christian, Muslim, or Druze, is entitled to enjoy full rights as well as

Torah breastplate, Jerusalem, 1945. Modern silver Torah breastplate, showing Tables of the Law. Jerusalem, Israel Museum, 148/190.

freedom of religion. Yet public opinion continues to be frequently agitated by discussions, controversies and further legal cases concerning the character of the state, and whether it should be secular or religious. A *de facto* situation has been accepted by the majority of the nation, with the exception of a small group of religious fanatics concentrated in Jerusalem.

◄ *The Western Wall today.* Since 1967 the Western Wall has again become a focus for Jews all over the world. A piazza has been laid out front of the wall and considerable excavations carried out along the sides. Photo Harris, Jerusalem.

Initially, Jewish Orthodox circles violently opposed Zionism. At the end of the 19th century, Jerusalem rabbis pronounced the anathema against Hebrew schools and Hebrew newspapers and against the ideals of the new immigrants. Enlightened rabbis in Central Europe as well as Hasidic Russian and Polish rabbis fought a long battle against those who sought to reconstitute a

Excavation, Southern Wall. Archaeological excavation at the Southern Wall of the Temple area in Jerusalem. The area being dug up by workmen was, in Temple times, a street along which were stalls where sacrificial animals could be purchased. The excavations over a wide area have given a clear picture of the approaches to the Temple and the routes by which the pilgrims entered its gates. Photo Harris, Jerusalem.

Jewish state by profane means. However, an opposite tendency also emerged in the circles of Orthodox Jewry. Leading rabbinical authorities were among those who initiated and founded the 'Return to Palestine' movement. Later, a Zionist religious party was constituted in the ranks of the Zionist Organization. This movement actively fought the predominant anticlerical tendencies but became a positive factor both in propagating the Zionist ideal and in promoting practical work in the Land of Israel. When mass immigration brought to the country thousands of Orthodox Jews from Eastern Europe and North Africa, religious influence over Israel society became stronger. It was further encouraged by systematic religious education and by the founding of religious youth movements.

Indifference toward religion, if not outright distrust, was the

Roman theater at Caesarea. Caesarea dates from the 1st century B.C. and was also an important center under the Crusaders; it has recently achieved new importance as a holiday resort when excavations revealed the full scope of the theater. It has today Israel's only golf course. Openair concerts and theatrical performances are periodically held in the theater, that had lain for centuries buried in the sand dunes. Photo Harris, Jerusalem.

Gasoline station near Avdat. Roadhouse near the ruins of the ancient Nabatean city of Avdat (central Negev plain), first built in the 1st century A.D. and destroyed in the 7th. The ruins, excavated and reconstructed, include Byzantine baths, a Roman camp, burial caves and churches. They can be seen on the hill behind the gasoline station, built by Nachum Zolotov. Photo J. Zafrir.

characteristic of young pioneers of the Second and Third Aliyot which respectively preceded and followed World War I. For them, Zionism was essentially a movement of national rebirth, a means to solve the problem of Jewish existence. They were the standard-bearers of social progress and individual liberty. They rejected the requirements of Orthodox Jewry and refused to put religious observance above everything.

In its essence, Zionism was basically a movement of return to the national past. Although it reflected the Orthodox conception of Judaism, it found its inspiration and its historical consciousness in Jewish tradition. Its main source of inspiration was the Bible. Biblical studies became a central subject, not only in Orthodox schools but in all the secular schools. A further source of inspiration was the Talmud and its legends.

The Israel way of life, though not subservient to the dictates of strict Orthodoxy, keeps traditional Jewish customs. The Sabbath came to be accepted as the national weekly holiday. Certain Jewish festivals returned to their original status of nature festivals or feasts commemorating historical events. Thus, Zionism and the new Palestine are largely responsible for the new significance of the *Hanukkah* festival, not only as the Festival of Lights but also as the feast commemorating the heroic victory of Judah the Maccabee over the Hellenistic oppressors.

In the same way *Lag ba-Omer* was given its true character of a festival commemorating the Bar Kokhba rebellion against the Romans (132-5 A.D.). Passover regained its character as a Spring festival, Pentecost (*Shavuot* or *Weeks*) was again regarded as the celebration of harvesting. The 15th of the month of *Shevat*, an almost forgotten festival was again the 'New Year of the Trees' in order to glorify the plantation of new forests. The traditional customs of ancient Israel again found their natural ambiance.

In a different field, biblical interpretation and the study of the Jewish past underwent considerable development with the rebirth of Israel. Until then, biblical exegesis had been the almost exclusive province of non-Jewish researchers. Confronted by the topography of the Bible, living on the very site of the biblical drama, the scholars of Israel often superseded foreign researchers reconstructing the historical truth.

Yehezkel Kaufmann was the initiator of a new approach to the evolution of the Mosaic religion and modern Israel interpretation of the biblical past is largely due to him. His doctrine was continued and completed by his numerous disciples. The study of the Bible infected all classes and almost became a national hobby. Circles of biblical studies sprang up everywhere while congresses and biblical quizzes drew large audiences.

In the same way, the passion for archaeology, another characteristic of the Israelis, must be attributed to their nostalgia for the remote past and to their secret longing to bridge the tremendous historical gap that, for centuries, separated the people of Israel from its land. New archaeological discoveries thus elicit enthusiastic reactions throughout the country. Hundreds of volunteers often participate in the excavations: soldiers and members of the *kibbutzim* often become amateur archaeologists. After

Hechal Shlomo, Jerusalem. Hechal Shlomo in Jerusalem is the seat of the Chief ▶ Rabbinate and headquarters of other religious institutions. Photo Harris, Jerusalem.

the discovery of the Dead Sea Scrolls, the interest in archaeology became even more widespread and even specialized archaeological congresses arouse the interest of the man in the street.

For the circles of Orthodox Jewry, Israel has also become an important center of research and study of talmudic and rabbinic literature. The destruction of East European Jewry and the forced liquidation of the Oriental Diaspora have contributed to make Israel practically the greatest center of Jewish religious studies.

The great *yeshivot* (religious academies) of Poland and Lithuania have been reconstituted there. Prayer-books, new editions of the Talmud and other sacred works are printed in Israel and distributed all over the Jewish world.

The fundamental dichotomy between the two basic conceptions of Judaism still exists but the differences between Orthodox and secular elements are often made less acute through identity of opinion on the great political problems facing the State. The

Synagogue at Hebrew University, Jerusalem. The striking synagogue of the Hebrew University on the campus at Givat Ram, Western Jerusalem. Architect: Heinz Rau. Photo Harris, Jerusalem.

Synagogue at Hebrew University (interior), Jerusalem. The synagogue is raised from the ground, as can be seen from the exterior view (previous illustration); the ceiling is completely covered, and there are no windows so that the interior is lit solely from daylight entering from below. Photo Harris, Jerusalem.

mutual intolerance of the two groups that marked the early stages of the creation of the new society in Eretz Israel gradually abated. Avraham Yitzhak Kook, chief rabbi of Palestine during the first years of the Mandate, largely contributed to this development. He constantly preached mutual respect and insisted on priority being given to national interest over all else. The appearance of a religious working class, and above all, the formation in the thirties of religious *kibbutzim* and *moshavim*, helped promote systematic cooperation between secular and religious elements. As the years passed, interest in Jewish traditions and Jewish thought began to preoccupy the young generations. A general tendency to return to spiritual values as well as the desire to find new forms of contact with Judaism and Jews is discernible. This has been further stimulated by the demonstrations of solidarity with Israel throughout the large communities of the Diaspora during the Six Day War in June 1967.

THE NEW LITERATURE

Before Palestine became Israel, Jerusalem and Tel Aviv were already on their way to becoming the main centers of Hebrew literary life in the world. A fateful turn of events speeded up this process: from 1920 onward, literary creation in the Hebrew language was no longer possible in Russia, where it had matured. Similarly, Jewish life in Poland was on the wane between the two world wars, until its complete annihilation in Nazi crematoria. With the disappearance of this Jewish world another great Jewish vernacular also came close to extinction. Yiddish, which for centuries had been the language of East European Jewry and had recently waged a desperate war against the cultural supremacy of Hebrew, now lay in its death throes under the debris of the world in which it had come into existence. Once Europe had vanished from the picture, the Diaspora of western countries

Hebrew University campus, Western Jerusalem. The Hebrew University was founded on Mount Scopus in 1925, on the hill overlooking Jerusalem. Access was barred between 1948 and 1967 and during that period a second campus was created in Western Jerusalem. At the end can be seen the National Library; in the far left-hand corner, the Shrine of the Book, part of the Israel Museum, that houses the Dead Sea Scrolls. In 1972, seventeen thousand students attended the University. Photo Harris, Jerusalem.

which was linguistically assimilated, had no need for a specifically Jewish tongue. The Yiddish papers and reviews which are now left are not very numerous and the last paper written in Judeo-Spanish (outside Israel) disappeared when the Salonika ghetto was razed to the ground.

There was no doubt that the future of Hebrew literature was linked with Israel, where it lost its exclusive status of a literary language and found its natural reading public for whom Hebrew was the only medium of culture and thought. Although numeri-

cally restricted, this environment had the advantage of direct contact with the readers. The tongue was constantly enriched and became more flexible. The new generations spoke Hebrew, thought in Hebrew and, for the most part, read only Hebrew.

For a long time, the poets and novelists who had settled in Palestine continued to weave the threads of their literary work around life in, or characters from, the Old World. Hayyim N. Bialik and Saul Tschernikhovski, the two main poets of that time, continued to sing of their youth and bygone days. The novelists

described Russia, their youth in the *stetl,* the small Jewish communities and so on. They had some difficulty in adapting their palette to the unfamiliar colors of their new lives.

But new themes soon began to appear in Hebrew writing. Yehudah Burla and several other writers revealed the strange, little-known world of the Oriental Sephardi Jews. Later, Hayyim Hazaz, one of the best stylists of modern Hebrew prose, who had become known through his descriptions of his native Ukraine, discovered the mysterious and fascinating world of the Yemenite Jews. Avraham Kabak wrote a historical novel around the tragic figure of Solomon Molkho, the Jewish mystic martyred in the 16th century. At the end of his life, Kabak wrote the

most successful of his novels, *The Narrow Path,* a historical evocation of Jesus.

Young writers looked for a new style and started exploring the hidden treasures of old Hebrew literature. The master of Hebrew prose, whose influence has been great on novelists and story-tellers ever since, was Nobel prizewinner Shemuel Agnon. His style, that skillfully blends elements from the Bible and talmudic literature, the symbolism of his descriptions, the graphic conciseness of his prose, left their mark on all the new literary movements in Israel. Though he mostly described the world of his native Galicia, *Temol Shilshom* (Only Yesterday) is a monumental description of Palestine at the time of the Second Aliyah.

pioneers, the famines, the constant struggle against Arab attackers, the sleepless nights in isolated villages, the atmosphere of siege and bloodshed, found their expression in the stories of that time.

The War of Independence caused the appearance of a new current known as the 'Palmah Generation'. For the first time, literature was in the hands of young writers who had been born and raised in Israel. This generation had not known the past from which its fathers had fled. To them Zionism was a remote ideal, for they had struck natural roots in their own land and did not need ideological justification in order to feel bound to it. They had been raised amid constant dangers. Before they had even reached manhood they had to drill with guns and grenades. It was they who won the War of Independence, using improvised weapons in pitiless battles, often in isolated groups in the midst of their enemies, sometimes alone. In these battles, many lost their comrades (the war took a toll of 7,000 of a population of 500,000). They emerged from it with a feeling of infinite sadness, a sadness pervading many of the literary works which appeared just after the war, and which finds its most typical expression in the great novel by S. Izhar, *Yemei Tsiklag* (The Days of Ziklag), telling of the actions and thoughts of a small group of fighters encircled on the top of a hill and doomed to certain death. Though not easy to read, this novel soon became very popular with the young generation whose feelings it expressed. Moshe Shamir followed the same line and produced a number of stories concerning life on the *kibbutz*. However, his reputation as a writer mainly rests on his historical novel *King of Flesh and Blood* which centers around the life of Alexander Yannai, one of the last kings of the Hasmonean dynasty.

Shemuel J. Agnon (1888-1970), winner of the Nobel prize for literature (1966), novelist and story writer, one of the most distinguished representatives of modern Hebrew literature. Born in Galicia, Agnon settled in Palestine in 1909, but spent twelve years in Germany. His writings deal largely with life in Galicia, though their scope is universal. He wrote in an original style of Hebrew, skilfully blending elements of talmudic and biblical literature. Government Press Office, Tel Aviv.

In the wake of the Third Aliyah, echoes of the literary revolution shaking the world after World War I brought about a revolt against Hebrew classicism. It was led by the poet Avraham Shlonsky, an innovator in the field of language and a virtuoso of the new Hebrew style. A multitude of disciplines joined him; the most important of them was Natan Alterman who, at a time when the Jewish population of Palestine was fighting for its very existence, helped in no small way to sustain the morale of the *Yishuv* and the courage of its young fighters with his poems revolving around topical themes.

From then on, Hebrew poetry acquired a new rhythm. Literary prose shed the successive historical layers, especially from the Bible, which had bogged it down. As with all new nations, poetry was the first province of literature to express the true character of the new society. The novel still had some difficulty in adjusting to the new reality. Yet, the hard life of the first

The Knesset chandelier. Bronze *menorah* (seven-branched candelabrum) symbol of the State of Israel opposite the Knesset entrance, sculpted by the British-Jewish sculptor Benno Elkan. The *menorah* is decorated with scenes from Jewish history and was given to the Knesset by British parliamentarians.

Yad Va-Shem memorial hall (exterior), Jerusalem. A memorial and study center on Memorial Hill adjoining Mount Herzl, dedicated to the 6,000,000 Jews who perished in Nazi Europe. The main memorial hall is built of Galilee stones and concrete; the big stones for the lower part of the building and the plain concrete top were chosen for their gaunt impact. Photo Anatol Lewkowicz, Jerusalem.

Later, the young Hebrew literature opened its gates to the influence of literary currents in Europe and America. With the creation of the State, contacts with the outside world became more frequent, the taste for foreign languages spread and led to experiments in new and easier forms of expression. The avant-garde schools in America with their tendency to indulge in introspection, even to the point of sickness, have left their mark on Israel literature.

ISRAEL ART

The search for original expression and the will to keep abreast of the intellectual currents agitating the modern world have made themselves felt in the other branches of culture and art — more even than in the field of literature. Hebrew literature represented only the continuation of a long tradition, but this was not the case of painting, music, and theater where everything had to be started from scratch.

In 1906 an artist, a former professor at the Sofia Academy of Art, settled in Jerusalem and set out purposefully to create an authentic Palestinian art. Boris Schatz founded a school of arts and crafts which he called 'Bezalel', after the artist, who, according to biblical tradition, had decorated the Tabernacle in the wilderness. He created a style which was long identified with Israel's artistic production. He also discovered the artistic genius of the Yemenites and encouraged them to produce fine metal objects decorated with silver and copper filigree, after Damascene models, but representing specifically Jewish symbols. A whole generation of young painters came out of his school. Some engaged in experiments and found their own original style, while others kept to decorative painting.

After World War I, a number of Jewish artists arrived in Palestine, especially in Jerusalem to which they were attracted by the fame of the Bezalel school. Some came with the British army, in the uniforms of the Jewish Legion. At the beginning of the 1920s, an exhibition, sponsored by the British governor of Jerusalem, opened in the vaulted rooms of the Citadel of David, in the walls of the old city. This marked the beginning of genuine Israel painting.

In the following years, a number of Palestinian painters who had not found in the country an atmosphere favorable to artistic creation left their jobs, their *kibbutzim,* or their working camps,

Yad Va-Shem Memorial Hall (interior), Jerusalem. To the left, the Eternal Flame. On the ground, plaques bearing the names of the death camps: Maidanek, Auschwitz, Mauthausen, and others. Ashes of the victims are buried underneath. Photo Anatol Lewkowicz, Jerusalem.

and went to study in Paris, under the direction of the famous masters of that time. As a result, the influence of the Paris school is still very strong in Israel art.

At first, the artists tried to give plastic expression to the ideas of their environment. However, in the field of painting (as in the field of art in general), these experiments proved unsuccessful because of the very character of that ideology, which resisted artistic representation.

Before abstract art came onto the Israel art scene, landscape was the main genre of all the different schools that sought to capture the harsh quality of Oriental light. Later, the artists endeavored to capture the spirit of antique Hebrew and Canaanite models, especially in sculpture and the graphic arts.

At the end of the forties, an exhibition called *Ofakim Hadashim*

(New Horizons) took place in Tel Aviv, which showed the impact of modern expressionist art and of abstract painting. As the population of the country increased, the number of those interested in art grew. Israel art now exhibits all the different trends current in modern painting, and the work of its artists is increasingly appreciated abroad. Dozens of galleries appeared in the country's main cities. A deserted Arab village, Ein Hod, near Haifa, was turned into an artists' colony. Similarly, the old quarter of the kabbalists, in the Galilean town of Safed was restored as a residential area for artists and soon became a center of attraction for art dealers and collectors. Most representative and sought after today are perhaps Reuven Rubin, Moshe Mokady, Mordekhai Levanon, Jakob Steinhardt, Mordekhai Ardon, Marcel Jancu, and Avigdor Arikha.

MUSIC MAKING

In this sphere, as in other aspects of culture, the artists have striven for, and to some extent achieved, a synthesis based on strong European training and influences, more exotic elements introduced by Jews emanating from Arab and Oriental lands, and the traditions of the Land of Israel itself. Jews that had never been aware of it discovered the beauty of the Sephardi liturgy and of the ancient Judeo-Spanish *romanzo*. The Yemenites brought all their collection of haunting melodies. And thus, from this mixture, the Israel song was born.

Symphonic musical activity began in earnest as early as 1936,

White from 80° to 180° by Buki Swartz. In the Billy Rose Art Garden, at the Israel Museum, Jerusalem. The museum was opened in 1965 and now consists of the Bezalel Museum, the Samuel Bronfman Biblical and Archaeological Museum, the Shrine of the Book, the Youth wing, and the Billy Rose Garden of Modern Sculpture, donated by the famous American entertainer. Photo Harris, Jerusalem.

239

'Capriccio' by Sorel Etrog. The Billy Rose Art Garden at the Israel Museum was designed by Isamo Noguchi, and its architecture follows the flowing lines of the Jerusalem landscape. The garden houses interesting specimens of modern sculpture. In the foreground Sorel Etrog's *Capriccio*. On the left Ezra Orion's *Sculpture* and on the right Picasso's *Profile*. In the background, sculptures by Vasarely, Karl Appel, Ossip Zadkine. Photo Harris, Jerusalem.

when the violinist Bronislaw Hubermann decided to create the Palestine Symphony (later the Israel Philharmonic) Orchestra. This was to provide employment for Jewish artists who had been expelled from German orchestras by the Nazi decrees. Previously, there had been numerous attempts at forming chamber orchestras and the few conservatories had already produced several young musicians who were later to achieve fame. The creation of the Philharmonic Orchestra was the starting signal for considerable development of Israel's musical life. The greatest conductors and the masters of modern music came to Israel concert halls and Toscanini himself directed the Philharmonic Orchestra during its opening concerts. This national orchestra also played a role in the

The John F. Kennedy Memorial outside Jerusalem. Built by the Jewish National Fund, in the center of a forest planted by US Jews in memory of President Kennedy. The building represents a truncated tree and has the same number of pillars as the US states. Architect: D. Reznik. Photo Werner Braun, Jerusalem.

historical events that agitated the State. During World War II, it gave concerts for the Palestinian soldiers in camps on the Egyptian front; it played in Eilat, after the liberation of the town; for the Israel Defense Forces during the Sinai Campaign; and in the amphitheater on Mount Scopus after the unification of Jerusalem. The Philharmonic Orchestra was invited to many foreign countries where it received a highly enthusiastic welcome.

Numerous other orchestras also rose to prominence, notably the Radio Orchestra and the Chamber Orchestra. Promising composers have begun writing authentic Israel music and expressing the national character of the country in modern musical idiom. The works of Menahem Avidom, Paul Ben-Haim, Ödön Partos (to name only a few) are frequently played abroad and a group of younger composers and conductors has achieved a reputation in the musical world.

When Israel society was in its infancy, there were already timid attempts at theatrical activity. Amateur groups performed in the Jaffa schools and in the larger settlements. After World War I, a few professional groups appeared. But real theatrical life did not begin until the arrival of the Ha-Bimah Company in Palestine. This theater, the first professional Hebrew-speaking theater in the world, was created in Moscow in 1918, during the Revolution. This experiment at producing a play in a language that was not spoken at such a period, appeared somewhat incongruous. The initiative was due to a handful of young and passionate actors determined to realize their ideal whatever difficulties they had to face. A genial director, the Armenian Vakhtangov (a disciple of

Independence day poster. For the twentieth anniversary of the foundation of the ▶ State of Israel, this independence day poster by Koppel Gorban, representing the *menorah* and the lions of Judah is a powerful evocation of the young nation with a long history. Photo Harris.

Stanislavsky, founder of Moscow's Art Theater) was won over to the idea. The enthusiasm for novelties and experiments which characterized the first months of the October revolution set a propitious mood. The first Hebrew theater in the world thus came into being in Moscow. When it staged S. An-Ski's *The Dibbuk,* a play based on Jewish folklore, it achieved immediate international fame.

But it soon became obvious that the Ha-Bimah Company could no longer pursue its artistic activities in Moscow where

Caesarea concert. A concert in the annual Israel Music and Theater Festival. Music enjoys enormous popularity in Israel today, with a process of amalgamation between musics of the different origins and generations. The elder generation brought composers and performers — some of the world's very greatest — with a rich European tradition; the middle seeks a stance between the music of Europe and the Orient, whilst the youngest composers try to base the language of their music on the inflections of Hebrew. Government Press Office, Tel Aviv.

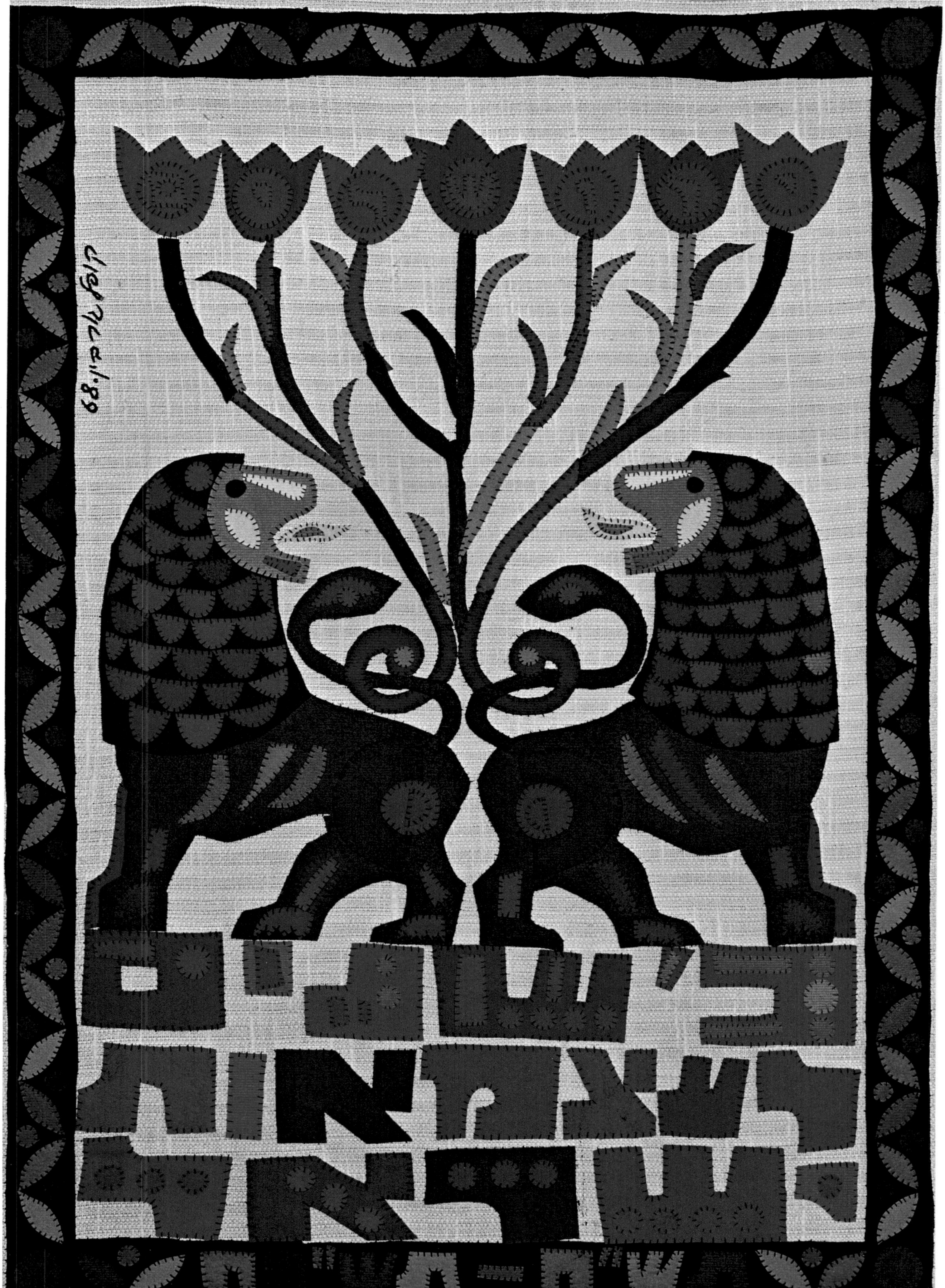

hostility toward Hebrew culture became increasingly apparent. After a short stay in America and a tour of Europe, the theater settled in Tel Aviv in the late 1920s. Its chief problem there was the question of repertoire for, at that time, Hebrew dramatic literature was very restricted. This state of affairs compelled the theater to fall back upon translations of classical plays with biblical subjects and on adaptations from Yiddish comedies and dramas. Later, however, classics of the international stage were produced. Its fame abroad, which glamorized it in the eyes of the Israel public, and its team of first-class actors succeeded in satisfying and maintaining the interest of a wide audience.

At about the same time, another theater, Ohel (The Tent), which was set up and maintained by the *Histadrut* (Labor Federation) opened its doors in Tel Aviv. Its company of talented artists came for the most part from the working class and many of its members had been among the masons who built Tel Aviv.

In the following years, new theatrical companies came into being. The most famous among these are the Cameri (Chamber Theater) in Tel Aviv and the Haifa Municipal Theater. These new theaters usually reacted against the taste for 'classicism' and the influence of the Russian theater which characterized the Ha-Bimah. Israel's theatrical life continues to be very intense. Many

Zionist Congress in Jerusalem. Festive opening of the 27th Zionist Congress in Jerusalem (June 1968). Since 1951 (the Twenty-Third Congress) Zionist Congresses are held in the capital of Israel. The congress is being addressed by Dr. Nachum Goldmann, and seated on his left is President Shazar of Israel. Central Zionist Archives, Jerusalem.

original Hebrew plays have been very successful although no indigenous style has yet been born.

ISRAEL AND WORLD JEWRY

This intense intellectual life which we have tried, however schematically, to describe here, reflects a feverish urge to create, as quickly as possible, as if the artists intended to fill the vacuum left by centuries when they were unable to create independently. However, this constant pursuit of originality and tendency to return to the sources do not mean that Israel has acquired the cultural leadership of the Jewish world. Translations of Israel books frequently sell well abroad, Israel actors often achieve fame outside Israel, and Israel orchestras are greeted by storms of applause, but Jewish masses in the West continue to live in the cultural environment of their native countries, without these achievements leaving a deep influence. Seen in a historical perspective, the State of Israel is still far from holding the central position in the world of Jewish thought and culture as was the case with talmudic or gaonic Babylon, or Spain during its Golden Age, or Champagne at the time of Rashi.

The Knesset, Jerusalem (exterior view). Israel's single-chamber parliament. The Knesset was built with money left by James de Rothschild. With 120 members, the building was inaugurated in 1966. The view here is from the Israel Museum. Government Press Office, Tel Aviv.

Unlike the authority of these ancient centers of world Judaism, Israel's authority is not unchallenged. In those remote periods, Jewish life completely centered on the religious principles and on the philosophy of Judaism, whereas modern Western Jews, whatever the strength of their Jewish feelings, are primarily interested in the intellectual life of the countries they live in. It is not, therefore, so much the cultural glamor of the Jewish State, as the very fact of its existence which has made its impact on the traditional basis of Jewish life.

It is not difficult to imagine what the fate of the Jewish people would have been in this tragic century, had the State of Israel not come into being. World Jewry stood on the brink of an abyss. The Nazi Holocaust had deprived it of its most active centers and of the communities that had been the most faithful to the values

The Knesset, Jerusalem (interior view). Government members sit round the table in the center. There is a portrait of Theodor Herzl on the wall at the back. Photo Hillel Burger.

246

Wall in Knesset chamber by Danny Caravan (detail). Photo Hillel Burger.

and traditions of Judaism. On the other hand, the newly acquired independence of Arab and North African nations was accompanied by eruptions of Muslim religious fanaticism and intolerance. Without the State of Israel, no trace would be left today of this ancient and individual world. Without the new state, millions of survivors, scattered through dozens of strange countries in complete isolation from their sources and without their traditions would never have been able to reconstruct their authentic way of life.

Without Israel, world Jewry would be represented by the great centers in the American continent, with the United States community in the leading position. But even there, the process of assimilation, which is in any case very strong, would have been bound to intensify to the point of endangering the existence of the Jewish community as a separate entity. As one modern thinker has put it: 'The hatred of the environment endangers the physical existence of the Jew while toleration endangers Judaism'. This is even more true when Jewish communities stray from their religious traditions or lack the centers that would ensure their cohesion.

The reality of Israel, its political, spiritual and security problems as well as the extraordinary achievements of its pioneers and the heroism of its soldiers, are a source of daily concern and of pride for millions of Jews all over the world. Russian Jewry, as has now been shown, sees in Israel a symbol of hope and a promise of survival.

One of the specific signs of the present revival of Judaism in Western countries is the extension of the school network which, for all its shortcomings, gives a Jewish and Hebrew education to an increasing number of young people, an unprecedented development since the opening of the ghetto gates. This education is based primarily on the teaching of modern Hebrew as it is spoken in Israel (besides the traditional Jewish subjects). The schoolteachers are trained in Israel's teacher training colleges or teach according to Israel methods; textbooks are composed of excerpts from modern Israel literature and the songs learned are Israel songs. '*Shalom*' has become the normal form of greeting. In meetings between Jewish youngsters, girls and boys can be seen wearing Israel costumes and dancing the *Hora*.

A new style of Jewish identification has come into being. In the remotest corners of the dispersion, the Jews have their own flag: that of the Zionist movement which is also the national flag of Israel. When anti-Semitism reappears and incidents occur, no Jew tries to stand by and ignore the offense: Israel's courage is there as a constant reminder.

Public life revolves around Israel. Charitable institutions and

Africans in Israel. Students from developing countries in Africa study at the Hebrew University and other institutions of higher learning in Israel. In addition, many Israelis have visited Africa for extended periods in the framework of the government's technical assistance programs. Photo Harris, Jerusalem.

women's organizations do all they can to help Israel. Jewish students, when they are not drawn toward the leftist ideologies which are the fashion in Western universities, turn to the only alternative: Israel, for the Return to Zion represents a genuine and positive element of that change which youth seeks.

The unity of world Jewry and mutual responsibility concerning the fate of the various branches of Judaism are all expressed in the common concern for Israel. When a community is in danger, the Jews are no longer content simply to appeal to the conscience of the world. They demand the right of the persecuted community to join their brothers in Israel. To everybody, this appears as the most natural and sensible solution. Though only 17 per cent of the world Jewish population actually lives in Israel, the Jewish State has thus become the universally recognized center of international Jewry.

The deep concern of all Jews for Israel comes out clearly whenever a danger threatens the Jewish State. Never did this solidarity express itself more strongly than at the time of the May 1967 crisis which led to the Six Day War. With the threats of destruction hanging over them brandished by the Arab leaders who boasted of the coming victory and promised extermination of the citizens of Israel, the Jews of all Western countries, who had lost their confidence in the capacity and will of the Great Powers to find a peaceful solution to the crisis and doubted the genuineness of their determination to go to the rescue of the Jewish State, were not prepared to accept this time again the role of passive and powerless onlookers, unable to prevent the disaster about to befall their brethren. They were no longer prepared to stand by and do nothing. This determination brought about the completely unanimous stand of world Jewry in defense of Israel. It was an unprecedented manifestation. Thousands of volunteers set out for Israel and tried to get there before the outbreak of the war. Whole communities mobilized their resources in order to help the State.

Then came the first news of Israel's victories. When, after a few days, the sound of the *shophar* was heard before the Western Wall, in the very center of a reunited and liberated Jerusalem, a messianic wind swept over the Diaspora. Feelings of relief and pride, the intoxication of unexpected victory, immense emotion welled up in men and women who, the day before, had been struck with the premonition of impending catastrophe.

Israel is the product of a hard struggle, of the patient progress through time, and relentless work of three generations of builders whom nothing would divert from their final aim. When Israel came into being, the friends of the young state wondered what new message the young nation was going to give the world. Twenty years later, this question is still without an answer. A message is not something made to order. And yet, does it not verge on the miraculous that a young nation, isolated on its glorious but barren land, doomed by circumstances to live in a constant state of alert, should have turned the scales of Jewish history and aroused new hopes and expectations for an ancient civilization that stood on the brink of an abyss?

We have traveled far through space and time in the pages of this book. Our authors have applied themselves to discerning the Jewish spirit and its specific expressions in vastly varying contexts. It has sometimes been difficult to see the wood for the trees—but the wood is there, in fact a majestic, monumental forest. And—to change the metaphor—if we pick out the major strands, we find them woven into the overall pattern of Jewish civilization.

The many special manifestations evident through Jewish history are rooted in the vision of the Fathers of the Jewish People which has served as the inspiration of their descendants throughout the ages. First of course was the vision of the One God. Scholars of Bible and of comparative religion may dispute as to whether this was a sudden revelation or a gradual development, but the origin is irrelevant. Whatever its genesis, the purity of its conception and its implications became the lodestar of Jewish life. The great values of Judaism all flowed from this supreme vision.

It was this uncompromising monotheism which inspired the great ideals of the prophets that have informed Jewish life under all conditions. The natural corollary of the fatherhood of God is the brotherhood of man, proclaimed already by the biblical prophets and the attainment of which is a constant objective of Jewish endeavor. This is the basis for the universalistic aspect of Judaism. Unfortunately the outside world has too often stifled the possibilities for the Jew to give full vent to this side of his spirit. For this reason it has been important in these pages to indicate the external forces that have all too forcibly molded so much of Jewish life and stinted natural developments. But this side of the Jew has refused to be quenched. The vision can be detected even despite the grimmest restrictions and persecutions, and it bursts forth most visibly and irrepressibly in the humanitarianism that characterizes so much of Jewish life and thought. It has led Jews and Judaism to the liberal tradition where they have played so vital a role.

Pure monotheism implies not only human brotherhood but also human dignity. All men being in the image of God, they inherit an innate dignity which calls for recognition and respect. The Jew sees man as the subject, not the object, of history. He has himself known only too well the pain of humiliation. One of his achievements has been the maintenance of his own dignity in the face of heart-rending trials and provocations. Others under similar circumstances have become animals; the Jew has stubbornly clung to his culture and tradition and demonstrated that civilization need not be a veneer but can become so deeply ingrained as to defy the most outrageous challenges. And this surely is one of the most striking lessons to be learnt from these pages, illustrated in the constant reiteration of the triumph of the spirit, evidenced for example by the unceasing cultural creativity or humane social structure maintained even in the degradation of the ghetto or in face of the callous deprivations that were so regularly the Jewish lot.

It is true that at the same time there has been a particularistic tradition in Jewish life. Its origins have been traced back to priestly circles but it has been nurtured by the external hostility to Jews and Judaism which inevitably turned the Jews in on themselves. Generally misunderstood from outside, it led to distorted pictures which reinforced the hatred, contempt, or mockery directed at the Jews, and this in turn only led to greater Jewish introspection. But even so the Jew knew that this image was a misrepresentation. He was criticized for his belief that Israel was a chosen people. There were times when the chosen people idea developed strong exclusivist overtones among the Jews but this was their escape from the horrors to which they were subject, from which they looked forward to the realization of their ideal to a time when their sufferings would no longer be in vain but would bring reward to them. But through them, all mankind would benefit. And the traditional view of the election of Israel was not a narrow exclusivism. On the contrary it imposed high moral duties and the Jew saw himself as the privileged bearer of the Divine vision—but the vision was open for all to behold and to accept. In fact the Jewish doctrine was far more tolerant than that of other faiths. 'Righteous men of all nations,' taught the rabbis, 'have a place in the world to come.' Salvation was not restricted to any one community.

And here is one of the cruxes of the Jewish condition. Faith as such was not enough. Indeed the very formulation of dogmas was a late development in Judaism and was only embarked upon to emulate external parallels. For the Jew the basis of his religion was action. Judaism was a way of life. This, too, had its particularistic side in the observance of the Commandments and the many special customs. The Law was basic and the respect for and veneration of Halakhah became a hallmark of the Jews. It engendered the discipline of Jewish society, which played such an important role in Jewish history and was one of the values communicated by the Jews to Western civilization. It sharpened the Jewish mind and in modern times conditioned the Jew for his prominence in the juridical profession.

But the universalistic application of the practical side of Jewish ideals has been one of the golden threads of Jewish life. One of the ringing messages of the Bible is that of social justice. From a modern viewpoint some of the provisions may appear primitive, but put in its own setting it remains a great document. It has only to be compared with other codes of its period for one to realize how progressive and forward-looking it is. And throughout the ages the Jews have applied that same spirit to their own situation and have always remained a few steps ahead of others. This has expressed itself in many ways. One recurring theme in this book has been the democracy of Jewish life. The Jews were one of the early democratic communities and their internal life has been conducted in a democratic spirit. It is therefore natural that Jews have been among the pioneers of democracy in general society and their inspiration can be detected in its development in countries such as England, the US and France where the founding fathers of democratic government were steeped in, and profoundly influenced by, Hebraic thought. It is therefore no accident that Jews have played a disproportionate role in the struggle for human rights. Here the Jew has been conditioned both by his long tradition and by the bitterness of his own experience as a perennial victim of social injustice.

A further basic ideal that we have seen emerge is the primacy of learning. The Jewish ideal is the scholar. The real leader is the sage versed in rabbinic lore who can draw on his knowledge for inspiration and guidance. Through him, the Law is personified. And the practical result is the predominant role of education in Jewish life. From the Babylonian academy to the Lithuanian *yeshivah,* from the Yemenite *heder* to the American day-school, education has been the keynote. When the surrounding society was boorish and ignorant, the Jew was literate and educated. Here, too, he has played a key role in handing down the vision of universal education and knowledge as the birthright of every individual. And when the Jew was admitted into non-Jewish society, he quickly shone by virtue of this tradition of literacy alongside the other qualities brought from his heritage, as well as a keen sensitivity, partly developed as a reaction to the negative factors which had forged so much of his history.

Ethics and morality have characterized Jewish life and this has been focused in the intimacy and healthy fabric of its family life. This is all part of the Jewish concept of Holiness which is another key to understanding the Jewish spirit. It is the result of their special relationship to God and was expressed biblically in the notion of the covenant—the acceptance of mutual obligations with God adopting Israel (together with all who would undertake the same obligations as Israel) while Israel agreed to a way of life embodying Holiness. Holiness permeates the life of the Jew. It is the reason for his acceptance of 'the yoke of the Commandments' which govern his every step and action. Some of the Commandments can be explained and accepted rationally, some not. But the Jew—at any rate traditionally—did not mind. It was the discipline of the holy life that was his special mission. Not only was he part of a Holy people but the Holy people had been granted a Holy land and the Holy land contained a Holy city. And apart from the people as a whole, the unit of Holiness was the family. The position of the woman in the Jewish world, it is true, retained many aspects of the Oriental attitude which had affected Judaism; but in the home her role was sanctified. And Jewish family life continued to be a model of its kind throughout the centuries when it could serve as an example and inspiration to others. It is only recently that the Jewish family—like so many other traditional Jewish ideals—is being seriously challenged. The danger to Jewish *mores* stems from the challenge of assimilation and acculturation which threaten to achieve what all the oppression, persecution and discrimination could not succeed in doing.

Beyond the family, the reader will have detected the emergence of the sense of community. Indeed from earliest times the Jews have lived as a community. Their prayers, for example, are uttered not in the singular but in the plural; their confession reads not 'I have sinned' but 'We have sinned'. Worship ideally is a communal act and the Jew went three times a day to the synagogue which was not only a place for communal prayer but the center for study, fellowship and communal activity. Its very informality provides a key to the Jewish character; religion was not a remote expression of respect but an act of communal participation, an acknowledgment not only of gratitude to God but of devotion to the Jewish way of life and membership of the Jewish people.

And there is a further characteristic which should be recorded—and that is the Jewish belief in the dignity of labor. Circumstances forced Jews into an unnatural occupational structure but they have always retained their respect for labor bequeathed by the Bible. And whenever they have had the opportunity they have eagerly become working men—from the ancient talmudic rabbis who earned their living by the sweat of their brows, to the craftsmen of the medieval Mediterranean areas and of Eastern Europe, and the agriculturalists of modern times in Russia and Argentina and today's Israel. And to working men elsewhere the Jews have bequeathed the great boon of the Sabbath day's rest.

As we have followed the story of the Jewish people, its unique spirit has been manifested in a myriad ways. Details which perhaps appeared unimportant and irrelevant acquire their own significance when seen in their full perspective. The Jewish spirit can be detected in the way Jews lived, in their attitudes, in their writings, in the occupations they pursued, in their participation in the lives of the lands to which they were scattered, and in their many contributions to world culture, both creatively in every sphere of human endeavor, and as transmitters and catalysts. And in their determination to live according to their own lights, whatever the pressures put upon them, they have given an example of nonconformity and an insistence on maintaining their minority views and beliefs at all costs.

The special features we have described came to the fore in connection with the two cataclysmic events of recent Jewish history. The very fact of the Holocaust can be seen as a tribute to the potency of the Jewish spirit. It is a universal tragedy that Hitler succeeded as he did—but his attitude revealed a correct understanding that the Jews embodied everything to which he was opposed. Judaism represented the very antithesis of his insane paganism, of his degradation of man, of his wild attempt at the glorification of a group of 'supermen' on the basis of race rather than spirit. This would have been fought by Jews and by all who had inherited the Judaic spirit even if they had not been singled out as the major victims. And the behavior of the Jew in that period reflected their tradition—not only the desperate revolts but the study classes in the Warsaw ghetto, the orchestral and operatic performances in the Theresienstadt concentration camp, the synagogues established under the most bestial conditions, and the song sung by the tragic victims as they were herded into the gas chambers... 'I believe with perfect faith that the Messiah will come... even though he tarry, I still believe he will come.'

And most recently in the State of Israel, for which Jews have yearned, dreamed and prayed at every possible opportunity over the centuries. We are here at the outset of a new development in the Jewish spirit, the future of which is not clear. Inevitably under the new sociological circumstances, the new Israeli is not the same as the Diaspora Jew in many respects. But the bonds remain fundamental. They are different branches of the same tree and although they may appear at some levels to be growing away from each other, the trunk and roots remain common to both. The Israeli springs from the same Jewish tradition and is in fact more profoundly imbued in it than most of the Jews elsewhere in the world. And though the expression may differ, his way of life is influenced and directed by the same major traits as we have outlined above. There is, for example, the feeling for the brotherhood of man (witness the many contributions made by Israel to the development of the welfare of African states); there is the stress on democracy (unparalleled anywhere in or near the Middle East); there is the awareness of social justice, dignity of labor, and a feeling for community (most outstanding in the growth of the collective way of life, e.g. in the *kibbutz*); there is the stress on education (expressed not so much in its traditional forms as in impressive institutions of higher learning); and there is the flowering of cultural activities of the most intensive quantity and sometimes of notable quality. The signs are unmistakeable. They are the same as those that have distinguished the Jewish people throughout its checkered history, and which are still basic to Jewish living, in its various vicissitudes, throughout the world.

And underlying all these manifestations is one other fundamental—Jewish optimism. As we have seen, Jews have refused to give way or despair under the most gruelling situations. They have not given in or gone under but have continued to plan for the future—confident that eventually the world will be a better place and that they have still a unique contribution to make in that direction.

Geoffrey Wigoder

BIBLIOGRAPHY

(This list is confined to complete works in English).

General Works dealing with Jewish Spirit and Civilization

The Legacy of Israel; planned by I. Abrahams and edited by E.R. Bevan and C. Singer (Oxford, 1948)

Great Ages and Ideas of the Jewish People; edited by L.W. Schwarz (New York, 1956)

The Jewish Contribution to Civilization; by J. Jacobs (Philadelphia, 1919)

The Jewish Contribution to Civilization; by C. Roth (London, 1956)

Jewish Thought as a Factor in Civilization; by L. Roth (Unesco, 1954)

Jewish Influence in Modern Thought; by A.A. Roback (Cambridge, 1929)

The Jews: Their History, Culture and Religion; edited by L. Finkelstein (New York, 1961)

The Hebrew Impact on Western Civilization; edited by D. Runes (New York, 1951)

General Reference Works

Encyclopaedia Judaica; edited by C. Roth and G. Wigoder (Jerusalem, 1971)

Jewish Encyclopedia; edited by I. Singer (New York, 1901-6; reprinted 1963)

New Standard Jewish Encyclopedia; edited by C. Roth and G. Wigoder (New York, 1970)

Encyclopedia of the Jewish Religion; edited by R.J.Z. Werblowsky and G. Wigoder (New York, 1966)

Jewish History

History of the Jews; by H. Graetz (Philadelphia, 1956)

A Social and Religious History of the Jews; by S. Baron (Philadelphia, 1952 ff.)

A History of the Jewish People; by M. Margolis and A. Marx (Philadelphia, 1947)

A Short History of the Jewish People; by C. Roth (London, 1970)

A History of the Jews; by S. Grayzel (Philadelphia, 1968)

The Course of Modern Jewish History; by H.L. Sachar (New York, 1963)

The Jewish Community; by S. Baron (Philadelphia, 1942)

Jewish Life in the Middle Ages; by I. Abrahams (Philadelphia, 1932)

Judaism and Jewish Thought

Judaism; by I. Epstein (London, 1960)

Judaism: A Portrait; by L. Roth (London, 1960)

The Essence of Judaism; by L. Baeck (New York, 1967)

The Evolution of Jewish Thought; by J.B. Agus (New York, 1960)

The Wisdom of Israel; by L. Browne (London, 1960)

Judaism; edited by A. Hertzberg (New York, 1961)

A History of Medieval Jewish Philosophy; by I. Husik (Philadelphia, 1916)

Philosophies of Judaism; by J. Guttmann (New York, 1964)

Major Trends in Jewish Mysticism; by G. Scholem (New York, 1946)

The Arts and Sciences

A History of Jewish Literature; by M. Waxman (New York, 1960)

Modern Hebrew Literature; by S. Halkin (New York, 1950)

The Story of Yiddish Literature; by A.A. Roback (New York, 1940)

Jewish Music; by A.Z. Idelsohn (New York, 1929)

Music of the Jews; by M. Rothmuller (London, 1953)

Jewish Art; edited by C. Roth (New York, 1961; new edition, 1971)

A History of Jewish Art; by F. Landsberger (Cincinnati, 1956)

The Architecture of the European Synagogue; by R. Wischnitzer (Philadelphia, 1964)

Jewish Costume; by A. Rubens (London, 1967)

A History of Jewish Crafts and Guilds; by M. Wischnitzer (New York, 1965)

The Jew in Science; by L. Gershenfeld (Philadelphia, 1934)

The Jews and Medicine; by H. Friedenwald (New York, 1967)

Ancient Near East

The Religion of Israel; by Y. Kauffmann (New York, 1960)

The Archaeology of Palestine; by W.F. Albright (London, 1960)

Hellenistic Civilization and the Jews; by V. Tcherikover (Philadelphia, 1959)

Hellenism; by N. Bentwich (Philadelphia, 1919)

Judaism in the First Centuries of the Christian Era; by G.F. Moore (Harvard, 1927)

Everyman's Talmud; by A. Cohen (London, 1949)

A Rabbinic Anthology; edited by C.G. Montefiore and H. Loewe (London, 1938)

The Legends of the Jews; by L. Ginsberg (Philadelphia, 1946)

Byzantium

The Jews in the Byzantine Empire; by J. Starr (New York, 1939)

Byzantine Jewry; by A. Scharf (London, 1971)

Muslim Lands

Jews and Arabs; by S.D. Goitein (New York, 1955)

Judaism and Islam; by E.I.J. Rosenthal (New York, 1961)

Between East and West; by A. Chouraqui (Philadelphia, 1968)

Spain

A History of the Jews in Christian Spain; by Y.F. Baer (Philadelphia, 1961-6)

The Jews in Spain; by A.A. Neuman (Philadelphia, 1942)

Marranos

A History of the Marranos; by C. Roth (New York, 1959)

Italy

The History of the Jews in Italy; by C. Roth (Philadelphia, 1946)

The Jews of Ancient Rome; by H.J. Leon (Philadelphia, 1960)

The Jews in the Renaissance; by C. Roth (Philadelphia, 1960)

The Makers of Hebrew Books in Italy; by D.W. Amram (Philadelphia, 1909)

England and its former dependencies

A History of the Jews in England; by A.M. Hyamson (London, 1928)

A History of the Jews in England; by C. Roth (Oxford, 1964)

Social History of the Jews in England, 1850-1950; by V.D. Lipman (London, 1954)

The Jews in the Literature of England; by M.F. Modder (New York, 1966)

The Jews in South Africa; edited by L. Hotz and G. Saron (London, 1956)

Germany and Austria

The Jews of Germany; by M. Lowenthal (Philadelphia, 1944)

The Jews of Austria; edited by J. Fraenkel (London, 1968)

Eastern Europe

History of the Jews in Russia and Poland; by S. Dubnow (Philadelphia, 1916-20)

The Jews in Russia; by L. Greenberg (New Haven, 1965)

The Jews in the Soviet Union; by S.M. Schwarz (New York, 1951)

The Jews in Soviet Russia since 1917; edited by L. Kochan (Oxford, 1970)

Jews of Czechoslovakia (Philadelphia, 1968-71)

The Golden Tradition; edited by L. Dawidowicz (New York, 1967)

Life is with People; by E. Herzog and M. Zborowski (New York, 1962)

Hasidic Anthology; edited by L.I. Newman (New York, 1934)

North America

Jewish Experience in America; edited A.J. Karp (New York, 1969)

Early American Jewry; edited by J. Marcus (Philadelphia, 1951-3)

The Jews in America; by R. Learsi (Cleveland, 1954)

The American Jew; edited by O. Janowsky (New York, 1942)

The American Jew: A Reappraisal; edited by O. Janowsky (Philadelphia, 1964)

The History of the Jews in Canada; by B.G. Sack (Montreal, 1945)

Latin America

Jews in Latin America; by J. Beller (New York, 1969)

Jews in Colonial Brazil; by A. Wiznitzer (New York, 1960)

History of the Jews in the Netherlands Antilles; by I.S. Emmanuel (Cincinnati, 1970)

Zionism and Israel

The Zionist Idea; by J. Heller (New York, 1949)

The Zionist Idea; edited by A. Hertzberg (Philadelphia, 1966)

The Zionist Movement; by I. Cohen (London, 1945)

A History of the Holy Land; edited by M. Avi-Yonah (London, 1969)

A History of Palestine from 135 A.D. to Modern Times (London, 1949)

The Jews in their Land; edited by D. Ben-Gurion (London, 1966)

GLOSSARY

Aggadah (adjective: aggadic)
The narrative and homiletical section of the Oral Law (Talmud and Midrash).

Aliyah
Immigration to the Land of Israel; in modern times, specific waves of immigration (First Aliyah, Second Aliyah, etc.)

Amora (pl. amoraim)
Jewish rabbinical authorities between the period of the compilation of the Mishnah and the completion of the Talmud.

Ashkenazi
Jews adhering to the culture and ritual that was developed in Central Europe and eventually carried especially to Eastern Europe and to Western Europe and the Americas.

Bar Mitzvah
Ceremony at which a boy, on his thirteenth birthday, is recognized as an adult and assumes responsibility for observing the Commandments. The corresponding ceremony for girls (aged 12 years and a day) is called Bat Mitzvah.

Bet Din
Jewish religious law court.

Bet Midrash
Place of assembly for study or prayer.

Converso
Jew who embraced Christianity under pressure but remained at heart faithful to Judaism (also called Marrano).

Dayyan
Religious judge.

Dhimmi
Person in Muslim land accorded protected status and allowed to retain his religion.

Exilarch
Head of the Babylonian Jewish community.

Gaon
Head of the Babylonian (and other) academies.

Gemara
Exposition of the Mishnah; the Mishnah together with the Gemara comprise the Talmud.

Genizah
Depository for worn-out, sacred books; especially, the Cairo Genizah, discovered at the end of the 19th century, containing a wealth of documents from the Middle Ages.

Haggadah
Home ritual recited on the eve of Passover.

Halakhah (adjective: halakhic)
The legal sections of the Oral Law.

Halutz
An agricultural pioneer in modern Israel.

Hasidism (adjective: hasidic)
Pietistic movement. One such movement flourished in medieval Germany but the best-known one was founded in East Europe in the late 18th century.

Haskalah
Enlightenment movement through which the Jews of Central and Eastern Europe encountered the world of general European culture.

Havdalah
Service at the conclusion of the Sabbath.

Hazzan
Cantor in the synagogue service.

Heder
School (often a single room) for teaching Jewish religion.

Kabbalah
Jewish mystical lore.

Kashrut
Regulations governing dietary laws.

Karaites
Sect rejecting talmudic authority and basing itself solely on the Bible.

Kibbutz
Collective settlement in Israel.

Kiddush
Sanctification of Sabbaths and festivals.

Marrano
Forced convert; see Converso.

Masorah
Body of tradition governing the punctuation and reading of the Hebrew Bible.

Midrash	Exegetical interpretation of the Bible.
Mishnah (adjective: mishnaic)	Codification of the Oral Law carried out in the 3rd century A.D.
Moshav	Cooperative settlement in Israel.
Nagid (pl. Negidim)	Head of the Jewish community in Egypt and in certain other countries (generally Muslim lands).
Nasi (pl. nesi'im)	Title used by president of Sanhedrin and head of Palestinian Jewish community; also used by Jewish communal heads in other countries.
Pale of Settlement	Territories in tsarist Russia where Jewish residence was permitted.
Patriarch	Nasi (q.v.)
Piyyut	Liturgical poem.
Rabbinites	Normative Jews who accepted rabbinic tradition (as opposed to Karaites).
Sabbetaian	Followers of the 17th century pseudo-Messiah, Shabbetai Tzevi.
Sephardi	Jews living in Spain or descendants of those expelled from the Iberian peninsula at the end of the 15th century (as contrasted with Ashkenazim).
Stetl	Small community in East Europe.
Takkanot	Rabbinical or communal regulation.
Tallit	Prayer shawl.
Talmud	Name of the two major compilations of Jewish Law (Palestinian or Jerusalem Talmud; Babylonian Talmud) comprising the Mishnah and discussions on the Mishnah (Gemara).
Tanna (pl. tannaim)	Rabbinical authority quoted in the Mishnah.
Torah	The Pentateuch; the entire body of Jewish religious teaching.
Tosafot	Explanatory glosses on Rashi's commentary on the Talmud; the rabbis who compiled these glosses were known as tosafists.
Tzaddik	Hasidic rabbi.
Yeshivah (pl. yeshivot)	Talmudic academy; Jewish traditional school.
Yishuv	Modern Jewish settlement in the land of Israel; a place of Jewish settlement in Israel; a Jewish settlement-group.

INDEX

Figures in Roman type refer to volume I, those in Italics to volume II

Printed in Switzerland

ACKNOWLEDGMENTS

We would like to extend our thanks to the museums and libraries throughout the world, who lent us their material. In addition to all the individual photographers who have contributed their work, we are in particular grateful to David Harris, Jerusalem, and Hans Hinz, Basle, who have provided a large number of illustrations. Most of the illustrations for the chapter on Latin and Central America were supplied by Dr. I.S. Emmanuel, author of *History of the Jews in the Netherlands Antilles,* while many illustrations for the chapter on Germany were provided by the Rheinisches Bildarchiv. For the chapter on the United States we are grateful to the publishers of *Contemporary Synagogue Art* for a number of illustrations. Finally we would much like to thank Mrs Irène Lewitt, photo archivist at the Israel Museum, for all her advice and assistance.

This book was printed
in August 1972 in the workshops
of Imprimeries Réunies S.A., Lausanne,
where the color illustrations and jackets in offset
were also printed.
The binding is by Roger Veihl, Geneva.
Editorial: Giles Allen.
Documentalist: Marie-José Treichler.
Layout and design: Franz Stadelmann.
Printed in Switzerland.